1994

A Cultural History of the American Novel relates and interweaves a number of novels, ranging from Henry James's *The Portrait of a Lady* (1881) to William Faulkner's *Go Down, Moses* (1942), with a series of cultural events as diverse as Buffalo Bill's Wild West Show and the "Southern Renaissance" of the 1930s. On the one hand, it examines novels as works of art that arise from and remain embedded in culture; on the other, it presents cultural events such as the making of Chicago's Columbian Exposition and New York's Armory Show as differing in degree but not in kind from novels. By bringing authors, texts, cultural events, and readers into varied and multivalent relationships, *A Cultural History of the American Novel* raises complex questions not only about the larger context of history, culture, art, and literature but also about such important issues as class, race, gender, and ethnicity.

Minter's broad and synthetic vision reconstructs literary history as a cultural drama in which novels and events emerge as related sites of cultural expression. Provocative fusions of the real and the imagined, the novels and the events considered here disclose a complex latent kinship between the structures and procedures of society in the United States and the structures and procedures of imagining during a critical period of national change and growth.

A Cultural History of the American Novel

A Cultural History of the American Novel

Henry James to William Faulkner

DAVID MINTER

CAMBRIDGE
UNIVERSITY PRESS

Published by the Press Syndicate of the University of Cambridge
The Pitt Building, Trumpington Street, Cambridge CB2 IRP
40 West 20th Street, New York, NY 10011-4211, USA
10 Stamford Road, Oakleigh, Melbourne 3166, Australia

First published 1994

Printed in the United States of America

Library of Congress Cataloging-in-Publication Data
Minter, David L.
A cultural history of the American novel : Henry James
to William Faulkner / David Minter.
p. cm.
Includes bibliographical references.
ISBN 0-521-45285-6 (hc)
1. American fiction – 20th century – History and criticism.
2. American fiction – 19th century – History and criticism.
3. Literature and anthropology – United States. I. Title.
PS379.M49 1994
813'.5209 – dc20   93-30651
                                                    CIP

A catalog record for this book is available from the British Library.

ISBN 0-521-45285-6 hardback

For Christopher and for Frances

. . . art may be of value purely through preventing a society from becoming too assertively, too hopelessly itself.

Kenneth Burke, *Counter-Statement* (1931)

Contents

A Preface in Two Parts   *page* xiii

Acknowledgments   xxi

A Note on Sources, Citations, and Bibliography   xxiii

PART ONE: A DREAM CITY, LYRIC YEARS, AND
A GREAT WAR

1. The Novel as Ironic Reflection   1

   Henry James and the novel in the "twilight of the
   absolute," in which George Santayana, W. E. B. Du Bois,
   and Huck Finn, among others, make brief appearances

2. Confidence and Uncertainty in *The Portrait of a Lady*   5

   The tension between technical confidence and moral
   uncertainty in James's The Portrait of a Lady, *in which*
   Alfred North Whitehead, Werner Heisenberg, and James
   Joyce make brief appearances

3. Lines of Expansion   11

   The play between two different lines of expansion, one out
   to the vagrant West, the other back to the incorporating
   East, as seen in Willa Cather's My Ántonia, O. E.
   Rölvaag's Giants in the Earth, *and Theodore Dreiser's*
   Sister Carrie, *featuring brief appearances by Christopher*
   Columbus and Henry Roth, among others

4. Four Contemporaries and the Closing of the West   21

   In which Chief Sitting Bull (1834?–1890), Henry Adams
   (1828–1918), Henry James (1843–1916), and William F.
   Cody (1846–1917) emerge as representative cultural figures
   during the twilight of the West and a variety of figures,
   including Michael Gold, make brief appearances

5. Chicago's "Dream City"   23

   The role of the World's Columbian Exposition of 1893 in the process of authorizing the New World's official lineage, in which Daniel Burnham and Henry Adams play major roles, and Candace Wheeler, Frederick Douglass, and others make brief appearances

6. Frederick Jackson Turner in the Dream City   27

   The Dream City as the scene of Frederick Jackson Turner's "Significance of the Frontier in American History," in which Willa Cather, Henry Adams, and Buffalo Bill, among others, make return appearances

7. Henry Adams's *Education* and the Grammar of Progress   31

   The city as scene in Henry Adams's Education *and Edgar Allan Poe's "The Man of the Crowd," with brief appearances by Karl Pearson, Werner Heisenberg, Paul Elmer More, Bertrand Russell, and Owen Wister, among others*

8. Jack London's Career and Popular Discourse   38

   The novel at the turn of the century, in which Henry David Thoreau and T. K. Whipple make brief appearances and Henry James returns

9. Innocence and Revolt in the "Lyric Years": 1900–1916   43

   Writing on the lyrical Left in the early twentieth century, in which a wide range of writers and artists appear and reappear

10. The Armory Show of 1913 and the Decline of Innocence   50

    The rise and fall of good hope, in which Frederick James Gregg, Arthur Davies, Mabel Dodge Luhan, Gertrude Stein, Ezra Pound, and Woodrow Wilson play important roles

11. The Play of Hope and Despair   54

    Tensions in Jack London's Martin Eden *and Edith Wharton's* The House of Mirth, *with brief glances at Stein's* Three Lives, *Dreiser's "trilogy of desire," and Norris's* McTeague

12. The Great War and the Fate of Writing   64

    In which Randolph Bourne, Alan Seeger, Edith Wharton, Ellen La Motte, Willa Cather, and Harry Crosby, among others, play prominent roles in ringing out the Lyric Years

PART TWO: FICTION IN A TIME OF PLENTY

1. When the War Was Over: The Return of Detachment   77

   Featuring The Education of Henry Adams *as a
   "textbook of American experience," with brief appearances
   by Woodrow Wilson, Henry James, John Hay, and Louis
   Kronenberger, among others*

2. The "Jazz Age" and the "Lost Generation" Revisited   81

   *In which Gertrude Stein, F. Scott Fitzgerald, Waldo
   Frank, John Peale Bishop, H. L. Mencken, and others
   make brief appearances; E. E. Cummings's* The
   Enormous Room, *John Dos Passos's* 1919, *and Sinclair
   Lewis's* Babbitt *emerge as exemplary texts; and "jazz" is
   featured as the era's appropriate accompaniment*

3. The Perils of Plenty, or How the Twenties Acquired a
   Paranoid Tilt   96

   *In which A. Mitchell Palmer, Lothrop Stoddard, Madison
   Grant, Nicola Sacco, Bartolomeo Vanzetti, and Walter
   Lippmann play important roles; Dos Passos reappears; and
   Sherwood Anderson's* Winesburg, Ohio *becomes a guide to
   "anti-success" as a mode of resistance to the "diffused
   prosperity" of the "New Capitalism"*

4. Disenchantment, Flight, and the Rise of Professionalism
   in an Age of Plenty   103

   *Featuring discussions of "big" and "little" magazines, with
   brief appearances by Henri Laurent, Ernest Elmo Calkins,
   Bruce Barton, John B. Watson, among others, and also
   featuring Fitzgerald's "The Scandal Detectives" as a guide
   to a world of loosened restraints and new indulgences*

5. Class, Power, and Violence in a New Age   110

   In which Dreiser and others reappear and Fitzgerald's The
   Great Gatsby *becomes a model of mythmaking as a form of
   resistance*

6. The Fear of Feminization and the Logic of Modest
   Ambition   117

   *In which Glenway Wescott, Malcolm Cowley, Alain
   Locke, Katherine Roof, Harold Stearns, Edward Bok,
   Charles William Eliot, Joseph Hergesheimer, Robert
   Herrick, Edmund Wilson, and others appear, and Gertrude
   Stein's art of splicing emerges as another form of resistance*

7. Marginality and Authority / Race, Gender, and Region   125

*In which F. Scott Fitzgerald, T. S. Eliot, W. E. B.
Du Bois, Henry Luce, E. E. Cummings, Bruce Barton,
and others appear, and John Dos Passos plays a major role
in setting the limits of resistance*

8. War as Metaphor: The Example of Ernest Hemingway   133

*In which John Dewey, Dorothy Canfield Fisher, and
Thomas Boyd appear; Lewis, Mencken, and Cummings
reappear; and Hemingway emerges as the endpoint of an era*

PART THREE: THE FATE OF WRITING DURING THE
GREAT DEPRESSION

1. The Discovery of Poverty and the Return of
Commitment   147

*In which F. Scott Fitzgerald, Josephine Herbst, Genevieve
Taggard, and others return to trace the move from
carelessness toward commitment*

2. The Search for "Culture" as a Form of Commitment   152

*In which explorations of the national mood like Nathan
Asch's* The Road, *"proletarian" novels like Edward
Dahlberg's* Bottom Dogs, *and documentary ventures like
Dorothea Lange and Paul S. Taylor's* An American
Exodus, *as well as Alfred Kazin's memoirs, are featured as
parts of the Angry Decade's effort to reclaim "culture" for
"the people" and also as fitting in unexpected ways FDR's
use of the radio in his "fireside chats"*

3. Three Responses: The Examples of Henry Miller, Djuna
Barnes, and John Dos Passos   160

*In which three very different writers are seen as disclosing
the limits of different forms of resistance*

4. Cowboys, Detectives, and Other Tough-Guy
Antinomians: Residual Individualism and Hedged
Commitments   167

*In which humor darkens, violence becomes public, and
Westerns and detective novels lead toward encounters with
James M. Cain and Horace McCoy*

5. The Search for Shared Purpose: Struggles on the Left   181

In which Kenneth Burke, Nathan Asch, Sherwood Anderson, Michael Gold, Josephine Herbst, and Tillie Olsen play small roles and Jack Conroy, James T. Farrell, Daniel Fuchs, Robert Cantwell, Henry Roth, John Steinbeck, and Nathanael West play larger ones in disclosing the forms and limits of protest fiction

6. Documentary Literature and the Disarming of Dissent   195

In which Nathan Asch, Dorothea Lange, and Paul Taylor, among others, reappear in the context of the New Deal's Federal Writers' Project and Federal Theater Project as exemplars of the search for "America as an idea," and James Agee and Walker Evans's Let Us Now Praise Famous Men *is featured as bringing the radical skepticism of the thirties to bear on the works of writers and photographers alike*

7. The Southern Renaissance: Forms of Reaction and Innovation   202

In which writers as different as Allen Tate, Robert Penn Warren, Erskine Caldwell, Margaret Mitchell, Ellen Glasgow, and Thomas Wolfe help us to see why the "peculiar" South could for a time become the nation's literary heartland

8. History and Novels / Novels and History: The Example of William Faulkner   215

In which Faulkner's fiction emerges as a culmination both of the formal preoccupations of literary modernism in the late moment of its turning back on itself in skepticism and critique, and of the thirties' engagement with poverty and violence as social problems and with race, gender, caste, and class as crucial correlates of selfhood

Notes   231

Bibliographical Notes   234

Bibliography   247

Index   253

A Preface in Two Parts

This book began as an extended essay commissioned as part of the Cambridge Literary History of the United States, and some of it will appear in that history. In accord with my original assignment, the focus is on "canonical" novelists from roughly 1890 to 1940. Like other contributors to the project, however, I was given considerable latitude in defining my task; and as I began thinking historically about novels of the period, I began reaching back in time and out in several directions, trying to trace two sets of reciprocal relations – one among novels that seemed to me crucial (from Henry James's *The Portrait of a Lady* [1881] to William Faulkner's *Go Down, Moses* [1942]) and another between novels and a series of cultural events (Buffalo Bill's Wild West Show, Chicago's Columbian Exposition, and New York's Armory Show, to cite a few early examples) that seemed to me to function as cultural texts in which questions having to do with history, culture, society, art, and literature, and thus with class, race, ethnicity, gender, family, and nationality, were being reflected upon and acted out. I hope to show that we can clarify the social, cultural meanings of novels by examining them in the contexts from which they emerged as "stories" worth telling and retelling, and that these contexts are broadly cultural rather than exclusively literary – that novels belong to and remain parts of the extended process that embraces everything we do to nature by asserting ourselves as expressive creatures and everything we do to ourselves by engaging in this transformative process.

Conceived in this way, literary history becomes a cultural drama in which authors, texts, and nonliterary events enter into multivalent relationships with readers. Since both the novels and the events that I examine represent interesting fusions of the real and the imagined, they provide ways of examining the structures and procedures of society as well as the structures and procedures of imagining during crucial years of the late nineteenth and early twentieth centuries. In them, the central and the marginal, the established and the revisionary find unequal expression.

Near the end of *The Rebel*, Albert Camus speaks of the "procedures of beauty," by which he means imaginative affirmations of "the value and the dignity common" to all human beings, and the "procedures of rebellion," by which he means all resistance to injustice, as ways of contesting "reality while endowing it with unity." Some of Camus's key terms – "beauty" and "rebellion" – are more extreme than my mood allows. But his words place aesthetic and political resistance within history as ways of contesting established relations; and, almost surreptitiously, they remind us that all of our contesting retains as one part of its motive the restoration if not the preservation of "unity."

While declaring itself the land of the free, the United States has repeatedly demonstrated its willingness to deal, as though in an emergency, with those who violate its written and unwritten rules limiting resistance. It tells us a great deal about the varied means and the vigilance of our society that novelists as different in background, social status, and disposition as Jack London, Edith Wharton, and William Faulkner have added protagonists as different as Martin Eden, Lily Bart, and Joe Christmas to its list of victims. But even when it has tilted toward the dream of perfect order – as it has in crucial moments throughout its history and did decisively in the 1920s, for example – it has continued to honor, however cautiously, the counterdream of total freedom, as though mindful that no culture can survive by embracing one of these dreams and abandoning the other. To avoid desiccation, cultures committed principally to the dream of order must tolerate some measure of change. Conversely, to avoid disintegration, those committed principally to the dream of freedom must impose limits. The oscillation of the culture of the United States in this regard, and the changing roles of its literature in this process, form part of the story I tell.

My ways of tracing reciprocities among novels and between them and cultural events require some explanation. In one motion, I read novels as cultural events, mindful that history shapes our writing and our reading as well as other aspects of our lives. In another, I read cultural events as different in degree, but not in kind, from novels. When we use words to record, report, or interpret events, we turn them into scenes, spectacles, or stories. Whether this process is elaborate, as it tends to be in art, or more modest, as it tends to be in journalism or history, it does violence to events because, as actions, events do not make meaning; they take possession of time. They fill the minutes of our days, command our attention for their duration, and then disappear. Once we take possession of them as storytellers, with words arranged in a certain order, we transform them. Furthermore, although writing and reading play different roles in this process, they have crucial things in common, as Ralph Waldo Emerson suggests in "The American Scholar" when he pairs "creative reading" with "creative writing" as activities of "labor and invention," put to the task of making words on a page become "luminous with manifold allusion."

When I began tracing reciprocities among novels and between them and cultural events, I assumed I would be able to create a well-wrought narrative that followed a traditional, linear, logocentric line. But I soon discovered that in order to discuss cultural events as different kinds of narratives and different kinds of narratives as cultural events without hypostatizing the events or idealizing the stories, I would have to give up that model and trace instead several broken lines. In what follows, I jump and shift as I go, engaging and reengaging novels in some moments and cultural events in others. From one angle, my narrative unfolds as an episodic cultural history built around a series of events that merges with a history of several novels; from another angle, it unfolds as a history of several novels that becomes, after its fashion, an episodic cultural history. In short, I present cultural events as a lens for reading novels, and novels as a lens for reading cultural events.

Between 1890 and 1940, the novel continued to reign, as Matthew Arnold noted in 1887 with considerable dismay, as "the most popular and the most possible" form of imaginative literature. Its means of dominance changed, however, pushed in part by Henry James's interest in refining it as an art form. With the work of the great historical sociologists of the nineteenth and early twentieth centuries – Karl Marx, Emile Durkheim, Ernst Troeltsch, and Max Weber, among others – came a new awareness of how history envelops human life. Even Troeltsch, whose subject was the social teachings of the Christian churches, found envelopment easier to imagine than transcendence. With the rise of psychology came an awareness of the ways culture shapes consciousness, and consciousness shapes "experience" – a term that James defined, in his preface to *The Princess Casamassima,* as "our apprehension and our measure of what happens to us as social creatures," as though to remind us that language is one of our chief means of apprehending and measuring our experience. Acquiring more force, psychology changed our sense of the social scenes in which we live and the lives we live within them. Working with new forms of linguistics and anthropology, it also deepened our sense of how our modes of discourse as well as our institutions change everything they touch. The rapid rise of cities ushered in a new recognition, as both Vachel Lindsay and Ezra Pound noted, that urban experience is more "cinematographic" than "narrative" in form and more fluid and "modern" than stable or "traditional."

Responding to these developments, novelists launched aggressive experiments in technique. They enlarged the range of dissonant noises they recorded, jeopardizing closure; they deepened our sense of the tension between lived time – the flow of human experience within the world – and words more or less fixed on the pages of a book; and they tilted the novel toward the formal self-consciousness and the open-ended improvisation that became in different moments the signature of the modern and the postmodern. Such moves kept the novel untamed. Recent novels embrace and resist the past; they also resist and embrace noises that defy closure and closure that tames noises. In *Sister Carrie,* Carrie Meeber practices the deliberate forgetting of her past. She seldom thinks of Drouet, Hurstwood, her parents, or her sister once they pass from her range of vision. In *The Great Gatsby,* Jay Gatsby transforms his past by turning remembrance into aggressive mythmaking. How such things mirror larger acts of cultural forgetting and remembering – why, for example, the twenties tilted more toward mythmaking as a form of remembering in which selective forgetting played a large role, and the thirties tilted toward remembering and reporting that merged surreptitiously with forms of mythmaking and its selective forgetting – constitutes another part of the story I tell.

In teaching us how language and culture work, novels carry us up into handsome drawing rooms and down into the mean streets of city slums. They give us a sense of how lives lived in other times and places differ from our own. They challenge us to register voices whose moral and cultural resonances – or gendered and racial resonances – differ from our own. By the range of our response, we reflect the range of our capacity for calling our own lives into question. One conviction that grew in me as I wrote this book, for example, is this: that despite the varied dreams and the many experiences of success that mark the culture of the United States, the burden of our history teaches us that we should not speak of that success unless we are prepared to confront its costs by seeing it as its victims – those sacrificed for it or excluded from it – saw it. Under proper pressure, the novels I discuss can make clear the slightly unusual logic of such a claim.

Novels, of course, do things other than cut across the grain. In the United States, they have worked in countless ways to authorize what should or should not be honored as "American." The need to form a consensus about such things and to make visible the interlinked ideas, assumptions, and beliefs that undergird it – the rhetoric, the rituals, the symbols – stems in part from the country's sense of belatedness vis-à-vis older cultures, which goes with its sense of being perpetually young; in part from its sense of being deliberately created as a nation, which goes with its sense of vast purpose; and in part from its sense of religious, moral, regional, racial, and ethnic diversity, which goes with its sense of being a confederation as well as a nation. The urge to consolidate and the urge to resist consolidation remained strong throughout the period I survey. "Dissensus" found expression within the shifting consensus, just as resistance to ideology found expression within the dominant ideology. Both the events and the novels that I examine remain openly conflicted. They champion things they criticize and criticize things they champion.

In trying to understand the role that literature and literary history can play in the cultural process of consolidation and resistance, I have taken my lead from Hannah Arendt's "The Revolutionary Tradition and Its Lost Treasure" in *On Revolution* (1963). The United States has lost touch with its revolutionary tradition, Arendt argues, because it has failed "to remember" it, and it has failed to remember it because it has failed to talk about it. One sign of this, she says, is our fear of the revolutions of others. If it is true, she continues, "that all thought begins with remembrance, it is also true that no remembrance remains secure unless it is condensed and distilled" in language. What saves our affairs from futility is "incessant talk about them, which in turn remains futile unless . . . certain guideposts for future remembrance, and even for sheer reference, arise out of it." This process, Arendt asserts, is political, cultural, and literary. "How such guideposts for future reference and remembrance arise out of this incessant talk," she adds in a footnote, "may best be seen in the novels of William Faulkner, whose 'literary procedure,' built around 'incessant talk,' is 'highly political.' "

For Arendt, Faulkner remains "the only author to use" incessant talk for these purposes. It is more likely that Faulkner, an intensely modern and American as well as a deeply Southern writer, was in this representative as well as extreme. Faulkner had no need to break through to some wholly new "literary procedure." He had only to remain conflicted and enmeshed; and that, as it turned out, was for him unavoidable. Like most of the writers I discuss, he remained divided – skeptical as well as committed – even about the force of "literature." Beyond that he and his contemporaries had only to put their internal conflicts to the task of recovering lost themes and forgotten voices, while remembering that, in Mikhail Bakhtin's words, "to be means to communicate," and that "absolute death (non-being) is the state of being unheard, unrecognized, unremembered." To be "means to be for another, and through the other, for oneself," Bakhtin adds, before going on to remind us that "authentic human life" may best be conceived verbally as "open-ended dialogue."

The writers I engage see the things they value as threatened by destruction or corruption; personal acts of recovery and catharsis lie for them near the heart of creativity. But many of them, including Faulkner, also think of the individual as what Kenneth Burke, in *Attitudes Toward History* (1937), calls the "corporate we." To them isolation means being excluded from the ongoing dialogue in which acts of articulation become empowering as well as interdependent or, more radically, become empowering because interdependent. But with this recognition came another: that for people who remain voiceless, history exists only as a force that impinges upon them. It is appropriate to think of the novels I discuss as helping to socialize readers. But those whom they help to socialize into culture as a dynamic process, or what Bakhtin calls "open-ended dialogue," constitute a privileged subset of the population. Even novels that try to speak for the voiceless essentially cannot speak to them, since the voiceless do not read their words, as James Agee painfully discovered in writing *Let Us Now Praise Famous Men* (1941).

If, however, reading texts and events remains for some of us a way of participating in incessant talking or open-ended dialogue, and if these activities are among those through which we form as well as discover our fears and desires, then it follows that by changing the books we read and our ways of reading them we shall change as well the things we fear and desire and our ways of fearing and desiring them. Contrary to the logic of much recent criticism – which (c)overtly valorizes itself by (c)overtly celebrating its prowess in forcing works of art back into the nexus of power relations from which they came, denying their status as "art" and exposing them as tools of the status quo – change is one lesson that the past insists on teaching us. Like those who think of themselves as rebels, those who think of themselves as champions of the status quo often serve ends different from those they espouse. The limited hope that history offers us does not lie in pure lines of action in which one set of forces wins and another loses the future. It lies in victories and defeats that are always more as well as less than we expect them to be precisely because the opposing forces that define them do not merely engage in conflicts; they also embody contradictions. Insofar as reading and writing play roles in changing the things we desire and our ways of desiring them, they enter the historical process and, in their own modest ways, change the world. It is in this sense that our knowledge, as Elizabeth Bishop reminds us in "At the Fishhouses," is so radically historical as to be "forever, flowing and drawn," and also forever "flowing, and flown."

Recent developments in criticism have helped to free us of reverential attitudes toward authors and texts that were neither necessary nor desirable; and they have made us aware of many ways in which as writers and readers we may be taken in and used by stereotypes or, on a larger scale, myths and ideologies – inflected by race, gender, and class, for example – that are hostile to our interests and thus to our lives. At their best, however, these developments also reiterate what we might call, borrowing another term from Kenneth Burke, the "spiritual motive" of the modern novel in the United States, by serving the ongoing task of spontaneously creating imperfect communities, knit together by imperfectly possessed and even painful memories, and by imperfectly shared and practiced values. In this process our conflicted novels can still play important roles. James's *The Portrait of a Lady* stops rather than concludes, with its author uncertain and its heroine still on the go; Dreiser leaves Carrie rocking in her chair as she gazes down from a hotel room onto an unfinished world; Fitzgerald leaves Carraway still searching for lost words with which to clarify the significance of the faces and scenes he remembers; several of Faulkner's best novels, from *The Sound and the Fury* to *Absalom, Absalom!* to *Go Down, Moses,* present themselves as stories still engaged in the process of their own formation. Even when such novels speak of the past, a spirit of contemporaneity infuses them; and even when they seem about to become narrowly self-involved, they continue to evoke the putative community they seek to serve.

In this book, I make considerable use of discoveries of our new hermeneutics of suspicion. But I have followed the lead of Tzvetan Todorov in trying to avoid the special terms associated with them. Having acknowledged that there is a sense in which "one is always talking to oneself when one writes," Todorov goes on to pose a crucial question: "Must we really write exclusively for members of our own profession?" "Only physicists can read physicists," he adds, but in "the humanities and social sciences, including literary criticism," we write about people, and what we write will interest some of them – provided we make our "discourse accessible and interesting" by avoiding "jargon better adapted for conveying to our colleagues which army we belong to than for conveying to our readers what we are talking about" and follow instead the examples of the "writers" who furnish us our subject matter. Todorov's aim in this admonition is to remind us that communities are always in the process of becoming and that they depend on ongoing dialogue – upon words spoken both for and against the "Law" that undergirds them, for and against both what is and is not permitted or privileged. To help this book's chance of contributing to that dialogue, I have followed the advice of a friendly reader and devised "a kind of Victorian contents list" which I hope will aid readers in coping with my unorthodox way of jumping and circling.

Finally, let me say a few words about my title. While writing this book, I began calling it "Heirs of Changing Promise." By "heirs" I meant to include both the novelists and the characters I discuss as well as their readers and mine. By "changing promise," I meant to include both the United States as a still unruly, shifting cultural scene and the novel as a still unruly, shifting genre. Implicit in my effort to reconstitute and juxtapose selected novels and events, I came to recognize, was the hope that this book might contribute to the ongoing process of defining who those changing heirs and what those changing promises might be. Convinced of the need for greater clarity, I have adjusted my title. But I still hold to the layered hopes that resonate in my earlier version of it.

Acknowledgments

I am indebted to Rice University for research support that enabled me to complete this book and to several graduate students at Rice – especially Kathye Bergin, Jane Creighton, Mylène Dressler, Caroline Levander, Peter Norberg, and Duco Van Oostrum – who have helped me, sometimes unknowingly, in thinking about the problems I deal with.

I also owe special thanks to Emory University, which provided support that enabled me to begin this book when I still carried heavy administrative responsibilities. In particular I want to express my gratitude for the friendship and support of President James T. Laney and the goodwill of the faculty and staff of Emory College. Of the latter, there are far too many to name. But I want them to know that working with them for ten years was one of the finest things that ever happened to me, that I remember them with lasting gratitude, and that, as I write these words, I am sitting in a study where both the certificate of honorary membership given me by the College Staff Consortium and "A Cowboy's Farewell" given me by the chairs and directors of the Emory College faculty hang on the wall under the watchful eyes of my wolf in sheep's clothing, an earlier, anonymous gift of the faculty. I am also indebted to four research assistants who helped me at Emory with this and other projects – Karen Johnson, Carolyn Dennard, Sally Wolff, and Glenn Kellum.

Among several scholars who worked with me on the *Columbia Literary History of the United States*, I want especially to acknowledge those who wrote on the prose of the period covered by this book: Daniel Aaron, Quentin Anderson, James M. Cox, Donald M. Kartiganer, Donald McQuade, Elaine Showalter, Wendy Steiner, Robert Stepto, Linda Wagner, and Michael Wood. I learned from all of them. I am also indebted to my colleagues on *The Harper American Literature* – Robert Atwan, Martha Banta, Justin Kaplan, Donald McQuade, Robert Stepto, Cecelia Tichi, and Helen Vendler. Working with them has been a privilege.

At an early stage, I presented parts of this work at Harvard University, where I benefited from the suggestions of several people, including Daniel Aaron, Frank Lentricchia, John T. Matthews, Werner Sollors, and Robert Stepto. At a later stage, Charles Altieri and Carolyn Porter read parts of the manuscript. I am grateful for their help and encouragement. Sacvan Bercovitch has offered suggestions and encouragement all along the way. I am deeply grateful to him.

Terry Munisteri of Rice University helped me in the last stages of this project, and I am grateful for her expert assistance. Andrew Brown, Susan Chang, Julie Greenblatt, and Mary Racine of Cambridge University Press made helpful suggestions, and I am grateful to them as well. Jo Taylor, a colleague for ten years and a lasting friend, has shared the ups and downs of this book from the first word written to the last revision. I hope she knows how grateful I am for all she has done. On another personal note, I want to mention two former students who have become fast friends – John Irwin and Carolyn Porter. In naming them I remember how blessed I have been in students for many years. I hope they and other students not mentioned here will find things in this book that they like.

Finally, I want to thank my large, extended family, several generations deep, who have been with me as I wrote this book, including four now dead whose lives spanned part or all of the period it covers: my parents, Kenneth Cruse Minter (1889–1948) and Frances Hennessy Minter (1892–1948); my sister, Mary Frances Minter Wright (1917–67); and my father-in-law, James Alfred Sewell (1899–1988). To Caroline, my wife, who has talked with me about this book from its beginnings to its end, I owe more than I can possibly say. Together, we dedicate it to our children, Christopher and Frances, with good hope, gratitude, and love.

A Note on Sources, Citations, and Bibliography

I have used notes in the text to locate longer quotations from the novels and other works that I directly discuss. When I refer to works or briefly quote from them to illustrate changing moods and tendencies, I provide basic information – names of authors, titles, and dates of publication – in the text. As a further aid to inquisitive readers, I have added bibliographical notes to each of the three major parts of my narrative. To simplify and supplement these notes, I have provided a four-part bibliography – a general bibliography of works pertinent to most or all of the period between 1890 and 1940, and an additional bibliography for each of the three major parts of this study, 1890–1918, 1918–29, and 1929–40. In my bibliographical notes I refer to books included in these bibliographies by name of author and brief title and, on the first reference only, refer the reader to the appropriate part of the bibliography. When I refer to books not included in the bibliography, books on a single author, for example, I provide full data in the bibliographical notes.

PART ONE

A Dream City, Lyric Years, and a Great War

1. THE NOVEL AS IRONIC REFLECTION

Novelists as different as Henry James and Theodore Dreiser began the twentieth century as they ended the nineteenth, torn by conflicting allegiances. On one side, their openness to what Henry James called the "strange irregular rhythm of life," and thought of as the "strenuous force" that kept fiction on its feet, drew them toward history and a shared story of conquest, the taming of a continent and the making of a new nation and a new people, as we see in a range of titles, including James's *The American* (1877), William Dean Howells's *A Modern Instance* (1882), Gertrude Stein's *The Making of Americans* (1925), Willa Cather's *O Pioneers!* (1913), Dreiser's *An American Tragedy* (1925), and John Dos Passos's *U.S.A.* (1938). On another, they were drawn toward what James called the "romantic" and described as the "beautiful circuit and subterfuge of our thought and our desire," things "we never *can* directly know." Like Flaubert, James wanted to tidy up the loose, baggy traditions of the novel. Even more than Flaubert, he associated looseness with history. Simply by placing human thought and desire under the aspect of the "beautiful," defined in terms of order and subtle indirection ("circuit and subterfuge"), James evoked the lyrical tradition of the nineteenth century, in which self-examination became a prelude to self-transcendence and the journey toward the self's interior became a covert preparation for a journey up and out of time itself, for the solitary reader as well as the solitary singer. The move toward the interior provided the means, but self-transcendence was the end of the lyric, the real work of which was to bring the solitary self's thought and desire into harmony with the timeless world of "great" poems and "noble" thoughts, the scattered notes of the "supreme" or "absolute" song, that had begun when human time began – or more drastically, into harmony with the timeless music of the spheres. All art "constantly aspires toward the condition of music," Walter Pater announced in *Studies in the History of the Renaissance* (1873). "The thinker feels himself floating above the earth in an astral dome," Friedrich Nietzsche added in *Human, All-Too-Human* (1878), in discussing Beethoven's Ninth Symphony, "with the dream of immortality in his heart: All the stars seem to glimmer about him and the earth seems to sink ever further downward." In the hands of the Poet, Stéphane Mallarmé added, in "Crisis in Poetry" (1886–95), unlike those "of the mob," language "is turned, above all, to dream and song."

I

None of these writers – Pater, Nietzsche, Mallarmé – advocated traditional forms of spirituality. But it was not foolish error that led "upholders of culture," including religious leaders, who often turned cold eyes on the novel, to prefer lyric poetry, particularly as represented by the "Genteel" tradition and the "Fireside" poets, nor an accident that they did so the more ardently as the nineteenth century's assault on traditional religious beliefs intensified. However secular or even pagan the lyric's enterprise might seem at times, it remained tilted toward the spiritual.

The novel, by contrast, remained the most terrestrial of literary forms. Even when it was drawn toward the voice of a single, solitary character caught in the act of flight – Huckleberry Finn's, for example – its own less sublime commitments to ordinary and even sordid aspects of human thought and desire and obdurate social realities held it. The novel's orientation flowed from its commitment to what James called the *real:* the world of actualities – the colloquial, the vernacular, and the regional; the daily rhythms of love and work and play; the pull of desire and the push of competition in the day-to-day tasks of getting and spending money as well as time – things, James added, that we can't not know sooner or later in one way or another and yet can never fully measure. If, furthermore, the first of these moves, toward sordid or seamy consciousnesses, opened the novel to a fuller but less pretty psychology, the second maintained its commitment to the force of history – and that, as Robert Frost might have said, has made all the difference.

The novel might be epic in reach, but it had less interest than the epic in valorizing the past. Whatever role it might play in valorizing social authority, it could not, in Genteel terms, be lyric. Many of the ministers and priests who praised the lyric's devotion to spirituality and transcendence warned against the novel, fearing that its allegiance to the historical, material world it purported to represent was likely to promote worldliness. Novelists might lament, as James did, the inadequate life and materialist values of the Gilded Age. Certainly they wrote more out of disenchantment than approbation. But they gave their deeper loyalty to what Walt Whitman – a reform-minded poet bent on claiming poetry for the same middle class that had claimed and been claimed by the novel – called, in *A Backward Glance o'er Travel'd Roads* (1888), "vivification" of contemporary facts and "common lives" and defined as "the true use for the imaginative faculty of modern times." The rising authority of the novel – which by the late nineteenth century posed so direct a challenge that William Dean Howells wondered aloud whether the lyric might not be dying – was thus grounded in its willingness to embrace an expanding "people," the middle class, and grapple with the force of history, even when such commitments meant confronting an incorporating, rampaging, ransacking business civilization, thundering "past with the rush of the express," as Andrew Carnegie put it in *Triumphant America* (1886) – and even when this willingness carried the risk of implicating it in the historical processes and materialist values of the class and culture it embraced.

As concept, history embraces both the natural world as primal and residual force, and the social, cultural world as constituted of all the things that humans have done to nature, including the transformations they have worked on themselves in the process of doing that work. But it also embraces art – if by art we mean, as Henry James did, the "maximum of ironic reflections" that humans can bring to bear on the scenes and spectacles of life. At the turn of the century, a wide array of interactive events and developments – periods of prosperity and depression; new technologies; waves of immigration; rapid urbanization; a new, centralized form of corporate capitalism; a Great War; big labor; bigger and bigger government; the rise of the professions; the cult of the therapeutic; the cult of personal pleasure; rapid communications and rapid transit; rapid transformations in the lives of black Americans as they struggled up from bondage; and the emergence of the "new woman" as writer and protagonist, as well as object of poorly repressed anxieties – changed society. But they also changed fiction by deepening the alienation and the fascination writers experienced as they confronted the nation's changing scene. Artists in general and novelists in particular became more self-conscious, self-absorbed, and self-referential between 1890 and 1940 in part because the pace of change seemed almost out of control and in part because, during what André Malraux called "the twilight of the absolute," the arts – and later the disciplines devoted to their study – were becoming their own absolutes. Writers and artists began thinking of their works as autotelic because their age was so convincingly dominated by other forces.

Revisiting the United States in 1904, for the first time in twenty-five years, Henry James encountered a greater array of items than he had ever before seen – greater, he added in *The American Scene* (1907), than his "own pair of scales would ever weigh." The problem James faced – of whether the maximum of ironic reflection could match the "maximum of 'business' spectacle" then looming in the United States in a mass too large for any known language – lingered at least through the first several decades of the twentieth century as *the* problem of the novel. If Nietzsche also has lingered, especially for literary artists, along with Darwin, Marx, and Freud, as a major precursor, it is because the question of art has lingered, stubborn and obdurate, as a question not merely about the cultural role of art but, more ominously, about the adequacy of art to any cultural role it might care to claim.

One problem had to do with continuities or, more accurately, with their loss, which became a great theme of James, as well as Gertrude Stein, Edith Wharton, Sherwood Anderson, Willa Cather, Theodore Dreiser, F. Scott Fitzgerald, Ernest Hemingway, and William Faulkner. For what loss of a sense of sequence threatened was narrative. In traditional village cultures, Ezra Pound observed, people acquired a sense of slow time and thus of sequence based on shared knowledge. Because they knew what they, their families, and neighbors had done before, during, and after "the Revolution," and then regularly related what they knew in stories, their lives acquired historical meaning as parts of a cultural narrative. As a result, their lives lent themselves to formal fictional narrative. Cities, by contrast, like modern capitalist economies, celebrated the new and the present. They bombarded consciousness with sensory impressions of changing objects and scenes that overlapped; they were, Pound said, "cinematographic." As a result, they threatened to defy narrative altogether. Yet it was not only the possibility of narrative that was at stake; it was also the adequacy of language. The spectacle of life seemed, as James put it in *The American Scene,* to be hanging there, suspended "in the vast American sky . . . fantastic and abracadabrant, belonging to no known language."

Hoping to resist what he once called (in a letter to Daniel Cory) "the alienation of the intellect from the milieu," George Santayana used the role of the outsider-as-insider to gain insight into the persons and places of the land that from 1872 to 1912 he more or less called home. There were, to be sure, important things that Santayana only glimpsed, including the special role of economic abundance in shaping this country's version of modernity and the peculiar way in which, having created and named itself as a nation and a people, and having built into its federal organization and its Constitution a set of provisions against both fragmentation and unionization, the United States had promptly set about testing, both in the Civil War and in unprecedented waves of immigration, whether it could resist the centrifugal forces working to fragment it without succumbing to the centripetal forces working to homogenize it. Still, what he saw, he saw clearly: that, given its tilt toward the future, unimpeded, as he put it, "by survivals of the past," the United States would embrace the modern, would become a modern instance, a window to the world's future. Offended by such hasty embrace, Santayana returned to Europe, where old traditions and institutions were slowing the march of time. But he stayed in the United States long enough to see, as though for the first time, how marked it was by its openness to change.

What Santayana both exemplified and grasped as insight was the peculiar authority, moral as well as aesthetic, that a sense of marginality would confer on writers shrewd enough or lucky enough to control it, particularly in a country where changing facts were coming increasingly to loom as too numerous and novel for any one mouth or any known language. In 1903, a year before James's last trip to the United States and nine before Santayana's departure, W. E. B. Du Bois published *The Souls of Black Folk* (1903), announcing that there was "dogged strength" as well as pain in the predicament of a people who, robbed of "true self-consciousness," were permitted to see themselves, in anger, pity, fear, or amused contempt, only "through the eyes of others," and so were doomed to feel "their twoness." Du Bois thus joined Santayana in recognizing, first, the extraordinary pressures that the United States would exert on the people it marginalized and dispossessed and, second, the peculiar authority that the voices of such people would come to possess as the twentieth century unfolded. In considerable measure, the nation's fiction recounts the plights and adventures of deprived, betrayed, or battered people, often still young, like Huckleberry Finn, who are forced to enter the social fray when the twin tasks of redefining reality and shaping a new language adequate to ironic reflection in a new age are becoming the tasks of life as well as art.

Seizing this task as art's challenge was Mark Twain's great achievement; living out its consequences was Huckleberry Finn's mixed fate. When Twain thought of writing a sequel to his masterpiece and saw Huckleberry Finn in middle age, standing on the edge of the twentieth century rather than on the edge of a boundless territory, he thought of him as having gone mad and fallen silent.

2. CONFIDENCE AND UNCERTAINTY IN THE PORTRAIT OF A LADY

The fiction of Henry James features "passionate pilgrims" who leave home in search of "chance feasts" and then proceed through life as "wondering and dawdling and gaping" seekers. But it also features people who scheme and design, pushed by economic competition and pulled by sexual desire. The discourse of imaginative contemplation, the discourse of profit and loss, and the discourse of sexual conquest merge in James's work, each converted, as it were, into the currency of the other. In *The Golden Bowl* (1904), Adam Verver's "majestic scheme" possesses "all the sanctions of civilization" and aims at meeting the needs of the "thirsty millions" who seek culture as people once sought faith. Behind his "strange scheme" lie two convictions: that "he had force" because "he had money" and that "acquisition of one sort" could become the "perfect preliminary to acquisition of another." Finally, we come to see both the majestic millions he has made and the majestic palace of art he envisages as products of his capitalistic gifts for "transcendent calculation and imaginative gambling," for "getting in" and "getting out" at the right times – in short, for the "creation of 'interests' that were the extinction of other interests."

In order to place Adam Verver's talent for accumulating money and power under the aspect of his talent for majestic scheming in the name of art and, conversely, his talent for majestic scheming under the aspect of his acquisitive talents, James employs a language in which erotic, political, economic, and aesthetic desires intermingle. His cosmic strategists want to rid themselves of his passionate pilgrims, just as his passionate pilgrims want to free themselves of his cosmic strategists. In the end, however, each discovers a need for the other. If, furthermore, some of his characters, including Isabel Archer, long to be free of history, so also does history, if by history we mean human experience as shaped by political economies, want to be free of resistive, dissenting individuals in full possession of individual consciousnesses. Intolerant of many things in James's novels, history is especially intolerant of genuine independence – this being one of James's great themes, at least from *The Portrait of a Lady* (1881) on.

The *Portrait* underwent a long gestation, during which James struggled to transform his story of "the mere slim shade of an intelligent but presumptuous girl" into a big subject. One way was to surround his heroine with a rich social context of people and events; another was to make her an heir of Romanticism's long effort to discover and name the private, incommunicable things we can never directly know, and so permit her to emerge as an independent figure of consciousness. In theory, James honored the second of these more than the first; in practice, he used both: he added characters and events that enlarge Isabel Archer's world, and he endowed her with a personal consciousness that carries her toward a sense of destiny.

These two strategies for making a small subject large – the one by incorporating social history, the other by tracing the emergence of a personal consciousness capable of measuring history – were in fact becoming central to James's notion both of himself as artist and of the novel as literary form, even as he wrote the *Portrait*. Like *Watch and Ward* and *The Bostonians,* the *Portrait* reflects the lingering influence of female novelists James read in his youth, especially Louisa May Alcott and Anne Moncure Crane Seemuller, and the lingering influence of his father's confused opinions about sex, marriage, and women. But the *Portrait* enlarges the play of James's conflicted imagination in two related ways, and so makes visible two strategies that have shaped the efforts of novelists to cope with a world of rapidly expanding and changing facts. James wanted to find some way of doing justice to the pressure of history as overdetermining force, while also exploring the fates of individuals who want to feel free. If abject failure was one possibility, unsuccess was another. Most of his passionate pilgrims begin, like Isabel Archer, as unsponsored children and then become isolated expatriates or marginalized observers of an alien world.

The *Portrait* begins with a description of a dense, palpable milieu that tends to incorporate everyone:

> Under certain circumstances there are few hours in life more agreeable than the hour dedicated to the ceremony known as afternoon tea. There are circumstances in which, whether you partake of the tea or not – some people of course never do, – the situation is in itself delightful. Those that I have in mind in beginning to unfold this simple history offered an admirable setting to an innocent pastime.[1]

James's emphasis here is on an imposing social order that has served as an effective medium of value. We see one token of its force in its ability to envelop people who prefer not to partake of it; another, in terms like "dedicated," "delightful," "admirable," and "innocent"; and yet another, in the self-assured voice of its narrator. As the *Portrait* unfolds, however, it leaves this world behind. First, we encounter Isabel Archer, a child of promise, who comes from the still new world of the United States. Since she is open and unaffected, and wants to experience life firsthand, Isabel is perfectly suited to serve as an exemplary protagonist of a cautionary tale in which the heroine suffers in order to become wise. Early in the novel, the narrator seems confident that society's lessons will turn out to be good as well as inevitable – as they are, more or less, for Jane Austen's Emma Woodhouse. Soon, however, we discover that the society undergirding England's tea parties suffers from some deep malaise: "There's something the matter with us all," Ralph Touchett says, reminding us that, although the gardens and drawing rooms of England and Europe demand accommodation and sometimes reward it, they no longer serve as the locus of value. Only Mr. Touchett, a dying citizen of a dying age, discloses what conviction, connectedness, and loyalty might mean. Each of the other characters seems somehow already to have learned, without remembering when or how, the lesson that Ralph Touchett lifts to visibility with his gift to Isabel: that money is the foundation of their social order. Simply by accepting the imperial process by which Isabel, upon acquiring a large fortune, becomes the center of their lives, they acquiesce to the economic imperative on which their society is based – and thus commit themselves to confronting the large question of whether freedom is to be defined in spiritual or material terms, as freedom from earthly entanglements and restraints or as possession of money and power.

Madame Merle and Gilbert Osmond differ from other characters in the *Portrait* primarily because they remain untroubled by what they know and so are prepared to make the most of it. Having noted that "the greatest invention of the nineteenth century was the invention of the method of invention," Alfred North Whitehead went on to describe the rise of the inventor as a fall into "disillusionment" or "at least anxiety." Having once thought of themselves "as a little lower than the angels," human beings had become servants "of nature," he said. Fulfilling the prophecy of Francis Bacon, he added, this turnabout had undermined "the foundations of the old civilisation." Socialized almost beyond the point of being human, Merle and Osmond show little interest in nature. Their world is social, their style imperial. In their attitude toward society, however, they mirror the same curious dominance-as-subservience that Whitehead locates in modern science's attitude toward nature. Moved by a desire similar to modern science's, they follow a similar strategy. They are realists who submit to society in order to give the appearance of dominating it.

The confrontation between Isabel and Madame Merle, in Chapter 19 of the *Portrait,* turns for Isabel on the role of appearances – the trappings of class, such as manners and accents, as well as the furnishings of life, teacups, gowns, and jewels – in representing the real thing: her unique, essential self. But it turns for Madame Merle on whether there is a self that precedes or even exists independent of its signs and the social conventions that govern them – the hope of semiautonomy as well as transcendence having already been surrendered. This debate, though of uncertain beginnings, is intensely modern, and Merle and Osmond are modern in nothing so much as this: that in them the line between being passive and being active dissolves. As master manipulators, they stage and direct scenes; as servants if not slaves, attendant lords, in J. Alfred Prufrock's phrase, they play out their lives as overdetermined creatures in a world they never made. "It still remains to be seen," Whitehead concluded, "whether the same actor can play both" the part of the inventor and the part of the servant. Having once pictured himself as the detached lord of his own creations, James Joyce came full circle in *Finnegans Wake:* "My consumers, are they not my producers?" Merle and Osmond know how to manipulate money and status, conversations and conventions, words, paintings, and people, including themselves, for their own amusement. They treat everyone the same: as pawns in a game played out in the twilight of purposive existence. Passion and pleasure as well as joy and wonder lie somehow already behind them. Amusement, precariously based on a sense of dominance, is their only anodyne for malaise.

By making Isabel's world their world, James turns his cautionary tale of youthful folly into the tale of an evil fate. Born a child of promise, Isabel falls into history, only to find herself "ground in the very mill of the conventional." In this story, which James almost certainly conceived as a version of the story of the United States and the modern world, "our heroine" suffers out of all proportion to her folly, largely because she is cleverer at doing what she wills – at having her way – than she is at willing what she wills – that is, at clarifying and naming her own desires. Isabel's problems have several sources, of course. Her money brings possessions that become something like a soft if not an iron cage; and since she is a child of the United States, she assumes that money brings responsibility because it appears to bring power. In addition, she is surrounded by people who are expert manipulators of themselves and others.

But Isabel's deeper problems revolve around her own uncertain impulses. Her "visions of a completed consciousness" – like Ralph Touchett's dream of seeing her soar above her world – turn less on a narrative desire to enter her world and take hold of it than on a lyric desire to transcend it. Even after she falls into history, she finds surrendering her separatist desires very difficult. Furthermore, as she begins to accept the fact of being enmeshed, her own consciousness emerges as strange, uncertain, and conflicted until it comes to resemble the ambiguous world in which she moves. In exploring what it means that humans in a technological age can more nearly do what they will than ever before yet cannot will what they will, the great physicist Werner Heisenberg quotes the Chinese sage Chang Tsu: "Whoever loses his simplicity becomes uncertain in the impulses of his spirit." And so it is with Isabel. Loss of simplicity not only changes her; it makes her story a tragedy of the socialization of consciousness – a development that seems to thrust itself on James's narrator almost as harshly as on his reader, making the *Portrait* a new novel.

Just after Isabel recognizes that Osmond's declaration of love is something she has invited as well as something that surprises her, James's narrative voice changes. Once sure of itself, it now finds itself moving over strange and threatening ground:

> What had happened was something that for a week past her imagination had been going forward to meet; but here, when it came, she stopped – that sublime principle somehow broke down. The working of this young lady's spirit was strange, and I can only give it to you as I see it, not hoping to make it seem altogether natural. Her imagination, as I say, now hung back:

there was a last vague space it couldn't cross – a dusky, uncertain tract which looked ambiguous and even slightly treacherous, like a moorland seen in the winter twilight. But she was to cross it yet.[2]

With the narrator's early assurance, and our own as readers, now relics of the past, like teatime at Gardencourt, what is left – for Isabel, her narrator, and her readers alike – is a world in which the representative structure is Osmond's "house of darkness," where life and art, ground in the mill of the conventional, seem moribund. Isabel's triumph consists in recognizing, first, that her world is one in which all human values are threatened and, second, that in its own conflicts her consciousness resembles her world. For it is the shock of this double recognition that initiates a moment of "liminality" in which she realizes that her old dreams for herself in that world must be relinquished. In her midnight meditation – in Chapter 42 – Isabel's internal life becomes the *other* side of a social scene that is slouching its way toward emptiness because it no longer understands its own desires. To salvage from that world and for it – and of herself and for it – all that can be salvaged, she must recognize that she is entangled and encumbered, that selfhood is a social issue as well as a private concern, and that to become a responsible social agent she must master words, customs, conventions, mores, and institutions that possess histories of their own that preclude their ever becoming wholly hers. Similarly, she must confront the "bitter" knowledge that she, too, has been used: "the dry staring fact that she had been an applied handled hung-up tool, as senseless and convenient as mere shaped wood and iron." This recognition becomes an extension of her rereading of her life, and it carries her away from the lyric desire for transcendence toward a narrative desire for entanglement, not as "renunciation," but as a deep "sense that life would be her business for a long time to come." Rome, she has come to realize, is a "world of ruins" where "people have suffered." These interrelated recognitions possess, as James presents them, a "very modern quality" that detaches itself and becomes "objective," allowing Isabel to see her own disappointments in a new light. First, "in a world of ruins the ruin of her happiness" becomes a "less unnatural catastrophe"; second, surrounded by things that have "crumbled for centuries and yet still were upright," she discovers a "companionship in endurance" that reinforces and enlarges her commitment to herself by making it a commitment to doing all that she can to rescue Pansy, until toward the end she becomes something like Pansy's earthly "guardian angel."

   In these interrelated discoveries, we observe the return of several things that Isabel has denied. The staying power of the denied as well as of the past is a part of what she learns for herself and teaches us about Osmond's world. In this way James reminds us that works of literature achieve one of their tasks by embracing the public thought of their time. This was not a new lesson, of course, but it was necessary, in part because it enabled James to remind us that a novel can expose the secret fears and hopes of an age even if it cannot resolve them. Only by confronting her own complicity and her own limitations can Isabel hope to find a way of countering Merle's duplicities and Osmond's manipulations and a way of replacing her empty dream of the "infinite vista of a multiplied life" with possibilities open to an implicated, conflicted, and used self. What Isabel thus inches her way toward resembles what James calls, in his preface to *The Lesson of the Master*, "the high and helpful public and, as it were, civic use of the imagination."

James was drawn to the drama of such discoveries because he felt the need of them. His sense of mounting technical confidence finds expression in the brilliant manipulations of Merle and Osmond. His uncertainties and confusions, which were moral as well as aesthetic, find expression in Isabel's predicament. As Isabel sits by the fire rereading her life, her problem emerges as a problem of perception, of consciousness, and, by extension, a problem of language. But it is also a problem of Isabel's conception of herself as an autonomous agent. The moment her crisis draws attention to the tools and processes of consciousness, and then recasts the self as neither coherent unity nor conflicted multiplicity but rather as the play among these possibilities, Isabel becomes a modern protagonist. Our preference for her over Gilbert Osmond and Madame Merle can be put in several ways. But it turns on her refusal to let disappointments, or more drastically "ruins," rob her of will and her refusal to let proliferating ambiguities and uncertainties persuade her that moral judgments always mask self-interest – the cynical position that Merle and Osmond fix as one of the major temptations of the modern world.

In the world of the *Portrait*, the lyric desire for transcendence makes itself felt in Isabel's longing to live the "infinite vista of a multiplied life" and in Ralph Touchett's desire to see her rise above her world. But Isabel acquires as well a narrative impulse toward entanglement that squares more fully both with living in the encumbered worlds of historical societies and with becoming the heroine of a novel in which the story of the United States becomes entangled with that of the modern world. That story was scientific, technological, philosophical, political, aesthetic, and literary, in ways the *Portrait* never directly engages. Like modern science and technology, literary modernism emerged as a fast-moving affair, fueled by dislocations and upheavals as well as innovations. It would be played out in major cities of Russia, middle Europe, western Europe, England, and the United States, and also in villages in Minnesota, Mississippi, and Argentina. In the United States – a "half-savage country, out of date," to borrow Pound's words, populated by people from a hundred lands, uprooted and even rootless – two very different styles, geared to ironic reflection in a new age, would dominate narrative expression. One was Mark Twain's discovery of the energy and cunning of vernacular English, particularly as expressed in the voice of Huckleberry Finn as he grapples with what it means to be enslaved or free, black or white, female or male, damned or saved. The other was James's grand style, which had its origins in Isabel's midnight vigil. In both of these, technical confidence would mingle with – and would serve both to counter and to stress – moral and spiritual confusions, evasions, and insights. We see them in the oblique confessions of Willa Cather's

Jim Burden and F. Scott Fitzgerald's Nick Carraway; in the self-conscious fluidity of Gertrude Stein's prose and the self-conscious restraint of Ernest Hemingway's; and in the audacity of William Faulkner's, where concealment matches disclosure, mystification matches expression, and evasion matches revelation. These and other acts of style acknowledge epistemological difficulties and imply that beauty has become almost impossible. They thus pay tribute to the dawning of an age, confident as never before of its technical powers yet unsure of itself, too.

It is, then, a new and colder darkness, in which values begin to fade and the world seems to be speeding up as it runs down, that forces itself upon us in *The Portrait of a Lady*. By situating his story of the modern self in a rich social context, James presents the problem of replacing lost values and countering spiritual impoverishment as society's problem and the novel's as well as the self's. The imagination's task of vivifying the facts of life becomes Isabel's no less than James's, and hers no more than her readers'. But Isabel is a model for us on another count, too. Back in New York, in a room whose only door to life's street has been sealed, she has read novels that filled her mind with impossible dreams. Yet we cannot say simply that that experience poorly prepares her for living in the only world given her. For what is it that she does, as she sits alone by the fire, if not to engage in reading and rereading both her life and her historical culture as historical novels that disclose and reveal as well as mislead and misguide. Sometime between her midnight vigil and the last paragraph of the novel, she is able to reconcile for herself the tension between freedom and consent. The freedom to defy her husband by turning away from him, she claims as her own. Having exercised her freedom once, however, she retains it as an option even when, at the end of her recorded story, she uses it as the basis for not turning away from Pansy, the stepdaughter who needs a "guardian angel" and has no hope of finding anyone else to play that role.

3. LINES OF EXPANSION

To grasp fully the authority of Isabel Archer's story, we must see behind it the force of history as felt in the interplay of two contrastive lines of expansion. The first of these lines carried people from Europe to the New World and its frontiers; the second carried immigrants to its cities and the children of farmers and ranchers back from its frontiers to its cities, or even across the Atlantic to England and Europe. Between 1820 and 1930, more than 62 million people uprooted themselves and resettled in "foreign" lands, dwarfing the great *Volkerwanderung* of the Teutonic tribes during the last centuries of the Roman Empire. Of these, roughly 52 million settled in the United States, Europe's and then Asia's main frontier, making it not only the most diverse country in the world but also, as Santayana saw, the home of descendants of the most restless peoples in the world. Interacting with this migration was another, from the soil of farms and footpaths of villages, in

Europe as well as the United States, to the sidewalks and streets of cities. If novels like Willa Cather's *My Ántonia* (1918) and O. E. Rölvaag's *Giants in the Earth* (1924–5 in Norwegian; 1927 in English) trace the first of these lines of expansion, Theodore Dreiser's *Sister Carrie* (1900) traces the second, toward the cities of the upper Midwest and the East – a line that James extended back across the Atlantic to Europe in scores of stories, including Isabel Archer's.

Political and economic as well as cultural, these lines of expansion yielded hundreds of stories in life as well as art: William Dean Howells's, Mark Twain's, Hamlin Garland's, and Edith Wharton's; F. Scott Fitzgerald's, Jay Gatsby's, and Nick Carraway's; Willa Cather's as well as Jim Burden's; Theodore Dreiser's as well as Carrie Meeber's; Henry James's as well as Isabel Archer's and Adam Verver's. In one way or another, furthermore, all of these lives were driven by dreams of possession – sexual, cultural, and economic. The "New World," early promoters promised, was a "*Paradise* with all her Virgin beauties," waiting to be claimed. The Scotch-Irish, as one formulation put it, landed on the eastern shores of the New World and spread out across the continent, keeping the Sabbath and everything else they could lay their hands on. "I take possession of the old world," says the protagonist of "The Passionate Pilgrim" (1871), one of James's early international tales, "I inhale it – I appropriate it!"

Adventure as taking possession and taking possession as adventure, and both of these as versions of living that can slide almost imperceptibly into versions of dying, became the nation's story, almost from the beginning. On his third voyage, having decided that the world was not round but pear-shaped and that he was standing near its highest point, Christopher Columbus wrote his sovereigns to report "that the Terrestrial Paradise" testified to in Holy Scriptures now lay before him like a dream – for him to explore and them to possess. "Your Highnesses have an Other World here," he wrote, one that would expand their dominion and wealth. Later, as English-speaking Protestants got into the act, the lines separating piety, patriotism, profit, and possession continued to blur. John Winthrop and his followers braved the "Vast Sea" of the North Atlantic on instructions from God in order "to possess" this "good land" and build there "a City upon a Hill" as a beacon to the world. Later still, as the literature of exploration became a literature of settlement, and so became "American" as well as Spanish, French, Dutch, and English, connotations multiplied. Writing at the end of the sixteenth century, Sir Walter Raleigh described "the sweet embraces of . . . Virginia," while another voyager depicted the New World as "a country that hath yet her maydenhead." Caught up in the possibilities of such discourse, Richard Hakluyt, the great collector of explorers' narratives, urged Sir Walter to persevere "a little longer" so that his "bride will shortly bring forth new and most abundant offspring" – without noticing that he had enlarged the role of male explorers and diminished the role of women. Even late in the nineteenth century, the daunting term "New World" and its cognates – "Wilderness," "Garden," "Virgin Land" – still carried connotations of some special sanction, as names given to a place chosen for some grand destiny. What could such terms as "America" and "American" mean if they did not mean something special? The "mission" of the American people was not only to civilize the New World, but also to experience renewal born of the process of conquest and then to bear witness, to all peoples everywhere, to the efficacy of such renewal. "The untransacted destiny of the American people is to subdue the continent," William Gilpin said first in 1846 and then in 1876, in *The Mission of the North American People.*

Such imperatives continued to echo in the literary and political discourse of the United States for generations: in Walt Whitman ("Seest thou not God's purpose from the first"), Hart Crane ("Terrific threshold of the prophet's pledge"), and Frederick Jackson Turner ("the richest gift ever spread before civilized man"), for example. Caught up in the Civil War's testing of the nation's survival, Congress passed the Homestead Act (1862), which granted free farms of 160 acres to all citizens and applicants for citizenship who occupied and improved the land for five years, in part to reiterate the nation's commitment to subduing and possessing the continent and in part to separate Thomas Jefferson's agrarian vision of the New World from the institution of slavery. And in the years following the Civil War, that double intent seemed about to be realized. Between 1860 and 1990, the number of farms and ranches rose from 2,000,000 to 5,737,000, adding 430,900,000 acres of settled land, more than had been claimed in all the decades before 1860 combined.

In fact, however, the increased pace of immigration did more to enlarge the cities than to settle the prairies, which is to say that it primarily fed the nation's second line of development, from the plains back to Chicago and the cities of the East. Between 1880 and 1890, Chicago tripled in size and New York grew from less than 2 million to more than 3.5 million. Begun as a nation of villages and farms, the country was becoming a nation of cities. In 1830 one of fifteen Americans lived in cities of 8,000 or more; by 1900 one of three; by 1910 nearly half; and by 1920 more than half. In 1860 there were 141 cities of 8,000 or more; by 1910 there were 778, often located on the sites of old mission churches, trading posts, frontier forts, or Indian battles. With this concentration of people went another: by 1910, 1 percent of the nation's business firms produced 45 percent of its manufactured goods. With both kinds of concentration came a new kind of diversification. By 1890, after two immense waves of immigration had brought millions of "strangers" to the nation's shores, one-fourth of the population of Philadelphia and one-third of the populations of Boston and Chicago were foreign-born, and four of five New Yorkers were either foreign-born or the children of foreign-born parents. Soon a third wave would swell to tidal proportions, bringing millions of people from southern and eastern Europe – a development reflected in Alfred Stieglitz's photograph "The Steerage, 1907." Following Stieglitz's lead, Henry Roth, in the prologue to *Call It Sleep* (1934), describes 1907 as "the year that was destined" to bring the greatest number of immigrants to the shores of the United States. Actually, however, although each year between 1909 and 1914 matched 1906 and 1907 by bringing more than a million immigrants to the United States, the peak year was 1913, when 1,285,349 arrived.

Each of these epic stories – the exploration and settlement of the West, the new immigration, and the migration to cities – found literary expression time and again. And each fed off the others. In Rölvaag's *Giants in the Earth* we follow Beret and Per Hansa as they pack their possessions in a few trunks and begin the great voyage from Norway across an ocean so wide it seems to have no end, to the "Promised Land." Docking in Quebec, they move through Detroit, Milwaukee, Prairie du Chien ("Had that been in Wisconsin?"), Lansing, Iowa, and Fillmore County, Minnesota, before they finally reach the Dakota Territory, a "vast stretch of beautiful land." There, fifty-two miles from Sioux Falls and so far from the world of their births that they have lost track, they stake a claim, which Per Hansa records on June 6, 1873, eleven years after the Homestead Act:

> This vast stretch of beautiful land was to be his – yes, *his* – and no ghost of a dead Indian would drive him away!... His heart began to expand with a mighty exaltation. An emotion he had never felt before filled him and made him walk erect.... "Good God!" he panted. "This kingdom is going to be *mine!*"[3]

Per Hansa is not a brutal man. His story, as Rölvaag signals both in his subtitle – "A Saga of the Prairie" – and in his dedication – "To Those of My People Who Took Part in the Great Settling..." – evokes the earliest story of the United States. But it is a story in which women play subordinate roles and suffer, as Beret does, great loneliness; and it is a story in which the dispossession and the deaths of Native Americans seem to be sanctioned if not by God at least by history.

Willa Cather's *My Ántonia* (1918), written earlier but set several years later, follows two related journeys. Jim Burden is an orphan who travels from an old Virginia farm through Chicago, across so many rivers that he becomes "dull to them." Ántonia Shimerda is a member of the first Bohemian family to journey "across the water" through Chicago to Black Hawk, Nebraska. Later, Burden, who becomes the narrator of Ántonia's story, journeys from the western edge of the New World through Chicago to New York. Later still, he goes back to visit Ántonia, in preparation for telling her story. Hamlin Garland wrote stories – *A Son of the Middle Border* (1920) and *A Daughter of the Middle Border* (1921) – that resemble Burden's and Ántonia's, and lived one that resembled Burden's. Born in Wisconsin, he moved to Boston, where he won the friendship of William Dean Howells, before going back to the Middle Border to write. Theodore Dreiser's *Sister Carrie* (1900) recounts the story of another child of immigrants who moves from the rural Midwest to Chicago, carrying her belongings in a small trunk and a satchel, and her savings, four dollars, in a yellow leather snap purse. "It was in August, 1889. She was eighteen years of age, bright, timid, and full of the illusions of ignorance and youth."

As poorly equipped for the move she makes and the strange new world she encounters as Beret and Per Hansa are for theirs, or Ántonia is for hers, Carrie, too, must learn by going where she has to go. Full of yearning though she is, she remains so vague as to seem almost passive, "A Waif Amid Forces." Drawn from Columbia City to Chicago and then to New York, she moves from one dry relationship to another. Even after she becomes a wealthy performer, she remains curiously blank. In one sense, life is something that happens to her; in another, it is something that is always about to happen. Early and late, we see her sitting in a rocking chair, moving yet going nowhere. On her first evening in Chicago, sitting in her sister's small flat on Van Buren Street, she feels "the drag of a lean and narrow life" and moves "the one small rocking-chair up to the open window," where she sits, "looking out upon the night and streets in silent wonder." Later we see her on stage, gazing out at audiences that gaze back at her, or sitting in other rocking chairs, observing the world's spectacles as they parade past her windows or through her mind's eye. In the novel's last scene, we see her in "her comfortable chambers at the Waldorf," reinforced by "her gowns and carriage, her furniture and bank account," still waiting for the "halcyon day when she should be led forth among dreams become real." During her performances, she goes down, into time and history, where she becomes a social creature and makes money. After or between performances, she moves up and out of the fray, protected by her jewels and furs and bank account, toward a kind of secular transcendence, where she can look down on the street life of her world and feel almost free of society and its requirements. Filled with yearnings that linger, she continues to move without going anywhere, as we see in the novel's last lines:

> In your rocking-chair, by your window dreaming, shall you long, alone. In your rocking-chair, by your window, shall you dream such happiness as you may never feel.[4]

Ántonia's story, like Per Hansa's, is the story of a family within a dispersed yet supportive community of families in which the family still functions as the basic economic unit. In 1787 it took nine farm families to feed one urban family. By 1940 one farm family could sustain eight city families. In 1954, in *The Dollmaker*, Harriette Arnow described one part of what the loss of the farm family as an economic unit meant to women:

> It wasn't the way it used to be back home when she had done her share, maybe more than her share of feeding and fending for the family. Then, with egg money, chicken money, a calf sold here, a pig sold there, she'd bought almost every bit of food they didn't raise. Here everything, even the kindling wood, came from [her husband].[5]

Ántonia lives a much harder life than Carrie. By the end of her story, she seems worn and even battered by time. But she remains the central member of a definable unit that is larger than herself. Carrie, by contrast, lives as a single separate self in a large, almost limitless city of performers and observers.

Neither Per Hansa nor Ántonia has anything we would call a career, though their lives are filled with deeds done – marriages made and sustained, homes and barns built, children born and reared, crops planted, harvested, and laid by. Carrie lives in rented rooms, apartments, or hotels, and her life is filled with activities that we associate with theaters, music halls, and sports arenas – with rehearsals that possess meaning only as preparation for performances that are intense yet ephemeral, intimate yet distanced, personal yet stylized. Her career and her possessions are in the end all she has.

Behind these contrasts lie vast differences. Per Hansa and Ántonia live in a world of forces and rhythms not made by human hands. Both of them – as James Dickey once remarked of Theodore Roethke – are animal enough to feel themselves half into unthinking nature yet human enough to be uncomfortable there. Their homes are shelters built to protect their human mortalities. They travel great distances and live full lives, but they never travel far enough or live long enough to encounter a world like Carrie's cities, where life is shaped by human hands to mirror human desires.

In *Giants in the Earth, My Ántonia,* and *Sister Carrie* elements of what James called the "real" and the "romantic" mingle, though it is probably fair to say that elements of "romantic" are more pronounced in *Giants in the Earth* and *My Ántonia* than in *Sister Carrie.* Yet in James's terms, these worlds divide in the opposite way. Ántonia and Per Hansa move amid forces that are real precisely because they do *not* conform to human desire, while Carrie inhabits a world that mirrors human longings. Insofar as her world remains *other,* it remains other despite being shaped by human hands. If her world fails her, as in some sense it surely does, it fails because it mirrors what Heisenberg calls uncertainties "in the impulses of the spirit." Having triumphed, Carrie becomes a woman of means who possesses to an unprecedented extent the capacity to do whatever she wills. Only her capacity for controlling or even understanding what she wills remains limited.

The sights and sounds of Carrie's world emanate from the concerted efforts of people to manipulate their environment in the name of will and desire – which is to say, power and longing. Ántonia and Per Hansa live in a land of the big sky and the great plains, of dry winds and great blizzards. Above them the great ball of the sun rises, grows enormous, and then retreats "farther and farther into the empty reaches of the western sky." "At the moment when the sun" disappears, "the vastness of the plain seem[s] to rise up on every hand," filling "the silence . . . with terror," until the "spell of evening" crowds in and lays "hold of them," taking possession of those who would possess it.

Like Carrie, Ántonia and Per Hansa look to the future, filled with hope and fear. But all of the grand spectacles of their world belong to nature. For them, task follows task; there is always work to be done. They live hard, unillustrious lives, and time scars and carries them as it does all things. Having left home to be married, Ántonia is driven back, deserted and pregnant. Carrie, by contrast, carries on extended affairs with Drouet and Hurstwood without apparent concern about pregnancy, as though she can control what happens to her body by will alone. Per Hansa dies in a blizzard, trying to return home from an errand undertaken to help a sick neighbor. Yet there is a sense in which both Ántonia and Per Hansa feel themselves to be the masters of their days. Though often heavy, their steps are measured in ways that Carrie's are not. When Per Hansa dies on the open prairie, leaning against a haystack, with his "eyes . . . set toward the west," his mind is filled, not with vague dreams of the future, but with memories of his wife and home as they "come, warm and tender" to make him laugh softly, and then of hope for his son. Although Ántonia's life is no more illustrious than Per Hansa's, she too becomes one of the earth's giants. She leaves images in the mind, Jim Burden remarks near the novel's end, that grow stronger with time, because she lends

> herself to immemorial human attitudes which we recognize by instinct as universal and true. I had not been mistaken. She was a battered woman now, not a lovely girl; but she still had that something which fires the imagination, could still stop one's breath for a moment by a look or gesture that somehow revealed the meaning in common things.[6]

Embedded in Jim Burden's celebration of Ántonia, however, is an oblique confession of his own internal confusions as well as the empty marriage he has made and the sterile life he lives – of which both his frenetic travels and his way of coming accidentally to tell the only story that matters to him are signs. The strengths he celebrates in Ántonia emerge as the other side of his own weaknesses. His seeming loyalty to nature is in fact another part of his sentimental, nostalgic loyalty to the past. Insofar as his celebration of Ántonia lifts her out of time, it allows him to claim possession of her, as the novel's title suggests. And in doing this, it does violence to her earned relationship to the cyclical world of nature, from which he is already alienated, in order to claim her for the linear world represented by the trains he rides and serves. In his hands, Ántonia is judged by a code of conscience not her own, a fact that reinforces our sense of the wide, never completely traversable distances that separate many things in *My Ántonia* – including act from word, event from memory, pioneer settlers from inheritors, hired girls from bourgeois families, West from East, land from city, and above all female heroine from male narrator. *My Ántonia* explores all of these distances; in its many juxtapositions of them, it may even be said to make each explicit exploration of one an implicit exploration of the others. But its structure stresses the last of them and thus brings each of them under its controlling aspect.

Jim Burden, as it turns out, is as incapable of fathering children as Carrie is of bearing them. But Carrie fills her life not with stories out of her past but with performances. Time carries her, as it carries Jim and Ántonia, but with a difference, in part because few characters in the history of the literature of the United States carry so few active memories with them. Carrie rarely mentions her family and never looks back longingly toward anything we might call "home." Once they have dropped out of her life, she scarcely thinks about Drouet or Hurstwood. Between performances, she practices, looking to the future; between practices, she rocks and waits, filling her life with formless yearning.

To understand Carrie's characteristic moment as one in which living becomes yearning, we must understand her urban world as one made to reflect human desires — for pleasures, comforts, and diversions as well as power — that have become indiscriminate, mixed, and confused, and thus insatiable. And we must understand it as having in the process acquired a forward-looking, expansive logic of its own:

> In 1889 Chicago had the peculiar qualifications of growth which made such adventuresome pilgrimages even on the part of young girls plausible. Its many and growing commercial opportunities gave it widespread fame, which made of it a giant magnet, drawing to itself, from all quarters, the hopeful and the hopeless — those who had their fortune yet to make and those whose fortunes and affairs had reached a disastrous climax elsewhere. . . . Its population was not so much thriving upon established commerce as upon the industries which prepared for the arrival of others. The sound of the hammer engaged upon the erection of new structures was everywhere heard. Great industries were moving in. The huge railroad corporations which had long before recognised the prospects of the place had seized upon vast tracts of land for transfer and shipping purposes. Street-car lines had been extended far out into the open country in anticipation of rapid growth. The city had laid miles and miles of streets and sewers through regions where, perhaps, one solitary house stood out alone — a pioneer of the populous ways to be. There were regions open to the sweeping winds and rain, which were yet lighted throughout the night with long, blinking lines of gas-lamps, fluttering in the wind. Narrow board walks extended out, passing here a house, and there a store, at far intervals, eventually ending on the open prairie.[7]

Chicago, Carrie's first city, is most fully itself as an inspired outline of what it will be. We feel its force most deeply in its forward-leaning crunch — in industries designed to prepare for the arrival of new industries, and buildings built to prepare for buildings yet to be built. It preempts because it is insatiable as well as unfinished. The reaching lines of streetcars and streetlights exist as lines of expanding force. They thrust into the open prairie and windy night "in anticipation of rapid growth." In this they recall *The Cliff-Dwellers* (1893) by Henry Fuller, whom Dreiser called "the father of American realism," in part because he set his novel in a skyscraper; and they anticipate Alfred Stieglitz's photograph "From the Shelton Hotel" (1932) in which the most striking feature of the city's skyline is the scaffolding of an unfinished building reaching up into the sky. Carrie lives in a world of human making that thrusts up into the sky and out along the earth, driven by gathered forces of its own. People hurry to it in order to observe the ongoing works of human hands and read in them their human reasons for being. Yet in Carrie and in the novel that bears her name those reasons have become vague by virtue of becoming indiscriminate, unrestrained, and insatiable, in all of which they resemble the capitalism that dominated the United States in the late nineteenth and early twentieth centuries. The lines that thrust out into the open prairie and up into the sky have no known destinations and no recognized boundaries, not because they are sufficient ends in themselves but because they are fed by and feed the large engines that drive their world.

Carrie's intimate relations to her present context, the remarkable extent to which she is a creature of the world around her, make her one of the most important characters in her nation's fiction. In one of her representative moments, she sits in her rocking chair, almost forlorn, dreaming and yearning yet going nowhere; in another she occupies a stage, where staring seems the only "proper and natural thing" to do. As a performer and celebrity who inhabits a "shiny plush-covered world" of things, she discovers both "the meaning of the applause which was for her" and "the delight of parading," of being seen and creating a stir, until her head is "so full of the wonder of it that she [has] time for nothing else."

In James's *Portrait,* when Isabel Archer sits through the night by the fire in her husband's "house of darkness" and discovers uncertain truths about herself, her husband, her marriage, and her world, we observe the power as well as the limitations of "motionless seeing." Isabel's "mere still lucidity" does little to alter her world. It acquires force by yielding insight. We never know to what extent effective action will flow from Isabel's vigil. In James's fiction, history as limiting force weighs heavily even on the lives of people born in the United States. But Isabel possesses an internal richness, a changing yet constituted life, that contrasts sharply with the rich, successful, yet attenuated life of Carrie, and there is a sense at least in which she also discovers her human connectedness.

Carrie, by contrast, comes to us as a largely vacant self – or, more drastically, as an object in a world of objects. She becomes "Carrie Madenda," a celebrity whose name blazes in incandescent lights at Broadway and 39th Street. She attains everything that had "seemed life's object" (gowns, a carriage, furniture, bank account, success, applause, celebrity) only to have "once far off, essential things" become in possession "trivial and indifferent." Her longings and yearnings, like her sad discoveries, are neither symptoms nor signs. She becomes the deep figure both of the novel that bears her name and of the larger world whose indiscriminately incorporating self inspired Dreiser to create it precisely because her intimacies, privacies, and secrets of self find expression only in theatricalities that commercialize and trivialize them. After publishing *Sister Carrie,* Doubleday, Page & Company tried to limit its distribution, apparently because Carrie's "fall" from virtue is never properly punished. But Doubleday's concerns were misplaced. Carrie is a dangerous character not because she lets her erotic instincts run riot but because she so perfectly sublimates them.

Carrie begins her travels as a young woman who is already manipulated by the desires of men, as opposed to the desire for them. Women in *Sister Carrie* remain to a large extent figments of male imaginations. They are sometimes (as with Hurstwood's wife) less and sometimes (as with Carrie) all that men desire, but they are never more. Carrie's life is shaped by her sense of what those desires mean and her assumption (acquired we can only guess how) that they are what matter, as force always matters. She is controlled not by her own sexual desires – something Dreiser seems incapable of imagining – but by her society's definition of her as a beautiful young woman. She learns to make her sexuality an asset by using it to please the men who look at her with desire. To manipulate them, however, she must also manipulate herself. After she gets to New York and Hurstwood's energies begin to fail, she takes charge of her life and becomes a star. Having learned from her incorporating ethos both an aesthetics and an economics of desire, she discovers that in cities sex, desire, entertainment, and money go hand in hand. Hurstwood's fall and her rise, turning as they do on work, money, and social position, are indicators not of a world of limitless possibilities but rather of one where one person's fall balances another's rise. Furthermore, whereas Carrie's lower-class status enhances her appeal to Hurstwood – by emphasizing not only her youthful yearning but also her vulnerability and dependence, in short, her "femininity" – his fall accentuates the difference in their ages, undermining his "masculinity" and robbing him not only of appeal but also of clear sexual identity.

Having learned the imbalance of power implicit in being watched and analyzed, Carrie also learns to protect her private life by living alone. She saves herself for prying eyes that are prepared to pay. When she performs, she watches and analyzes the crowd that watches and analyzes her. Gazing at those who gaze at her, what does she see? What Dreiser can safely leave us to imagine: herself as she exists for the crowd, as though in a mirror. For Carrie is at one and the same time the creator of an image and the image of her own creation. She thus becomes a savvy exploiter both of herself and of her capitalist, sexist society. Yet the more proficient she becomes in meeting the needs of her social and economic self, the more her private self regresses until it exists only as a neglected, exploited, still yearning child within her, crying, "Watch me, watch me!" not simply out of familiar egotism or insatiable appetite for attention but rather because, as a child of present sensation and yearning, she depends on admiring eyes and clapping hands to confirm her existence. They see me and love me, she seems to say. They will hold what I look like and what I do in their minds. They will remember it and make it true.

Though attractive and sensuous, Carrie never becomes a creature of sexual desire. In her merge three different senses of what a distinctively American self might be. She is a "performing" self, an "incorporating" and an "imperial" self: she lives in part to stir applause for herself, in part to take possession of things "for herself as recklessly as she dared," and in part to become preeminent. Yet in her rocking chair, surrounded by possessions and awaiting another performance, she seems beleaguered, as though afraid, as Tocqueville prophesied, that time is running out on her pursuit of happiness secured by money, possessions, status, and power. Between performances, her face becomes almost blank in its beauty, with no expression and little to express, and her life becomes a weatherless one of waiting. In all of this – in her pastlessness; in her name, given her by a man; in her accidental discovery of herself as a performing self; in her desire for celebrity and her affinity with the city and the new century's changed form of capitalism; and in the curious blankness of her inner life – she becomes the representative creature of her world and also, as its title suggests, a sister to us all.

4. FOUR CONTEMPORARIES AND THE CLOSING OF THE WEST

Both the pioneering move into the lands of the West and the urbanizing move back into the cities of the upper Midwest and the East yielded, as I have noted, stories in life as well as in fiction. To gauge the force of these contrasting lines of development, which were social, economic, and political as well as cultural, we need to keep three facts before us: first, that Henry Adams (1838–1918) and Henry James (1843–1916) were younger contemporaries of the great Sioux leader Sitting Bull (1834–1890) and Buffalo Bill Cody (1846–1917), as well as older ones of Isabel Archer, Ántonia Shimerda, Jim Burden, and Carrie Meeber; second, that the same Congress that devised Radical Reconstruction in order to secure the rights of black people of the South also enacted and funded a policy of radical subjugation and segregation of the original inhabitants of the West in order to conquer and dispossess them; and third, that the same group of eastern industrial and banking interests that underwrote the cultural achievements of the Northeast became the chief beneficiaries of these policies as well as of the Homestead Act, which was rationalized as a reading and implementation of Thomas Jefferson's agrarian dream.

In the summer of 1868, three years and a few months after Appomattox, the federal government launched a relentless campaign against Native Americans and appointed General William T. Sherman, one of the deliverers of the black slaves of the South, to head it. Some soldiers, like General George Crook, West Point '52, known among the Indians as the Gray Fox, continued to feel conflicted about the push to annihilate Native Americans. "Yes, they are hard," he said of the wars. "But the hardest thing is to go out and fight against those who you know are in the right." Yet the policy of total war prevailed: "I will urge General Sheridan to push . . . for the utter destruction and subjugation" of all Indians of "hostile attitude" outside the reservations, Sherman wrote. "I propose that [Sheridan] shall prosecute the war with vindictive earnestness," until "all hostile Indians . . . are obliterated or beg for mercy." "The only good Indians I ever saw," Sheridan later stated, "were dead" – a line that gave birth to an aphorism.

Soon the frontier was transformed into what Walt Whitman, in "A Death-Sonnet for Custer," called the "fatal environment": a scene of mortal conflict between people to whom the land belonged and people determined to seize it in the name of profit, piety, and progress. In the late 1870s, after two hundred battles and countless skirmishes – after the Red River War (1869–74), the Battle of Little Big Horn (June 1876), and Chief Joseph's Rebellion (1877) – resistance virtually ended. By the early 1880s, the great buffalo herds, numbering more than 13 million in 1865, had been essentially annihilated, depriving Native Americans of the Plains of food, clothing, and shelter. "Kill every buffalo you can," the army instructed. "A buffalo dead is an Indian gone." The last act in a struggle that virtually ended in the late 1870s came in 1890 when, shortly after Sitting Bull died at Standing Rock, two hundred Dakota men, women, and children danced their last Ghost Dance and then were massacred by U.S. Army troops in the Battle of Wounded Knee. "Nits make lice," ran one justification for the killing of Indian women and children. "Kill the nits, and you'll get no lice."

Even before the West had been won, its herds destroyed, and its original inhabitants either killed or forced onto reservations, its story was being incorporated for profit. At age thirteen, William F. ("Buffalo Bill") Cody began working as a pony express rider. Later he worked as a buffalo hunter, a stage coach driver, and a prospector before joining the Union Army and winning the Congressional Medal of Honor. From 1868 to 1872, he was chief scout for the Fifth U.S. Cavalry. In 1869, the year in which he participated in the defeat of the Cheyenne, Edward Zane Carroll Judson, writing under the name of Ned Buntline, wrote the first of twenty dime novels that made Cody a national hero. Lured by Buntline to appear in Chicago in a melodrama called "Buffalo Bill, King of Bordermen," Cody spent eleven years on the stage before he followed Buntline's example and began turning fictional versions of his experiences into a marketable narrative of his own.

In its first version, Cody's story featured a cast of cowboys, Indians, horses, and buffalo and was called "The Wild West, Rocky Mountain, and Prairie Exposition." After opening in Omaha, Nebraska, in 1883, it moved across the country to Coney Island, where it played to capacity crowds. A year later, dubbed "Buffalo Bill's Wild West Show," with a hundred more Indians, a hundred more horses, and an enlarged cast of cowboy stars (including Buck Taylor, "Mustang Jack," "Country Kid" Johnny Baker, "Squaw Man" John Belson, and Annie Oakley), Buffalo Bill opened in St. Louis, moved to Chicago and then east, playing to one sellout crowd after another. In 1887 he took his story to England, France, Spain, and Italy, on one of the most successful tours of Europe ever made by an American storyteller. During one remarkable recounting in London, at Queen Victoria's Jubilee, he loaded the kings of Belgium, Denmark, and Greece on the Deadwood Coach and drove them safely through an "Indian attack," with the Prince of Wales riding shotgun. Later, hoping to hold off a group of aggressive competitors, he added episodes from other frontiers – from the Battle of San Juan Hill, for example, and the Boer War. But the story of the West – a story of overt subjugation and covert incorporation – remained the core of his tale. By the time he died in 1917, he had left his mark on the circus and the movies and had made his name known over much of the world.

In Buffalo Bill's narrative, the West, once an expanse no eye could measure, acquired a different kind of eternalism. Though ostensibly historical, Cody's story recorded something like a human triumph over history and thus reminds us that historical narratives, like philosophy, religion, and literature, can serve submerged social, political ends. For it celebrated as a triumph for humankind both the virtual annihilation of Native Americans and the hardship of the pioneers. Looking back on himself as a boy still named Itshak Isaac Granich – before the Palmer Raids of 1921 forced him to change it – Michael Gold, author of *Jews Without Money* (1930) and editor of *New Masses,* described himself as "disappointed" that he could find no "Messiah who would look like Buffalo Bill." What Gold wanted, and may even be said to have needed, was a hero who could "save" his people and "annihilate" their enemies while making the hardships of the one and the destruction of the other seem right.

5. *CHICAGO'S "DREAM CITY"*

Ten years after his first tour of the United States and six after his first tour of Europe, Buffalo Bill brought his Wild West Show to the World's Columbian Exposition in Chicago for one of his last triumphant presentations. Once a small Indian village on the shores of Lake Michigan, Chicago pushed and promoted itself past older eastern rivals who wanted to host the nation's Columbian celebration by recounting its quintessential American rise from meager beginnings to a bustling center of trade, commerce, stockyards, and railways, and by insisting that it was the nation's window to the future. Chicago might have no culture, one citizen remarked, but when it got some it would make it hum.

Persuaded, Congress gave Chicago exclusive rights to official commemoration of the four hundredth anniversary of Columbus's discovery of the Americas, and then passed a bill authorizing the World's Columbian Exposition of "arts, industries, manufactures, and the products of the soil, mine, and sea," which President Benjamin Harrison signed in the spring of 1890, the first year in which the value of the nation's manufactured goods surpassed that of its agricultural commodities. A year later, six thousand workers were employed on projects sponsored by forty-four nations and twenty-six colonies and provinces. "Make no little plans," instructed Daniel Burnham, the Chicago architect charged with coordinating the mammoth effort to transform seven hundred acres of Jackson Park into a wonderland of promenades, canals, lagoons, plazas, parks, streets, and avenues as well as four hundred buildings.

To assist him in planning Chicago's "Dream City," Burnham assembled a group of advisers that included the park builder Frederick Law Olmsted, the painter Kenyon Cox, and the sculptor Augustus Saint-Gaudens. Do "you realize," Saint-Gaudens asked at a planning session, "that this is the greatest meeting of artists since the Fifteenth Century?" But the real business of the Exposition was competitive cultural politics, national and international. Burnham's planners took for granted that their exposition would surpass Philadelphia's Centennial celebration of 1876. Their serious competition was the great Paris Exposition of 1889, and their aim was total victory. Theirs would be the best-planned, best-operated, most dazzling exposition ever.

On all counts, Burnham and his advisers succeeded. Replicas of scenes from around the world – a Parisian café, a Bohemian glass factory, a Moorish palace, a Cairo street, a Japanese bazaar – sprang up on the Exposition's clean, well-lighted grounds, illuminated, William Dean Howells reported, by "myriad incandescent bubbles" made possible by alternating-current electrical power. Miniature replicas of whole villages, complete with native inhabitants, including Germans, Turks, Chinese, and Dahomans, also found space. Above the grounds soared a conspicuous display of U.S. technological prowess, conceived by a young Chicago civil engineer, George Washington Gale Ferris, as a direct challenge to the Eiffel Tower: an enormous illuminated wheel that lifted its passengers high into the air to see the New World's newest city rising from the plains. "[Before] I had walked for two minutes," Owen Wister wrote in his diary, "a bewilderment at the gloriousness of everything seized me . . . until my mind was dazzled to a standstill."

The Exposition's planners welcomed tourists in record numbers, proud that their endeavor had inspired Karl Baedeker of Leipzig to publish the first Baedeker's guide to the United States. Working from mixed motives, they viewed their Exposition as another phase in the nation's plan for dominating and converting the world. They welcomed people like the Dahomans, whom they thought of as cruel and barbarous, in order to teach them how a people of energy, ingenuity, and discipline could transform, in Burnham's words, a "desolate wilderness" and a "dreary landscape" into a glittering world of technological wonders. Enlightened, the Dahomans could return to their primitive homes with new images of the "influences of civilization" in their minds.

Burnham and his colleagues thought of themselves as disciples of Matthew Arnold. A new alliance between business and government, on one side, and culture, on the other, was one of their avowed aims. But what could such an alliance mean to people who were as tradition-bound and backward-looking about art as they were present-minded and forward-looking about politics, business, and technology? Burnham had helped to establish Chicago as an architectural center. In the first stages of planning, he supported the innovative plans of his friend John Root for making architecture the principal cultural focus of the Exposition. But both men wanted national participation; and when they called in Richard Hunt, acknowledged dean of architecture in the United States, the firm of Peabody and Stearns from Boston, and that of McKim, Mead, and White of New York, Root found himself outnumbered. Before the end of the first conference, Burnham had abandoned Root's hope for an eclectic, experimental approach in favor of celebrating eastern formalism, a triumph signaled when McKim lowered Saint-Gaudens's twenty-foot Diana from atop New York's Madison Square Garden and raised her above the Pantheon-like dome of his new building in Jackson Park.

To Burnham and his advisers the results were gratifying. The architectural focus of the Exposition was the White City, and the center of the White City was the reflection pool of the Court of Honor, surrounded by massive "Greek" temples. The "Fair," Burnham boasted, "was what the Romans would have wished to create, in permanent forms." To Louis Sullivan, whose Transportation Building was the only nonclassical structure on the grounds, the results were an "appalling calamity" and a "betrayal of trust": a "suavely presented" and "cleverly plagiarized" but deeply "fraudulent . . . use of historical documents."

In correspondence, Henry Adams described the Exposition's buildings as "fakes and frauds" that seemed mischievous in their deception of "our innocent natives." Walking the grounds, he spent most of his time studying innovative "dynamos and . . . steam-engines." Later, in his *Education,* he described the Exposition as an astonishing "scenic display," more spectacular than anything in Paris or North America, from Niagara Falls to the Yellowstone Geysers. But its lessons came from its "industrial schools," where one acquired "the habit of thinking a steam-engine or dynamo as natural as the sun." The questions posed by its "half-thoughts and experimental outcries" were whether the new creations "could be made to seem at home" on the shores of Lake Michigan and whether their maker, the American, could be "made to seem at home in it."

To such questions, Burnham's creation had nothing directly to say. The dissociation of art from history that Sullivan and Adams decried – "lesions" was Sullivan's term, "rupture" was Adams's – was precisely what Burnham desired. "The influence of the Exposition architecture will be to inspire a reversion to the pure ideal of the ancients," he said, not in despair but in hope. Standing on Burnham's grounds, Hamlin Garland delivered a lecture titled "Local Color in Fiction." But for Burnham even architecture, the most terrestrial of the arts, was decorative and ornamental except when it bodied forth the timeless, transcendent ideals of the ancients. If, furthermore, this was Burnham's problem on one level, it was Chicago's on another, and the nation's on another. Vulgar forms of art could serve vulgar ends. Dime novels, Horatio Alger's books, and Buffalo Bill's story of the West, which Chicago's Dream City helped to promulgate, were useful in justifying the nation's conquest of the continent and in teaching its young boys manly aspirations. In its own way, even the Dream City admitted that "art" could also serve crass ambitions. California's strange contribution – a "knight on horseback" made entirely of California prunes – was billed as a "unique departure in statuary." Descended from knights of the American plains and chivalric knights of old, it evoked ideals of a near as well as distant past. But California's knight, the *Guide* to the Exposition makes clear, belonged to the future, by signaling that the United States was prepared to expand its markets abroad. California's prunes, it notes, were already being "introduced victoriously into all lands, to the discomfiture of the products of other countries." A few years later, the nation commenced, in Howells's haunting words, "to preach the blessings of [its] deeply incorporated civilization by the mouths of [its] eight-inch guns."

But in Chicago's Exposition, true "art" belonged to the Court of Honor, where "Greek" temples spoke of the past to the ages, without challenging the Exposition's aggressive nationalism, or its emphatic exclusion of the poor, or its emphatic control of Native Americans, women, and black Americans. Outside its gates, one hundred thousand victims of the panic of 1893, the nation's worst depression to that time, wandered the streets, searching for food and shelter. "What a spectacle!" the journalist Ray Stannard Baker exclaimed, observing the pitiful throng outside the fairgrounds. "What a downfall after the magnificence and prodigality of the World's Fair." In that same year, as though in ironic commemoration of the Exposition's grand opening, Stephen Crane published *Maggie: A Girl of the Streets,* a nightmare vision of the cruel consequences of urban poverty. Like London's *Martin Eden* (1909) – and more obliquely, both Kate Chopin's *The Awakening* (1899) and Edith Wharton's *House of Mirth* (1905) – Crane's story ends in suicide. But Maggie's march to the river in which she dies is even more harrowing than Martin Eden's dive into the sea, or Edna Pontellier's long swim away from society's shore, or Lily Bart's drift into unconsciousness, in part because it comes to us as the logical outcome of a young woman's life in a world ruled by exploitation.

Thousands of laborers, of "half a score of nationalities and of as many trades," had built the Exposition, wrote Walter Wyckoff, who worked there as a road builder. But the Exposition's *Official Manual* saved its accolades for Burnham and the stout bankers, lawyers, and politicians who served as advisers and sponsors. In *Midway Types: A Book of Illustrated Lessons . . .* (1894), Native Americans appear as "well-known thorns in the side of Uncle Sam." Offended by the Dream City and the story it sought to tell, Chief Simon Pokagon walked the grounds, distributing a pamphlet called *Red Man's Greeting,* which reminded visitors that "the land on which Chicago and the Fair" stood still belonged to the Potawatomis, "as it has never been paid for." But the Exposition's official story, which defined American Indians as a nuisance finally got rid of, was reiterated in its "Ethnology Department," which presented them as representatives of "primitive" peoples destined to extinction in the name of progress. Less a vanishing than a vanished people, North America's first inhabitants were at last wholly "other."

Having lost hope of achieving parity with men in planning the Exposition, women settled for a single building, adjoining the Children's Building and situated on the border between the exalted art of the White City and the varied amusements of the garish Midway. Although assigned to Sophia Hayden, the design of the building was controlled by a "Board of Lady Managers" – a designation set by the U.S. Congress and resented by its own members. Elizabeth Cady Stanton, Susan B. Anthony, and Jane Addams were among the many women who spoke there, backed by two large murals, given equal status: Mary Fairchild MacMonnies's *Primitive Woman,* depicting women engaged in traditional tasks of service and nurturance, and Mary Cassatt's *Modern Woman,* depicting young women in a garden, enjoying the fruits of nature and the arts. The effect of the whole, said the artist Candace Wheeler, was to present "a man's ideal of woman – delicate, dignified, pure, and fair to look upon," terms that recall Burnham's notion of "culture." But these two images of women – as performers of domestic tasks and as guardians of culture and refinement – in fact represented assumptions and interests so deeply embedded in the culture at large that most men and many women came "naturally" to share them. In 1927 the writer Mary Austin (1868–1934) recalled the culture of her early years as one in which women were regarded as too refined to be driven by worldly ambitions or carnal desires. Focused on the immediate and the eternal, on the needs of hearth and home and the thought of heaven, women were taught to shun the push of competition and the pull of desire that both drove and entitled men to run the world.

Despite repeated petitions – for a building, a department, an exhibition – black Americans were forced to settle for a day. In 1893 Scott Joplin, a native of Texarkana, Texas, moved from St. Louis to Chicago and organized his first band, launching a career that made him the "King of Ragtime." One year earlier, Anna Julia Cooper, a native of South Carolina living in Chicago, had published a book called *A Voice from the South,* comparing the fate of being a black woman to living with one eye bandaged and darkened. But the fathers of White City showed little interest in black men or black women, except as menials hired to work on grounds and cleanup crews; granting them a "day," which black Americans renamed "Darkies' Day," was for them a concession. Noting that the Exposition and the civilization it celebrated had been built by the labor of thousands of black men and women, Frederick Douglass used the occasion to rename Chicago's White City the "whited sepulcher." And in fact the Exposition's treatment of black Americans reiterated a theme that was implicit in its version of the "official" lineage of the nation's people. Speaking at the Exposition's World's Parliament of Religions, Lyman Abbott called Chicago "the most cosmopolitan city" and Americans "the most cosmopolitan race on the globe." But foreign peoples were given space only along the garish Midway, outside the Dream City itself, in a series of villages arranged in an order whose ethnic logic was clear: the exhibits of the Teutonic and Celtic races came first, then the Mohammedans, the West Asian peoples, the East Asian peoples, and the Africans of Dahomey. The continent's first settlers, Native Americans, came last. "Let no one fear," added John Henry Barrows, of the First Presbyterian Church of Chicago, "that the solar orb of Christianity is to be eclipsed by the lanterns and rush lights of other faiths" – sentiments that squared perfectly with the Exposition's clear definition of "American" culture and its subordination of other civilizations to its own.

6. FREDERICK JACKSON TURNER IN THE DREAM CITY

Standing in the Dream City – within "the greatest city of modern times: Chicago, the peerless," as John Flinn's *Official Guide to the World's Columbian Exposition* (1893) called it – before members of the American Historical Association, Frederick Jackson Turner, a young professor from Wisconsin, delivered his famous address, "The Significance of the Frontier in American History." The dominant traits of the nation – strength and inventiveness of mind, buoyancy and exuberance of spirit, "restless, nervous energy," and "dominant individualism" – Turner said, were "traits of the frontier, or traits called out elsewhere because of the existence of the frontier." "The true point of view" in U.S. history, therefore, was "not the Atlantic coast" but the "Great West." Since the days when Columbus sailed, he added, in a line that embraced the nation's emerging political economy as well as its storied past, "America has been another name for opportunity, and the people of the United States have taken their tone from the incessant expansion" virtually forced upon them by their environment. The "expansive character of American life," he predicted, would go on demanding "a wider field for its exercise."

At times, Turner seemed to be looking forward, anticipating the war that would come in 1898, when, following President McKinley's "Open Door" policy, the nation started seeking "wider fields." When his gaze fixed on the past, however, it almost stopped short, arrested by the sense of an ending: "Never again will such gifts of free land offer themselves." Despite his exuberance, Turner's tone is often elegiac. Part discovery and part invention, his "thesis" draws on words of earlier writers – from explorers and early settlers through Jefferson and Jackson to George Bancroft, Francis Parkman, and William Gilpin – as well as on selected facts of history. It remains controversial due in part to its active biases and in part to its convenient omissions. His story of the United States revolves around white male explorers and settlers, modeled on Daniel Boone and Leatherstocking, as we see when he describes "the wilderness" mastering "the colonist" by stripping "off the garments of civilization and array[ing] him in the hunting shirt and the moccasin." Women, black and brown Americans, the violent destruction of ancient civilizations, and the quick exploitation of the land and its resources play minor roles in his story, a fact that strikes with added force for being not only convenient but also consonant with the logic of Chicago's Exposition. Furthermore, although Turner speaks of the "composite nationality" of the people of the United States, he largely ignores new immigrants. He knew that the lessons of the West were mixed – that coarseness went with strength, expediency with inventiveness, and a lack of artistic sensibility with a "masterful grasp of material things." And he worried that frontier violence and exploitation might inculcate violence and greed. But he believed that his nation stood at a critical juncture and concluded that it needed its hard frontier virtues to meet new challenges. In speaking of the past, he in fact spoke to the present about the future. In this special sense, he was as much a moralist as a historian. His underlying and overriding purpose lay in creating a usable past for an uncertain future. In 1914 he was still reiterating what he had announced in 1893:

> American democracy was born of no theorist's dream; it was not carried in the Susan Constant to Virginia, nor in the Mayflower to Plymouth. It came stark and strong and full of life out of the American forest, and it gained new strength each time it touched a new frontier.[8]

The appeal of Turner's story owed something to its status as another declaration of independence from Europe and something to its assertion of a distinctive past. But it also owed something to its reassuring "modernity." From Chicago, Henry Adams returned to Washington in time to watch Congress repeal the Silver Act. Bankers and "dealers in exchange" supported a single gold standard, Adams reported, the silver minority opposed it, and "the people" continued, as they had for a hundred years, to vacillate, torn between "two ways of life": one, that of an agrarian republic based on a dispersed form of entrepreneurial capitalism, to which Chicago had been a gateway, and the other, that of an urban, industrialized nation based on a centralized form of corporate capitalism, "with all its necessary machinery," to which the Dream City was a window. But Adams knew where the future lay, and so as we shall see did Turner. He knew that, despite the trust-busting reforms of the late nineteenth and early twentieth centuries, the future belonged to a world dominated by the means and ends of corporate capitalism, as the strange fate of the Homestead Act had already made clear.

After the Civil War, advertisements of "free land for the landless" spread around the world. But few landless families could finance long journeys, and of those that could, few were prepared to cope with the ecology of the Great Plains, where the bulk of public lands lay. Nearly two-thirds of all homesteaders who filed between 1870 and 1890 lost their farms. Meanwhile, the bulk of public lands dispersed served other interests. Of 3,737,000 farms and ranches established between 1860 and 1900, fewer than 600,000 (roughly 16 percent) came from homestead patents, accounting for only 80,000,000 of 430,900,000 acres (less than 19 percent) of new land claimed. The rest went to ranchers set on expanding their empires or to rail companies set on expanding theirs – results that fit perfectly the aims of eastern bankers and industrialists who opposed the Jeffersonian ends of the Homestead Act.

Major parts of the United States remained rural and agricultural well into the twentieth century, and many farming communities as well as most of the South remained poor. But a new way of life was emerging, and it was urban, industrial, commercial, affluent, and secular. Dominant first in the East, it spread across the upper Midwest and then incorporated the nation's heartland. Eventually, it triumphed even in the South. Chicago, "or rather the World's Fair City," Howells wrote, "was after all only a Newer York, an ultimated Manhattan, the realized ideal of that largeness, loudness and fastness, which New York has persuaded the Americans is metropolitan."

Having begun her career by writing stories about frontier Nebraska, where she had moved at age nine, after a journey that took her through Chicago, Willa Cather later turned to stories – *A Lost Lady* (1923), *The Professor's House* (1925), and *Death Comes for the Archbishop* (1927) – that trace the decline and fall not simply of the "frontier" but of the preurban, preindustrial, premodern world to which Chicago was saying good-bye. Writing as one fearful that the early days of the United States might also have been its best, Cather presents her novels as archaeological digs that unearth the shards, rituals, folkways, and memories of worlds almost lost. In them, customs, mores, manners, and accents as well as turns of speech vary, but other things, including the sense of being in tune with nature and inheritors of traditional wisdom, do not. In them culture comes to us through inarticulate artisans who know their tools and inarticulate farmers who know their fields and animals. Or it comes in rituals preserved in the inherited phrases of ancient languages, which remain authentic because they convey an interpretive framework, a way of organizing reality, that endows communal existence and individual existences with purpose and meaning.

To people like Adams and Cather, "progress" seemed little more than an honorific term for change. For Turner, as for Chicago's Dream City, its validity as concept seemed self-evident. What Turner sought was a new mode of discourse with which to save what he saw as valuable lessons of the nation's past, and he found it in Darwinian thought:

> The buffalo trail became the Indian trail, and this became the trader's "trace"; the trails widened to roads, and the roads into turnpikes, and these in turn were transformed into railroads . . . until at last the slender paths of aboriginal intercourse have been broadened and interwoven into the complex mazes of modern commercial lines; the wilderness has been interpenetrated by lines of civilization growing ever more numerous. It is like the steady growth of a complex nervous system for the originally simple, inert continent.[9]

Turner's story fit, on one side, the story told by Buffalo Bill in his Wild West Show and, on the other, the story told by Burnham and his advisers in their Dream City. Turner knew that growth was only one part of the story because he knew that the nation was already working its way free of its religious and political moorings. He sensed, moreover, what Emile Durkheim saw: that interests can connect people, but that they "can only give rise to transient relations and passing associations," not to a sense of community. Turner's larger aim was to preserve a sense of community, grounded in history and made manifest in cultural practices, so that his people could go forward, thinking and acting in consort. His thesis is programmatic as well as explanatory.

Like Chicago's Exposition and Buffalo Bill's show, however, Turner's thesis reminds us that the forging of national identities always involves a process of exclusion, negation, and suppression as well as inclusion and affirmation. In saying what the United States willed to be, what it willed to give its name to and incorporate, Turner virtually shouted what it willed to control, exclude, or suppress. He thus added his words to the mixed discourse of self-confidence and self-doubt that continued to echo through the early decades of the twentieth century, as the nation continued its search for an adequate identity. To Buffalo Bill's language of showmanship and Chicago's of technology, he added his own, taken in part from words and deeds of the past and in part from Darwin and biology, and put it to the purpose of propounding the pertinence of frontier virtues to the new order signaled by Chicago. His thesis promises a way of reconciling the natural and the civil, individualism and egalitarianism, separatism and civic-mindedness, secession and union – without altering the power structure of his world, except by enlarging his country's share of it. When he reaches back to evoke a lost world, to celebrate pioneer sturdiness and frontier independence, he laments the passing of an era, and his tone becomes elegiac, echoing the era of the early republic. But when he fixes his gaze on the scene emerging around him and then begins to speak of progress, he moves from the nation's earlier modes of discourse toward a discourse informed by the sciences, especially Darwin, and the social sciences, including the one at whose meeting he delivered his most celebrated address. Armed in this way, he invented an image of his country as still a New World, whose future lay before it like a dream and whose people remained heirs according to promise.

For Turner, therefore, the answers to Adams's questions – whether the scenic display of the Dream City could be made to seem at home in Chicago and whether "the American" could be made "to seem at home in it" – were clear and reassuring. Adams's sense of the past left him believing in accelerating change but confident of little else. Turner's version of it enabled him to face the future with contained alarm, sustained by faith in the grammar of progress – from simplicity to complexity, from frontier to society, from wilderness to civilization, from the "slender paths of aboriginal intercourse" to the "complex images of modern commercial lines." It was, therefore, stunningly appropriate that he should deliver his first great address when and where he did. Chicago's Dream City, which helped to launch his spectacular career, not only gave him a platform; it also reinforced his themes with its celebrations and endorsed his omissions with its exclusions. In the decades that followed, the interests bodied forth in the World's Columbian Exposition continued to sponsor him and his thesis.

7. *HENRY ADAMS'S* EDUCATION *AND THE GRAMMAR OF PROGRESS*

Adams might well have conceded Turner special authority, for he thought of people like Turner as allied with the future. He may even have felt some sympathy for Turner's purpose: few episodes in the search for some "form of religious hope" or "promise of ultimate perfection" left him wholly unmoved. Still, in his own reflections he remained ambivalent about the consolidated forces that were shaping the modern world and skeptical about the several theories – "formulas," "arranged sequences," and "convenient fictions," he called them at various times – that proposed to explain them. In a chapter of the *Education* called "The Grammar of Science" (a title of a book by Karl Pearson published in 1899), he follows Pearson in contrasting the precision of our knowledge of the world made available through sensory experience to science with the uncertainty of our knowledge of all relations between our deepest human needs and the world we inhabit:

> Pearson shut out of science everything which the nineteenth century had brought into it. He told his scholars that they must put up with a fraction of

the universe, and a very small fraction at that – the circle reached by the senses, where sequence could be taken for granted. . . . "Order and reason, beauty and benevolence, are characteristics and conceptions which we find solely associated with the mind of man."[10]

In his sense of the allure and the threat of dissociation between nature and culture, in which nature becomes an object of analysis, manipulation, and exploitation, while culture becomes the creation of human hands directed by "characteristics and conceptions . . . solely associated with the mind of man," Adams locates the origin of the "modern" mind – including "American" versions of it. It was at virtually this same moment that pragmatism was emerging in the United States as a philosophical movement charged by the demand that philosophy continue to meet our deepest needs as human beings even if that meant placing the process of knowing within the process of conduct and replacing the search for ultimates with a search for effective means of coping with the present. In Adams's context, even Lyell and Darwin are more premodern than modern in the problems they address because, unlike Pearson, they attribute to nature not change but evolution, not accidental collocations of atoms but meaningful selection – or, more precisely, selection that corresponds to human conceptions of what selection might mean. In one of his most telling depictions of himself – "a child of the seventeenth and eighteenth centuries" forced "to play the game of the twentieth" – his most striking act is to treat the century in which he was born and lived most of his life as an interim between an old world in which people could believe that the earth had been created for their habitation, and a new world in which they recognized that order, reason, beauty, and benevolence – as characteristics and conceptions associated only with their own minds – were as doomed to extinction as they.

The "modern" moment, if by that we mean the artistic, literary, and philosophic "modernisms" that emerged in the late nineteenth and early twentieth centuries, thus arose not only in the great cities of Europe, but also along the ragged edges of the New World. And it found different expression, including the effort to hold traditional values, customs, and forms in mind while modifying or abandoning them in practice. Such contradictions enter novels by Edith Wharton and Jack London as well as Cather and Dreiser, and they dominate Buffalo Bill's tale and Turner's thesis. They even lie behind Burnham's separation of art from life, which served the dual purpose of protecting "interests" from exposure to what James called the "maximum of ironic reflection" and of protecting art from being exposed as another elaborate, disguised, or even sinister expression of mere "interests." These and other versions of "modernism" arose, furthermore, only in part because energy abounded. They also arose because interests abounded. No single version, as it turned out, could meet all of the needs at hand.

Despite the popularity of Darwinism, the deeper implications of evolutionary theory for understanding ties between human thought and human culture, on one side, and human origins in nature, on the other, would be decades unfolding. Despite the power of Marxist thought to inspire critiques of culture, its implications for understanding the conflicted relations between history and culture as expressions of human will and history and culture as shapers of human will were only beginning to emerge. Finally, despite the growing popularity of Freudian thought, its implications for understanding the haunting discrepancy between the ability of the human will to do what it willed and its ability to will what it willed had scarcely been glimpsed. Such fundamental tensions as these, the "modern" moment addressed: including a tension between nature as a realm from which human life had evolved and culture as a product of human hands doing the work of human minds and so giving expression to needs associated with those minds alone; and then between culture as the product of peculiarly human needs and culture as a historical scene that was unlike anything humans ever much wanted to see. One result, present in poetry as well as fiction, took shape as a separation of literature from history as well as from nature and even from the personal voice and self of the writer. In theory at least, "literature" began separating itself from history, culture, and self as well as from nature by declaring itself a special realm of detached, impersonal, and even transcendent discourse, hoping, strange as it may seem, to name itself the peculiar realm of everything distinctive in the human spirit.

Behind the pathos of the present that lies so deep in Adams's thought as to constitute its mysterious armature lay his conviction that the "Grammar of Science" had forever divided human beings against themselves by defining them as human animals whose deepest needs, though met for a time by human inventions, must in the end be forfeited. Having suddenly become inventors of all formulas having to do with "order and reason, beauty and benevolence," humans might fancy themselves exalted inventors of all the gods, and authors of all their words. But the price paid for such exaltation struck Adams as severe, if only because purely human formulas, lacking divine or even natural sanctions, were certain to fail in meeting the human needs that inspired them. "Our nada who are in nada," one of the characters in Hemingway's "A Clean, Well-Lighted Place" (1933) says to himself, as he begins to turn out the lights in a cafe, "nada be thy name thy kingdom nada they will be nada in nada as it is in nada. . . . Hail nothing full of nothing, nothing is with thee."

Adams's anxiety was, then, no less "American" than Turner's, but it was more fully "modern," and it made his sense of the critical juncture at which the United States stood more inclusive as well as different. Like Turner, Adams saw the nation moving from the dispersed, agrarian world toward an urbanized, centralized, and mechanized world. He, too, realized that this new world would be driven by "the capitalistic system with all its necessary machinery." In addition, however, he saw the emerging culture as one in which faith in purpose was becoming more difficult, skepticism more preemptive.

In his sense of the implications of a dissociation between the sensory world of nature and the motions of human minds (and, by extension, the tools, instruments, and formulas devised by them to meet their needs), Adams glimpsed what Heisenberg later saw clearly. In picturing for ourselves the nature of the existence of elementary particles, Heisenberg said, "we may no longer ignore the physical processes by which we obtain information about them" since "every process of observation" causes disturbances in the field of observation. "In consequence," he continued, "we are finally led to believe that the laws of nature which we formulate mathematically in quantum theory deal" not "with the particles themselves but with our knowledge of" them. In short, Adams sensed about the science of Lyell and Darwin what Heisenberg observed about science generally: "In science, also, the object of research is no longer nature in itself," Heisenberg says, "but rather nature exposed to man's questioning, and to this extent man here also meets himself." Even in the study of nature, "one sees what one brings." Adams understood, furthermore, that working hypotheses can meet the needs of science more easily than those of philosophy. Where philosophical inquiry was concerned, he had little interest in partial success or workable solutions, including those promised by pragmatism.

In 1917, a year before Adams died, Bertrand Russell reiterated the harsh implications of modern skepticism he had first articulated in 1902:

> Such, in outline, but even more purposeless, more void of meaning, is the world which Science presents for our belief. Amid such a world, if anywhere, our ideals henceforth must find a home. That Man is the product of causes which had no prevision of the end they were achieving; that his origin, his growth, his hopes and fears, his loves and his beliefs, are but the outcome of accidental collocations of atoms; that no fire, no heroism, no intensity of thought and feeling, can preserve an individual life beyond the grave; that all the labours of the ages, all the devotion, all the inspiration, all the noonday brightness of human genius, are destined to extinction in the vast death of the solar system, and that the whole temple of Man's achievement must inevitably be buried beneath the debris of a universe in ruins – all these things, if not quite beyond dispute, are yet so nearly certain, that no philosophy which rejects them can hope to stand. Only within the scaffolding of these truths, only on the firm foundation of unyielding despair, can the soul's habitation henceforth be safely built."

Two years later, Joseph Conrad wrote to Russell describing his own "deep-seated sense of fatality governing this man-inhabited world," a sentiment later echoed in Hemingway's revision of the Lord's Prayer. Toward the end of the *Education,* especially in the chapter called "The Grammar of Science," Adams describes the modern self in terms even bleaker than Russell's because he saw darknesses within the modern self that matched those without. Like Russell, Adams presents life as coming "inexplicably out of some unknown and uni-maginable void" into which it is doomed to disappear. But other constraints haunt his "tired student," who feels so pushed by the force of history and the work of culture ("external suggestion") and driven by the force of nature ("nature's compulsion") that nothing – not his art, his philosophy, or even his internal dream world – can be called his own. More than most writers of his time, Adams realized that the interactions between biology and culture, or nature and history, in shaping individual human lives and determining the fate of humankind were something people had only begun to understand. He took some consolation in thinking that what Lionel Trilling later called a "hard, irreducible, stubborn core of biological urgency, and biological necessity, and biological reason" might in some measure place us beyond culture's powers to control us with enticements and threats. But the self as scene of balancing compulsions, some welling up from within, others felt from without, seemed to Adams cold consolation. He persisted in his effort "to invent a formula of his own for his universe" because he thought the effort deeply human. But he assumed that the contours of human hope had forever changed.

In 1868 Adams had landed in New York to see "American society as a long caravan stretching out towards the plains." In 1904 he again landed in New York to find an urban world of almost frantic energy:

> Power seemed to have outgrown its servitude and to have asserted its freedom. The cylinder had exploded, and thrown great masses of stone and steam against the sky. The city had the air and movement of hysteria, and the citizens were crying, in every accent of anger and alarm, that the new forces must at any cost be brought under control. Prosperity never before imagined, power never yet wielded by man, speed never reached by anything but a meteor, had made the world irritable, nervous, querulous, unreasonable and afraid. All New York was demanding new men, and all the new forces, condensed into corporations, were demanding a new type of man.[12]

Like Chicago's Dream City, Adams's New York is a product shaped by human hands to meet human needs. But since it is also driven by forces and interests that have outgrown their servitude, it threatens to turn its makers into servants shaped to its requirements. In 1921 Ezra Pound described city life as "cinematographic." A few years earlier, Vachel Lindsay had predicted that city life would give unprecedented authority to visual media – to images, signs, and symbols, to drawings, cartoons, illustrations, and photographs – that were creating a "hieroglyphic civilization." Earlier, cities had undergone explosive growth that both required and generated concentrations of capital that could fuel industrial growth and the creation of new technologies. New York, like Chicago's Dream City, expressed the human desire to dominate space and master natural forces. But control accompanied expansion. Country clubs, landscaped city parks, amusement parks, and wilder, more expansive national parks further extended social control over human contact with nature and human use of leisure. As modern cities became more coextensive with human activities, they also became more authoritative in shaping and even creating human desires, as we see in Adams's New York and much earlier in Poe's "The Man of the Crowd" (1840).

Natural science presupposes human beings, Niels Bohr once noted, as both spectators and participants on the stage of life. The city, as represented by Poe's almost anonymous and interchangeable London, is so preemptive along

these lines that the distinction between being an observer and being a participant virtually dissolves. By surrendering concern for things inside him in
order to observe the "scene without," Poe's nameless protagonist emerges as
a model of the evacuation and objectification of the modern self. The external
world of the city, its street life, provides the only life he knows. Having
studied people in groups, he begins examining details of their clothes, gaits,
faces, and expressions. Although he possesses considerable learning, some of
it arcane, he remains internally impoverished. Finally, having studied the
crowd, he fixes his attention on one stranger – a worn man of searing coun-
tenance. And from this drama of spectator and participant comes a moment
of recognition in which the two figures merge as related versions of a single,
almost anonymous figure: the "man of the crowd."

The "man of the crowd" – both as narrator/spectator and as participant/
actor – is a modern, urban hero. His contacts with other people are brief,
impersonal, and superficial; and since interests alone create them, they remain
external and transient. Though intimacy is sometimes insinuated, none is
conceivable. Personal commitments, together with the claims and expectations
that go with them, no longer exist. Social life consists of a succession of
unrelated yet almost interchangeable scenes. Poe's London, like Adams's New
York and Baudelaire's Paris, is unreal yet vivid – ever shifting yet almost
predictable, crowded yet lonely, diseased yet energetic, splendid yet squalid.
It is in Adams's terms a scene "from which every trace of organic existence
had been erased." To speak of what Poe's protagonist is, we must speak of
the roles he plays. He is part spectator as participant and part participant as
spectator. In one sense his seeing is narcissistic: everywhere he looks, he finds
images of his own empty self. In another, it is imperial: hounded by his own
internal blankness, he incorporates other figures. All of his surviving needs
are thus fed by what Vachel Lindsay called "crowd splendor." In him the
forlornness and the bravado of the modern city merge.

Turner sought to salvage the story of the frontier as a set of experiences
and a set of words that people might use in confronting the novel demands
of the nation's emerging cities. A bit earlier, Buffalo Bill had begun telling
his version of that story for his profit and the world's edification. In *The
Virginian* (1902), Owen Wister presents as a model citizen a socialized fron-
tiersman whom both Turner and Cody would have recognized on the spot.
Wister's hero, another hero without a name, is at once traditional and modern
– traditional in his personal code, modern in his social ethic. He heroically
faces danger not simply because he is brave but also because he is free of
internal conflicts: even under maximum pressure, he never doubts that his
code is right. He values his honor and his reputation neither less nor more
than he values the institution of personal property, which he accepts as essential
to the social order. In the early scene in which he confronts Trampas, he is
prepared to kill a man who insults him. Later he leads a group of men in
hanging an old friend named Steve, who has become a cowboy-rustler, proving
that he is willing to kill in order to protect his employer's property, or more

broadly the institution of property. If in his personal code he holds fast to an old sense of honor, in his social ethic he defends a conception of society bluntly spelled out by Paul Elmer More, who taught at Harvard, alma mater of both Owen Wister and Theodore Roosevelt, to whom Wister rather elaborately dedicated *The Virginian*. Looking "at the larger good of society," More asserts in *Aristocracy and Justice* (1915), "we may say that rightly understood the dollar is more than the man" and that "*the rights of property are more important than the right to life.*" Earlier, such thinking had been used to justify slavery. But once the Virginian commits himself to it and then marries Molly Wood, a native of Vermont and a descendant of heroes of the American Revolution, he is ready to become one of Wyoming's leading citizens, a member of a new elite whose task – of continuing to make manifest the destiny of the United States – flows directly from shared interests.

In fact, however, the world for which Cody, Turner, and Wister sought to save the story of the frontier was only in part a presupposition and consequence of a certain conception of the importance of property and capital. It was also a world shaped by the grammar of science and the logic of technology, which, as Heisenberg has noted, were forever changing the relation between nature and man by holding "incessantly and inescapably . . . the scientific aspect of the world before his eyes." The engineer emerged as one of the heroes of Chicago's Columbian Exposition because of his crucial role in transforming a "desolate wilderness" and "dreary landscape" into a "Dream City." From one angle, technology may be defined as a step-by-step process by which people impose their desires on their environment. With each technical advance, people enlarge their material power over their lives and their world. Max Weber once spoke of material possessions as an "iron cage," and F. Scott Fitzgerald later suggested that possessions might become possessors: "The Victor belongs to the Spoils," he wrote. But at the century's turn, the goal of technological advance remained unchallenged, except by inconstant mavericks like Adams.

Adams knew that the modern city made manifest the desire of human beings to imprint versions of themselves on the world. But in describing New York of 1904 as "unlike anything man had ever seen – and like nothing he had ever much cared to see," he identified what Heisenberg later defined as the moment when technology ceases to be "the product of conscious human effort for the spreading of material power" and begins to outgrow its servitude and assert its freedom. Having become a process driven by forces of its own, technology reminds us, Heisenberg notes, that large forces attract large forces and that human beings remain limited in nothing so much as this: that, even when they can do what they will, they cannot perfectly control what they will. In developing this notion, Heisenberg quotes the Chinese sage Chang Tsu:

> When a man uses a machine he carries on all his business in a machine-like manner. Whoever does his business in the manner of a machine develops a machine heart. Whoever has a machine heart in his breast loses his simplicity. Whoever loses his simplicity becomes uncertain in the impulses of his spirit.

Uncertainty in the impulses of the spirit is something that is incompatible with truth.[13]

Adams knew that machines were here to stay and that technology was not the only source of uncertain impulses. But he doubted that even Turner's continent-striding nineteenth-century American could control the massed forces of the modern world.

Writers of the twentieth century – from Frank Norris and Jack London to Ernest Hemingway and Ken Kesey – have gone on looking to the nation's early frontiers for models. The frontier, Norris said, is an "integral part of our conception of things." Jay Gatsby owns a library full of books he has never read. But Fitzgerald lets us know that he has read both Benjamin Franklin's *Autobiography* and a book called *Hopalong Cassidy*. In *One Flew over the Cuckoo's Nest,* Kesey evokes loggers, trail hands, and wagon masters – figures of frontier folklore – as heroic models. And in moments of maximum pressure, with life as well as freedom at stake, his protagonist, Randall Patrick McMurphy, rubs his nose with his index finger, then thrusts his thumbs into the pockets of his jeans, imitating the character that the actor John Wayne became. First in Chicago and later in New York, Adams observed a "breach of continuity," a rupture in historical sequence, so profound that it left the world demanding a new type of man, "born of contact between the new and the old energies." Opening the last chapter of his *Education,* he defines this new man as the "sole object of his interest and sympathy." But he also pictures him as almost disappearing ("the longer one watched, the less could be seen of him"), as though to explain why the task of seeing him required the play of imagination as well as the work of observation.

Adams's search for a new protagonist for the modern world was in part – like Gatsby's search, and McMurphy's – a search for a new code of conduct. In *The Sun Also Rises,* Jake Barnes suggests that modern codes must follow experience: "I did not care what it was all about," Jake says. "All I wanted to know was how to live in it. Maybe if you found out how to live in it you learned from that what it was all about." But traditional philosophy, not pragmatism, still held Adams's loyalty, and he knew that commitment to it meant trying to get to the ground of truth itself, even if that ground was shifting. In presenting the mind engaged in that search, and thus in the act of creating meaning, Adams anticipated the general blurring of generic lines that has characterized the twentieth century. His *Education* is part philosophy, part intellectual and cultural history, and part autobiography, and it makes wholesale use of novelistic techniques. In the process it sets the discovery of some new kind of self-originating discourse as the task of art in the twentieth century.

8. JACK LONDON'S CAREER AND POPULAR DISCOURSE

In outlook, Jack London was closer to Cather and Dreiser than to James and closer to Turner than to Adams. But in his talent for turning personal adventures into remunerative art and culturally illuminating narrative, he resembles Buffalo Bill. Born in San Francisco on January 12, 1876, the illegitimate son of William Henry Chaney, an itinerant astrologer, and Flora Wellman, a spiritualist, London was named for his stepfather, John London. In 1886 his stepfather's farm failed, and the family moved to Oakland, the workingman's city of which another Oakland artist, Gertrude Stein, later said, "There is no there there." But Stein had lived in Pennsylvania and Europe before her family moved to Oakland, and her privileged life had given her very different standards. The vacancies of Oakland were the closest thing to home that London ever found. At age fourteen, he quit public school and began spending his days working in a laundry and then a cannery, and his nights frequenting libraries and saloons or working in San Francisco Bay as an oyster pirate. Later, older and tougher, he signed on as an able-bodied seaman on the *Sophie Sutherland,* a sealer bound for the Siberian coast and Japan, and began a life of remarkable adventures. Later still, in 1901 and 1905, he tried to become Oakland's first Socialist mayor.

In 1894, one year after Adams's trip to Chicago and Stein's matriculation at Radcliffe College, London joined Kelley's Industrial Army, a group of unemployed workers that marched with Coxey's Army on Washington, hoping to force the government to help the unemployed. Back in Oakland, he studied briefly at the University of California, Berkeley, as a special student and then left to go prospecting for gold in the Klondike. Back in Oakland again, his pockets still empty, he began the adventure of writing about his adventures. His first book, a collection of stories called *The Son of the Wolf* (1900), catapulted him to fame. By the time he died sixteen years later, he had published forty-three books and made several small fortunes as one of the most popular, highly paid writers of his time.

One explanation for London's emergence as a writer-hero of the years before World War I lies in his talent, like that of Herman Melville, for transmuting his adventures into fiction. He worked as a sailor, an oyster pirate, and Klondike prospector. He was arrested for vagrancy in Buffalo and again in Niagara Falls, where he spent thirty days in jail. Preparing to write *The People of the Abyss* (1903), he lived for several months as a tramp in the East End of London. During years of national adventurism and imperialism, he kept on finding new frontiers to write about. Not even great success stilled his restlessness. After *The Call of the Wild* (1903) and *The Sea Wolf* (1904) had made him famous and earned him large sums of money, he left for Japan and Korea to cover the Russo-Japanese War for the Hearst newspapers. When the Mexican Revolution broke out in 1914, he headed for Veracruz to cover the war for *Collier's* magazine.

When London began writing, he intended simply to recount his adventures. But he soon found himself caught up in a remarkable unfolding in which his desultory reading played an obtrusive role. Traces of his reading – in Hobbes, Bacon, Locke, Kant, Laplace, and Freud, in Swinburne, Shaw, Conrad, and Kipling – are scattered throughout his writings. In addition, he relied heavily on popularizers like Ernst Haeckel, whose *The Riddle of the Universe* (1899) applied the doctrine of evolution to philosophy and religion, and Herbert Spencer, who saw evolutionary thought as the key to understanding all change in the knowable universe, including ethics and social organization. But Darwin, Marx, and Nietzsche were his great heroes. From his readings of and about their works, he emerged with ideas, often reductive, that shaped his sense of everything he had experienced. His writings thus inscribe three adventures: his effort to make money by recounting his experiences, his effort to find meaning in his experiences, and the struggle among three giants to shape his interpretive venture.

To true disciples of any one of London's intellectual heroes, his appropriations are sure to seem unsatisfactory. His desire for social justice and his sympathy for society's outcasts reinforced the influence of Marx. But nothing could displace his fascination with nature as a scene of the struggle for survival, or with human beings as animals shaped by primal forces that can never be obliterated. In his repeated attempts to enter the consciousness of animals, his fascination with the human urge to recapture elemental, ecstatic forms of consciousness, through moments of struggle with primal forces, survived. Believing that such moments belonged to an elite who were willing to risk everything, he continued celebrating them, despite their clash with his politics.

In the "blood longing" that Buck feels in *The Call of the Wild,* we see traces of Nietzsche as well as Darwin. Having come to embody the skills and traits of his primal animal community, Buck becomes its leader because, as a courageous, skilled killer, he knows how to survive "triumphantly in a hostile environment where only the strong survived." Buck is a natural aristocrat who commands the life around him by virtue of his superiority. Even Nietzsche's notion of racial superiority had a lasting impact on London's mind: "I am first of all a white man," he wrote, "and only then a socialist." Given the basic thrust of his writings, in which women remain as subordinate as they do in Turner's, it is important to feel the narrow, exclusionary sense of the second of his operative terms ("man") as well as the first ("white").

As a result, mixed and even contradictory elements entered virtually everything he wrote. In *The People of the Abyss,* the modern city's slum becomes a frontier of savagery that stands as an indictment of the money-based, class-ridden society promoted by modern capitalism. There are a half-million or more human beings "dying miserably at the bottom of the social pit called London," London reports. Yet in writing about society's victims, London presents himself as a heroic superman. *The Call of the Wild* traces the reprimitivization of Buck, a "civilized" and thus partially denatured aristocrat among dogs. By obeying the call of the wild and surrendering his civilized restraints, Buck becomes again a primal animal who survives "triumphantly in a hostile environment." In *White Fang* (1905), the sequel to *The Call of the Wild,* London reverses this process. While Buck's journey carries him toward nature, White Fang's carries him toward civilization.

"I love the wild not less than the good," Thoreau says in *Walden.* "What

really happened to" the people and the children of people "who left civilization
and traveled the wilderness road?" asks T. K. Whipple in *Study Out the Land*.
"All America lies at the end of the wilderness road, and our past is not a dead
past but still lives in us," he adds; "thus the question is momentous."

> Our forefathers had civilization inside themselves, the wild outside. We live
> in the civilization they created, but within us the wilderness still lingers. What
> they dreamed, we live, and what they lived, we dream.[14]

London believed that the wilderness still lived within people like himself, and
he thought of this as representative rather than exceptional. For, like Thoreau,
he regarded the savage and the civilized as contending principles, not as fixed
scenes or as fixed states of being. He valued both the capacity to be changed
by "socialization" in the name of the "good" and the capacity to remain
"natural" by retaining one's affinity for the "wild." More than Thoreau,
however, he thought of the wild, in the city of London no less than in the
Yukon, as a truly savage realm where there was "no law but the law of the
club and the fang" – a phrase in which the distance between nature and its
weapons ("the fang") and civilization and its weapons ("the club") almost
vanishes. In fiction and nonfiction, he presents life in frontier terms, as a
struggle of instincts and wills as well as weapons. Society mirrors nature in
his writings because it is dominated by elemental struggle. He thus locates in
societies of the modern world disguised versions of the tangled skein of conflicting impulses and desires that he observed in nature.

London wrote plain prose that makes a direct appeal to experience, and he
possessed a gift for narrative. But his works owed some of their popular appeal
to the way in which they served the cult of the "strenuous life" that arose as
a counter to the fear of "gentility" and "femininity," which increased around
the turn of the century. In short, though London thought of himself as a rebel,
and in some ways was one, he served the culture of which he was a critic in
ways that he never fully understood – except imaginatively in *Martin Eden,*
where such knowledge leads to despair. And he served it by constructing
stories beneath whose simple surface lurked confused, destabilizing issues that
neither he nor his society could tame.

Given the almost magisterial control of his later novels, Henry James is
sometimes thought of as epitomizing the lessons of form, or even those of
transcendent art. Given the exposed seams and sheer noisiness of his work,
London is often thought of as epitomizing the culture-bound artist. Yet in
very different ways both writers remind us that social and economic forces
play shaping roles even in art. James's novels depend on a language of interests
and investments, of power, manipulations, and economic status, and thus on
a specific political economy that seems almost to flaunt its capacity for shaping
modes of understanding and habits of expression as well as habits of the heart;
habits of desire, aspiration, and wonder as well as habits of industry; and thus
social, moral, and aesthetic as well as intellectual reflexes. There are, of course,
several explanations for James's reiterated, self-aware relinquishing of the sense

of fixed meaning and unambiguous tone that faith in the possibility of absolute truth demands. Some of these explanations are philosophical, others aesthetic. But James's insistence on knowing every mind through another mind, and his habit of treating even the pretense of knowing clearly and directly as dangerous, illicit, or vampirish, had social as well as epistemological and aesthetic roots. He avoided primal social and economic scenes as well as primal sexual scenes, not simply out of reticence or because he was unfamiliar with them, but also because he thought of language and sensibility as always already too deeply conditioned by and implicated in them. What was lost in advance was the possibility of their serving as anything more than radically imperfect tools for gaining the perspective that full understanding required. From the *Portrait* on, language and sensibility were for him at once necessary and unreliable – the locus of illumination and understanding, and the locus of error and deceit. In his style, in which engagement and evasion coexist, he enacts the predicament of a writer who recognizes that his most essential tools are potentially deceitful and destructive as well as creative. And since he saw his predicament as modern rather than merely personal, he learned to confront it by sharing it with characters like Isabel Archer. The language of power and the power of language merge in his fiction. But his is also a world in which control as power and control as impotence coexist, drawing sublime triumph and abject failure closer together than they had ever been before.

Not understanding himself or his predicament as well, London approached nature instinctively, as a scene of adventure and as a haven. He identified with the wild, and especially with his wolflike dogs, by signing letters to close friends "Wolf" and by building a home he named "Wolf House." Ideas, by contrast, he approached as he approached society: in wary confrontation. Yet his novels owe their popularity in part to the ideas he never fully mastered. Even the novels (*The Call of the Wild, The Sea Wolf, White Fang*) and stories ("To Build a Fire") that struck readers as "pure" adventure are filled with crudely interpreted action. Where ideas were concerned, London remained an amateur in the double sense of being unprofessional and enamoured. Yet he became a teacher to his nation more easily than James in part because he was less disciplined and less concerted, a fact we must understand if we are to understand his success and the culture that made it possible.

The Call of the Wild begins by forcing us out of our anthropocentricism. "Buck did not read the newspapers," runs its first line. Through Buck, his St. Bernard-shepherd hero, London reconnects us with the natural world from which we are descended and to which we still belong. London's cause is in a sense primitivistic: he wants to reawaken our ties to unthinking nature. "There is an ecstasy that marks the summit of life, and beyond which life cannot rise. And such is the paradox of living, this ecstasy comes when one is most alive, and it comes as a complete forgetfulness that one is alive." Behind his primitivism, or vitalism, lay a conviction that, in their effort to conquer nature, modern industrial-commercial-bourgeois societies have created a false relation between humans and nature, and thus between humans and themselves.

Crudely yet tellingly, he insists that the underlying motives for the creation of such societies are economic, as we see early in *The Call of the Wild* when Buck is sold into captivity for profit. In *White Fang,* Beauty Smith is "a monstrosity," "the weakest of weak-kneed and sniveling cowards," who, seeing the strength and beauty of White Fang, the wolf-dog for whom the book is named, "desired to possess him" – in order to beat him for pleasure and exploit him for profit: "Beauty Smith enjoyed the task. He delighted in it. He gloated."

London tried, after his fashion, to be faithful to all of his heroes, Darwin, Marx, and Nietzsche, because he felt that he and his society needed them. As a result, there was something in his writings for admirers of people as different as Theodore Roosevelt, Eugene Debs, and Herbert Spencer. He traced and retraced actions that evoked the frontier myth in the hope of fostering moral and spiritual renewal. In his own forays into "virgin" territories, he found what earlier explorers had found in theirs: an economic as well as heroic potential. For he discovered in the process of launching an amazingly remunerative career a discourse that blends heroic self-dramatizations, clear evocations of his culture's frontier experiences and frontier myths, authentic political concerns, and self-taught (if also half-digested) ideas about nature and society.

9. *INNOCENCE AND REVOLT IN THE "LYRIC YEARS": 1900–1916*

London wrote during a period of rapid, uneven economic recovery. Between 1900 and 1910, the nation's population jumped from 67 million to 92 million, with much of the gain coming in cities, where the rate of growth was three times faster than that in rural areas. Both average per capita wealth and average personal income increased, as did the unevenness of their distribution: in a period of strong economic expansion, the average real income of laborers fell. Investors, even those with modest capital to invest, were the winners, as both expansion and consolidation of industries pushed profits up – especially in railways, iron and steel, copper, meat packing, milling, tobacco, and petroleum. By 1910, the men in charge of the nation's largest business firms possessed enormous political as well as economic power. "We have no word to express government by monied corporations," Charles Francis Adams, Jr., noted in 1869. Forty years later, the nation was still looking for words to describe its new political economy, which was dominated, Henry James observed, by the "new remorseless monopolies." Meanwhile, the poor were becoming poorer and more hopeless – "oxlike, limp, and lead-eyed," as the poet Vachel Lindsay put it. Some skilled laborers prospered, but others suffered, especially the new immigrants from Asia and southern and eastern Europe. In the North and the South, black Americans continued to be victimized by inferior schools, poor housing, and segregation that was vigilantly enforced in schools, churches, unions, and workplaces, as well as society at large.

Such contrasts quickly spawned a literature of protest. Having begun his career as a writer of adventure stories for boys' magazines, Upton Sinclair turned to reform fiction in 1906, in a novel called *The Jungle,* set in the bars, tenements, and packinghouses of a Chicago ghetto, where death hangs in the air like a "subtle poison." "What *Uncle Tom's Cabin* did for the black slaves," Jack London declared, *The Jungle* had a chance of doing "for the white slaves of today." On one side, Sinclair's fiction resembles social exposés like Lincoln Steffens's *The Shame of the Cities* (1904), John Spargo's *The Bitter Cry of the Children* (1906), and Ida Tarbell's *History of the Standard Oil Company* (1904). On another, it resembles novels like Stephen Crane's "two experiments in misery," *Maggie: A Girl of the Streets* (1893) and *George's Mother* (1896), Abraham Cahan's *Yekl: A Tale of the New York Ghetto* (1896) and *The Rise of David Levinsky* (1917), Paul Laurence Dunbar's *The Uncalled* (1898) and *The Sport of the Gods* (1902), James Weldon Johnson's *The Autobiography of an Ex-Colored Man* (1912), and Anzia Yezeirska's *Bread Givers* (1925). Similarly motivated, the painter John Sloan and other members of the "Ash Can school" and the "Revolutionary Black Gang" – Everett Shinn, William Glockens, and George Luks – sought to make painting "unconsciously social conscious." To genteel critics, Sloan and his associates were "apostles of ugliness." But urban life, not ugliness, was their subject, vernacular honesty their aim, as they scouted the dark alleys, dank saloons, and squalid tenements of New York in search of thieves, drunkards, and slatterns.

In fact, however, even as they studied the harsh world of the nation's cities, writers like Sinclair and painters like Sloan were lifted by hopeful winds of change. By 1912, when Woodrow Wilson announced his "New Freedom," *new* had again become a talismanic word, as it had off and on for several centuries, beginning with the early explorers of the "New World." The nation's tilt toward the dreamer and the tinkerer reflected its sense of itself as an unfinished scene; and in the first two decades of the twentieth century, an aggressive experimental mood, conscious of itself as revisionary, took hold. Spawning a "New Poetry," a "New Theater," a "New Art," and a "New Woman," it fractured the cultural scene. On one side stood devotees of the "Genteel Tradition," a term coined in 1911 by George Santayana. On the other stood young rebels imbued by a sense of urgency and high calling. Men in gay clothing joined "smoking women" in flaunting the younger generation's victory "over the prostrate body of puritanism." Working "with knives in their brains," they examined the prejudices and inhibitions of their parents, determined to cast off everything that seemed to them petty, provincial, timid, or bland.

Mabel Dodge Luhan, author of *Movers and Shakers* (1936) and leader of the "rebel rich," as the novelist and journalist Floyd Dell called them, knew that some of the "Genteel Custodians" were tough-minded on some issues and of two minds on others. Several of them had enlisted in the mixed army of men and women fighting for women's suffrage; others worried about the diverse problems that had placed every "human relation," as Walter Lippmann wrote in the *New Republic* in 1914, "whether of parent and child, husband and wife, worker and employer," in a "strange situation." A few were even trying to address what Ludwig Lewisohn, in *Upstream* (1922), called the silent conflict between the interests of the established classes and "the sense of life and scale of values brought by the yet inarticulate masses of immigrants." But Luhan and the rebels could not help thinking of the Genteel Custodians as timid people bent on using their drawing rooms, private clubs, and country estates to shield them from the energy and problems of the new United States. Not only were the Custodians too fastidious, they had lost their nerve. They shrank from the poor, industrial working classes, the new immigrants, and black Americans, fearful of what their stirrings might mean. Their talk about "invasions of the darker types" hid two interconnected fears: fear that their racial "purity" might be lost if the new "strangers" were assimilated, and fear that the "strangers," left unassimilated, might become dominant, displacing their privileged descendants. As a result, they evinced fear of every person or idea that had, as H. L. Mencken put it, an "alien smell" about it, lest they, the chief beneficiaries of the nation's abundance, should lose status and power as others gained them.

During the nineteenth century, the parents and grandparents of the Genteel Custodians had placed their interests and concerns at the top of the nation's official list. Having achieved a more or less coherent rationalization and justification of their ascendancy, they had become expert in using both descent relations, defined by blood, and consent relations, defined by marriage, partnership, or other agreements under law, to consolidate and enlarge the wealth and to secure the privileges that, in their eyes, they had earned and possessed the right to bequeath. Some of them admired the uses to which the energetic, aspiring young protagonists of Horatio Alger put consensual relationships; others realized that much of the nation's energy depended on its ability to inspire people with great expectations. But having arrived, they wanted to tilt their society and its political economy away from openness toward stability and privilege. Some of them enjoyed watching the antics of the rebels, and even helped finance them. But in doing so, they were following a strategy familiar at least since France in the heyday of Voltaire and Rousseau: the upper-class strategy, described by Talleyrand, of taking delight in one's critics, confident of one's ability to tame their words and pictures with applause, money, and kisses. Recognition of the power of that strategy gave Jack London the story of *Martin Eden* and filled him with despair.

At stake were the rights, privileges, and spoils that the Custodians thought of as theirs. At stake, too, was their ability to co-opt the rebels and subvert the subversives. Their insistence that art remain aloof from local desecrations meant, first, that Beauty and Truth must be respected, and with them Tradition; second, that reticence and "good taste" must govern human relations; and third, as Henry Van Dyke put it, that the "spiritual rootage of art" must be preserved. In short, like Burnham and his advisers, they wanted to make lyric poetry, as the Genteel Tradition had defined it, normative for all art – a move that reflected deep commitments and protected clear interests, the extent of which can best be judged by the rebels' targets. It is, however, both ironic and telling that rebels like Floyd Dell and Genevieve Taggard, looking back on the heyday of their rebellion, would call it the "Lyric Years," without wondering what kind of independence they had achieved.

For a brief time, the assault appeared to be frontal. In 1911 Frederick Winslow Taylor, the "father" of "systematic management," published *The Principles of Scientific Management,* celebrating efficiency as an ideal that should be

> applied with equal force to all social activities: to the management of our homes; the management of our farms; the management of the business of our tradesmen, large and small; of our churches, our philanthropic institutions, our universities, and our governmental departments.[15]

Twenty-five years later, John Dos Passos included a portrait of Taylor in *The Big Money* (1936), called his plan "The American Plan," and ended with Taylor lying "dead with his watch in his hand," as though to signal what worship of efficiency might lead to. In fact, however, the ideas associated with Taylor's name were widespread before Taylor systematized them, just as the critique of them was widespread before Dos Passos satirized them, and even before D. H. Lawrence, in *Studies in Classic American Literature* (1923), attributed them to Benjamin Franklin, as the nation's first secularized Puritan. In 1917 Randolph Bourne, in "The Puritan's Will to Power," framed one of several indictments that described industrial capitalists as descendants of a life-denying Puritanism and its dream of total control. Other diagnosticians named the Puritan as the chief carrier of repression, and repression as the nation's most enervating disease. In "Puritanism," James G. Huneker announced, "the entire man ended at his collarbone." By teaching themselves to refer to all natural acts euphemistically, to enclose all personal and especially all sexual relations in arduous formalities, and to make all social relations instrumental and exploitative, disciples of gentility and efficiency had turned maturation into a process of desiccation and made themselves victims of life-denying formulas. They were Puritans, and Puritans were money-hungry, life-denying neurotics who had forgotten how to laugh, feel wonder, or trust pleasure: "and down they forgot as up they grew," E. E. Cummings later wrote, in "anyone lived in a prettyhow town."

Meanwhile, in her salon on Fifth Avenue, Luhan was staging "Evenings" where writers as different as Edwin Arlington Robinson, Lincoln Steffens, Mary Austin, and Carl Van Vechten encountered journalists like Walter Lippmann and political radicals like John Reed, Emma Goldman, and Bill Haywood. One thing Luhan's guests shared was a sense of the immediate past as what Joseph Freeman called a "dark age" across which the "meteors of Nietzsche, Whitman, Darwin, and Marx" had flashed; and another was the sense of the Lyric Years as a period in which barriers were going down and people were reaching out to communicate new thoughts in new ways. Gone forever was the world of the "vanished village" where God's commandments reigned with such authority that rebels who broke them assumed they had sinned. Now, Freeman said, you "had to make up your own right and wrong; you had to decide everything for yourself" – especially about sex but also about honoring your parents and accepting their authority. Gone, too, was the sense that the system of corporate capitalism must not be changed.

At times, the new art, the new sexuality, and the new politics seemed to go hand in hand. In Chicago, Van Wyck Brooks reported, "splendidly pagan" refugees of the drab farms, dried-up villages, and stagnant towns of the Midwest were gathering to discuss "art and socialism and the finer emotional forces that were to prevail in the future." The Midwest, Ford Madox Ford later reported from Paris, "was seething with literary impulse." Meanwhile, back in New York, Isadora Duncan – "what genius is," Luhan wrote – had become the high priestess of sexual revolution that rebels assumed would sweep the land. Following her triumphant appearance in Carnegie Hall, Duncan's admirers hatched a scheme for having her dance in Harvard Stadium or the Yale Bowl before crowds of children too young to have been corrupted by puritanical repression. Duncan was more than the "greatest living dancer" and more than the "symbol of the body's liberation" from outdated mores. She was a "sublime cult" that looked toward an era ever-more-about-to-be when life would be "frank and free" and people would believe in the "beauty of [their] own nature." "To die happy," the rebels said, one had to glimpse the future by seeing Isadora Duncan dance.

In fact, however, the rebels were not as liberated as they thought. A mix of pagans, aesthetes, and reformers – "earnest naive anarchists . . . labor leaders, poets, journalists, editors, and actors," as Luhan called them – they were also less unified than their enemies. It was very confusing, Luhan confessed; though the rebels "were all part of one picture," they were also "jumbled and scattered." One split set those who valued politics more than art against those who valued art more than politics. Another set those more concerned with social justice against those more concerned with personal freedom. Both anarchism and vagabondage were popular and both "spat indiscriminately upon all group life." Writers who saw the poet-artist under the aspect of the orphan, the wanderer, the outcast, and even the derelict favored those who chose the solitary way and rejected the "doom of being a joiner." Some settled for leading what Freeman called a dual life, supporting art with one hand, political reform with the other; others, including Freeman and Dell, turned to *Masses* in the hope of reconciling their "warring selves" and "connecting literature with revolution." Other magazines – including the *New Republic,* founded in 1914 by Herbert Croly and edited by Walter Lippmann, and *Seven Arts,* founded in 1916 and edited by James Oppenheimer – sprang up to promote other versions of unity. Even established magazines – including *Smart Set,* edited after 1914 by H. L. Mencken with George Jean Nathan, and *Masses*, edited from 1913 to 1917 by Max Eastman – sought to make unity their cause. But in practice unity proved to be difficult.

Mencken was an early champion of the "crude" art of Dreiser, and he had written a controversial book on Nietzsche, adding his voice to the chorus fomenting revolt against the "denatured Brahmins," who seemed to him blind and deaf to everything "honest, interesting, imaginative, and enterprising" in life as well as art. But he had limited use for the complex if not deliberately obscure "modernist" works of writers like Ezra Pound, and even less for the reformers he called "birth controllers, jittery Socialists, and other such vermin." James Oppenheimer started *Seven Arts* in part because *New Republic* seemed to him, in its two short years, to have become one-sided in its concern for the "values of life" as opposed to art's concern with form and technique. The problem with Dreiser, Dell insisted, was the "Passive Attitude" he inculcated by presenting life in Darwinian terms. Louis Smith preferred the reformers Mencken called "vermin" to aesthetes who refused to make art socially responsible. Hutchins Hapgood, author of *The Spirit of the Ghetto* (1902), thought Stein and Pound as well as postimpressionists irresponsible in their abandonment of the idea that art should represent the "real" world.

What prevailed, when unity failed, was a more or less good-spirited truce. Although Mencken preferred his own accessible essays to obscure poems, he occasionally published Pound and Joyce. And he preferred even "vermin" to "Brahmins." Smith and Hapgood remained skeptical of those they called "aesthetes" and critical of nondoctrinaire radicals like Max Eastman. Eastman was a "half-ass intellectual," Smith said, "not a real revolutionary socialist." But like Hapgood, he preferred mild iconoclasts and even hedonists to the Genteel Custodians on grounds that any disturbance was a good one. Disturbances shake foundations, Hapgood wrote, and lead to new life, "whether the programs and ideas have permanent validity or not."

The result was what Pound called an "American Risorgimento," by which he meant a "whole volley of liberations" directed in more or less the same direction – against the Genteel Tradition. For years, rumors had been drifting across the Atlantic about a panoply of uprisings against authority. At stake were not only fundamental aesthetic values but also social traditions and ethical conventions, including, for Tristan Tzara and dadaism, the value of "Art" and the idea of achieved culture as transmitted by what W. B. Yeats called "Monuments of unageing intellect." Caught up in their "volley of liberations," the rebels of the Lyric Years concentrated on the enemies they had named and, in a sense, created – "the denatured Brahmins," "the Puritan," "the Genteel Custodians" – and avoided the issues that divided them. American provincialism was one of their pet peeves, especially when it took the virulent form of fearing anything that had an alien look or smell about it. In the manners and dress displayed in their enclaves, as well as in the books they carried around and read, they were self-consciously cosmopolitan. One of their goals was recognition of what Randolph Bourne called "trans-nationality" – "a weaving back and forth, with other lands, of many threads of all sizes and colors."

At the same time, however, virtually all of them wanted to contribute to the creation of a distinctly "American" culture. Van Wyck Brooks, an editor of *Seven Arts* and author of *America's Coming of Age* (1915), spoke for many when he insisted that there could be no true revolution until native writers had brought their readers "face to face with [their] own experience." Brooks's indictments of the puritanism and materialism of culture in the United States owed much to European thinkers. Yet he remained convinced that a "world of poetry" lay "hidden away" in the nation's past and that it might yet "serve, as the poetry of life should serve," to bring about the reconstruction of the nation's life. With this largely unexamined hope before them, he and his friends spent much of their time reading their precursors and reading one another: Brooks read Dell, Dell read Brooks, both read Bourne, and Bourne read both. They read the fiction of Norris, Sinclair, London, and Dreiser as well as Cather, Wharton, and Stein. And they read the verse, to cite Freeman's list, of "Robert Frost, Edgar Lee Masters, Vachel Lindsay, James Oppenheimer, Amy Lowell, Ezra Pound, T. S. Eliot, [and] . . . Carl Sandburg," as well as "Walt Whitman, whose revolutionary message was expressing itself in the new freedom of our literature."

Caught up in the possibilities of renewal, the rebels skirted problems they could find no way to resolve, including the tension between identifying a national culture and creating a trans-national culture. And they assumed, as Floyd Dell put it, with what now seems stunning innocence, that the "new spirit" abroad, generated by the "search for new values in life and art," would "logically . . . lead to a socialist society," accomplishing "Great Change" through "gradual conversion." For a time, particularly between 1913 and 1917, when Max Eastman edited it, *Masses* presided over radicalism in the United States as no magazine before or since. But *Masses* was nothing if not both commodious and evasive. It brought politics cheek to jowl with the early love poems of E. E. Cummings. Through its pages, as a faithfully uncritical Freeman put it, the winds of change "released by Omar Khayyam, Friedrich Nietzsche, Edward Carpenter, Walt Whitman and finally Sigmund Freud blew across America . . . to rescue us from the crushing oppression of puritanism, from the implacable sense of guilt." Even when its focus became explicitly political, its revolutionary amalgam included the gospel of "Comrade Jesus." As a rule, however, its reach – the irreverent cartoons of Art Young, the iconoclastic essays of Dell, the proclamations of the labor agitator Arturo Giovannitti, the exposés of Mary Heaton Vorse, and the travel reports of John Reed – remained broadly cultural rather than concertedly political.

To Dell, writing in the bleak aftermath of the Great War, 1912 became the "Lyric Year" in which renewal seemed almost at hand. For Taggard, looking back from 1925, the crucial date was March 1906, when the first issue of *Mother Earth* – founded, edited, and published by Emma Goldman – had appeared. But Taggard's sense of the era as a "Joyous Season" – a "holiday" in which "zealous social work, backed by optimistic social theory" had pitted young, hopeful, high-spirited reformers against enemies that seemed old and pale and tired – was consonant with Dell's. And so, too, was her sense that it ended when the federal government, too hurried to wait for Talleyrand's form of co-optation to work, suppressed *Masses* and put an end to the energizing innocence that sustained the Lyric Years.

10. THE ARMORY SHOW OF 1913 AND THE DECLINE OF INNOCENCE

No event more fully captures the rebellion, the divisions, and the evasions of the Lyric Years than the Armory Show that opened in New York on the evening of February 17, 1913, shortly before the Woolworth Building, standing 792 feet high, became the tallest building in the world. In *Movers and Shakers,* the third part of her four-part autobiography, *Intimate Memoirs* (1933–7), Luhan discusses several "Revolutions in Art" – and also reprints her own piece, "Speculations, or Post-Impressions in Prose," written on the occasion of the Armory Show, in which she asserts that "Gertrude Stein is doing with words what Picasso is doing with paint" – "impelling language to induce new states of consciousness." Luhan thus reinforces her broader claim: that the spirit that inspired the era's artists also imbued the planners of the Armory Show. Frederick James Gregg and Arthur Davies were co-conspirators with Stein and Picasso in a plot to open the eyes of "the great, blind, dumb New York Public" to art that is "really modern." Planning the exhibition, they talked "with creepy feelings of terror and delight" about their plan to "dynamite America." "Revolution – that was what they felt they were destined to provide for these States – and one saw them shuddering and giggling like high-spirited boys daring each other." The show itself, Luhan concluded, was the most important thing of its kind "that ever happened in America" precisely because it had touched the "unawakened consciousness" of people, allowing artists to set them free.

In some respects, including the furor it created, the Armory Show almost matched the dreams of its makers. Some art critics, including Frank Mather for *Nation,* reassured readers that the hullabaloo would die down and sanity prevail, keeping art pure and society safe. Others followed Norman Hapgood in the *Globe,* who described the New Art's wanton violations of "ideal forms" and "noble subjects" as morally and aesthetically offensive, and Duchamp's *Nude Descending a Staircase* as a barbaric deformation of the human body. Kenyon Cox, adviser to Burnham in the building of Chicago's Dream City, described Cézanne as "absolutely without talent and absolutely cut off from tradition." But the most important denouncements came from Royal Cortissoz, a man with close ties to such formidable institutions as the Century Club, the National Academy of Design, and the American Academy in Rome.

Cortissoz was a biographer of Augustus Saint-Gaudens (1907), another of Burnham's advisers, and John La Farge (1911). In 1913 his attacks on the Ash

Can school and the Revolutionary Black Gang had established him as the most effective enemy of the new "barbarism." Following the Armory Show, he described Cézanne as ignorant, Van Gogh as incompetent, and "Picasso the Spaniard" as the creator "of a kind of Barnumism." Behind his message about the dangers of "Picasso the Spaniard," Gauguin "the stupid Frenchman," and Van Gogh the "tormented" Dutchman lie poorly repressed ethnic anxieties, the logic of which surfaces in his reference to the imminent threat that "foreign influences" pose to "American" society as well as "American" art. What "Post Impressionism" attacks, Cortissoz insists, is the notion of art as a timeless "manifestation of the eternal ideal" – in defense of which he names "Mr. Roger Fry, an English critic," and John S. Sargent as his allies. As it turns out, furthermore, the most invidious enemies of art – so-called artists who display technical "incompetence suffused with egotism" in subjects that are "dirty," styles that are "brutal," and results that are "obscure" – are also the most invidious enemies of "America."

Aided by notoriety, the Armory Show became a boisterous success. People rushed to see it. After it closed in New York, major parts of it moved to Chicago, where, attacked by the Law and Order League, it held its own in head-to-head competition for crowds with Lilly Langtry in vaudeville and George M. Cohan in *Broadway Jones*. From Chicago it moved to Boston. Back in New York, Gregg, Davies, and their co-conspirators staged a victory celebration. They marched through the halls where the show had opened to the music of fife and drum, raising their glasses in toast after toast. "Don't cheer, boys," John Quinn said, repeating the words of Captain Philip at Santiago as he and his crew watched a disabled Spanish ship sink, "the poor devils are dying."

The repercussions of the Armory Show lasted for years. Impressionist and postimpressionist works had been shown earlier by Alfred Stieglitz in his gallery at 291 Fifth Avenue – "the largest small room of its kind in the world," Marsden Hartley called it. Although Bill Haywood thought Stieglitz narrow, artists thought him broad: having no narrow program of his own, he made convention his enemy and artists who defied it in interesting ways his friends. In 1908, 1910, 1911, and 1912 he had presented Rodin's drawings, Matisse's nudes, Toulouse-Lautrec's color lithographs, Cézanne's lithographs, and Picasso's drawings. But the Armory Show marked a turning point in lifting fauvist, cubist, and early futurist works to visibility. Of the several hundred paintings sold during its run, one was Cézanne's *The Poor House on the Hill*, purchased by the Metropolitan Museum. It was the first Cézanne acquired by a public institution in the United States.

Another set of repercussions came, however, from within the ranks of the rebels. To those who shared Brooks's commitment to native traditions, the show's concentration on Europe was disturbing. But the deeper issue had to do with the purpose of art. To Luhan, the paintings of Picasso were no more dangerous than the prose of Stein. What one was doing with painting the other was doing with words: using art "to induce new states of consciousness."

But when Luhan went on to say what this meant – for Stein, Luhan observed, language becomes "a creative art rather than a mirror of history" – not even the talismanic word "new" could save her from offending socialists who insisted that art have social purpose or writers who regarded mimesis as an indispensable part of art's legacy. Formalists might be content to see individual artists like Stein dedicate themselves to reshaping the perception, sensibility, and thought of an elite group of aficionados. But to young idealists who hoped to fuse art and politics, the separation of art from social and economic ac-tualities, and thus from "the people," spelled defeat. The failure of *Masses* to reach the masses was already an open secret. One wit wrote:

> They draw fat women for *The Masses*
> Denuded, fat, ungainly lasses –
> How does that help the working classes?[16]

But the ideal of unity persisted. To surrender it was unthinkable to the editors of the *Masses* and to scores of rebels who remained committed to the idea of social reform, however uncritical they remained about the political implications of their aesthetics or the aesthetic implications of their politics.

Ezra Pound sat out the Armory Show in rural England and in general showed little interest in cultural disturbances masterminded by people like Gregg and Davies. To writers like Mencken and Lippmann as well as revolutionaries like Louis Smith and social critics like Hutchins Hapgood, Pound had all the markings – in costume, manner, and style – of an aesthete who cared little about material culture, let alone political realities and the plight of the masses. But Pound's concerns were more inclusive than most people thought, as his later career made clear, however sadly.

In his early years, Pound's concerns converged on the possibilities, problems, and powers of language. Later, after the Great War began killing off some of his friends, including the sculptor Henri Gaudier-Brzeska, his interest in pol-itics and economics became more overt. In "Hugh Selwyn Mauberley" – which he described as "a study in form, an attempt to condense the James novel" – his enterprise embraces the task of saving culture as well as language not only from politicians, bankers, and warmongers but also from decadent aesthetes and hyperrefined literati. Later still, looking back from his confinement in Pisa at the end of World War II to his own version of the Lyric Years – the years he spent between 1913 and 1916 living with W. B. Yeats at Stone Cottage near Coleman's Hatch in Sussex – he thought of them as an innocent age, "before the world was given over to wars," when life seemed fresh and politics had not yet been born.

But Pound's eye for cultural politics in fact dated back to early disappoint-ments with the commercial magazines and publishing houses that dominated literature in Western democracies, including the United States. The survival of art mattered, as Pound saw it, because art's fate was inseparable from the fate of *all* forms of originality, freedom, and individuality. The seamlessness of culture convinced him that the forms of discipline dictated by commercial civilization (maximum efficiency, standardized products, interchangeable parts and interchangeable workers, repetitious processes, and systematic management) were inimical to life as well as art. Sensing that the broader economic process – in which corporate capitalism inspired "systematic management" and "systematic management" reinforced corporate capitalism – he identified a threat to individuality that was simultaneously a threat to artistic creativity, and so made resistance the center of his life. Unable to resolve the issue of how politics and art might be conjoined not only in fact, which at some level they were, but also in conception and intent, which they were not, Pound worked in fits and starts. His public persona as an aesthete, which was only partially true to his writings, triumphed over them, because it was easier for him communicate and for the public to grasp. But he knew what he desired, and it was not that art be separated from politics or that the United States try to turn back the clock. It was that the United States seize the artistic as well as the political promise of its democracy before its incorporating economy further diminished them, as his little book, *Patria Mia,* written in 1913, makes clear.

Pound's unsuccess, like that of the editors of the *Masses,* whose choice ran in the opposite direction in search of the same end, was prepared by his own failure of will. But it was sealed by the coming of World War I. The outbreak of a general war in Europe was the fruit of decades of competition for markets and colonies. Fueled by industrial growth that it in turn fueled, that competition gave rise to frustrated as well as triumphant nationalism and spurred a mounting arms race. Within the United States, antiwar feelings ran highest among German-Americans and Irish-Americans, to whom fighting on the side of allies that included France and England was repugnant. The virulent anti-Semitism of the czarist empire made Jewish-Americans reluctant to do anything that might help Russia. But many people in the United States, including most of the young idealistic rebels, watched Europe with shocked disbelief. Keeping a safe distance seemed the only wise course of action, lest their "Joyous Season" become a fool's paradise. As conflict led to conflict and atrocity to atrocity, however, hope of keeping Europe's madness at a safe distance died. In the end, most of the rebels accepted what Henry James expressed in a letter: that the war, "this abyss of blood and horror," and not the Lyric Years of good hope, was what the treacherous nineteenth century had all along been working toward.

The United States entered the Great War reluctantly, it entered late, and it remained uncertain of its motives almost to the end. "The world must be made safe for democracy," President Wilson said. "We are going to war upon the command of gold," countered Senator George Norris of Nebraska. Still, by the time Congress voted (the Senate on April 4, 1917, and the House, two days later, on a bleak Good Friday morning), most people supported the decision: the vote on the resolution to recognize the existence of a state of war with Germany was 82 to 6 in the Senate, 373 to 50 in the House. Americans remained divided about the origins of the war. "I voted for Woodrow Wilson,"

John Reed said in the summer of 1917, "mainly because Wall Street was against him. But Wall Street is for him now. This is Woodrow Wilson's and Wall Street's war." But such skepticism was more than balanced by enlistments in Wilson's "great crusade."

The full costs of waging what Wilson called "the most terrible and disastrous of all wars" emerged slowly. But one cost, anticipated by Wilson, surfaced early. War, he told a confidant in 1917, as though foreseeing the witch-hunts, spy scares, and kangaroo courts that lay ahead, will "overturn the world" we know; it will impose "illiberalism at home," instilling a "spirit of ruthless brutality" in the very "fibre of our national life." A year earlier, the government had banned *Masses* from the mails; a year later, in April and again in October 1918, it prosecuted, without success, Max Eastman, Floyd Dell, and Art Young for "conspiracy against the government." As late as 1916, when he launched *Seven Arts,* James Oppenheim still held to the faith of the Lyric Years: that "the lost soul among the nations, America, could be regenerated by art" or, as Van Wyck Brooks put it, that "a warm, humane, concerted and more or less revolutionary protest" could free the country of "whatever incubuses of crabbed age, paralysis, tyranny, stupidity, sloth, commercialism, lay most heavily upon the people's life." But such innocence faded. Within a year, the government had driven *Seven Arts* out of circulation, primarily because it opposed the war, and the Lyric Years – also called the "Little Renaissance," the "Confident Years," and the "Joyous Season" – had died, killing the hope shared by people like Luhan, Oppenheim, Brooks, Taggard, and Dell of bringing about "Great Change" through "gradual conversion."

11. THE PLAY OF HOPE AND DESPAIR

Like poetry and art, fiction of the Lyric Years got caught up in the play of hope and despair. In his early correspondence, describing his day-by-day struggles to get his fiction published in East Coast magazines and by East Coast publishers, Jack London complains, as Pound had, about the cost of postage as well as rejections. Later he began to flaunt his great success with macho swagger and then to analyze it with growing ambivalence, fearful that he had paid for it in the coin of corrupting compromise. In *Martin Eden* (1909), he confronts his writer-hero's confused ambitions and locates ties between them and the ambitions of his nation: "In the moment of that thought," he says of Martin Eden, "the desperateness of his situation dawned upon him. He saw, clear eyed, that he was in the Valley of the Shadow. All the life that was in him was fading, fainting, making toward death."

Martin Eden is the story of a writer whose life bears striking resemblances to London's own. One part of *Martin Eden*'s significance lies in the persistence with which it suggests that, despite its doctrine of impersonality, modern art often revolves around the interplay between artist and protagonist and between artist and work. Like London in his fiction, Gertrude Stein in hers, and Ernest Hemingway in his, Eden treats everything that happens to him – poverty and wealth, obscurity and fame, neglect and celebrity, adventure and boredom, injury and good fortune, health and disease – as things that are alien to him and yet are his own idea. He thus makes acts of attention acts of possession as well as creation. Through Nietzschean striving, he becomes a lionized and wealthy writer, forcing his materialistic, class-conscious society to acknowledge his superiority. In a sense, he appropriates the Horatio Alger plot: his is a story of a young man who rises from obscurity to fame, from rags to riches, from slum streets to fancy hotel suites. But he turns this familiar plot against the society that gave it birth and then made both its creators and its protagonists enormously successful by making his hero a social critic as well as an artist. The more his society honors and rewards him, the more he despises it.

London clearly took delight in making the story he was writing resemble the one he had lived. He also took delight in posing as a lonely rebel who exposes society (both his own and Martin's) as having neither soul nor integrity left to lose. As a young man, full of passionate hope, Martin Eden becomes a writer and falls in love with a young woman named Ruth Morse, whose upper-middle-class parents are anxious about their own social standing and, therefore, about their daughter's suitors. Because he has neither money nor status – not even "a job" let alone "a position," as Ruth's parents teach her to put it – Ruth rejects him. Embittered, Martin takes consolation in believing that "Nietzsche was right," that the "world belongs to the strong" who are too noble to "wallow in the swine-trough of trade and exchange." When success comes to him, and money and fame pour in and he flashes, "comet-like, through the world of literature," he is amused. Like Rousseau, he learns how to market his bad manners and angry words. Having learned how to market so much, however, he begins to realize that the value of his achievements has been established by the world that publishes, buys, and praises them. Soon he stops writing and starts selling the yellowing manuscripts of discarded work that he no longer believes in; feeding his bank account, he also feeds his contempt for the publishers who print his work and the readers who buy it.

When Ruth and her family change their minds about his value, Eden's despair deepens. In the Morse family's first overture, Mrs. Morse sends Mr. Morse to Martin with a dinner invitation. When Martin rejects it, they send Ruth to his hotel room to persuade him of her love. What Martin already believes, he now sees clearly: that Ruth and her family are bereft of values. It "makes me question love, sacred love," he says to Ruth. "Is love so gross a thing that it must feed upon publication and public notice?" Finally, however, it is not simply the crassness of the Morse family that offends him; it is the power of society to shape human lives and human values, including his own. Nothing Ruth has "done requires forgiveness," he concludes, because she has always acted in accord with what society has taught her, "and more than that one cannot" ask. When he also recognizes that it was an idealized Ruth that "he had loved," one made beautiful in part by the glamour of her "station" and in part by the "bright and luminous spirit of his love-poems," he loses everything. "It is too late," he says, "I am a sick man. . . . I seem to have lost all values."

Unable to find any means of rereading his life, Eden sinks further into despair that eventually swallows everything. "I'm done with philosophy. I want never to hear another word of it," he says, not long before he sees that art, too, is duplicitous, presenting a false face of hope to the poor and a smug face of security to the rich. Finally, so emptied of belief that he loses "any desire for anything," he drifts toward death as desire and fulfillment: "All the life that was in him was fading, fainting, making toward death." Overcoming a natural, atavistic "will to live" that aborts his first suicide attempt, he succeeds in his second.

London wrote *Martin Eden* in 1908–9 while sailing his homemade yacht the *Snark* from California to the South Seas. In it he depicts a direct confrontation between two very different conceptions of culture – one built on the dream of interests powerful enough to impose virtual order and to absorb or co-opt minor disturbances, which is the dream of the Morse family; the other built around the dream of values pure and noble enough to achieve expression and force recognition on their own, which is Martin's early dream. London's hope clearly lay with his protagonist, but his experience spoke to him in different terms. And it underwrote both the strategies of co-optation that the Morse family practice and the strategies of despair that engulf Eden. On the morning of November 22, 1916, seven years after he finished his most important novel, London died at the age of forty, apparently of a self-injected overdose of morphine. During the sixteen years between his first book and his death, he published forty-three books and piled up manuscripts from which editors and publishers fashioned seven more. He wrote as he lived, we may fairly conclude, as a man pursued. And he wrote as he thought, as a man grasping for hope as well as ideas: "Tell me," he seems to ask again and again with Laurel and Hardy, "why can't *we* ever get ahead?" His was an old man's rage even when he was still young. By the time he died, his body, once so beautiful that he described himself as being "proud as the devil of it," was a map of devastation: in his last years, he suffered from gonorrhea, insomnia (probably related to his heavy drinking), a severe skin condition, probably psoriasis, a syphilitic-like condition known as "Solomon sores," pyorrhea that forced him to have all his teeth removed, recurring dysentery, and chronic uremia. To cope with his maladies, he regularly took both arsenic (apparently to ease the pain in his bowels) and morphine. Yet he continued to eat raw fish and meat, which he loved, and, despite repeated warnings, to drink heavily – in obedience to something he once called, in *John Barleycorn* (1913), the "White Logic" of a "long sickness." In its pathos as well as its contours, dotted with excesses, in its desperate search for some accomplishment or idea that would suffice, and above all in its poverty and its riches and the telling way in which its poverty gave rise to hope and its riches to despair, London's life found expression in the story of Martin Eden. Like all good stories (including the story of the garden from which Martin got his name), Eden's story is many stories. But at bottom it is the story of a man who, having lost a home he can scarcely be said ever to have possessed, discovers that he can find no place he wants to call his own.

It is a long way from the world of Jack London to that of Edith Wharton, and from the story of Martin Eden to that of Lily Bart in *The House of Mirth*. But London's struggle, like Wharton's, was a struggle with form rather than for it. And it was troubled because it seemed to him that form and structure, in their striving to reconcile and integrate, were always already conservative. Art celebrated Dionysus but worshiped Apollo; it praised unruly eloquence but desired closure; it played at breaking forms but worked at creating them. London's art, like his identity as a writer, was troubled by his sense that literature was dedicated to suppressing both the social classes and the natural realities to which he was devoted. This is, of course, another way of saying that his identity crisis as a writer remained unresolved. And it is probably worth noting that his great commercial success, reflecting as it did national confusions that mirrored his personal confusions, had the effect of redoubling rather than resolving that crisis, as *Martin Eden* suggests. London remained a homeless child who wanted to claim art as well as life for dispossessed people. But he could find no way of succeeding as an artist without betraying his causes. His significance lies in the stark way in which the experience of feeling excluded drove him to seek inclusion that he could purchase only in the coin of betrayal.

If in London's life and art we observe the perils, for a man, of being born outside the nation's privileged circle, in Wharton's we see the perils, for a woman, of being born inside even the most privileged of circles. If, further-more, London speaks as a man for whom inclusion held out the compromising promise of power, Wharton speaks as a woman for whom inclusion necessarily meant confinement. Born in 1862 into an elite family that counted itself among New York's "Four Hundred" – a number set by the size of Mrs. Vanderbilt's new ballroom – Wharton had all the advantages that position and education could provide. Yet because she was a woman bent on becoming a writer, she was no less self-made than London, though for her self-making meant trying to slough off cultural baggage while his meant trying to acquire some. It tells us much about London that "home" was a concept the weight of which he felt precisely because he had never experienced it, and much about Wharton that her earliest recorded memory was familial. Wharton's respectable family was a web of aunts, uncles, and cousins reinforced by a larger web of friends. The only cloud hanging over it came from a late, unsubstantiated rumor that she was the daughter not of her businessman father but of a young Englishman who tutored her two brothers. That Wharton chose to take the rumor seriously points to her need to legitimize her felt marginality.

Reared as a well-bred daughter of a well-established family, Wharton came to a life of privilege that was also a life of constraints, several of which took the form of expectations. Wharton's family was prepared for many things, including her decision to come out into society at age eighteen and to make a suitable marriage at age twenty-three. But it was not prepared to see her act withdrawn in her youth (when she was in fact writing surreptitiously) or later to see her make her energies, conflicts, and ambitions public as a writer. The wealth of Wharton's world intensified its force. At no level of society was the proper role of women more clearly defined, and in none did terms like "proper" and "lady" carry more weight. For those able to accept and master propriety, her society allowed some play, even to women. But for those tilted toward resistance, it meant trouble, especially if they were women. Though Wharton knew her society well, she was never on easy terms with it, especially after she decided to become a maker as well as a consumer of culture. Her social world resembled the one that had given Henry James his great "international" theme and then authorized him to explore and exploit it. And it readily gave Wharton the right to live versions of some of the actions that James's novels trace. Once she had determined to be a writer, however, her world gave her the theme of women trapped between an established order and an emerging order. On one side stood a fading world that offered women place – as daughters, wives, mothers, and readers – but denied them voice, especially voice raised to an active social pitch. On the other stood a new order, too amorphous to provide place, yet palpable enough to call forth a voice.

The cost of Wharton's career lay, therefore, less in the large effort of writing her books than in the perilous effort of forging a self that necessarily constituted an act against family and society. The repeated periods of debilitating self-doubt that Wharton experienced in her thirties resulted at least in part from the conflict between her residual loyalty to her heritage and her emerging loyalty to herself as a woman determined to become a writer. Her decision to live abroad was less crucial for the distance it put between her and New York than for the distance it put between her and her family, though both were necessary to her effort to see and expose the falseness of the rich and sometimes elegant society that she saw Americans devising for themselves as a prisonhouse.

In *The House of Mirth,* in the "malice of fortune" that shapes Lily Bart's fate, we see an analogue to Wharton's own predicament. For it is a historical as well as familial malice that Lily Bart points to – one that takes several forms, the most inclusive being a fatal disjunction between her needs as an individual and the logic of the social world in which she tries to make her way by following the teachings of her mother. Like Edna Pontellier in Chopin's *The Awakening* (1894), Thea in Cather's *Song of the Lark* (1915), Dorinda in Glasgow's *Barren Ground* (1925), and Anna Leath in Wharton's *The Reef* (1912), Lily is a descendant of Hawthorne's Hester. She, too, is torn by the tension between what Chopin calls the "outward existence which conforms" and the "inward life which questions." But when she fails to find any place for herself – as a lover, a wife, a prophet, or a witness – she ends as Martin Eden ends, with the discovery that there is no place for her to go. She thus becomes a model of how hard effective resistance to one's milieu can be.

Lily Bart is, to be sure, much more likable than Martin Eden, in part because her requirements of life are more recognizably human. She wants genuine intimacy, yet she values her independence; she wants a full life, but she wants it as a consenting party and partner, not as an invited guest or an indulged wife. And since she is thoroughly modern, she also expects comfort. Her dream includes a "day of plighting," we are told, and also a "haze of material well-being." Lily's world offers her the plighting and the comfort she seeks by holding out to her a woman's traditional role in the "house of mirth," as a proper wife of an appropriate man. But in making this offer, it insists that all her requests come either as pleas to be "spoken for" by a properly empowered man or as pleas to be "spoken about" by properly empowered women – alternatives that rule out intimacy as well as independence by implicitly insisting that Lily accept herself as a desirable object rather than a desiring subject.

The social class whose interests dominate Lily's world demonstrates its powers of enforcement repeatedly. It controls marriages in order to concentrate property and wealth. Against minor dissenters such as Lawrence Selden and Gerty Farish, it follows a policy of tolerant marginalization. Once it is clear that Rosedale's fortune is going to continue to grow, not even his being a Jew can deter its policy of shrewd co-optation. But when Lily persists in resisting the pressure to play the part assigned her in its rigid, arid social narrative by undermining her chances to make the kind of marriage expected of her, it connives in a plot to discredit and ostracize her. At times Lawrence Selden seems to stand above the interests of the class he serves. But in fact he remains timid and inconstant both in resisting his monied world and in advocating his rarefied "republic of the spirit," whose trademark is freedom from all pressures and entanglements: "from money, from poverty, from ease and anxiety, from all the material accidents" of life.

By spoiling her chances of making a proper marriage, Lily in effect declines her ticket of admission into the "house of mirth." Her resistance to that world centers on its tendency to turn everything, including human beings – and specifically her – into commodities. About Selden's more ethereal "republic of the spirit," she remains of two minds – in part, we may assume, because it offers her no language of female mastery and growth and so cannot empower her either to understand herself or to insist that she be understood, and in part because it seems too genteel and rarefied to meet her human needs. Left to make her way in a world in which her own best inclinations and desires go against everything that her parents as well as her society – her father by abnegation, her mother by indelible instruction – have taught her, she becomes internally conflicted and makes one self-defeating mistake after another. At no point does she discover a language free enough of the money- and status-conscious world of the house of mirth to enable her to review and recast her life. Toward the end she begins to suffer from neurasthenia, a condition that troubled Wharton herself off and on throughout the 1890s. Finally, drifting toward death, carried by a "physical craving for sleep," which becomes "her only sustained sensation," she carelessly consumes a lethal dose of sleeping drops. To the end we cannot be certain whether her act, like that of Edna Pontellier in *The Awakening,* stems from an impulse of the self to find affirmation beyond society's reach, even at the expense of death, or more simply from some assent to dismissal from a world she cannot accept, though the novel clearly tilts toward the latter.

Theodore Dreiser possessed disaffections of his own, including several that ally him with London and a few that ally him with Wharton, and like them, he remained committed to fiction as a form of cultural criticism. But he possessed in abundance an ability that Wharton and London possessed only in measure: the ability to accept on its own terms the society into which he was born. As a result, he spent little time trying to reform society and less rejecting it. He saw the suffering that surrounded him and did not like it. But necessity seemed to him to rule life, and he saw no point in pretending it did not. While Adams continued to write as one convinced that the force of nature ("nature's compulsion") and the force of history ("external suggestion") were things humans had been put on earth to overcome, Dreiser wrote as one convinced that nature would get you even if history did not. Such knowledge pushes Martin Eden toward despair. But Dreiser drew different lessons and few morals from his experiences and readings. In a world in which "nothing is proved," he said, "all is permitted." History, whatever else it was, was not principled. People were simply caught, or "caged" as Adams had put it, like "frightened birds." "We suffer," Dreiser wrote, "for our temperaments, which we did not make, and for our weaknesses and lacks, which are no part of our willing or doing."

Born into a family of fifteen, Dreiser pulled away from both his rigid, dogmatic German Roman Catholic father, whom he learned to dislike, and his kind, ineffectual mother, whom he learned to pity. Dogged by poverty, the family moved from one small Indiana town to the next. To Booth Tarkington (1869–1946), rural Indiana was the "Valley of Democracy." To Dreiser (1871–1945) and, so far as we can judge, several of his siblings as well, rural Indiana was a slough of despond. Two of his brothers became alcoholics and two of his sisters "fell" early from virtue into scandal – including one whose story Dreiser transmuted into the story of Carrie Meeber, as the "sister" of his title, *Sister Carrie,* suggests.

Sister Carrie (1900) begins where youth ends, with Carrie on the road and on her own. In the early chapters of *An American Tragedy* (1925), we feel the pain of Dreiser's own childhood and youth more directly. Running from the poverty of his youth, Clyde Griffiths spends the whole of his short life acquiring the values of the successful people who inhabit the glamorous world he hopes to enter, which means that he learns to fear failure and worship success. Yet will plays a surprisingly small part in his life, in part because a harsh sense of necessity hovers over it. In the end, he drifts toward murder as Lily Bart drifts toward suicide. In a deep sense, both Lily and Clyde have always already done the one big thing, of embracing or inflicting death, that neither of them ever quite does, which means, among other things, that their stories resemble Jack London's even more than they resemble Martin Eden's.

Dreiser tumbled into writing *Sister Carrie* in the summer of 1899 – after a decade of newspaper experience in Chicago, St. Louis, Toledo, Pittsburgh, and New York – when his friend Arthur Henry decided to try his hand at writing a novel and asked Dreiser to keep him company. On one side, Dreiser worked from within the "realist" tradition that had served as one of the principal means of assimilating and transmitting the family-centered, morally ordered social world that Henry Adams associated with Thomas Jefferson and John Adams. On the other, he drew on the "naturalist" tradition that informed both journalism's effort and the novel's to adjust determinist elements present in Darwin's view of nature and in Marx's view of history to the poverty and squalor of modern cities. Although he accepted these traditions as grounded in capitalist political economies, Dreiser associated realism with a dispersed, entrepreneurial, and largely agrarian capitalism, and naturalism with the new urban, corporate capitalism. The process of painful transition from one of these to the other is a part of what *The House of Mirth* may be said to chart. It is a "breach of continuity" or "rupture in historical sequence" (to use Adams's terms) that leaves Lily Bart with no place to go. To the fading world of gentility, Lily Bart appears too "modern" – particularly in her concern for physical comfort and pleasure and in her careless disregard for propriety. To the world emerging around her, however, her moral sensibility seems too concerned with candor and especially independence. If Lily Bart's needs and desires may be said to mirror Wharton's discontent with the world into which she was born, her fate may be said to mirror Wharton's residual loyalty to that world – a conflict out of which Wharton made fiction again, first in *The Custom of the Country* (1913) and then in *The Age of Innocence* (1920).

Dreiser, by contrast, fit the United States emerging on the near side of the historic shift that Adams located in 1893, and that Wharton limned, as perfectly as any writer of his time. His America is industrial and commercial, it is centralized, and it is affluent enough to make poverty all the more painful to those trapped in it. Above all, it is urban, and it is fast becoming secular. "We are unsettled," Lippmann observed in the *New Republic* in 1914, "to the very roots of our being. There isn't a human relation . . . that doesn't move in a strange situation." Having made "personal growth" its byword and "self-realization" its end, Dreiser's America imposes large burdens, especially on the young. Recalling his own youth during the first two decades of the twentieth century, Joseph Freeman spelled out that confusion clearly:

> All this was very complicated. In the vanished village you knew where you stood. There were God's commandments and you obeyed or broke them; but at least you knew what was right and what was wrong. Now nobody knew. You had to make up your own right and wrong; you had to decide everything for yourself.[17]

In Freeman's vanished village, organized religion played a crucial role in promulgating constructions of reality and authorizing codes and rituals that gave meaning to life and provided practical instructions about how to live it. Such formulas claimed divine authority on the basis of their origins, and they had acquired historical authority and become culturally sanctioned. In the new world Freeman describes, however, in which individuals are free to construct their own formulas and choose their own ways, they feel both empowered and burdened, both liberated and dispossessed. Like London's and Dreiser's protagonists, Wharton's and Stein's inhabit such a world and inherit its problems. In the *Custom of the Country,* Wharton's heroine, Undine Spragg, makes peace with this new world. Spragg is more openly erotic than Lily Bart, and she also sees her commodified world more clearly, which means that she accepts herself as possessing a clear trading value and a definite "trading capacity." In short, she knows what her resources are and learns how to use them. She thus succeeds where Lily fails. Yet having worked her value out successfully, acquiring money, rank, and power, she remains haunted by her longing for some "more delicate kind of pleasure" and even for "beauty."

With *Three Lives* (1909), Gertrude Stein began her long effort to adjust the structure and rhythm of prose to the fluid world emerging around her, in which everything seemed suddenly cut loose. Set against the backdrop of realist and naturalist prose, her fluid prose – full of participles and verb-nouns – provides a countertext. By focusing on the individual consciousnesses of two poor immigrant servant women and one sensitive young black woman, *Three Lives* also helped to announce an age in which the points of view of marginalized people would become increasingly important, in part because the risks of self-realization would vary inversely with society's authorization of the self. Stein works to capture the rhythms and intonations of almost silenced or lost voices. And she also works from a deep rapport with the cinematographic quality of modern life – its interplay of beginnings, repetitions, and endings – that anticipated several developments of the twenties. A sobering distance remains, however, between Stein's delight in finding new ways of conveying the fluid rhythms of the modern world, which can be appealing in their variety even when they are baffling in their slipperiness, and her protagonists' pain in trying to find ways of living among them.

Dreiser, by contrast, punctuated the early decades of the twentieth century with novels about the determined efforts of men and women to realize themselves within the new urban secular world of corporate capitalism. His novels belong to a nation scaled more to openness and change than to defined roles or fixed places. His men and women show little interest in family life. Pulled hither and yon by sexual desire or social ambition, they change apartments, partners, jobs, and cities. Physical as well as social mobility fascinates them, along with a love of the new and the novel – the romance of invention and change – even when fluidity and temporality threaten to engulf them. They live unsettled lives, moving up and down the social ladder, surrounded by buildings that are erected only to be razed. They live in boardinghouses, rented flats, or hotel rooms rather than homes; they have affairs rather than make marriages; they hold jobs or positions rather than pursue vocations; and they play roles rather than fashion identities. In short, they feel at home in the world we see emerging in *Martin Eden, The House of Mirth,* and *Three Lives,* a world in which "personality" is rapidly replacing "character" as the keyword to the only kind of selfhood that seems possible.

Dreiser's "trilogy of desire," especially *The Financier* (1912) and *The Titan* (1914), traces Frank Cowperwood's rise to wealth and power. In Cowperwood's story, Dreiser turns the Horatio Alger plot into the ultimate expression of an acquisitive affluent society. Twenty-five years earlier, in *Looking Backward* (1888), Edward Bellamy had imagined Boston in the year 2000 as a society in which people devoted themselves to possessing "the good things of the world which they helped to create." In the secular world of Cowperwood's Philadelphia and New York, the desire to possess things and the gratification of possession already signify more than galloping materialism because the accumulation of objects and especially of money – or, more abstractly, of "stocks and bonds" – has become the only way of keeping score in the only game that matters – the center, William Carlos Williams later observed, of this country's "whole conception of reality."

Cowperwood despoils the jungle world in which he lives, running through wives, friends, and rivals remorselessly and tirelessly. Yet he is not alone in embodying the United States T. S. Eliot described as a nation in which "the acquisitive, rather than the creative and spiritual instincts are encouraged." Even those whom Cowperwood exploits, defeats, or victimizes envy his brutal energy for the simplest of reasons: because it works. His rivals share his goal of dominance, without remembering when they absorbed it. They live in cities, made worlds of made objects, where life is so dominated by *things* that the desire to possess crowds out the desire to share and the desire to control crowds out the desire to protect. Early in Norris's *McTeague* (1899) we see McTeague respond to the sight of Trina lying helplessly in the dental chair in his office after he has given her gas. "Suddenly," Norris writes, "the animal stirred" in McTeague and the desire for total possession possessed him. In Trina as well as McTeague, furthermore, desire always circles back to possession. In both Norris's and Dreiser's novels, sex and money rule, and in their rule become confounded. Late in *McTeague* we see Trina, caught up in her own merged desires, wildly pressing gold coins to her body.

Even as he worked to transmute the United States in which he lived into fiction, Dreiser also worked to remind his readers of what both he and they were doing. The Cowperwood stories are based on the spectacular career of Charles T. Yerkes (1837–1905), who became one of the most dazzling financiers of his day by seizing control of Chicago's street-railway system. *An American Tragedy* is based on the case of Chester Gillette, which Dreiser studied with care. A lesser novelist might have disguised his historical sources. Dreiser's openness confirms what the way he tumbled into the writing of fiction suggests: that, remarkably unencumbered with theories about it, he felt at home with fiction. He had done considerable reading, of Nietzsche, Darwin, Freud, and Spencer, as well as Dickens and Zola. But he was less hounded by his reading than London was and probably had done less of it than Wharton, Stein, Cather, or Rölvaag. As a result, his encounters with the decentered world in which he lived seem less mediated than theirs. He felt the great shift that had overtaken the United States not as some "malice of fortune" but as a fact. Most of what he knew about the old ways, he had learned from his parents, and he found neither the harshness of his failed father nor the weakness of his failed mother appealing. His newspaper experiences, as he moved through Chicago, St. Louis, Toledo, and Pittsburgh to New York, had taught him much about the poverty, corruption, and slippery ethics of the nation's communities. But nothing he learned caused him to look back nostalgically on the string of small Indiana towns where he had lived as a young boy. Cities had come to him as a deliverance. Their ruthlessness bothered him, but their crassness scarcely fazed him, and he reveled in their hope, energy, and expansiveness. The ambivalence he felt toward life in the United States ran deep, but his openness to it ran deeper still, as the spilled-out clumsiness of his prose shows. As the country he labored to understand becomes ever more cautious, calculating, and self-protective, that openness may well come to seem more and more valuable.

12. THE GREAT WAR AND THE FATE OF WRITING

"It is the glory of the present age that in it one can be young," Randolph Bourne wrote in 1913, four years before World War I engulfed the United States and five before he died at age thirty-two. Scarred and disfigured at birth by a botched delivery, then crippled by spinal tuberculosis that deformed his back and stunted his growth, Bourne learned early to think of himself as too "cruelly blasted" to live a full life. Yet he wrote – *Youth and Life* (1913) and *Education and Living* (1917) and a series of essays for *New Republic, Masses, Seven Arts,* and *Dial* – as a fully engaged critic about the major concerns of the Lyric Years: youth, rebellion, education, politics, literature, and the arts. When it happened that he could not survive that age (he died in December 1918 of influenza), his friends came to regard him as the writer who best embodied its lost hope. After his death, both James Oppenheim and Van Wyck Brooks edited collections of his essays – *Untimely Papers* (1919) and *The History of a Literary Radical* (1920) – designed to establish him as its representative cultural critic.

Had Bourne written about himself, as several critics of his time did, such a development might seem less odd. In fact, however, though he took Walt Whitman as one of his prophets, Bourne avoided himself as subject. He focused instead on the aspirations and anxieties of his age, as though hoping vicariously to live them, and so made its yearnings his yearnings, its despair his despair. For him values are always social as well as personal. Even his passion for truth remains overtly historical and so manifests itself as an effort to speak both of and to a particular historical people. He writes not as a prophet speaking to the ages but as a citizen speaking to citizens. Only in 1918, with his world so mired in "Mr. Wilson's War" that the possibility of formulating a viable political aesthetic seemed lost, did he veer toward the kind of separatism that was for him the form of despair: "The enhancement of life, the education of man and the use of the intelligence to realize reason and beauty in the nation's communal living," he said, "are alien to our traditional ideal of the State," which "is intimately connected with war."

The Great War was, of course, one thing for a man like Bourne, who essentially could not enter it, and another for those who entered it as a grand crusade or great adventure. It was one thing for men and another for women, one thing for whites and another for blacks, one thing for volunteers and another for conscripts. But it engaged and provoked almost everyone, especially the thoughtful young, for many of whom it became either a life-shattering or a life-shaping experience. In 1914 Howells predicted that war would mean "death to all the arts." But Americans started writing about the war before their country officially began fighting it, and haven't stopped yet, in part because Bourne's sense of it as the death knell of the Lyric Years of good hope has prevailed.

Half a century earlier, a large number of literate men had fought as officers and as common soldiers in the Civil War, and many literate women had been engulfed by it. During the Great War, numerous literate and even literary men and women either opposed the war or served near or in its battle zones. As the war became the crucial issue in the cultural debate between the Genteel Custodians and the "League of Youth," new voices arose – some, like that of John Dos Passos (b. 1896), on the side of the League, and others, like that of Richard Norton, on the side of tradition. But the Great War united the children of tradition, in part by giving them another tradition to draw on, while it divided the rebels. The suppression of *Masses* and *Seven Arts* retarded public dissent. Several rebels – including Alexander Berkman and Emma Goldman – were arrested and convicted under the Espionage Act (June 1917). Still others were intimidated by private threats and public lynchings, or "patriotic murders" as they came to be called. In Missouri in April 1918 a young German-American named Robert Prager, whom the navy had rejected as physically unfit, was stripped, beaten, and then lynched while five hundred "patriots" cheered. Such acts, the *Washington Post* observed, were signs of "a healthy and wholesome awakening in the interior of the country." With "a hideous apathy, the country has acquiesced," John Reed reported, "in a regime of judicial tyranny, bureaucratic suppression and industrial barbarism."

In the face of such pressure, divisions among the rebels deepened. Many rebels thought of war as the "curse of mankind," a sign that the disease of nationalism was not "confined to Germany." But such views lost credibility in a world in which almost everyone – traditionalists, anarchists, and socialists alike – began to act like "trained soldiers," as Freeman put it. Some rebels followed Wilson from his peace campaign into his crusade; others advocated some form of accommodation; and a few, including Upton Sinclair, turned about completely by joining the "hate the huns" campaign. "One after another," Freeman noted, the same people who had opposed the war started supporting it, sometimes in terms so hysterical that they "made reactionaries like Elihu Root appear sober and logical."

Heartened by the rebels' disarray, the Genteel Custodians promptly reclaimed the moral high ground that they had always assumed was properly theirs. Evoking an old tradition of glorious self-sacrifice, they started dispatching volunteers to France even before the nation entered the war. Founded in 1914 by Richard Norton, son of Charles Eliot Norton of Harvard, the Norton–Harjes Ambulance Service and other such organizations drew volunteers from universities as far away as Stanford. James Harold Doolittle, of World War II fame, left the University of California, Berkeley, to join the Lafayette Escadrille, an air unit financed by private funds from the United States but led by French officers. Other young patriots found their way into regular British or French fighting units.

Like John Reed, Walter Lippmann, and T. S. Eliot, Alan Seeger was a member of the Harvard class of 1910. Fresh out of Harvard, Seeger went to Greenwich Village, donned a long black opera cloak, and became, in Reed's words, an "eager/Keats–Shelley–Swinburne Mediaeval Seeger." From there he moved to Paris, planning to live the life of a poet. But in 1914, he volunteered for the French Foreign Legion and two years later was killed in action, by which time he had already become the voice of young men drawn by duty into the Great War. "It is for glory alone that I am engaged," he wrote, speaking for countless young men who went forth believing that they knew what honor, glory, and duty meant and hoping that Wilson's grand crusade would save their country from its drift toward ruin. The "sense of being the instrument of Destiny" was what he sought, Seeger said, adding that he pitied "poor civilians" who would never see or know the "things that we have seen and known" and so would miss the "supreme experience."

Seeger and his friends, many of them "young acquaintances" of such elder statesmen as Theodore Roosevelt and Oliver Wendell Holmes, Jr., left early for the field of battle because they were convinced of the grandeur of war. In exclusive prep schools and venerable colleges, they had learned a code of honor that they thought of as reaching back beyond Sir Walter Scott and the Crusades to the glory and grandeur of Rome and Greece. One of the characters in Edith Wharton's *The Marne* (1918) turns specifically to ponder Horace's famous phrase, "Dulce et decorum est pro patria mori," as though to remind us of one of the ways in which tradition can work. The Civil War had come not only as a great ordeal but also as a "great good fortune" to young men of his generation, Oliver Wendell Holmes, Jr., observed, precisely because it had quickened their sense of life as a "profound and passionate thing." Even "in the midst of doubt, in the collapse of creeds," Holmes said, "there is one thing I do not doubt," the sublime beauty of a soldier who surrenders his life in the name of "a cause." Seeger wanted, he said, "to be present where the pulsations are liveliest" – and that meant facing war and even death, "the largest movement the planet allows . . . a companionship to the stars." "I have a rendezvous with Death," he wrote in his most famous poem, in which traditional verse serves traditional ideas:

> I have a rendezvous with Death
> At some disputed barricade,
> When spring comes back with rustling shade
> And apple-blossoms fill the air.
> I have a rendezvous with Death
> When spring brings back blue days and fair.[18]

"And I to my pledged word am true –" Seeger ends his poem, "I shall not fail that rendezvous."

Such sentiments led many Americans, women and men, to see the war principally in terms of its heroic potential. Even if it failed to free the world of tyranny and make it safe for democracy, it could still reinvigorate a culture that had grown soft, confused, artificial, and "unmanly." Devotion to a great cause, H. W. Boynton wrote in The Bookman (April 1916), had a "purifying influence." Anguish and suffering, Robert Herrick predicted in "Recantation of a Pacifist," in New Republic (October 1915), would bring about a "resurrection of nobility." Movies like Pershing's Crusaders and books like The Glory of the Trenches (1918) and My Home in the Field of Honor (1916) presented the war as a great adventure made noble by patriotism. Such sentiments spread through the culture as though history had prepared the way. "No kind of greatness is more pleasing to the imagination of a democratic people," Alexis de Tocqueville noted, "than military greatness, a greatness of vivid and sudden luster, obtained without toil, by nothing but the risk of life." Richard Harding Davis's story "The Deserter" (1916) promotes commitment to the war on similar grounds, as does Mary Brecht Pulver's "The Path to Glory" (published in Saturday Evening Post in March 1917), in which a poor family wins a community's respect when a son dies driving an ambulance in France. Ellen Glasgow's The Builders (1919) presents another brief on behalf of the war, though rather more in Wilson's terms than in Holmes's. Edith Wharton had already demonstrated – in The House of Mirth (1905), Ethan Frome (1911), The Custom of the Country (1913) – literary talents that included a gift for satire. When World War I came, however, Wharton made France's cause her own. She organized large relief programs and wrote prowar novels in terms inculcated by the class whose expectations had once stifled her own deepest needs. It is as though the soldiers' "great experience had purged them of pettiness, meanness, and frivolity," she writes in Fighting France (1917), echoing Herrick and Holmes, "burning them down to the bare bones of character, the fundamental substance of the soul."

In Patriotic Gore (1962), Edmund Wilson, a Princeton graduate who volunteered for the ambulance corps, looked back to find in the Civil War what he had observed firsthand in World War I: the rapid conversion of a divided nation into an "obedient flood of energy" that could "carry the young to destruction and overpower any effort to stem it." Some rebels protested to the end; a few followed Mike Gold to Mexico to avoid the draft. But as patriotic sentiments spread, more and more young men rushed to volunteer. "What was war like? We wanted to see with our own eyes," said John Dos Passos, another of Harvard's sons. "We flocked into the volunteer services. I respected the conscientious objectors, and occasionally felt I should take that course myself, but hell, I wanted to see the show." Soon the propaganda campaign took aim at women as well as men. One poster showed European women beseeching women of the United States to send their husbands and sons "to save our children"; another urged women to fulfill themselves by working in munition plants; and another, aimed at those still young at heart, featured a sexy, scantily clad young woman riding orgiastically across the skies on a large projectile. By late 1917, there were 175,000 troops in France. Six or seven months later, in the summer of 1918, nearly 10,000 per day were boarding troop transports bound for Europe. By November 11, 1918, when the Great War ended, 4,000,000 Americans were in uniform, nearly half of them in France, and roughly 1,300,000 had come under fire. Hundreds of others saw duty in combat zones as members of Norton–Harjes or the American Ambulance Field Service. Together they shifted the balance of power significantly, hastening an Allied victory.

Books like Wharton's *The Marne,* movies like *The Glory of the Trenches,* and verse like Seeger's, as well as other best-sellers, such as Robert W. Service's *Rhymes of a Red Cross Man* (1916) and Arthur Guy Empey's *"Over the Top"* (1917), offended some returning veterans, including Ernest Hemingway, another of those who joined the volunteer services. But patriotic works continued to come after the Great War had ended and disillusionment had begun. In Wharton's *A Son at the Front* (1923), a son teaches his father to see the war as a "precious responsibility" offered by Destiny to his generation: "If France went," his son says, "Western civilization went with her; and then all they had believed in and been guided by would perish." "The German menace must be met," the father adds, and "chance willed that theirs should be the generation to meet it." Later, quickened by the death of his son, the father is born anew as an artist. In Willa Cather's *One of Ours* (1922), Claude Wheeler, a successful yet unfulfilled son of the West, looks at a "statue of Kit Carson on horseback . . . pointed Westward" and mourns the loss of a life of adventure that he has been born too late to experience. Disappointed by his sense of being left to live in a diminished world where "there was no West, in that sense, any more," and convinced that adventures essentially never happen to those who stay at home, he heads for the trenches of France, where he finds fulfillment when he "falls" still holding to his "beautiful beliefs." "For him," his mother says, "the call was clear, the cause glorious."

As both the terrible toll of the Great War (1.8 million killed for Germany; 1.7 million for Russia; 1.4 million for France; 1.2 million for Austria-Hungary; 947,000 for Britain; 48,000 killed, 2,900 missing, and 56,000 dead from disease for the United States) and its fruits (not the renewal prophesied by people as different as Woodrow Wilson and H. G. Wells, in *The War That Will End War* (1914), but a botched peace, continued turmoil in Europe, and renewed isolationism in the United States) became clear, however, a new disillusionment set in, especially among writers. Europe had emerged so decimated, depleted, exhausted, and debt-ridden, so torn by inflation and political unrest, that it was hard to see what the sacrifices had been for. Still reeling from their losses, the victors faced embarrassing disclosures of the atrocities they had committed in the name of "saving" civilization. Here is a list, jotted down in 1922 by Winston Churchill, then secretary of state for war for Great Britain:

> All the horrors of all the ages were brought together, and not only armies but whole populations were thrust into the midst of them. . . . Neither peoples nor rulers drew the line at any deed which they thought could help them to win. Germany, having let Hell loose, kept well in the van of terror; but she was followed step by step by the desperate and ultimately avenging nations she had assailed. . . . The wounded died between the lines: the dead mouldered into the soil. Merchant ships and neutral ships and hospital ships were sunk on the seas and all on board left to their fate, or killed as they swam. Every effort was made to starve whole nations into submission without regard to age or sex. Cities and monuments were smashed by artillery. Bombs from the air were cast down indiscriminately. Poison gas in many forms stifled or seared the soldiers. Liquid fire was projected upon their bodies. . . . When all was over, Torture and Cannibalism were the only two expedients that the civilized, scientific, Christian States had been able to deny themselves: and they were of doubtful utility.[19]

Having emerged as a new world leader, blessed with an expanding economy and the prospect of unmatched prosperity, the United States decided to protect what it had by turning its back on the rest of the world, and so refused to sign the Treaty of Versailles or join the League of Nations, the only hope the world had for new order.

At home, furthermore, the "obedient flood of energy" that had turned a divided nation into a concerted force had in fact been bought at a considerable price, including many betrayals of principles. Once the aristocrats of recent immigrants, German-Americans had become the targets of "strident rant," to use Bourne's phrase. Sauerkraut and pretzels were declared "un-American"; coleslaw was renamed "liberty salad"; orchestras stopped playing German music; schools stopped teaching German language and literature; and the Metropolitan Opera House dropped all German operas from its repertoire. By the war's end, virtually every immigrant group had felt the impact of propaganda and abuse – spy scares, witch-hunts, kangaroo courts, and even lynchings. President Wilson talked loosely of foreign-born Americans as "creatures of passion, disloyalty, and anarchy" who "must be crushed out." The National Security League, originally formed to lobby for national defense provisions, aimed a barrage of name calling and accusation at "imported people" and "hyphenated-Americans," imploring "100 percent Americans" to defend national security – an effort joined by such organizations as the American Protection League, the American Defense Society, the Boy Spies of America, and the Sedition Slammers. The result was an assault on foreign influences that rippled through the decade of the twenties, sometimes with terrible results.

Drawn into the war effort in record numbers, women assumed that an era of rapid progress had dawned. A few prominent leaders of the prewar years, notably Jane Addams, held firmly to their pacifist convictions, but most struck compromises that allowed them to support the war. The National American Woman Suffrage Association endorsed Wilson's initiatives even before the nation declared itself at war. Later, with the war under way, Carrie Chapman Cott, president of the association, declared women "opposed to anything that will bring a peace which does not forever and forever make it impossible that such sufferings shall again be influential on the world." Giving the vote to women, Wilson promptly told Congress, was "vital to the winning of the war." Some women served abroad in the American Expeditionary Force as nurses or telephone operators. Nearly a million took up war work, fueling hopes that a new day of employment as well as emancipation had come. Some, including Wharton, had the heady experience of making major contributions to what Wharton called "the greatest need the world has ever known." Others, including Cather, made writing about the war a way of making contact with it.

With such experiences behind them, women greeted passage of the Nineteenth Amendment as the culmination of a century of struggle that signaled a new era. What followed, however, was neither the reconstitution of society that supporters of suffrage had prophesied nor the disintegration that its enemies had predicted. Suffrage had little discernible influence on the nation's politics, and less on its economy. In 1923 the National Women's Party, led by Alice Paul, proposed the nation's first equal rights amendment as a logical next step after suffrage. But far from becoming a new, unifying cause, the proposal drew fire from men and divided women. It set upper-class women against working-class women, and radical leaders, who scorned the jobs traditionally assigned to women, against moderates, whose first priority was to improve the pay and working conditions of women in jobs they already held. Both the new sexuality and the new technology proved to be mixed blessings – the first by pressuring women to be more physically appealing to men, the second by pressuring them to be more efficient in running their houses so that they could give more time to charity.

For a time, women had felt "no longer caged and penned up." Through the sacred glamour of nursing, they had gained self-esteem and had learned things about men that "reduced their inhibitions." In factories, they had "stepped into the shoes" of absent men and even "worn their pants" for a time, gaining access to new jobs at fair wages. When the war ended, however, the patriotism used to call them into factories was used to send them back home so that veterans could take their jobs. In 1920 women constituted a smaller percentage of the labor force than they had in 1910. As disillusionment mounted, suspicion spread – among women of men, and among men of women. In literary circles gender-based fear increased after the war.

Early in the war, advocates insisted that the war would do quickly what peace would take years to accomplish: not only would it advance women's rights, it would dehyphenate the "hyphenated-Americans." "The military tent where they all sleep side by side," Theodore Roosevelt announced, "will rank next to the public school among the great agents of democratization." Conscription and compulsory military training (estimates hold that roughly one of five draftees was foreign-born) were widely defended on grounds that they would transform the many peoples of the country into one "new nation." In fact, however, drafting new immigrants severely tested the fairness of military leaders, while the drafting of black Americans completely outstripped it. Strict racial segregation remained the unexamined rule, despite Roosevelt's description of the military tent, and proper training of black soldiers by white officers presented problems that no one was prepared to address. Several brutal courtmartials and executions resulted, in Houston, Texas, and elsewhere. Those black soldiers who survived training were quickly assigned menial tasks. W. E. B. Du Bois and other leaders had hoped that the war would give black men a chance to earn advancement, first in the military and then in the labor market. Instead, new versions of old patterns prevailed. Abroad, black soldiers were discriminated against and even brutalized by other U.S. troops and some allies as well as the enemy. When they returned home, they found that the Deep South remained the Deep South and that the industrial North, the new "Land of Hope," was already torn by white fear and black frustration.

Coupled with the carnage, atrocities, and betrayals that took place during the Great War, both the botched peace conference in Versailles and the Senate's rejection of the League of Nations compounded disillusionment. In Cather's *One of Ours,* Claude Wheeler dies believing the war a noble cause. But in his mother's mind, a window of doubt soon opens. "He died believing his own country better than it is, and France better than any country can ever be," she says, before adding words that present her son's faith as illusion and her wisdom as disillusionment: "Perhaps it was well to see that vision, and then see no more." Like Cather, Dorothy Canfield Fisher supported the war, but in her novel *The Deepening Stream* (1930), we encounter a young American woman who, having struggled to save her beloved France, is left walking the streets of Paris, her head filled with reports of behind-the-scenes deals that are aborting the peace talks. In the world being born, she realizes, she will always be a "refugee."

As their disillusionment deepened, survivors of the Great War turned to writers like Bourne as their guides. But they also found support in unexpected places. Ellen La Motte was born in 1873 in Louisville, Kentucky. In 1915, shortly before Seeger joined the French Foreign Legion, she went to France to serve as a nurse with the French army. A year later she filed her report – *The Backwash of War: The Human Wreckage of the Battlefield as Witnessed by an American Hospital Nurse* – which focuses on the pain and slime she encounters in the backwash behind the lines. Her "Heroes" are soldiers who face the bitter realization that they are anonymous parts of a "collective physical strength" dedicated to a Pyrrhic advance of "Progress and Civilization." This knowledge makes some of them contemptuous of life, including their own; and it turns others into lonely victims. La Motte tells, for example, of a young aviator who, a few days after being decorated for destroying a Zeppelin, kills himself flying drunk. In "A Citation," she recounts the last terrible days of a young soldier who holds onto life, waiting for a general to come to honor his heroism with medals, only to die "after a long pull, just twenty minutes before the General arrived with his medals." War, she observes, in direct contradiction to the discourse of glorious self-sacrifice, is not a filtering process "by which men and nations may be purified." It is lonely, senseless dying in the "backwash" of the world.

During the twenties, literature dealing with the Great War followed La Motte's lead more than Seeger's; setting terrible losses against dubious gains, it countered the discourse of honor with a discourse of disillusionment. "There died a myriad," Pound wrote in "Hugh Selwyn Mauberley" (1920),

> And of the best, among them,
> For an old bitch gone in the teeth,
> For a botched civilization,
> Charm, smiling at the good mouth,
> Quick eyes gone under earth's lid,
> For two gross of broken statues,
> For a few thousand battered books.[20]

Behind such words lay a suspicion that the Great War had finally laid bare a secret about modern technological societies: that they depend on economies that in turn depend on the preparation of war to stimulate invention and production and on the execution of war to stimulate consumption, including the heightened form of consumption called destruction. The Great War was not merely another episode in an endless conflict; it was a sign that sooner or later nations will do whatever their weapons make possible. Pound knew that "civilized" nations had used "old men's lies" to attract young recruits. Writing years later, echoing Robert Graves's reminder that patriotism died in the trenches, William March, a Marine from Alabama who won the Distinguished Service Cross, filed another brief against the Great War, in a novel called *Company K* (1933), in the form of a brutal parody of a commanding officer's letter to a bereaved parent:

> Dear Madam: Your son, Francis, died needlessly in Belleau Wood. You will be interested to hear that at the time of his death he was crawling with vermin and weak from diarrhea. His feet were swollen and rotten and they stank. He lived like a frightened animal, cold and hungry. Then, on June 6th, a piece of shrapnel hit him and he died in agony, slowly. . . . He lived three full hours screaming and cursing by turns. He had nothing to hold on to, you see: He had learned long ago that what he had been taught to believe by you, his

mother, who loved him, under the meaningless names of honor, courage and patriotism, were all lies.[21]

Such bleakness descended on relatively few Americans, of course. Most Norton–Harjes and American Ambulance Field Service volunteers and most combat troops held fast to the set of beliefs that led them to volunteer. Some of them dismissed the works of writers like Pound, Dos Passos, and Hemingway as unrepresentative. But there were widespread signs of disillusionment in the culture at large. One came in 1920, when the Senate turned its back on Europe, repudiating the nation's avowed purposes for entering the war and forfeiting its chance of claiming world leadership on the basis of vision rather than power. Another came with the rapid repudiation of the reform spirit and the progressive faith of the Lyric Years. People like H. L. Mencken and George Jean Nathan were soon bragging about being self-absorbed rather than high-minded. "The great problems of the world – social, political, economic and theological – do not concern me in the slightest," Nathan wrote. "What concerns me alone is myself, and the interests of a few close friends. For all I care the rest of the world may go to hell at today's sunset." At the same time, overtly sexist and racist discourse began to spread, while toleration, even as a laudable idea, lost ground.

Writing in 1936, Cather remarked that "the world had broken in two in 1922, or thereabouts," naming the year in which *One of Ours* was published. In *A Lost Lady* (1923), her affection for an already vanished America, and her disillusionment with the United States of the twenties, emerged in a portrait of Ivy Peters as the perfect bourgeois real-estate developer of the emerging nation. Having followed "dreamers" and "adventurers," Peters has learned how to get "splendid land from the Indians some way, for next to nothing," and then develop it for profit:

> Now all this vast territory . . . was to be at the mercy of men like Ivy Peters, who had never dared anything, never risked anything. They would drink up the mirage, dispel the morning freshness, root out the great brooding spirit of freedom. . . . The space, the colour, the princely carelessness of the pioneer they would destroy and cut up into profitable bits, as the match factory splinters the primeval forest. All the way from Missouri to the mountains this generation of shrewd young men, trained to petty economies by hard times, would do exactly what Ivy Peters had done.[22]

For Cather, the lost world that had come earliest in her own life, as well as that of her nation, suddenly seemed almost blessed. But there is more than nostalgia in her evocations. She reminds us of the power of places and of landscapes that are not of human making, just as Dos Passos reminds us of the power of those that are. Stein, living in Europe, dated the breaking point in 1914. Several writers favored 1919, the year for which Dos Passos named one of his novels. But even those who resisted the bleak term "Waste Land" agreed that the Great War had changed the landscape of life. In *Death Comes for the Archbishop* (1927), Cather describes the Southwest of the early nineteenth century as a place where "death had a solemn social importance," not as "a moment when certain bodily organs" of an isolated individual "cease to function, but as a dramatic climax" to a life lived in a community. "Among the watchers," she adds, "there was always hope that the dying man might reveal something of what he alone could see." For Cather as for many other writers, war had made injury and death more terrible by making them so completely personal that no discourse could convincingly tie them to purpose or insight. The turnabout that Cather limns makes the mass anonymous deaths of the Great War's trenches a perfect introduction, if not to life in the twentieth century, at least to the literature of the twenties.

The *War Letters* (1932) of Harry Crosby are considerably more direct. In them we follow the transformation of another son of Harvard – a nephew of J. Pierpont Morgan – who became an ambulance driver. Convinced that God has "ordained the war" in order to make the world a "finer, cleaner, and squarer place," Crosby's early reports are good-spirited. Gradually, however, he begins to describe, with obsessive and even perverse delight, landscapes ravaged by war, the surreal horror of nighttime warfare, and horrific images of the dead and dying. Having survived the war, Crosby was decorated by France and the United States for his heroism. But having lost his hold on the old world he associated with St. Mark's and Harvard, he had become, his wife Caresse remarked, "electric with rebellion." In June 1927, at a Four Arts Ball in Paris, he turned ten live snakes loose during a wild dance and then stepped back to watch the show. "I remember," he wrote in his diary,

> two strong young men stark naked wrestling on the floor for the honor of dancing with a young girl . . . and I remember a mad student drinking champagne out of a skull which he had pilfered from my Library as I had pilfered it a year ago from the Catacombs . . . and in a corner I watched two savages making love . . . and beside me sitting on the floor a plump woman with bare breasts absorbed in the passion of giving milk to one of the snakes![23]

Two years later, on December 10, 1929, in a hotel room in New York, Crosby shot and killed himself. Having already left, in his letters and diary, a record of how the Great War had emptied him of beliefs, leaving him with nothing but a hunger for exotic visual stimulation and a deeply spectatorial disposition, which he used to manipulate his fascination with danger and death, he left no further note of explanation.

One part of the story of the twenties would be played out in the lives and deaths of people like Harry Crosby. Hart Crane would become a casualty of the times, and so would Zelda Fitzgerald. The mood of the decade would cultivate a tone and style so ironic and haunted as to seem almost paranoid: "At the start of the winter came the permanent rain and with the rain came the cholera," Hemingway writes in *A Farewell to Arms* (1929). "But it was checked and in the end only seven thousand died of it in the army." Nothing any longer seemed sacred, least of all the platitudes of official patriotism. "I was always embarrassed," Frederic Henry remarks in *A Farewell to Arms* (1929), by the words sacred, glorious, and sacrifice and the expression in vain. We had heard them . . . and we had read them . . . , and I had seen nothing sacred, and the things that were glorious had no glory and the sacrifices were like the stockyards at Chicago if nothing was done with the meat except to bury it. There were many words that you could not stand to hear and finally only the names of places had dignity.[24]

People emptied of beliefs remained rare, of course, even in the aftermath of the Great War. Soon a spirit of energy and exuberance, quite different from that of the Lyric Years, began reaching out to embrace writers as old as Gertrude Stein (1874–1946) and as young as Langston Hughes (1902–67) in what seemed for a time a single "younger generation," united by the sense of being survivors, exiles, and refugees as well as geniuses together. Their brief engagement in the Great War had taken them a long way from the moment during the Lyric Years when the world seemed just to have begun and the promise of transforming society and reinventing the United States seemed at hand. And it had taught them to regard big, hallowed words and the social uses to which they could be put with suspicion. But in the process, it had deepened their belief in the power of words – a belief that the wholly disillusioned can never know. If language possessed force, everything lay open to inspection – not only myths of heroism and old customs and mores, but the force of history and the authority of fiction. In addition, the war had given them a new sense of parity with Europe. Europe lay devastated, with many of its great writers dead or shattered. The United States had been catapulted into a position of international prominence that promised finally to free it of lingering cultural colonialism. Writers continued to regard their culture with mixed fascination and disappointment, but they assumed that the future belonged to the United States, and by extension to them as well. "The war . . . or American promise!" Bourne had said. "One must choose. . . . For the effect of the war will be to impoverish American promise." And much of the promise of the Lyric Years had in fact died during World War I. In particular, few writers of the twenties spoke with confidence about the possibility of reforming their society. But another task – that of cutting their ties with the past in order to invent the future of their literature – still seemed to them bright with possibility. To it, as well as the pursuit of pleasure, they were ready to give themselves with rare exuberance.

PART TWO

Fiction in a Time of Plenty

1. *WHEN THE WAR WAS OVER: THE RETURN OF DETACHMENT*

Henry Adams died in Washington, D.C., on March 27, 1918, less than eight months before World War I ended. Two years earlier he had authorized a posthumous edition of *The Education of Henry Adams,* one hundred copies of which had been printed privately in 1907. As it happened, then, the *Education* was published on September 28, 1918, one day after President Woodrow Wilson opened the Fourth Liberty Loan campaign with a stirring speech to a crowd of five thousand at the Metropolitan Opera House in New York. "At every turn . . . we gain a fresh consciousness of what we mean to accomplish," Wilson asserted. The war must end with the "final triumph of justice and fair dealing," and the League of Nations must be established as an integral part "of the peace settlement itself." The next morning, the *New York Times* urged people, "Back the Right and Might of Wilson and Pershing with the Dollars of Democracy!" Six weeks later, on November 11, the armistice was signed in a railroad car in Compiègne Forest. "By a kind of irony, just at the greatest moment in history," the *North American Review* announced in its December 1918 review of the *Education,* "appears this prodigy of a book."

Widely reviewed, the *Education* became a best-seller. For twenty-five years, Adams had been writing his friends bleak letters, predicting that the United States would follow Europe's drift toward catastrophe. Early in 1914, Henry James responded to one such letter, describing it as a "melancholy outpouring" of "unmitigated blackness." Still Adams persisted. "When one cares for nothing in particular," he said, even disaster "becomes almost entertaining." A great show is about to begin, he wrote John Hay, "the *fin-de-siècle* circus." What he wanted was the best possible seat for seeing the show, whether it be in Washington, New York, London, Paris, Berlin, or Calcutta. "To me it is amusing," he said, "because I said and printed it all, ten years ago."

In one sense, it was appropriate that Adams should die so near the end of the war that struck him as the final gasp of the world into which he had been born – "the past that was our lives," as James put it, paraphrasing Adams's "melancholy outpouring." In his early years, he had hoped to help reform that world. What we need, he wrote his brother Charles at age twenty-five, is new energy and vision "not only in politics, but in literature, in law, in society, and throughout the whole social organism of our country." Gradually, however, and then emphatically with the election of Ulysses S. Grant – who made the theory of evolution ludicrous, he said – history had rejected his ambition. "We have lived to see the end of a republican form of government," he observed shortly before he died. But it was also appropriate that his voice should survive the war. For while grieving "the past that was our lives," he had continued to wonder what the world replacing it would yield. "A great many things interested Adams," T. S. Eliot told readers of the *Atheneum*, in a review of the *Education*, "but he could believe in nothing."

The divisions that found expression in Adams's bleak outpourings also shaped his efforts to present himself as a detached observer of his world. *Mont-Saint-Michel and Chartres* (1904) enacts, among other things, a lyric aesthetic of flight. For us, Adams says, "the poetry is history, and the facts are false." But his retreat into the past also became a covert preparation for his examination of the world emerging around him. In the *Education*, his companion piece to *Mont-Saint-Michel and Chartres*, he uses another distancing device – that of telling the story of his own life in the third person – in order to make it the story of his age. In the *Education*, he becomes a disinterested interpreter – a theatergoer, a traveler, or, more radically, a posthumous observer – recounting the spectacle of his life and times. Having placed failed versions of his social self at his story's center, he places surviving, reflective versions of himself on its periphery.

As a social self, Adams acts as a "realist" bent on analyzing society and finding new ways of influencing it. He wants to be a "statesman" rather than a "politician" – that is, a principled servant of society rather than an opportunistic exploiter of it. But he also wants to be a man of affairs, and in this role he acts as an enlightened positivist. He knows that culture is grounded in profane history, but he wants moral purpose to inform it. In this endeavor he fails repeatedly, in part because his world no longer shares his concern with moral purpose and in part because he possesses little talent for mastering the language of power. The power of language imaginatively employed becomes his principal resource. As a social creature or man of affairs directly engaged in shaping history as event, he fails repeatedly. Only as a disembodied voice engaged in acts of style does he become a creature of force: a self-sufficient, surprisingly resourceful master of words.

During the thirties, as a way of looking back on the twenties, Malcolm Cowley and Bernard Smith edited a collection of essays titled *Books That Changed Our Minds*. George Soule wrote on Sigmund Freud's *The Interpretation of Dreams;* Charles Beard on Frederick Jackson Turner's *The Frontier in American History;* John Chamberlain on William Graham Sumner's *Folkways;* R. G. Tugwell on Thorstein Veblen's *Business Enterprise;* C. E. Ayres on John Dewey's *Studies in Logical Theory;* Paul Radin on Franz Boas's *The Mind of Primitive Man;* Max Lerner on Charles Beard's *Economic Interpretation of the Constitution;* David Daiches on I. A. Richards's *The Principles of Literary Criticism;* Bernard Smith on V. L. Parrington's *Main Currents in American Thought;* Max Lerner on Nikolai Lenin's *The State and the Revolution;* and Lewis Mumford on Oswald Spengler's *The Decline of the West.* The second essay of the book, behind Soule on Freud, is Louis Kronenberger's on the *Education.*

To "intellectuals of the twenties," Kronenberger reports, the *Education* was "a perfectly *conscious* study of frustration and deflected purpose" by a writer equipped to disclose to them "the plight of the modern world." Born an heir to power, Adams had given up "being a participant," choosing "instead, a place on the sidelines," where he could turn the story of his life into a story of and for his age. The *Education* recounted "personal weakness" as well as "social disorder." What set it apart was Adams's ability to make language serve several purposes simultaneously. "Henry Adams, who lived life in a minor key, took every precaution to write about it in a major one. The *Education* is a completely full-dress performance," Kronenberger asserts. It belongs among "the textbooks . . . of American experience."

The tensions with which the *Education* grapples – between humans as social, pragmatic, analytical, interdependent, consensus-seeking creatures, on one side, and private, idealistic, intuitive, imaginative, self-sufficient, mythmaking creatures, on the other; and between language as referential, demystifying, authenticating, discrete, analytic tool, on one side, and as self-referential, merging, blurring, generative, contriving, unruly, synthetic medium, on the other – remained broadly cultural as well as deeply literary through the twenties and beyond. By splicing two versions of himself, by simultaneously acknowledging and then blurring the lines between (auto)biography, cultural history, and fiction, and between social documents and personal narrative, and by employing language as itself several changing things, Adams introduced himself into the culture of the twenties as a member of the first generation of modernists. *Mont-Saint-Michel and Chartres* was, among other things, his way of ransacking culture, shoring fragments against his ruins, to borrow a phrase from Eliot, and his way of writing a prose "poem including history," to borrow from Pound. In the *Education,* he pieces together fragments of failed dreams that are social and familial as well as personal. In one motion, he depicts the present as shaped by the past; in another, he shows how we reshape the past to meet the needs of the present. On behalf of himself and his society, he creates a sense of the present and its possibilities by inscribing the present's sense of the past and its thrust. At the same time, he adds to art's social, mimetic commitment a psychological and epistemological commitment. In the first of these moves, he makes art's processes an imitation of the processes of the external world; in the second, he traces the processes of consciousness as it engages in the act of knowing that world. He thus blends his effort to reach an understanding of the processes of the world with his effort to reach an understanding of the processes of his own consciousness.

The *Education* arrived on the public scene at a time when the self's efforts to find some free space – independent of the great determinants of nature as defined by Darwin, of family as reconstituted by Freud, and of society, culture, and history as reconceived by Marx – were becoming more problematical.

This development proved particularly troublesome in the United States, where confidence in the simple, solitary self as free – bolstered by a Renaissance confidence in the modern self's powers of self-fashioning and by an enlightened confidence in the modern self's freedom from fealty to emperors and kings and its freedom to dominate nature through science – had gone largely uncontested, especially among white males. In democracies, where the fixed relations of aristocracies are broken, people "acquire the habit of always considering themselves as standing alone," Alexis de Tocqueville remarked,

> and they are apt to imagine that their whole destiny is in their hands.
> Thus not only does democracy make every man forget his ancestors, but it hides his descendants and separates his contemporaries from him; it throws him back forever upon himself alone and threatens in the end to confine him entirely within the solitude of his own heart.[1]

For Tocqueville, isolation and freedom go hand in hand. But for Henry Adams, who had never been able to decide whether his prominent family had marked him more deeply by branding him as a youth or by deserting him as a young man, solitude came from other sources and took different forms, and so did his hedged sense of freedom. As a result, his life became a search for other possibilities.

In that search, Adams made three interrelated discoveries: first, as Albert Einstein later put it, that the "history of an epoch" is the "history of its instruments"; second, that institutions like the church and icons like the "Virgin," or even presidents and first ladies, no less than dynamos, must be numbered among a culture's instruments; and third, that our instruments not only empower but also control us. Madeleine "found herself," he wrote in *Democracy* (1880),

> before two seemingly mechanical figures, which might be wood or wax, for any sign they showed of life. These two figures were the President and his wife; they stood stiff and awkward by the door, both their faces stripped of every sign of intelligence, while the right hands of both extended themselves to the column of visitors with the mechanical action of toy dolls. . . . There they stood, automata, representatives of the society which streamed past them. . . .
> What a strange and solemn spectacle it was. . . . She felt a sudden conviction that this was to be the end of American society; its realization and its dream at once. She groaned in spirit.[2]

In the *Education*, Adams's sense of his social predicament, like Madeleine's, is complicated by his sense of nature, family, and history as shaping and mis-shaping forces, and by his sense that the loss of religious faith has deprived consciousness of its moorings. No one can find an object worthy of worship, Madeleine notes. There "will be no other," she adds. "It is worse than anything in the 'Inferno.' "

By 1918, the rapid shift from a discourse of patriotism to one of disillu-sionment, reinforced by an increasingly intrusive advertising industry, was making virtually every reflective American more alert to culture's manipulative force. In the *Education,* Adams's life unfolds both as an effort to find some margin of freedom and as a record of the erosion of his confidence in that venture. Eventually his story calls into doubt virtually everything except the force of nature and culture in shaping individual and collective existence. Even playfulness of the kind that he practices in attributing his "Editor's Preface" to Henry Cabot Lodge and in dating his "Preface" on his birthday, February 16, 1907, seems strained. At last, he had written his brother Brooks in 1899, "life becomes . . . a mere piece of acting" in which one goes on behaving as if seeing, talking, acting, and writing really matter. In the form he gives the *Education,* he inscribes the moment when the performer as hero of action and the spectator as heir of consciousness become representative figures of modern culture. By positioning active versions of his "self" at the center of his story, as its ostensible subject, and contemplative versions of his "self" on its periphery, as observer or reporter, and then presenting the life of the first through the consciousness of the second, he prefigures other novels that juxtapose performers and spectators, actors and critics, the doers of deeds and their interpreters, in works as different as E. E. Cummings's *The Enormous Room,* F. Scott Fitzgerald's *The Great Gatsby,* and William Faulkner's *Absalom, Absalom!* In *U.S.A.* (1930–6) John Dos Passos combines the writer's role with aspects of the spectator-manager-director that we have learned to associate with architects, engineers, and movie directors. Having created this several-sided spectatorial role for himself, he balances it with episodes in the "Camera Eye" sections in which he becomes an actor in the spectacle he has designed, structured, and directed. Like Adams, he modifies the hyperrefined aloofness of the observer-spectator by acknowledging complicity and seeking involvement in a culture that he knew he could not escape.

2. THE "JAZZ AGE" AND THE "LOST GENERATION" REVISITED

Of several descriptions of the culture of the twenties, two – F. Scott Fitzgerald's "Jazz Age" and Gertrude Stein's "Lost Generation," the one stressing involvement, the other detachment – have proved most durable, and both have paid a price for their durability: they have lost their power to spark recognition. In the letters, diaries, and journals of the era as well as the published memoirs – Joseph Freeman's *An American Testament* (1936), Mable Dodge Luhan's *Movers and Shakers* (1936), Margaret Anderson's *My Thirty Years' War* (1930), Sylvia Beach's *Shakespeare and Company* (1959), Janet Flanner's *An American in Paris* (1940), Edith Wharton's *A Backward Glance* (1934), Robert McAlmon's *Being Geniuses Together* (1938), Harold Loeb's *The Way It Was* (1959), Matthew Josephson's *Life Among the Surrealists* (1962), Ernest Hemingway's *A Moveable Feast* (1964), and Malcolm Cowley's *Exile's Return* (1934) and *A Second Flowering* (1973), to name a few – anecdotes abound: of the lost "exiles" who shared Paris as a "moveable feast"; of Pound's efforts to make things new; of Sherwood Anderson's rejection of business for art; of Stein's, Anderson's, and Hemingway's struggles to perfect their style; of Hemingway's and Stein's divisive competitiveness; of John Freeman's, Dos Passos's, and Genevieve Taggard's lonely efforts to sustain the spirit of social reform by broadening the special disillusionment of the postwar years into a general disillusionment with the cultures of corporate capitalism; of the stunning effulgence, particularly in music and literature, in the flats, clubs, speakeasies, and cabarets of Harlem; of the rise that Zelda and Scott Fitzgerald shared and the crack-ups that divided them; of the suicides of writers as different as Dorothea and Gladys Cromwell, Harry Crosby, and Hart Crane; and of William Faulkner's singular decision to return to the place of his birth, as a kind of resident exile who would always feel "at home" there, "yet at the same time . . . not at home."

If, however, we attend the ways in which Stein's and Fitzgerald's terms reinforce each other, they acquire fresh meaning. The Jazz Age, Fitzgerald said, "had no interest in politics at all." It "was an age of miracles, it was an age of art, it was an age of excess, and it was an age of satire." "That's what you all are. . . . You are a lost generation," Stein said to Hemingway, referring specifically to the young people who had survived the war. Used by Fitzgerald in the title of his fourth book, *Tales of the Jazz Age* (1922), the term "Jazz Age" caught the exuberance of the era's wild parties. But even for Fitzgerald, who had not seen the killing and dying in France, disillusionment preceded exuberance. In his first book, *This Side of Paradise* (1920), he depicts his generation as doomed to shout old cries without meaning them and to fear poverty and worship success with a new, naked intensity, as though possessing money might somehow help to stave off disillusionment and keep alive a sense of beauty. For Hemingway, who had seen some of the killing and dying, the term "Lost Generation," used as an epigraph for *The Sun Also Rises* (1926), carried special authority because it conveyed a sense of how indelibly the Great War had marked the young who survived it. Both Fitzgerald and Hemingway knew, however, as Malcolm Cowley later observed, that the "Lost Generation" also felt "wrenched away from . . . attachment to any region or tradition" by the colleges they attended and the cities they flocked to as well as the publishing houses they relied on, which, "like finance and the theater," were cutting regional ties and "becoming centralized after 1900." Determined to make the most of their predicament, writers began thinking of themselves as the nation's first generation to be wholly unsponsored disciples of the "new." They were both branded and free, forsaken and chosen. They were refugees of a general wreck, yet their prospects as artists were boundless. In describing their predicament, they characteristically combined remarkable self-pity with grandiose self-consciousness. It "was given to Hawthorne to dramatize the human soul," John Peale Bishop announced. "In our time, Hemingway wrote the drama of its disappearance."

In claiming for themselves the special charm – to borrow another of Fitzgerald's titles – of the beautifully damned, they named themselves prophets of their age, a role they clearly preferred to that of social reformers. They were by turns sentimental, fun-loving, and almost carefree, stricken, proud, stoic, and defiant. But they realized that the national habit of feeling special meant nothing if it did not include doing something special. To take possession of their predicament, they wrote stories they thought of as disclosing the secret truth about the century with which they had been born and with which they identified. "After the war we had the twentieth century," said Gertrude Stein, who also suggested that she (born in 1874) had belonged to the twentieth century even before it officially began. Many aspects of life in their new century offended them, but others fascinated them, including its speed and technology. They practiced and even promoted some of the excesses they condemned. But they remained disappointed that world leaders, especially those in the United States, were more adept at corrupting language than enlarging human happiness; and they found in their divisions, doubts, and estrangement the ground for declaring themselves prophets, explorers, and mappers of the modern world.

At the heart of their project lay the task of restoring freshness to a much-abused language. Stein became a teacher of writers as different as Sherwood Anderson, Ernest Hemingway, Carl Van Vechten, and Richard Wright precisely because she saw clearly that the task of renewing language was certain to become a ground theme of the twentieth century. We see similar awareness in *U.S.A.*, where Dos Passos uses several strategies – juxtaposition, collage, the splicing of sketches, and the splicing of different narrative modes – in order to make words behave like forms on a cubist surface; we see it in *The Great Gatsby* (1925), where Fitzgerald uses Nick Carraway's voice to evoke tunes of the twenties and fragments of words heard long ago; and we see it in *The Sound and the Fury* (1929), *As I Lay Dying* (1930), and *Absalom, Absalom!* (1936), where Faulkner juxtaposes, splices, and even overlays voice on voice and style on style.

E. E. Cummings's *The Enormous Room* (1922) grew directly out of his experience in the Great War, which began when he volunteered to serve in France as an ambulance driver and culminated when he was wrongfully incarcerated for six months in the Camp de Triage de la Ferté Macé on suspicion of treasonable correspondence. In Cummings's mind, that experience, initiated and administered by bureaucratic paranoia and incompetence, became yet another sign of a world botched almost beyond recognition. In response, he wrote letters and then a book. But the first models for his response, in which playfulness mingles with near hopelessness, he locates on the walls of the first cell in which he is confined. There, in semidarkness, he discovers a "cubist wilderness" created by artists and writers who have covered the cell's walls "with designs, mottoes, pictures," as well as selections from Goethe; "a satiric landscape"; an "exquisite portrait"; a drawing of a "beloved boat"; and a strange picture, masterful in its "crudity," of "a doughnut-bodied rider" on a "totally transparent sausage-shaped horse who was moving simultaneously in five directions." Later, with the example of the imprisoned John Bunyon before him, Cummings lifts his eyes and sees the bars of his cell as his "own harp." More immediately, he resolves "to ask for a pencil at the first opportunity," in the hope of finding new ways of using old words so that he can turn the deprivations and intimate violations of his imprisonment into art.

In his effort to make experiences forced upon him his own, Cummings draws words and phrases from several languages ("My *cellule* was cool, and I fell asleep easily"); allegorizes foes ("Turnkey-creature," for example, which he then cuts to "T-c") and friends alike ("The Delectable Mountains," as he calls three heroes "cursed with a talent for thinking"); and borrows most of the structural apparatus of his narrative from Bunyan's *Pilgrim's Progress.* Yet he writes with mounting confidence that his words can make alien experiences his own and that his experiences can renew borrowed words.

On November 11, 1921, the third anniversary of the armistice, a few months before the publication of *The Enormous Room,* President Harding led a group of cabinet members, Supreme Court justices, members of Congress, and military leaders into Arlington Cemetery to bury an unknown soldier in his "native soil garlanded by love and covered with the decorations that only nations can bestow." Years before, Henry James had termed Theodore Roosevelt's patriotic pronouncements "crude and barbaric." But Harding's assumption that he could ensure that a soldier's "sacrifice, and that of the millions dead, shall not be in vain," combined with his curious celebration of the state – as an entity capable of feeling love, powerful enough to survive wars, and wise enough to select those whom it should decorate – seemed to many writers to push the abuse of words to a new low. Earlier, in *One Man's Initiation: 1917* (1920), his first response to the Great War, Dos Passos had decried "the lies, the lies, the lies, the lies that life is smothered in," calling on people to "rise and show at least that we are not taken in." Later, he ended *1919* (1932) – the second volume of his trilogy *U.S.A.* – by revisiting Harding's burial of the unknown soldier, "in the memorialamphitheatreofthenationalcemeteryatarlingtonvirginia," with a defiant act of style:

> In the tarpaper morgue at Chalon-sur-Marne in the
> reek of chloride of lime and the dead, they picked
> out the pine box that held all that was left of
>   enie menie minie moe plenty other pine boxes
> stacked up there containing what they'd scraped up
> of Richard Roe
>   and other person or persons unknown. Only
> one can go. How did they pick John Doe?
>   Make sure he aint a dinge, boys,
>   make sure he aint a guinea or a kike,
>   how can you tell a guy's a hundredpercent
> when all you've got's a gunnysack of bones, bronze
> buttons stamped with the screaming eagle and a pair
> of roll puttees?[3]

Writers of the twenties, including Cummings and Dos Passos, felt betrayed by the political leaders who presumed to represent them. They also felt cut off from older writers who had not shared their adventures or suffered their disillusionment. They were, they proclaimed, members of a "Lost Generation," citizens of an era that had begun when the war ended. T. S. Eliot's *The Waste Land* (1922) was scarcely published before writers adopted it as the only possible name for the scarred world left to them. The 1890s and the Lyric Years had in fact anticipated many things writers of the twenties claimed as peculiarly theirs, including their sense that all the significant things that had happened to them were unique and their assumption that their art must therefore be wholly new. A "new classic," Hemingway announced almost casually in *Green Hills of Africa* (1935), "does not bear any resemblance to the classics that have preceded it." The drawings of John Held, Jr., which helped to make the Flapper and the College Joe of Fitzgerald's novels trademarks of the era, were widely regarded as radically new – despite the fact that they owed almost as much to drawings on pre-Columbian sculpture and Greek vases as to the fine-line drawings of the richly illustrated French weekly *La Vie parisienne*. Yet the Lost Generation's feeling of being at once branded and abandoned touched so much that it acquired authority of its own, despite its being historically ill-grounded.

Jazz, perhaps the most distinctive artistic creation of the era, embodied the contradictions of the age in instructive ways. Its harmonies were drawn from old hymns, marches, and work songs, while its varied rhythms and changing beat depended on improvisation. Its aim was the creation of spontaneous communities of listeners and performers – or, more radically, of performers willing to become listeners and listeners able to become performers – who engage simultaneously in active remembering and deliberate forgetting. Jazz is sensuous and even sinuous; it is illicit, spontaneous, and unpredictable; it is ungenteel and uninhibited; it scorns pretense, endorses protest, and celebrates change. Offended by its sexuality, A. C. Ward called it a "dance of death" for Europe as well as the United States. Yet even as it celebrates the present moment of new creation, jazz evokes and echoes old words and rhythms that it treats as almost sacred. This doubleness made jazz the appropriate music of the twenties. In one mood it exemplifies a radical principle of origination. Like the United States and modernism, it is obsessed with the possibility of wholly new beginnings. It defines true artists as those able to shake themselves free of history long enough to engage in pure improvisation, and it therefore defines true art as work in which anteriority seems almost to vanish. And yet, like other forms of modernism, it works subtly to call into question the possibility of the modern so construed. In celebrating its generative powers, it acknowledges its own historicity, founding itself in contradiction: it declares its independence of the past, claiming the present as its own, but in doing so it defines its predicament as the historical one of trying to make a wholly new start in a world so old that everything that can happen has happened.

People heard jazz everywhere. From orchestras on boats and in ballrooms; from bands in speakeasies, dance halls, and high school gymnasiums; on radios and wind-up phonographs at home; over loudspeakers in stores and at work. Jazz's harmonies, born of contradictions, were one thing, however, while contradictions actually lived were another, as the strained and even tortured lives of scores of jazz musicians remind us. Compared with the exuberance of the Lyric Years – which was buoyed by a sense that old barriers were falling, that workers were marching, and that geniuses were sprouting while Isadora Duncan danced – the exuberance of the Jazz Age seems forced. In some moods, it reflects the sadness of a world already black and blue; in others, it reflects the anxiety of people so uncertain of what lies ahead that they seem afraid to let the party end.

Similar strains and contradictions showed even in the witty proclamations of older writers like H. L. Mencken and his disciple George Jean Nathan, who shared a poorly controlled need to appear outrageous: love, Mencken said, is a "minimum of disgusts"; "If I am convinced by anything, it is that Doing Good is in bad taste"; the "ignorant should be permitted to spawn *ad libitum,*" to provide a "steady supply of slaves" for talented people like him and his friends. Mencken, Nathan, and other survivors of the Lyric Years kept alive the Puritan as scapegoat. When he published *A Gallery of Women* (1924), Dreiser announced that it would make "the ghosts of the Puritans rise and gibber in the streets." But a *Gallery* presents a far more male-dominated view of female sexuality than Dreiser supposed, and a bleaker one as well. Similarly, Mencken and Nathan remained secret agents of things they despised. In their balancing act, important elements never quite balanced. Mencken's most ambitious work, *The American Language* (1919), is a brilliant as well as eccentric historical analysis of the origins and growth of the second of two major "streams of English." As such, it is a celebration of the new. Yet as Mencken continued to correct, enlarge, and rewrite *The American Language,* adding several supplementary volumes, it became clear that his desire to celebrate the new was matched by his desire to control it. His working assumption that he and his friends were entitled to money, power, and pleasure often made him sound like an ad man of the self-absorbed, consumer-oriented bourgeois culture that he criticized. Compared with Fitzgerald's downward spirals into darkness – from fame and fortune into alcoholism, depression, and neglect; from *Flappers and Philosophers* (1920) to *Tales of the Jazz Age* (1922) to *All the Sad Young Men* (1926) to *Taps at Reveille* (1935) – both Mencken's mocking essays and much of the satiric fiction he most admired, such as James Branch Cabell's *Jurgen* (1919), now seem shallow.

An amateur sociologist and anthropologist, Sinclair Lewis displayed an almost inexhaustible enthusiasm for recording the surfaces of modern life. The many catalogues and lists that he made helped him win Mencken's praise as a collector of examples of the venality, hypocrisy, demagoguery, and vulgarity that Mencken called "Americana." Lewis, Mencken announced, was "the one real anatomist" of "American Kulture" of the "booboisie." Neither as polished nor as sophisticated as *Jurgen, Main Street* and especially *Babbitt* are far more important examples of what Matthew Josephson, in *Portrait of the Artist as American* (1930), called "resistance to the milieu" epitomized by Harding. In them, Lewis mixes satire, parody, and caricature with yearning that is cultural rather than merely personal; and he presents them in prose that tilts the novel toward the kind of sociology practiced by people like Robert and Helen Lynd in *Middletown* (1929). Even tensions that Lewis never fully controls prove to be telling, in part because he re-creates the sadness of having to choose between alternatives as inadequate as Wilson's high-sounding idealism and Harding's crass appeal to selfishness and greed. "Stabilize America first, prosper America first, think of America first, exalt America first," Harding said in 1920 – the same year in which he coined the term "normalcy." "Not nostrums, but normalcy," he said, launching a splurge of self-indulgence that lent itself to easy satire.

Published in 1920, with the inauguration of "normalcy," *Main Street* focuses on a small midwestern town called Gopher Prairie. Published in 1922, two years after the first U.S. census to report that a majority of the population lived in cities, *Babbitt* is set in a growing midwestern city of 250,000 to 300,000 named Zenith, "the Zip City – Zeal, Zest and Zowie – 1,000,000 in 1935." In *Main Street* the principal conflict is between its protagonist, Carol Kennicott, and the dull, intolerant townspeople of Gopher Prairie, who seem determined, as Edith Wharton observed, to expose the poverty of the nation's life in the midst of plenty. But *Babbitt* is divided against itself, just as its protagonist, George Babbitt, is divided against himself. Its weaknesses as a novel shadow Babbitt's as a man. Finally, however, it possesses the force of its flaws and so becomes most compelling, not in the satire that made it famous, but in the tensions it never fully controls.

Lewis pokes fun at almost everything about the people of Zenith: their slang ("everything zips" "Oh, by gee, by gosh, by jingo" "Gotta hustle" "Service & Boosterism"); their fascination with new possessions – cars, gadgets, clothes, and furniture; their tastelessness, as seen, for example, in Zenith's "Athletic Club," which features a Gothic lobby, a Roman Imperial washroom, a Spanish Mission lounge, and a Chinese Chippendale reading room; their "Romantic Hero," not "the knight, the wandering poet, the cowpuncher, the aviator, nor the brave young district attorney, but the great sales-manager, who had an Analysis of Merchandising Problems on his glass-topped desk"; their churches, private clubs, and "civic" organizations; and their values – habits of mind and heart.

> Here's the specifications of the Standardized American Citizen! Here's the new generation of Americans: fellows with hair on their chests and smiles in their eyes and adding machines in their offices. We're not doing any boasting, but we like ourselves first-rate, and if you don't like us, look out – better get under cover before the cyclone hits town![4]

Zenith's citizens give new meaning to Chicagoans' promise to make culture hum once they got some; and they also reiterate the prejudices of the "Dream City." Among the advantages they claim for Zenith over older, more sophisticated eastern cities, one is the preponderance of "Ideal Citizens" ("first and foremost," Babbitt says, "busier than a bird-dog") and "Regular Guys" ("whooping it up for national prosperity!"), as opposed to long-haired types who call themselves "liberals," "radicals," or "intelligentsia," and "foreign-born" types with their "foreign ideas and communism." Inspired by such thoughts, Babbitt and his "Regular Guys" look forward to a civilization that has finally rid itself of all the wrong types, leaving "Regular Guys" free to live in a paradise of shiny gadgets and private clubs, as hollow as the world Waldo Frank later described in *The Re-Discovery of America* (1929), one of several important jeremiads of the twenties:

> Our success does not make us happy, our loyalty to State or Corporation does not enlarge, our cult of sport does not invigorate, our cult of crime does not release; our education does not educate, our politicians do not govern, our arts do not recreate, our beauty does not nourish, our religions do not make whole. Yet it is our energy that feeds these practices and cults. With our spirit we give them life and blood, in order that they should fulfill us. *And they do not touch us.*[5]

Babbitt reminds us that in fact such things can touch us without fulfilling us. Yearning born of emptiness inflects Lewis's satire from the start. At night Babbitt dreams of a "fairy child" who sees him as "gay and valiant" and who waits for him "in the darkness beyond mysterious groves." Even during the day, when pressures to conform burden him, he protects his friendship with Paul Riesling, whose name "sounds foreign" and whose discontent shows itself in daylight. Paul sits apart from the Regular Guys and encourages Babbitt to question their boosterism. Babbitt remains a middle-aged, middle-class American, but side by side with his materialism, boosterism, vulgarity, and poverty of mind and spirit, he retains a capacity for affection and loyalty, a desire for affiliation, a gift for hope, and an almost sacred discontent with life devoid of these things. Moved by the affection he feels for Paul and his own son – inspired by the example of one and the promise of the other – he tries to rebel: he flaunts the mores of his society, chooses the bohemian Bunch over the Regular Guys, publicly supports his unpopular friend Seneca Doane, and defends a group of strikers.

There is, of course, something pathetic about Babbitt's rebellion. His clichéd dreams, particularly those revolving around his "fairy child," belong to a male preserve, and even in rebellion, he remains timid. He and Zenith's other rebels are almost as culturally deprived as its conformists. Possessing little strength and no independent imagination, he is from the outset overmatched by his world. Still, his weaknesses coexist with yearning and discontent that Lewis never completely discredits. Babbitt mouths precepts he cannot believe. He fears the power of his administered society, which offers rewards (security, position, gadgets, property, slogans, and clubs) for conformity and threatens punishment (being ostracized "from the Clan of Good Fellows," which enjoys and controls society's spoils) for resistance. "The independence seeped out of him," we read, "and he walked the streets alone, afraid of men's cynical eyes and the incessant hiss of whispering." Putting "his late discontent" behind him, he becomes a parody of the "Good Fellow": he joins the "Good Citizens' League," which is spreading "through the country," and gets "fired up" about "the wickedness of Seneca Doane, the crimes of labor unions, the perils of immigration, and the delights of golf, morality, and bank accounts." Still, having reclaimed his place among "the best-loved men in the Boosters' Club," he continues to feel trapped. "They've licked me; licked me to a finish!" he says to himself, as he sees the pathos of his life reaching out into the future: "I'm going to run things and figure out things to suit myself," he says, "when I retire." "But I've never − . . . I've never done a single thing I've wanted to in my whole life!" he admits to his son, in a speech that tries to turn confession into moral imperative. "I don't know's I've accomplished anything except just get along," he says, as his voice fades out. "Well, maybe you'll carry things on further," he adds, with no apparent awareness of the haunting ambiguity hidden in the word "further."

In *Babbitt*, as in much of the fiction of the twenties, the century is still young, particularly in its confused efforts to cope with new attitudes toward human sexuality and new techniques of manipulation used by its culture. Yet at times it also seems too old to hope with conviction. Assuming, as it were, Freud's discoveries, on one side, and Marx's, on the other, Lewis subjects both family and society to overt suspicion by depicting them as institutions that divide people against themselves. Babbitt desires union yet fears it, longs for intimacy yet shuns it, wants adventure yet dares not seek it. Sick with desire and sick with fear, he oscillates, failing to resolve anything. His dreams of a "fairy child" are clichés before they enter his consciousness, just as his hopes for his son are clichés before they touch his lips. Having rebelled against his society, he shrinks back, accepting the protection it offers him against the perils of intimacy and adventure. Both his vague yet obdurate discontent and his vague yet obdurate hope become signs not of life lived but of life deferred to the next generation, despite the likelihood that deferral will mean carrying his abnegations rather than his resistance "further."

Babbitt's story remains his own, but his story bears his name, which has become a part of American English, as a continuing reminder of just how insecure and anxious the nation's middle class is, poised between the threat of falling and the hope of rising. Babbitt puts everything he can find − alcohol and drugs, enclaves and clubs, the feel of new gadgets and the thrill of power and speed, a rhetoric of union and a rhetoric of resistance, a rhetoric of love and a rhetoric of outrage − to the task of controlling the contradictory longings that leave him internally conflicted. As his will to resist yields to his will to survive, his life bends toward resignation and deferred hope.

It was business and businessmen, not rebels or dissenters, who ruled the twenties, as Lewis makes clear. Calvin Coolidge differed from Warren Harding in several important respects, but he changed the nation's priorities only by making them more respectable. Harding's regime (1920–3) was noted for the cronyism of its own "Clan of Good Fellows" and "Regular Guys," even before conspicuous corruption tumbled it into disgrace. Charles R. Forbes, head of the Veterans Bureau, was tried, convicted, and sentenced to prison for mal-feasance; Jesse Smith, a close associate of Henry Dougherty, the attorney general, killed himself to avoid a similar fate; Thomas W. Miller, Harding's alien property custodian, went to jail for accepting a bribe; and Albert Fall, secretary of the interior, was both fined and sentenced to jail for bribery. Only death, on August 2, 1923, following a heart attack, saved Harding from sharing disgrace with his friends. Coolidge, by contrast, was noted for asceticism and personal integrity both as Harding's vice-president and during his own admin-istration (1923–9). But he shared Harding's deep faith in the nation's business civilization. He had spent years working hard, saving his money and currying the favor of people in positions of wealth and power, waiting for his big chance. When it came with Harding's sudden death, he seized it as something both ordained and earned.

"The business of America is business," Coolidge announced. "The man who builds a factory builds a temple. . . . The man who works there worships there." He was, William Allen White observed, "sincerely, genuinely, terribly crazy" about wealthy men like Andrew Mellon, in part because he believed, like the Episcopal bishop William Lawrence, that "godliness [was] in league with riches." The wealthy deserved their wealth, the poor, their poverty. If money and power were visible signs of virtue, however hidden, and poverty and powerlessness visible signs of slothfulness, however disguised, it followed as night the day that the nation's important affairs should be entrusted to men who respected wealth even if they did not possess it.

Even more than Harding, Coolidge presided over an era of unprecedented prosperity. Led by him, the nation became so single-minded in its desire to establish a "businessman's government" and a "businessman's culture" that little else seemed to interest it. Here, for example, is the world according to Edward Earl Purinton, who sounds like one of Babbitt's or Coolidge's friends:

> What is the finest game? Business. The soundest science? Business. The truest art? Business. The fullest education? Business. The fairest opportunity? Busi-ness. The cleanest philanthropy? Business. The sanest religion? Business.[6]

Reinforced by prosperity, such thinking gained credibility. Major portions of the United States remained rural and agricultural throughout the twenties, and the South remained so poor that it later came to think of itself as having been ahead of the rest of the nation, waiting for it, when the Great Depression hit. But under Harding and Coolidge, the nation's new pattern of life – urban, industrial, commercial, affluent, and secular – swept across the land, powered by success. Tensions between the affluent and the poor, the house of have and the house of want, persisted. But the power and authority of the affluent, and their mounting skill in marketing hope, executed by an increasingly sophisticated advertising industry, muted protest during the twenties. Between 1920 and 1929, the population grew from 106,466,000 to 121,770,000 (+14.35 percent) and the gross national product jumped from $73 billion to $104 billion (+42.5 percent). More striking, however, was a drastic redistribution of wealth and significant changes in the tax structure. In 1920 the top 5 percent of the population controlled 23.96 percent of the nation's wealth; in 1929 the top 5 percent controlled 33.49 percent of the wealth and their taxes had dropped from approximately 11.5 percent of their income to 3.5 percent.

As the drive to make and spend money accelerated, "conspicuous consumption" and "pecuniary emulation" gained more authority. Freedom of choice meant the freedom to choose from an expanding range of goods, commodities, and activities, and the freedom to pay for them on installment plans. Soon a new "consumer ethic" and "leisure ethic" that stressed immediate gratification began to displace an older "work ethic" that stressed working and saving and the importance of self-discipline and self-restraint. Slowly and then more quickly, the value of restraint, which Coolidge continued personally to practice, began to lose its hold as a principle allied with success and respectability. Acting on impulse, doing whatever one wanted, began to gain acceptance as a "natural" and therefore desirable way of achieving self-fulfillment. In the challenged ethos, self-denial preceded self-realization. In the emergent ethos, with the promise of plenty eroding the authority of asceticism, self-assertion, self-realization, and even self-indulgence established themselves as respectable goals. A burgeoning advertising industry and a whole set of therapeutic enterprises catered to the notion that people were entitled to prosperity as well as psychic and physical well-being. One sign of this shift was the rapid rise of the term "personality," modified by such words as "fascinating," "attractive," "magnetic," "charismatic," "sweet," "charming," "dominant," "impressive," and "forceful." For unlike the word "character," "personality" claims no intrinsic value. It exists to be noticed, named, judged, and rewarded. At once modern and public, it centers on display and performance.

Several aspects of the nation's changing ethos, already dominant in *Babbitt*, were surveyed by Robert and Helen Lynd in *Middletown*, which sets the vanishing culture of independent citizens who retained strong traditional restraints against the rising culture of new business types who believed in utilitarian individualism. Both corporate capitalism, as it came increasingly to dominate the political economy, and proliferating bureaucracies, as they came increasingly to dominate a broad range of professional organizations and social clubs, including those devoted to the study of history and literature, as well as local, state, and federal governments, became effective instruments of the "New America." The tasks associated with controlling the vast resources of the nation, as well as legitimizing the new ethos, were formidable. With bureaucracy went a new managerial style and a new professionalism that extended tentacles of control, making every profession or craft more thoroughly regulated and administered. New marketing and advertising techniques began to focus on the process of manipulating – of stimulating and creating as well as directing – consumer "needs" for movies, magazines, and books as well as radios, automobiles, appliances, bathtubs, clothes, jewelry, cosmetics, and deodorants.

Implicit in this large-scale transformation was the analytical model that science and technology presented as defining the individual's relation to nature, which made the new century increasingly an age of analysis. "The utilitarians," Irving Babbitt wrote in *Rousseau and Romanticism* (1919), have "been able to stamp their efforts on the very face of the landscape." The people of the United States remained restless, always on the move; and they had long since announced that they no longer had a king. But they were also becoming increasingly conscious of their power for science and of their power through it. Science's claim of being able to reach "out into the whole cosmos" with its analytical method of classifying phenomena made itself felt with mounting authority because it worked. As science went "forward from relationship to relationship" and from scene to scene, Heisenberg noted, so also did technology go forward, step by step, transforming the environment by impressing "our [human] image upon it." By enlarging the "material power of man," science and technology reinforced human confidence in human power. At the same time, however, they increased human dependence upon it, creating new problems. "In earlier times," Heisenberg notes, man

> was endangered by wild animals, disease, hunger, cold, and other forces of nature, and in this strife every extension of technology represented a strengthening of his position and therefore progress. In our time, when the earth is becoming ever more densely settled, the narrowing of the possibilities of life and thus the threat to man's existence originates above all from other people, who also assert their claim to the goods of the earth. In such a confrontation, the extension of technology need no longer be an indication of progress.
>
> The statement that in our time man confronts only himself is valid in the age of technology in a still wider sense. In earlier epochs man saw himself opposite nature. Nature, in which dwelt all sorts of living beings, was a realm existing according to its own laws, and into it man somehow had to fit himself. We, on the other hand, live in a world so completely transformed by man that, whether we are using the machines of our daily life, taking food prepared by machines, or striding through landscapes transformed by man, we invariably encounter structures created by man, so that in a sense we always meet only ourselves.[7]

If one secret to understanding the culture of the twenties lies in recognizing the difficulties people faced in adjusting to new technologies and a changing ethos, another lies in understanding the ways in which delight gave way to dismay when people saw their desires more and more clearly stamped on their world. George Babbitt's world is homemade; it is made by humans to reflect human desires. Nature scarcely exists for Babbitt. Yet whether he stands inside the invisible walls of his social world in compliance or outside them in resistance, his world remains *alien*. In this respect he becomes an extreme extension of certain traits we see in Sister Carrie; in him, her curious blankness, her passivity, and her endless vague yearning lead to a life that is almost wholly deferred.

Although Lewis's art is often crude, Babbitt's confusions are not shallow. His experience is mixed not merely because his homemade world remains imperfect, or because it seems imperfect in unexpected ways, but also because the old familiar bipolar characterizations of his world – into subject and object, inner and outer world, body and soul – somehow no longer apply. As subject, Babbitt merges with his world as object. He sees it in himself and himself in it. In addition, he sees both in people around him – in fellow members of the Good Citizens League and the Boosters' Club – and in his own conflicted self what his forgotten ancestors had seen principally in nature or in historical enemies: the hostile, adversarial, imperfectly repressed or suppressed *other*. Viewed in this light, his confusions are both earned and modern.

Triumphant first in the East, Babbitt's new America spread easily across the upper Midwest. Then, following lines of trade, travel, and communication, it crossed the Great Plains and converted the vagrant West. During the twenties it gained ground even in the recalcitrant South. In the brief span between the beginning of the Civil War and the end of World War I, the erosion of the authority of the church and family had accelerated, as had the growth of cities and the expansion of the nation's most successful businesses into national or international markets – first in cities, the easier targets, and then, as canals, railways, and telegraphs extended their networks, in towns and villages. After World War I, the national economy, once again stimulated by wartime production, moved through a period of brief adjustment toward one of unprecedented boom. Cosmetics and cigarettes, refrigerators and porcelain bathtubs, along with scores of gadgets designed to reduce drudgery and provide entertainment began to appear and disappear. In addition, concoctions advertised as prolonging youth, promoting health, and ensuring social acceptability (by curing bad breath, poor complexion, or body odors, for example) crowded the market. Having entered World War I as a debtor nation, the United States emerged as the world's largest creditor nation. Over the next ten years, national income as well as the gross national product soared, giving the country the highest standard of living the world had ever known. Between 1900 and 1930, the number of telephones installed rose from 1.4 million to 20.2 million and the number of automobiles produced soared from 4,000 to 4.8 million. By 1929 the United States accounted for 34.4 percent of total world production, compared with 39.6 for Great Britain, France, Germany, Russia, and Japan combined.

As the nation's economic growth gained momentum, two infatuations that the world's poor essentially cannot know took hold – a fascination with new possessions, from autos and gadgets to trinkets and jewels, and a fascination with the future. In 1909 Americans purchased 2 million horse-drawn carriages and 80,000 automobiles. In 1923 they bought 10,000 horse-drawn carriages and 4 million automobiles. Soon a frenzy of speculation was lifting the new age of corporate capitalism to unheard-of heights. In 1923 new capital issues totaled 3.2 billion dollars, and shares traded totaled 236 million. In 1927, after Congress helped the rich by cutting the real estate tax in half and reducing the surcharge on individual income, new capital issues exceeded 10 billion dollars and total shares traded reached 1,125 million. With the promise of prosperity before them, more and more people made the dream of becoming rich their way of reaching out to touch the future.

Sooner or later, the cultural shift touched everything. It shaped the detachment and arrogance of remote manufacturers and stockholders who were shielded from the actual scenes of labor and production, as well as the attitudes of laborers who were separated from the objects they made. And it touched consumers not only by shielding them from the human costs of production but also by making them dependent on transient, depersonalized forms of possession. Writing in 1925 to his Polish translator, Witold von Hulewicz, Rainer Maria Rilke noted that "the Great War [had] completely interrupted" his writing of the *Duino Elegies*. Begun in 1912, resumed in 1914, and then taken up again in 1922, the *Elegies* had undergone a shift. "The 'Elegies' show us" engaged, Rilke wrote, in the "continual conversion" of our fragile and transient earth. When possessions were few and change was slow, the transformations worked by human hands acquired a certain seemliness: they created "not only intensities of a spiritual kind, but – who knows? new substances, metals, nebulae and stars." Now, Rilke said, the nature of such conversions had been altered. To shared objects such as houses, wells, and towers, as well as personal possessions, including books and clothes, our forebears added something of their shared humanity, making them signs of hope and meditation. "We are perhaps the last" generation to have "known such things," he added. For now "empty, indifferent things, pseudo-things," crowd "over from America."

Rilke's nostalgia turns in part on a break between the nineteenth century and the twentieth. But it also possesses spatial connotations. Empty, indifferent, anonymous objects are for him American. In fact, however, the shift that he describes (from objects made authentic by "the hope and the meditation" of those who made and possessed them to objects mass-produced anonymously and then casually and even fleetingly possessed) originated in Europe, not the United States. It is peculiarly American only insofar as this country is peculiarly modern. "America has become the wonder of the world," Kenneth Burke noted in an essay in *Vanity Fair* in 1923, simply because it "is the purest concentration point of the vices and vulgarities of the [modern] world."

To judge the importance of the correlation between the United States and the "modern," and between the modern and the rush of new mass-produced objects, we must recognize that the parts of life most deeply touched by mass production had little to do with the cheap, vulgar imitations, the "empty, indifferent things" that Rilke deplores. They had to do with work and play and love, with the conditions of life and the rhythm of living it, for those who made things and those who bought them. Traditional craftspeople made objects from start to finish, one or two at a time. Modern workers assemble them by repeating segmented tasks. Their goal is standardization – which, in its deepest logic, makes workers replaceable, parts interchangeable, and products identical. In its dream of perfect efficiency, the moment to which it aspires, mass production does to work what trench warfare did to fighting and dying: it robs it of meaning by making it anonymous.

For consumers, mass buying, the synergistic partner of mass production, also changed everything – from clothes and houses, to travel and communication, to games and vacations. One "industry" after another experienced a "revolution" that in turn spawned revolutionary changes in fashion and taste. And with each succeeding revolution came an acceleration in both the economics and the psychology of change. The need to see new techniques and new products displace old ways and old possessions touched everything, including literature, music, and painting, where tradition had once counted heavily. The characteristic claim of every avant-garde movement of the twenties was that it made some earlier technique, genre, or theory "old-fashioned" if not obsolete. In short, the modern valued what it depended on – not permanence but change. It privileged the "new" or "new-fangled" over the "old" or "old-fashioned." It counted on the unspoken promise of the "new" – the stunning promise that nothing lasts.

People of the twenties – ordinary people as well as the thoughtful young – felt the impact of modernity's infatuation with impermanence, and many of them felt it with unprotected intensity. Like Babbitt, they felt more hurried as well as more confused, as though time were going to run out on them before it ran out on their newest gadgets. In A Backward Glance, Edith Wharton describes her writing of The Age of Innocence (1920) as a "momentary escape," a "going back to . . . childish memories of a long-vanished America," by which she meant New York of the 1870s. In French Ways and Their Meaning (1919), she pictures the world since 1914 as "like a house on fire," with the lodgers standing on the stairs in disarray, their doors wide open, their furniture exposed, and their habits revealed. In her images of haste and loss and her image of the world's residents as lodgers, as temporary residents of changing quarters, Wharton captures the sense of the modern that reaches back to Sister Carrie and forward to Daisy and Tom Buchanan, who buy and sell mansions as well as rent flats in apartment buildings or suites in hotels. For it follows from the logic of what Wharton called the "roaring and discontinuous universe" inaugurated by the Great War that what matters most is changing possessions, preferably by increasing their number, but if necessary simply by changing their arrangement. One response, seen more in Lewis than in Wharton, was to expose the emotional poverty of such plenty. A second, closer to Rilke's letter and to Wharton's practice in The Custom of the Country (1913), was to decry the "invading races" of vulgarians who were displacing the rightful heirs, the "vanishing denizens," of the world or, as Wharton does in A Back-

ward Glance, to bemoan the ways in which vulgar immigrants are soiling the hitherto unnoticed "purity" of North American English. A third, close to Cather's practice in *Death Comes for the Archbishop* (1927), was to explore or celebrate lost worlds where tradition still mattered. And a fourth was to confront the discontinuous world directly by focusing on crippled or even ghost-like creatures who drift through attenuated lives, speaking a language like Babbitt's, which blends archaic phrases with strained slang and empty slogans.

3. THE PERILS OF PLENTY, OR HOW THE TWENTIES ACQUIRED A PARANOID TILT

As the twenties lurched back and forth between salvaging the old and embracing the new, a series of interrelated developments – including the rise of the Ku Klux Klan, the long, divisive trial of Nicola Sacco and Bartolomeo Vanzetti (1920–7), and the passage of the National Origins Act of 1924 – exposed conflicts that gave the era a paranoid tilt. In the Black Sox scandal of 1919, the greed of gamblers and Charles A. Cominskey, owner of the Chicago White Sox, merged with the resentments of the players to besmirch baseball, the "national pastime," and ruin the careers of innocent as well as guilty players. A. Mitchell Palmer, Hoover's attorney general, once a devout Quaker and prewar Progressive, took the lead in promoting postwar hysteria by accusing recent immigrants of bringing the nation to the edge of "internal revolution." In his campaign, Palmer found supporters among avid nativists, resurgent fundamentalists, and men bearing distinguished names and occupying high offices. "The Nordic race" must fight "against the dangerous foreign races," wrote Madison Grant, the patrician New Yorker who headed the Museum of Natural History, in *The Passing of the Great Race* (1916). Other socially prominent sorts, including Senator Henry Cabot Lodge, President F. A. Walker of MIT, Professor John W. Burgess of Columbia, and Professor N. S. Shaler of Harvard, voiced similar sentiments. An "alien usually remains an alien no matter what is done to him," the less polished Hiram Wesley Evans wrote shortly after the war, no matter "what veneer of education he gets, what oaths he takes." In "instincts, character, thought and interests . . . – in his soul – an alien remains fixedly alien to America and all it means." Amplified by people like Palmer, such fears spread quickly. Both the Red Scare (1919) and the Palmer Raids (1919–20) led to wholesale violations of civil liberties, including widespread harassment, unjustified arrests, and illegal deportations, of "dark," "foreign" threats. Soon "*they,*" Palmer said, soldiers of the "alien invasion," will "outnumber us." "Out of the sly and crafty eyes of many of them," he added, "leap cupidity, cruelty, insanity, and crime; from their lopsided faces, sloping brows, and misshapen features may be recognized the unmistakable criminal types." A "stream of alien blood" has diluted our power "to maintain our cherished institutions," added Congressman Albert Johnson, chair of the House Committee on Immigration.

Alarmed by people like Palmer, Evans, and Grant, as well as Lothrop Stoddard's *The Rising Tide of Color Against White World-Supremacy* (1924) and Shane Leslie's *The Celt and the War* (1917), which Fitzgerald reviewed for *Nassau Literary Magazine* in May 1917, a group of concerned citizens – reformers like Helen Keller, Norman Thomas, and Jane Addams, ethicists like Harry Ward of Union Theological Seminary, pacifists like Jeanette Rankin, labor leaders like Duncan MacDonald and Julia O'Connor, publishers like B. F. Huebsch of Viking Press, and lawyers like Felix Frankfurter – gathered on January 20, 1920, to form the American Civil Liberties Union. But while the ACLU grew slowly, people flocked to the Ku Klux Klan, a white-hooded army of night riders dedicated to obliterating what Evans called "radicalism, cosmopolitanism, and alienism of all kinds." Between 1919 and 1925, the Klan's membership rose from 5,000 to 5 million.

Among thousands of people who were ridiculed or terrorized for not being native-born, white, gentile, Protestant "Americans," two – Nicola Sacco and Bartolomeo Vanzetti – became the most famous. Arrested in May 1920 on charges of murdering a paymaster and a guard while committing a payroll robbery at a shoe factory in South Braintree, Massachusetts, Sacco and Vanzetti endured a long series of hearings, trials, and appeals. By the time they were finally executed, on August 23, 1927, they had become national symbols – for some, of the threat posed by dark, sly aliens intent on fomenting an "internal revolution" and, for others, of the threat posed by a ruthless society determined to destroy those who threatened its ruling classes.

Both Sacco and Vanzetti, the one a "good shoemaker," the other a "poor fish peddler," in Vanzetti's words, were Italian immigrants, and both were convinced anarchists whose radical affiliations reached back through the Lyric Years of Emma Goldman's *Mother Earth* and Bill Heyward's IWW to a deep-seated distrust of government acquired in their peasant homes in Italy. During World War I, they fled to Mexico, hoping for the day when Italy would finally be free of the tyranny of government. Back in Massachusetts, their hopes for Italy's reclamation dashed, they joined other immigrant anarchists in planning and executing demonstrations and bombings aimed at keeping alive what they called the "beautiful Idea" of a world free of government. They were, however, almost certainly innocent of the South Braintree robbery and murder; and they were clearly denied a fair trial. While sitting as judge on the case, Webster Thayer worked with other government officials to orchestrate sustained, systematic violations of their constitutionally guaranteed rights – by withholding and suppressing evidence and by conniving with the district attorney, Frederick G. Katzmann, to exploit their "alien blood," their broken English, their opposition to the war, and their unpopular social philosophy – in order to arouse against them, as Felix Frankfurter put it, a riot of "political passion and patriotic sentiment." By 1927, when Sacco and Vanzetti were executed, most of the Italian-Americans who shared devotion to their "beautiful Idea" were deported, jailed, or dead, victims of a formidable campaign waged by native-born men and women, including Attorney General Palmer, Judge Thayer ("those anarchist bastards," he privately called them, while still conducting their trial), Katzmann, the governor of Massachusetts, the presidents of Harvard and MIT, and many members of the best old families of Massachusetts. Observing the spectacle, Edmund Wilson concluded that it "raised almost every fundamental question of our political and social system."

Another result of the widespread campaign was the splintering of reformers into small, ineffective groups. United, radical reformers would have remained a marginal force; divided, they possessed virtually no power. For a time the Sacco–Vanzetti case – the most famous of its kind in the history of the United States – almost pulled reformers, writers, artists, and prewar suffragists into a concerted political force. Abroad, sympathetic workers rioted in Lyons, marched in London, and burned U.S. flags in Casablanca. At home, Michael Gold tried to place Sacco and Vanzetti at the center of a larger class struggle. To become martyrs in that struggle – "a legend for millions of fishermen, coolies, peasants, miners, steel workers . . . war cripples, hounded girl prostitutes, prisoners, negro slaves, poets, Einstein, Barbusse, able-bodied seamen and Jewish tailors" – was a "beautiful fate," he told readers of New Masses in October 1927. But the trial and execution of Sacco and Vanzetti produced as much art as action, most of it forgotten. On the evening of their execution, Edna St. Vincent Millay, Lola Ridge, John Dos Passos, and Powers Hapgood joined a motley group of other writers, artists, laborers, and friends in a vigil at Charlestown Prison. Later, Cowley, Dos Passos, Babette Deutsch, and Witter Bynner wrote poems; Millay wrote both the best-known poem about the case, "Justice Denied in Massachusetts," and an impressive poetic essay, "Fear"; Upton Sinclair wrote Boston (1928), a careful historical record of the case; and Maxwell Anderson collaborated with Harold Hickerson in writing the play Gods of the Lightning (1928) and wrote the play Winterset (1935). In May 1929 in New Masses, Gold published a "worker's Recitation" based on the public speeches and letters of Vanzetti, including the famous words Vanzetti spoke to Philip D. Strong, a reporter for the North American Newspaper Alliance, in late April 1927:

> If it has not been for these things, I might have live out my life, talking at street corners to scorning men. I might have die, unmarked, unknown, a failure. Now we are not a failure. This is our career and our triumph. Never in our full life can we hope to do such work for tolerance, for joostice, for man's understanding of man, as now we do by an accident.
>
> Our words – our lives – pains – nothing! The taking of our lives – lives of a good shoemaker and a poor fish peddler – all! That last moment belong to us – that agony is our triumph.[8]

Not long after the execution of Sacco and Vanzetti, Dos Passos began writing The 42nd Parallel (1930), the first volume of U.S.A. In its third and final volume, The Big Money (1936), Dos Passos brings his long work full circle, back to the shoemaker and the fish peddler, through a character named Mary French, who joins in the vigil at the prison where the two martyrs are executed. In one of the "Camera Eye" sections, Dos Passos speaks in his own voice of having watched as his nation split into two conflicting camps:

they have clubbed us off the streets   they are stronger   they are rich   they hire and fire the politicians the newspapereditors the old judges the small men with reputations the collegepresidents the ward heelers (listen businessmen collegepresidents judges   America will not forget her betrayers)....

all right you have won   you will kill the brave men our friends tonight....

America our nation has been beaten by strangers who have turned our language inside out who have taken the clean words our fathers spoke and made them slimy and foul....

all right we are two nations[9]

In the twenties, however, about which Dos Passos wrote these words, as opposed to the thirties, in which he wrote them, reformers remained demoralized and divided. Nothing, not even the long trial of Sacco and Vanzetti, succeeded in unifying them.

In 1919, when Congress extended wartime prohibition by passing the Volstead Act over Wilson's veto, the nation found itself divided along very different lines. Prohibition intensified tensions between "highbrows" and evangelical Protestants; but it also set law-enforcement officers against many citizens who became casual lawbreakers, both in the countryside, where they associated bootlegging with old-fashioned self-reliance, and in the cities, where they thought of it as a new way to get rich. Soon stills, bootleggers, and speakeasies were feeding big money into organized crime, while gangsters fought openly on country roads and city streets to control the profits of vice. In Washington, D.C., three hundred licensed saloons gave way to seven hundred speakeasies supplied by four thousand bootleggers. Boston had more than four thousand speakeasies, Detroit more than twenty thousand, as millions of Americans, including regular churchgoers, began breaking the law. In Chicago, where "Scarface" Al Capone headed a 60 million dollar empire and an army of nearly one thousand, unsolved murders became commonplace: in 1926 and 1927 there were no convictions in 130 gangland killings. In many instances cheap liquor – bearing names like Jackass Brandy, Panther Whiskey, and Yack Yack Bourbon – crippled or poisoned drinkers. Observing the spectacle, E. B. White proposed that the government nationalize speakeasies in order to provide citizens with "liquor of a uniformly high quality" and Congress with enough money to enforce Prohibition.

Prohibition began, of course, as another crusade to make the world safe by ensuring, to borrow one of Nick Carraway's lines in The Great Gatsby, that people would stand "at a sort of moral attention forever." Carried away by their own ardent rhetoric, leaders of the temperance movement tied "demon rum" to horrors ranging from venereal and hereditary diseases to the crimes and licentiousness that their listeners associated with dark foreigners. But their larger defeat came after victory, when Prohibition did more to increase lawlessness than moral restraint.

Prohibition was in part a story about the awkwardness of a people trying to cope with rapidly changing rules, and it marked the end of an era in which local institutions like the family and church felt they could ensure moral restraint with less help from the federal government. But Prohibition also demonstrated how effective forces of change would be in converting victories by parties of the past to its own ends. And in this sense, it was simply another story coming out of 1919 reiterating the triumph of the new. It promoted new forms of lawlessness and new ways of getting rich quick, as Fitzgerald makes clear in *The Great Gatsby*. Currents of energy seemed to be "breaking out everywhere," Dos Passos wrote in *Three Soldiers* (1921), "as young guys climbed out of their uniforms . . . ready for anything turbulent and new." Veterans used their "separation checks" as civilians used the proceeds from their "liberty" bonds: to launch a record-breaking party and buying spree. The year 1919 struck many people, including Dos Passos, who returned to it in the second volume of his trilogy *U.S.A.*, as marking a shift from a politics of reform (now become "nostrums") to a politics of splurge (now become "normalcy"), a turn from a kind of residual innocence toward new fears and prejudices, and the dominance of increasingly manipulated needs and stimulated desires. Taken together, the results gave life in the twenties artificial intensity and frenetic pace. Looking back on his own meteoric rise, Fitzgerald called it "unnatural, unnatural as the boom itself."

As the country moved with scarcely a blink from the scandals of Harding's regime to the excesses of Coolidge's, more and more writers began to feel "like aliens in a commercial world," Cowley wrote in *Exile's Return* (1934). They were "restless, uneasy, and disaffected," Walter Lippmann added, "world-weary at the age of twenty-two." Some took refuge in enclaves in Memphis, New Orleans, Chicago, or New York. Others followed the examples of James, Wharton, Stein, Eliot, H.D., and Pound and left the United States for Europe as soon as they had enough money for steamer tickets. Still others, most conspicuously Fitzgerald, joined extravagant parties on both sides of the Atlantic. Even those who prospered tended to identify with writers bent on saying "No!" to what Lippmann called the "diffused prosperity" of the "New Capitalism" and what Dos Passos called the "bastard culture" of Henry Ford and Andrew Mellon. Among several exemplary tales of the era, a favorite focused on the day – November 27, 1912 – when a thirty-six-year-old man named Sherwood "Jobby" Anderson walked out of his paint factory in Elyria, Ohio, and headed for Chicago, turning his back on his successful business and his bourgeois family in order to devote his "life" to "art." "I hardly know what I can teach," Anderson wrote his brother Karl, "except anti-success."

Standing near the end of the long transformation of Romanticism into Modernism, Anderson made authenticity and sincerity the twin pillars of his conception of himself as an artist. Sensing that the story of his conversion might serve as a model for others, he tidied up the facts. His break with business was among other things a nervous breakdown that his marriage temporarily survived; after arriving in Chicago he wrote advertising copy to make a living. But the pattern he needed was there, and it enabled him to present himself as the prototype of the vulnerable yet tough citizen who values his aesthetic sensibility, and thus his immortal soul, enough to avoid settling for the inadequate fate of mere success.

In the letters he wrote, the tales he told about himself, and his autobiographical writings – *A Story-Teller's Story* (1928), *Tar: A Midwest Childhood* (1926), and the posthumous *Sherwood Anderson's Memoirs* (1942) – Anderson mixed memory and desire by adjusting the facts of his life to the requirements of his self-appointed role. His autobiographical narratives bear some resemblance to novels like *Babbitt,* where the protagonist tries and fails to break away, and considerable resemblance to novels like Zona Gale's *Preface to a Life* (1926), which focuses on a businessman who discovers the emptiness of everything he has desired – success, a family, admiring friends – before escaping "into something real." Such parallels help us to understand how close Anderson came to creating himself as a fictional character for the edification of his contemporaries and to recognize that his motives were social and didactic as well as personal and literary. His story of dropping out and breaking away not only demonstrates the value of "anti-success." It also defines art as an act of resistance that combines intrusion and embrace and so becomes an act of love that "forces us out of ourselves and into the lives of others." "In the end," Anderson said, as he neared the end of his own life, "the real writer becomes a lover."

Anderson's dramatic conversion found expression in *Windy McPherson's Son* (1916), his first published novel, where he recasts memories of his father in light of his own disillusionment with the world of business. His second novel, *Marching Men* (1917), celebrates the militant brotherhood of industrial workers in ways that veer disturbingly toward totalitarianism. But in *Winesburg, Ohio* (1919), he turned toward something he had experienced more directly: the lonely half-life of a small midwestern town. Though small, Winesburg is no longer a community. Its people are divided by competing interests rather than knit together by shared purposes; they have nothing to look backward to with pride or forward to with hope. The feeling of being trapped in a cultural wasteland and of being isolated haunts and even cripples them. What they share is being grouped together by their maker as "grotesques."

Stylistically, Anderson was indebted to Gertrude Stein's *Three Lives* (1909). "She is making new, strange and to my ears sweet combinations of words," he said of Stein – whose reliance on simple diction and whose experiments with different forms of repetition and juxtaposition proved particularly helpful to him in his own fumbling search for new ways of rendering the shrunken lives of his inarticulate characters. Such breakthroughs as he records belong more to him than to his characters. In their struggle to express themselves verbally, as in their struggle to cope with their unfocused feelings and forbidden desires, most of his characters, including Wing Biddlebaum, remain locked in timid failure. Blighted speech, awkward silences, and compulsive gestures dominate their lives and relationships. Such hope as survives lies with the young who, like George Willard, summon enough energy to break away.

Formally, *Winesburg, Ohio* reflects the influence of Ivan Turgenev's *A Sportsman's Sketches* (1852), James Joyce's *Dubliner's* (1914), and Edgar Lee Masters's *Spoon River Anthology* (1915). Anderson uses a version of literary collage to give form to his discontinuous narrative. Several of his stories and characters, "The Tales and the Persons" of *Winesburg, Ohio,* create smaller patterns of their own; together, they contribute to the larger framework of Anderson's "Book of the Grotesque," which gradually becomes more than the sum of its parts. By permitting jumps and gaps, Anderson's discontinuous narrative allows him – as it later allowed Ernest Hemingway in *In Our Time* (1924), Jean Toomer in *Cane* (1923), and William Faulkner in *Go Down, Moses* (1942) – to omit some things and avoid others. In this sense, it simplifies his tasks in advance. In addition, it anticipates the more drastic jumps and shifts as well as the fragmentation and collage that, on a different scale, dominate Dos Passos's *U.S.A.*

In Anderson's hands, however, discontinuous narrative serves primarily to reinforce the theme of isolation. Repressed needs, thwarted desires, failed communications, and misshapen lives fill his work. His characters are not only cut off from one another; they are at odds with themselves and their own bodies. Wing Biddlebaum, for example, Anderson's "obscure poet," is represented by his "Hands," which seem to live a life of their own. Like many of Anderson's stories, "Hands" begins and ends abruptly, as though it has been amputated. The principle of fragmentation that pulls toward disintegration works against the principle of integration which is essential if *Winesburg, Ohio* is finally to become the story of a town. Reinforcing this tension as he goes, Anderson imposes an enlarged role on his readers, of whom he remains acutely conscious. As his part in the literary transaction, he creates a sense of fragmented simultaneity before he begins the move toward continuity, or sustained narrative, by foregrounding the story of George Willard and making his tales interactive. But he assigns much of the task of continuity to his readers, whose role he also foregrounds. Having observed that relations stop nowhere, Henry James went on to say that the artist's task was to make them appear to do so. In Anderson's world – of severed ends, dangling lives, deferred words – relations are imperiled. "It's just as well," says one character, thinking of a speech not made. "Whatever I told him would have been a lie." To read *Winesburg, Ohio* on its own terms, as the narrative of a town, the reader must discern relations, finish communications, and fashion connections out of hints and suggestions that lie impacted in awkward silences and blighted speech. And in this sense, the reader becomes another version of the artist as lover, or at least as matchmaker and healer, sharing the roles that Anderson creates for himself as a writer.

As much as any writer of his time, Anderson combined the fate of remaining a flawed writer ("For all my egotism," he remarked late in his life, "I know

I am but a minor figure") and becoming a major force ("He was the father of my generation of American writers," William Faulkner said, "and the tradition of American writing which our successors will carry on"). One explanation for this discrepancy lies in his origins. During the years in which New York was replacing Boston as the cultural center of the United States, the center of literary creativity was also shifting. The East was still home to many critics and readers and most of the major publishing houses, but many important writers were coming from the provinces, from the South and especially from the Midwest. Margaret Anderson and Janet Flanner came from Indianapolis; Dorothy Canfield Fisher from Lawrence, Kansas; Zona Gale from Portage, Wisconsin; Josephine Herbst from Sioux City, Iowa; Harriet Monroe and John Dos Passos from Chicago; Fitzgerald from St. Paul; Hemingway from Oak Park, Illinois, near Chicago; Lewis from Sauk Center, Minnesota; Ruth Suckow from Howarden, Iowa; and Langston Hughes from Joplin, Missouri – to name a few. Soon even Van Wyck Brooks, whose work as a literary historian presented New England's literature as "American literature," was convinced "that the heart of America lay in the West" and that Sherwood Anderson, who came from Camden, Ohio, "was the essence of his West."

Anderson opened up a large part of that essence, including the human ordinariness of the tender yet jealous sexual lives of children and of the touching yet grotesque sexual lives of repressed adults, in *Winesburg* and then passed it on to writers like Hemingway, Fitzgerald, Faulkner, and Thomas Wolfe. Related to this, the legacy of Freud's great work, was Anderson's exploration of the loneliness of the modern world as manifested in the social, cultural, and spiritual desiccation of small twentieth-century towns. The isolation that cripples his characters is social as well as psychological, and it possesses an economic history as well as an erotic one. His characters want to touch other lives and explore other worlds because they need a sense of purpose and a sense of human connectedness. For Anderson, all acts of reaching out – even efforts to speak and hear – are also acts of reaching back, undertaken in hope of reestablishing ties with some lost or forfeited self and some lost or forfeited community.

4. DISENCHANTMENT, FLIGHT, AND THE RISE OF PROFESSIONALISM IN AN AGE OF PLENTY

Some of the writers and artists who sailed for France or joined enclaves back home had read enough of Henri Murger's *Scènes de la vie de bohème* to think of themselves as bohemian artists. Others, inspired by the example of Flaubert, longed to make the "quaint mania of passing one's life wearing oneself out over words" their own. Joseph Hergesheimer, to take one example, became so enamoured of Flaubert's admonitions that he wrote, Edmund Wilson remarked, nearly as badly in a studied way "as Dreiser did in a crude one." Others drifted from place to place, experimenting, or like Babbitt, moved in and out of bohemian enclaves as troubled or merely curious visitors.

Lacking political edge, their discontent often seems shallow. Even among those who shunned possessions and traveled light, serious commitments to reform politics remained rare. Cultural critics like Brooks, Cowley, and Wilson thought of themselves as "men of letters," not academic critics. During the twenties, they remained for the most part present-minded, caught up in the literary scenes they wrote about. When they turned toward the past, they looked for writers who spoke to the stranded condition of their generation. By a "useable past," they meant one useful to writers who wanted to continue culture. What held them together, beyond the abandonment of old restraints and a glamorization of new indulgences, involving sex and alcohol, was a sense of shared predicament and common endeavor: their feeling that they had been left alone together to experiment "in a void."

In addition, they remained young professionals on the make. The inadequacy of mere success and society's hostility to art, or more generally to the needs of the human spirit, coalesce in the story of Anderson. But Anderson's version of "anti-success" included large ambitions built around his effort to become a professional writer. Immortality was one aim they shared. "I want to be one of the greatest writers who ever lived, don't you?" a young Fitzgerald said to a young Wilson. Recognition and money were others. Several of the writers we remember, including Fitzgerald, Hemingway, and Dos Passos, and several we have almost forgotten, like Louis Bromfield, built substantial reputations before they were thirty, and a few made large sums of money doing it. Even those who lagged behind in reputation or fortune were for the most part able to make a living in jobs connected with writing, without having to give their energies to alien pursuits.

They worked for magazines or presses or in bookstores, in London, Paris, or New York, Chicago, Memphis, or New Orleans, and they sold their work to presses as well as magazines, a few of which, like the *Dial,* offered prestigious annual prizes. Some "little magazines" lasted for years. Others were launched with a splash only to lead shrinking lives. But even those that were short-lived – *Double Dealer, Broom, Transition, Fire, Harlem, The Messenger,* to name a few – played important roles by publishing the work of little-known writers side by side with experimental work of well-known writers, by paying the writers who edited them modest salaries, and by helping to re-form the taste and reading skills of the nation's most adventuresome readers, including emerging writers.

At the opposite end of the spectrum was the *Saturday Evening Post.* Having achieved an average weekly circulation of 2,500,000 during the twenties, the *Post* commanded large advertising fees and paid large publication fees – as much as $6,000 per story or $60,000 for a serial. By 1928 most of its issues were running over 200 pages, with roughly half devoted to advertisements. Shunning ads for alcohol and cigarettes, the *Post* welcomed ads for automobiles and household items -- Premier Duplex vacuum cleaners, Kohler plumbing fixtures, Victor radios, Singer sewing machines, Kelvinator refrigerators, and Toastmasters. Like the *Post,* the *Ladies Home Journal* promoted and profited from the nation's affluence and consumerism. When the Lynds surveyed Muncie, Indiana, in 1924, as *Middletown, U.S.A.*, they found that the aggregate circulation of the *Post* and the *Journal* was sixty times greater than that of *Harper's* and *Atlantic*. Both the *Post*'s slogans – "soberness of living" and "evenness of mentality" – and the *Journal*'s preoccupations – domestic efficiency and civic virtue – interacted with two prominent themes: gossip about wealthy people and advice about how to join their ranks. What the *Post* celebrated – businessmen and engineers as creators of wealth and as shapers of the new world – the *Journal* endorsed; and what the *Journal* celebrated – attractive yet genteel women as servants of society and guardians of virtue – the *Post* endorsed. In addition, both offered "free" advice, implicit and explicit, on a range of themes prominent in Henri Laurent's *Personality: How to Build It* (1916): how to be aggressive and original without forfeiting "the esteem of others"; how to widen acquaintances and make connections; how to acquire poise and style while making and spending money. In short, they helped to define what being a successful man or woman meant by catering to an audience that increasingly depended on the advice of strangers about everything from morals and mores to hygiene and manners. And in their advertisements they made wholesale use of the fluid, nonlinear, nonrepresentational techniques that were beginning to dominate fiction. In 1915 Vachel Lindsay had announced, in a book titled *The Art of Motion Pictures,* that the civilization of the United States was growing "more hieroglyphic every day." The fast-paced life of the city as well as the art of the motion picture had something to do with the transformation that was under way. But so, too, did the young, rapidly growing advertising industry.

"Modernism offered the opportunity of expressing the inexpressible," said the advertising executive Ernest Elmo Calkins, "of suggesting [and selling] not so much a motor car as speed, not so much a gown as style, not so much a compact as beauty." In a whole range of books (*More Power to You, It's a Good Old World, What Can a Man Believe?, On the Up and Up,* and especially *The Man Nobody Knows,* the remarkable best-seller that presents Jesus Christ as the "founder of modern business"), Bruce Barton used advertising to press the claims of a culture in which consumerism and self-realization went hand in hand. What was involved in advertising, however, as a tool for marketing products, including Jesus Christ, was the crucial dissociation of words and concepts from specific or clear referents that the French sociologist Henri Lefebvre has described as "the decline of the referentials."

One sign of the power, sophistication, and opportunism of the young advertising industry came with the move of John B. Watson, author of *Behaviorism* (1924), after he had lost his position as professor of psychology at the Johns Hopkins University, following a scandal involving one of his graduate students, to an executive position with the J. Walter Thompson Company, a large and still powerful advertising firm. Watson thought of "consciousness" as a vague abstraction. Tangible stimuli and measurable responses – "observed facts" – he believed in. Properly studied, such things could lead to the "prediction and control of behavior." Advertising, he said, enabled him to bring two decades of basic research in behavioral psychology to bear on problems "connected with markets, salesmanship, public resistances, types of appeal, etc."

Popular culture of the twenties – the stories and advertisements found in the *Post* and the *Journal,* big-time spectator sports, radio programs, and picture shows challenged serious literature by providing competing diversions. But popular culture also enhanced the prospects of professional writers. Following the formation of Alfred A. Knopf in 1915, Boni & Liveright in 1917, and Harcourt, Brace in 1919 came Viking in 1925 and Random House in 1926, the same year in which the Book of the Month Club and the Literary Guild were established. Advertising not only manipulated buyers; it attracted readers and helped to train them. Big-time sports made heroes of Jack Dempsey, Babe Ruth, Bill Tilden, Bobby Jones, and Red Grange, and movies created a series of idols: Gloria Swanson in *Male and Female;* Douglas Fairbanks in *The Mark of Zorro;* John Gilbert and Greta Garbo in *Flesh and the Devil;* Rudolph Valentino in *The Son of the Sheik.* Furthermore, all of these – radio broadcasts, sports contests, and movies alike – bathed the minds of the nation's people in stories and serials that had discernible beginnings, middles, and endings and yet made wholesale use of jumps and shifts as well as blurred, coalescing images in order to tell stories of dramatic discoveries which promoted the idea that instant stardom was the truly modern way of achieving fame and fortune.

In 1922, 40 million people bought tickets to see movies; by 1930, an average of 100 million were buying tickets each week, making the movie theater, in Glenway Wescott's phrase, the "imagination's chapel in the town." The new dream of instant stardom – of being singled out, renamed, and transformed into a star – began to rival the older dream of attaining wealth by working hard and saving money. Stardom was something that happened to people, like war and disease, as the careers of characters as different as Buntline's Buffalo Bill and Dreiser's Carrie Madenda remind us. And like the dust and the dew, it was known to fall on thistles as well as roses – on the profligate Babe Ruth as well as the upright Lou Gehrig – which meant that virtue and hard work were but one route to fame. Once discovered or created, furthermore, stars existed to be seen and emulated. They entertained by exemplifying success and its rewards and by inspiring hope. In literature as well as in movies and sports, stardom was something that could happen to anyone, anywhere, at any time, and it could happen to writers as well as to their characters. Even those too old or battered to hope for it themselves could share in it vicariously for the price of a ticket to the local chapel of the imagination.

Few writers made fortunes, but few felt hounded by dollars. "The Jazz Age," Fitzgerald said, seemed to race "along under its own power, served by great filling stations full of money. . . . Even when you were broke, you didn't worry about money, because it was in such profusion around you." Many writers, including some of those who longed for prosperity and attained it, remained ambivalent about what Joseph Freeman, who had come of age during the Lyric Years, called the nation's "money culture." Hoping to free themselves from the habits it instilled by visible and invisible means, of judging yourself and everyone else by a single standard, "your income," they tried to make their enclaves counterworlds where "rhymes were more precious than dollars" and creativity counted more than greed. But on this score as on others, they met with mixed success, in part because, having appropriated the nation's old belief that individuals could reinvent themselves and so become anything they wanted to be, they simplified their task in advance.

Even Fitzgerald, whose interest in enclaves was limited and whose faith in new beginnings was tempered by an imagination tilted toward disaster, found himself drawn to stories of fresh starts and dramas of self-fashioning, as we see in *The Great Gatsby*. He also found himself fascinated by a spectacle he wanted to explore rather than reform:

> The uncertainties of 1919 were over – there seemed little doubt about what was going to happen – America was going on the greatest, gaudiest spree in history and there was going to be plenty to tell about it. The whole golden boom was in the air – its splendid generosities, its outrageous corruptions and the tortuous death struggle of the old America in Prohibition. All the stories that came into my head had a touch of disaster in them. [10]

Fitzgerald's proprietary instincts centered less on a world than on a generation: "my contemporaries," he called them. The same paths that no longer connected young people to anything, even one another, seemed to Fitzgerald to lead to him and his contemporaries. Their task, and their fate, to borrow a phrase from his story "The Scandal Detectives," consisted of "experimenting in a void," using "the first tentative combinations of the [new] ideas and materials they found ready at their hands." Since most writers of the twenties came from middle-class homes, they found it hard to judge success without regard to money. The more they exaggerated the distance between the world into which they had been born and the one in which they lived, the more their dream of success became the principal thing they had to fall back on. Nostalgia, a harking back to some lost, remembered place or some warm feeling, marks their words. But so, too, does the thrill and even the terror of the future. Loss, whatever else it might be, was a spur to experimenting in life and art. Here, again, is Fitzgerald in "The Scandal Detectives":

> Some generations are close to those that succeed them; between others the gulf is infinite and unbridgeable. Mrs. Buckner – a woman of character, a member of Society in a large Middle-Western city – carrying a pitcher of fruit lemonade through her own spacious back yard, was progressing across a hundred years. Her own thoughts would have been comprehensible to her great-grandmother; what was happening in a room above the stable would have been entirely unintelligible to them both. In what had once served as the coachman's sleeping apartment, her son and a friend were not behaving in a normal manner, but were, so to speak, experimenting in a void. They were making the first tentative combinations of the ideas and materials they found ready at their hand – ideas destined to become, in future years, first

articulate, then startling and finally commonplace. At the moment when she called up to them they were sitting with disarming quiet upon the still un-hatched eggs of the mid-twentieth century."

Contrary to the subversive connotations of this passage, what Mrs. Buckner's son and his friend are doing has more to do with books than with bombs or bodies, and as much to do with preparing for careers and getting money, if not exactly earning it. They are behaving scandalously by collecting data on local scandals. "Ripley Buckner, Jr., and Basil D. Lee, Scandal Detectives" are working on "THE BOOK OF SCANDAL," in which they have "set down such deviations from rectitude on the part of their fellow citizens" as they have been able to unearth. Some of these deviations – or "false steps," as they are also called – have been authored by grizzled old men and have become part of the community's folk literature. Other "more exciting sins," based on everything from confirmed reports to mere rumors, would bewilder or anger the town's caretakers; still others, based on "contemporary reports," would, if known, fill "the parents of the involved children with horror or despair."

The book is Basil's idea, and reading it requires "the aid of the imagination," for it is written in ink that becomes visible only when it is held close to a fire. Both boys are preoccupied with desirable girls and dangerous rivals, and they delight in pranks that require careful planning and clever disguises. Like Tom Sawyer and Jay Gatsby, they have read a few books and have drawn models as well as ideas from them. Basil's favorite character is Arsene Lupin, "a romantic phenomenon lately imported from Europe," who has inspired Basil's dream of going to Yale and becoming a great athlete in preparation for fol-lowing Lupin's example as "a gentleman burglar." Fitzgerald thus creates a more illicit version of a story he clearly knew, Owen Johnson's *Stover at Yale* (1912), in which Ricky Ricketts, sitting in Mory's, entertains Dink Stover by explaining his plan for becoming "a millionaire in ten years": find "something all the fools love and enjoy," convince "them that it's wrong," concoct a substitute, patent and advertise it, then "sit back, chuckle, and shovel away the ducats."

Like Ricky Ricketts's imagination, Basil's moves back and forth between the familiar and the scandalous – between life governed by accepted rules and life as illicit adventure directed by the imagination toward success that is to be measured in terms of style as well as dollars. If an older, ceremonious life has prepared Mrs. Buckner for crossing spacious lawns and serving lemonade on soft summer afternoons, another, still tentative and unhatched, is carrying her son and his friend away from home as she knows it. Fitzgerald juxtaposes these possibilities, knowing in advance, as the reader does, what the boys' choice must be. But there is irony, humor, and even pathos in their predic-ament. Although the town needs shaking up, the boys' dreams and methods are shallow as well as illicit. Their only real gain – learning what it is like to feel "morally alone" – is cloaked in loss. At the end of the story, Basil is left with little more than callow confidence in the "boundless possibilities of summer," which holds out the promise of easy sex and even easy love as well as easy adventure, easy money, and easy fulfillment.

Fitzgerald set out, like several of his contemporaries, hoping to live with intensity, have a grand time, and become a great writer. By 1925, with the publication of *The Great Gatsby,* he stood on the edge of doing just that. By 1928, when he wrote "The Scandal Detectives," he was already showing signs of feeling battered and disillusioned. Yet in many respects he remained an aging boy. Buoyed by his residual innocence, he still took delight in acting out, in part because he was convinced that artists, like art, should be allied with the illicit. To his indignant perception, modern culture was at odds with human fulfillment, especially in the repressive mores with which it governed pleasure in general and sexual pleasure in particular. He took pride in believing that his generation had emerged from the war steeped in disillusionment and schooled, in the "mobile privacy" of the automobile, in what he called acts of "sweet and casual dalliance." What followed, he later reported, was an "intensive education" designed to make the members of his generation devotees of pleasure. "Let me trace some of the revelations," he wrote, looking back on the twenties from November 1931.

> We begin with the suggestion that Don Juan leads an interesting life (*Jurgen,* 1919); then we learn that there's a lot of sex around if we only knew it (*Winesburg, Ohio,* 1920), that adolescents lead very amorous lives (*This Side of Paradise,* 1920), that there are a lot of neglected Anglo-Saxon words (*Ulysses,* 1921), that older people don't always resist sudden temptations (*Cytherea,* 1922), that girls are sometimes seduced without being ruined (*Flaming Youth,* 1922), that even rape often turns out well (*The Sheik,* 1922), that glamorous English ladies are often promiscuous (*The Green Hat,* 1924), that in fact they devote most of their time to it (*The Vortex,* 1926), that it's a damn good thing too (*Lady Chatterly's Lover,* 1928), and finally that there are abnormal variations (*The Well of Loneliness,* 1928, and *Sodome and Gomorrhe,* 1929).[12]

Alarmed by the spectacle that delighted Fitzgerald, Joseph Wood Krutch, who was only three years older than Fitzgerald, complained that the new barbarians had come as "barbarians have always come, absorbed in the processes of life for their own sake . . . begetting children without asking why they should beget them, and conquering without asking for what purpose they conquer." But Fitzgerald's problem was of a different kind. Beginning with the publication of his first novel, *This Side of Paradise* (1920), he fancied himself ringleader of a revolt that embraced music and literature as well as sex and alcohol and that was laden with social and moral as well as aesthetic implications. Yet he continued to think of his art and his career as apolitical. The crucial ties that undergirded the money culture of the twenties – or the "diffused prosperity of the 'New Capitalism,'" as Lippmann put it – he grasped only subliminally and disclosed only in his finest fiction: namely, that the splurge of the young, their unleashing of the erotic will in the pursuit of pleasure, was part of a larger national splurge in which their parents and political leaders were unleashing their political will in pursuit of power and their economic will in pursuit of money. This recognition gave him the core story of the rise and fall of Jay Gatsby, a self-made, self-named "star" who learns to trust power and possession more than pleasure even before he falls victim to the cynical manipulations of the chief beneficiaries of his world's political economy, the very rich. But Fitzgerald's art – and in this, too, it is representative – played a reinforcing as well as a countering role in the process it exposes to view – a fact Fitzgerald disclosed in Nick Carraway's curious combination of hesitation and readiness, diffidence and arrogance, guilt and smugness, and then more fully explored in his only other enduring novel, *Tender Is the Night* (1934).

5. CLASS, POWER, AND VIOLENCE IN A NEW AGE

In *Workers: An Experiment in Reality – The West* (1899), Walter Wyckoff surveys the harsh consequences of being poor in a land of plenty, particularly when poverty begins to close in as something remorseless and final, enforcing a sense that one is a "superfluous human being" for whom "there is no part in the play of the world's activity." Dreiser glimpsed such moments as a boy and never forgot them. The diaries he kept between *Sister Carrie* (1900) and *An American Tragedy* (1925) show little sympathy for blacks and Jews and less interest in the plight of the poor than in his own string of sexual conquests. But memories of his own painful childhood stayed with him. "Any form of distress," he once remarked – "a wretched, down-at-heels neighborhood, a poor farm, an asylum, a jail," or people without "means of subsistence" – was sufficient to inflict something close to actual "physical pain."

Dreiser begins *An American Tragedy*, his first commercial success, with Clyde Griffiths, a young boy full of yearning, enclosed by "the tall walls of the commercial heart of an American city." He then traces Clyde's brief rise to no great height and ends with him locked in a prison cell, waiting to be executed. Enticed by his society's major inducements – wealth, status, and power, meretricious glamour and beauty – Clyde becomes an easy victim of its failure to provide him any values by which to live, other than hope of entering, as a member rather than as a hired hand or guest, the world of the very rich. His money-conscious, pleasure-seeking world teaches him to admire people above him and to use those below. Part victim and part victimizer, he resembles both a doomed Carrie Madenda and a failed Frank Cowperwood, the protagonist of Dreiser's "trilogy of desire": *The Financier* (1912), *The Titan* (1914), and *The Stoic* (1947). His most representative moment is one in which he so little knows his heart's desire that he can neither act nor stop acting, as he wavers and hesitates before clumsily and almost unintentionally completing a murder he has carefully planned.

An American Tragedy, which was banned in Boston but celebrated in Russia, makes an interesting comparison with another ironic and haunting story about the fate of the American dream, also published in 1925 – Fitzgerald's *The Great Gatsby* – in part because the latter has worn better. In one respect, Fitzgerald mirrored his nation's new attitude toward money: he was considerably more interested in making and spending it than in accumulating it. Even when he made large sums by selling stories to the *Post,* he and his wife, Zelda Sayre Fitzgerald, author of *Save Me the Waltz,* found ways to spend it on glamorous parties and gay sprees held in hotels, rented houses, or flats. Yet long before the crack-ups that began the last chapter of their lives, strong undertones of sadness ran through Fitzgerald's stories, as though the temporariness of things and uncertainties about himself, his life, and his world haunted him. What sustained him, enabling him to go on "experimenting," beyond his ambition and his gift for hope, was a belief in work: "I'm a workman of letters," he said in one of his most telling self-characterizations, "a professional."

Jay Gatsby wants, as it turns out, much of what Scott and Zelda wanted – not mere success (a mansion, fabulous millions, and a beautiful life), but success enlarged and even sanctified by a dream that gave it purpose. Clyde Griffiths lives in a bleak rented room; Carrie Madenda lives in a suite in the Waldorf; Jay Gatsby lives in a mansion on Long Island. The work of a failed "plan to Found a Family," Gatsby's mansion fits both the history he has invented for himself and the dream he hopes to live. As it turns out, however, his newly purchased "ancestral home" is another temporary address. For he lives in a world whose secret logic Dreiser glimpsed in *Sister Carrie:* of waifs in a field of forces, of lives that are at once self-invented and overdetermined. Bearing assumed names (call me Carrie Madenda, call me Jay Gatsby, they seem to say), they live lives that are not so much careers as performances filled with words, gestures, and yearnings that just miss being absurd.

In some moments Gatsby stands under a "wafer of a moon" amid "blue gardens," breathing air in which "yellow cocktail music" and the sounds of "chatter and laughter" seem almost like an "opera." Wild rumors circulate about him, lifting him into a kind of celebrity as well as notoriety. In other moments, he moves in the "unquiet darkness" of a world represented by a desolate "valley of ashes" that is shaped by driving winds and so remains fluid and insubstantial:

> a fantastic farm where ashes grow like wheat into ridges and hills and grotesque gardens; where ashes take the forms of houses and chimneys and rising smoke and, finally, with a transcendent effort, of men who move dimly and already crumbling through the powdery air.[13]

On both the first and last times we see him, isolation and silence enclose him, setting him apart. Toward the end, he reminds us that silence can be a shield of the defeated as well as the suppressed. But when he speaks, as in his striking remark that Daisy Buchanan's voice "sounds like money," he reiterates his isolation by speaking as a self-fashioned creature who wants language to serve less as a medium of social exchange than as a means of evoking essences that he alone recognizes, validates by his attention, and names – to which we, like Carraway, can only assent. In his love for Daisy, he evokes the love of a serf for a fair and beautiful princess, or of a poor man for the "golden girl." Money and class are linked in *The Great Gatsby,* as they are in *An American Tragedy;* and in both novels they serve as effective barriers to the fulfillment of desire, and also as strong intensifiers of it. In a curious way, they even elevate Gatsby's love of Daisy and, while it lasts, Daisy's love of Gatsby.

More than any of his contemporaries with the exception of Faulkner, Fitzgerald made the history and myths of the United States – promises kept and betrayed – his own. Even late in his life, amid mounting despair, he could write words such as these: "France was a land, England a people, but America, having about it still that quality of the idea, was harder to utter – it was the graves at Shiloh and the tired, drawn, nervous faces of its great men, and the country boys dying in the Argonne for a phrase that was empty before their bodies withered. It was a willingness of the heart." One source of exuberance that comes through in his fiction, especially his short fiction, flowed from the satisfaction he took in knowing that some people who had been excluded had finally got into the money, the excitement, and the spotlight. Fitzgerald became the voice of the "Jazz Age" and the poet of the great party. Yet he retained what he called a "presentiment of disaster" that had several sources, including his sense that his party-like world was too mercurial to last, that its boom, like his own rise, was "unnatural."

During the Great War, Fitzgerald served a stint in the army at a base in Kansas, where Dwight D. Eisenhower was his commanding officer, and one in Alabama, where he met Zelda Sayre. But the war, which was for him more a lark than an ordeal, hovers over his fiction. "All my beautiful lovely safe world blew itself up here with a great gust of high explosive love," Dick Diver says to Rosemary Hoyt during a tour of Europe's battlefields in *Tender Is the Night* (1934). "This land here cost twenty lives a foot that summer," he says a bit earlier.

> See that little stream – we could walk to it in two minutes. It took the British a month to walk to it – a whole empire walking very slowly, dying in front and pushing forward behind. And another empire walked very slowly backward a few inches a day, leaving the dead like a million bloody rugs.[14]

In *The Great Gatsby,* the war enters as a moment of recognition between Gatsby and Carraway. But the desperation that Fitzgerald directly knew found expression in frenetic parties built around the desire to say yes to money and pleasure and no to moral restraints. He and Zelda were by turn romantic lovers, glamorous dreamers, and rootless, world-weary lost souls. Their extravagances were told and retold in the gossip columns of the magazines and newspapers as well as the memoirs and fiction of their era, including Carl Van Vechten's *Parties* (1930). It was a part of their mystique that they always said no to the mores of the past and never said no to a party, a drink, or a dalliance. But both of them were too sensitive and vulnerable, and in some ways too old-fashioned, not to sense that they might have to pay a high price for their extravagant goings-on. By 1930, when Fitzgerald said we have "no ground under our feet," their presentiments had become facts.

Jay Gatsby, a veteran of the Great War, lives in a "gross, materialistic, careless society of coarse wealth spread on top of a sterile world," to borrow a line from *Tales of the Jazz Age* – where almost all values seem to be dying. What sets him slightly apart from other characters – the Buchanans, the Wilsons, Jordan Baker, Nick Carraway, and Meyer Wolfsheim, co-conspirator in fixing the 1919 World Series – is his "heightened sensitivity to the promises of life," a "romantic readiness," a "gift for hope." Gatsby springs, we learn, not from his poor parents named Gatz and his lowly birth in the Midwest, but from his Platonic conception of himself. In his commitment to self-invention, he makes contact with a tradition, dating back to the Renaissance, that has helped to shape modern lives in history as well as fiction. "In any real sense of the word," the British drama critic Kenneth Tynan once remarked, turning his back on his birth in lowly Birmingham, April 2, 1927, "I was born at Oxford." "I have no more connection with my early life and Birmingham than I have with Timbuctoo."

Although Jay Gatsby is almost an "Oxford man," he takes his own practical methods of self-fashioning from Benjamin Franklin's *Autobiography,* as we see in his "SCHEDULE" of self-improvement, dated September 12, 1906, which he has copied on the flyleaf of a "ragged old copy of a book called Hopalong Cassidy." "I came across this book by accident," Gatsby's father says to Nick Carraway, holding it, not wanting to close it. "Jimmy was bound to get ahead. He always had some resolves like this or something." But Gatsby takes his romantic self-conception, as opposed to his social, pragmatic one, from versions of national dreams that owe more to Hopalong Cassidy than to Benjamin Franklin. Born James Gatz, son of "shiftless and unsuccessful farm people" from the Midwest, he becomes Jay Gatsby, heir of the nation's promise. Unlike Carrie Madenda, who recounts nothing of her past, Jay Gatsby recalls his only as he has fabricated it. The vagueness with which he presents himself leaves us as well as Carraway to imagine most of his history. Yet his restraint gives him a strange kind of authenticity. "They're real," says the little owl-eyed man of the books in Gatsby's library.

> "See!" he cried triumphantly. "It's a bonafide piece of printed matter. It fooled me. This fella's a regular Belasco. It's a triumph. What thoroughness! What realism! Knew when to stop, too – didn't cut the pages."[5]

Near the end of one of his parties, we see Gatsby, the perfect "figure of the host," standing with his hand lifted "in a formal gesture of farewell" that he has picked up somewhere along the way. He remains vague about how he amassed his fortune in part because it is a quintessential American fortune: money got no matter how for the purpose of rising in a society that worships it. But he also remains secretive about the larger dream he has pieced together from his nation's past. From moment to moment, he reflects the blend of confidence and insecurity that marks him as a "nobody" who has become a "star."

When Nick Carraway first realizes that Gatsby's mansion is situated across the bay from Daisy's home not by "strange coincidence" but by design, Gatsby's life takes on new shape. "He came alive to me," Carraway says, "delivered suddenly from the womb of his purposeless splendor." Both an "appalling sentimentality," associated with his romantic side, and an appalling materialism, born of his utilitarian individualism, touch almost everything Gatsby says and does. Yet we hear in his words echoes of "an elusive rhythm, a fragment of lost words" heard long ago, that date back to the dreams and letters of the original discoverers and settlers of the New World. Like the silence in which he often moves, his sentimentality and his materialism evoke a dream to which his plan – to make millions, buy a mansion, and win Daisy Buchanan away from Tom Buchanan – remains an inadequate correlative. The secret to Gatsby's failure lies, however, only in part in the inadequacy of his dream and his plan for realizing it, both of which, like him, always just miss "being absurd." It also lies in the fact that his world, which pretends to be receptive to dreamers, in fact protects those who have been born to riches and power.

The Great Gatsby is in part a regional story of displaced Midwesterners who come East, where the action is, and then discover a world so corrupt that it kills Gatsby, among others, and sends Carraway back home, hoping to find a world that still stands at moral attention. But it is also a story of class conflict between "little" people who yearn to enter the privileged world of wealth, power, and status, and "big" people like Daisy and Tom Buchanan who have been born into that world and have no intention of relinquishing their hold on it. The "very rich . . . are different from you and me," Fitzgerald had written in "The Rich Boy." "Yes," Hemingway replied snidely, "they have more money." But Fitzgerald was right. The very rich of the twenties were set apart by their determination to claim as their own the right of casual indifference to the consequences of their actions. Having made themselves models to be emulated, they became expert in protecting themselves from the competition of those who tried it. As members of the first generation to have grown up with what Caspar W. Whitney called (in 1894) "the blessings of the country club," that "really American institution," Tom, Daisy, and their golfing friend Jordan Baker assume that they have a right to spend vast sums of money without even pretending to make any. And if wealth is one of their entitlements, power is another. Nick Carraway, who has been born into a privileged class but has been left no real money and so must work, is marginal by fate as well as disposition. He is related to Daisy and, like Tom, is a Yale man. But he lives in a small house on the edge of Gatsby's estate and is employed handling the stocks and bonds of the very rich.

As poorly born, we may assume, as James Gatz, Myrtle and George Wilson live and work in the "valley of ashes," in an apartment above their garage: "Repairs. George B. Wilson. Cars bought and sold. –." Unlike her already defeated husband, Myrtle still hopes to enter the rich, exciting world of the Buchanans. Though she differs from Gatsby on many counts, she too is full of yearning; and she too learns that the glamorous world she longs to enter knows how to exploit her but remains indifferent to her. Gatsby seeks to reconstitute his life by bringing it into accord with a dream he possesses in haunting if degraded form. Myrtle Wilson simply wants to enter the heedless, selfish world of the very rich. As it turns out, however, the two things she and Gatsby share (their impoverished beginnings and their acquired hopes) are larger determinants of life, and thus of fate, than the different textures of their dreams. Gatsby's dream comes more from his culture's past, Myrtle's from its present. But they pay the same high price for being presumptuous – for wanting, as Daisy Buchanan says of Gatsby, "too much." Myrtle dies as the hit-and-run victim of Daisy's careless driving; Gatsby dies as the victim of George Wilson's mistaken revenge after Tom and Daisy conspire to protect Daisy by telling Wilson "the truth": that Gatsby is the owner of the car that killed Myrtle.

Nick Carraway, another privileged survivor, remains marginal to the end, and then returns to the Midwest with a story to tell. The Buchanans, however, walk away unscathed, Daisy looking for another party, Tom for another polo match:

> It was all very careless and confused. They were careless people, Tom and Daisy – they smashed up things and creatures and then retreated back into their money or their vast carelessness, or whatever it was that kept them together, and let other people clean up the mess they had made.[16]

Tom epitomizes an aristocracy of such wealth and power that it can afford to be careless as well as narrowly self-interested. When he disappears from our sight, both his string of polo ponies and his prejudices, which involve gender and race as well as class, remain intact – and so too does his not quite articulated assumption that people like Jay Gatsby and Myrtle Wilson have been put on earth to entertain him, and people like George Wilson, to run his errands. "That fellow had it coming to him," he says to Carraway about Gatsby. "He threw dust into your eyes just like he did in Daisy's" – trying to convince Carraway that as a threat to their status and power Gatsby had to be taken care of. Daisy, though far more winning than Tom, rediscovers her dependence on him and so moves inevitably toward the moment when she imitates his carelessness and then becomes his willing co-conspirator in self-protective deceit and crime. In killing Gatsby, Wilson betrays Myrtle, to whom he wants to remain loyal, and serves Tom and Daisy, his own and his wife's twin destroyers. He remains to the end a bland, ineffectual, nondescript, almost ghostlike creature who acts decisively only when he acts as a tool of the rich. He thus suffers an extreme version of the fate that Sherwood Anderson rejected and that George Babbitt halfheartedly resists.

The Great Gatsby owes some of its staying power to the way in which it presents the twenties as a deeply "American" decade. In addition, it draws on the texture and plot of a story – that of the young man from the provinces – which, as Lionel Trilling observed, has figured prominently in history and in the novel since the late eighteenth century. By presenting Gatsby's story through the mind and voice of Nick Carraway, however, Fitzgerald distances himself from his novel and also establishes several sets of tensions: between the East and the Midwest; between a world of grim, ashen poverty and one of careless, ruthless wealth; between Gatsby's dream and Myrtle's yearning; between a past in which the United States inspired the poor to dream and then gave them space in which to live their dreams and a present in which it manipulates the hope-driven energies of the poor while offering them meager rewards; and, thus, between an era in which the American dream remained an enabling myth and one in which it was becoming a cultural lie. Carraway possesses the special self-consciousness of one who is aware that history, however lost or forgotten it may be, continues to shape the present. At scattered points within the novel, and especially in the frame provided by its first two pages and its last page, he evokes a historical context for his readers, or more precisely, as if for his readers, as a surrogate historian who is also a surrogate artist. He thus brings imagination into the novel as a faculty that is always moral and historical as well as aesthetic, complicit as well as provisionally independent, and shared as well as personal. Jay Gatsby is a failure who dies, but *The Great Gatsby* remains his story in part because his effort to recreate himself in an overdetermined world allies him with the narrator and the novelist. Gatsby knows that it is meaning he seeks, not mere facts. He senses, too, that society should function as a repository of noncoercive codes and models that transform facts into meaning. He even senses that no simple sequence, taxonomy, or hierarchy for arranging facts will suffice to meet his needs for meaning. And so he fashions a dream – made up of models, charts, and lost fragments of words – on the basis of which he tries to fashion a life.

For Gatsby and Carraway, *The Great Gatsby* becomes a story about several forms of resistance. For Tom Buchanan, a truly modern, nomadic ex-Midwesterner, it is a story about power. Though obtuse about many things, Tom possesses a bone-deep understanding of the centripetal forces that dominate his world. Power-smart as well as power-hungry, he focuses his resistance on those – Gatsby and the Wilsons, and now and again Carraway and Daisy – who threaten his domination either by trying to turn back the clock ("Of course, you can," Gatsby says, hoping to undo events that have made Tom triumphant) or by trying to wrest control from him. Despite occasional setbacks, furthermore, he wins every contest he enters, including the one for Daisy. As a result, the hope held out to us in *The Great Gatsby* is very limited. It is aesthetic, insofar as Carraway learns imperfectly how to make something of an inadequate past and present; and, to a lesser degree, it is moral, as we see in Carraway's mixed efforts to wrestle with moral issues. But the novel's hope is not in any larger sense historical. The possibility that Daisy might claim independent control of her own life never enters the picture. She and Tom move on as though Jay Gatsby and Myrtle and George Wilson had never existed, without even attending their funerals.

Jay Gatsby is not, however, a victim of Tom Buchanan alone. We may think of Franklin's *Autobiography* as in part a story of how one man learned to protect himself from his culture by running away from his home in Boston and by learning to keep his own counsel, protect his privacy, and make his way without accepting either his society's sexual mores, stressing monogamy, or its economic imperative, stressing the need of men to go on making more and more money. Similarly, we may think of Hopalong Cassidy, Gatsby's other model, as a modern knight of the plains whose life is informed by a romantic code of honor and gallantry. But the chief cultural work of these models – one a social pragmatist, the other a romantic idealist – as played out in Gatsby's life, is to make him vulnerable to the machinations of the rich. In particular, they make him an easy victim of Tom Buchanan, which is to say that they serve the nation's monied classes. Myrtle's dream, of marrying into wealth and power, is no less literary than Gatsby's; its origins are less specific only because they are newer. And it serves the same class that Gatsby's serves, and leads to the same end.

Virtually ignoring Myrtle Wilson, whose manner, dress, speech, and dreams continue to reflect her lower-class origins, Nick Carraway overcomes his snobbish scorn for Jay Gatsby and "takes care" of him by trying to elevate his story. In the process, however, he simplifies it, in part because he wants to contain as well as celebrate Gatsby. As Carraway's voice becomes more intrusive, particularly in the novel's first and last pages, Gatsby's resistance becomes more a grand gesture. Only by altering Carraway's voice do Gatsby's subversive hopes survive. At times his story also seems used by his cultural models – Franklin's schedule, Hopalong Cassidy's code, and his mentor's (Dan Cody by resonant name) example. Finally, however, Gatsby's story uses them as it uses Carraway's voice. To the end Jay Gatsby goes on struggling for as well as with James Gatz and the cultural models given him, and for as well as with Daisy and Nick, in a never completely lost contest with Tom Buchanan, in which a part of Fitzgerald's art, and almost silently, Myrtle and George Wilson's lives, are also joined.

6. THE FEAR OF FEMINIZATION AND THE LOGIC OF MODEST AMBITION

At times Fitzgerald and his contemporaries gained enough perspective on their sense of feeling dispossessed to recognize it as an old story – as we see, for example, in Glenway Wescott's *Goodbye, Wisconsin* (1928) where displaced Midwesterners become "a sort of vagrant chosen race like the Jews." But for the most part they left such ties unexplored. Rather than reach out to recent immigrants, women, or African-Americans, they remained almost as jealous of their status and control as Tom Buchanan is of his. Cowley notes, for example, that "the admired writers of the generation were men in the great majority" and adds that they were also "white, middle-class, mostly Protestant by upbringing, and mostly English and Scottish by descent," without stopping to wonder whether such a configuration was more created than given and, if created, by whom and in whose interests and, further, why, once created, it gained such easy acceptance in the United States during Coolidge's presidency. In the process, he ignores issues that now seem to leap out at us.

Cowley's "admired writers" thought of themselves as rejecting the prejudices and provincialisms of their day. They bemoaned the Senate's acts in the aftermath of the war; denounced the KKK, the Red Scare, and the persecution of Sacco and Vanzetti; and condemned the vulgar materialism and ruthless profiteering of businessmen. Such pronouncements fit their sense of themselves as an oppressed minority of cultural loyalists. Yet many writers, including some Cowley admired, harbored and even expressed versions of the ambitions and prejudices they thought of themselves as rebelling against, a fact that may help to explain why their society rewarded them in ways that it never rewarded black writers of Harlem, Jewish writers of New York's East Side, or women writers anywhere, from New Orleans to Chicago to New York to Paris, many of whom it pushed into the marginalized tasks of running bookstores, editing small journals, and writing diaries.

In *The New Negro: An Interpretation* (1925) Alain Locke and his collaborators – including Jean Toomer, Zora Neale Hurston, Countee Cullen, Claude McKay, James Weldon Johnson, Langston Hughes, W. E. B. Du Bois, and Jessie Fauset – declare the language of race to be a part of the nation's strategy of subjugation, and then work to overturn it by exploring the moral authority and aesthetic possibilities of imposed marginality. In Harlem, a growing number of artists were working to make the diversity of African-American life visible. Striking political organizations, such as Marcus Garvey's Universal Negro Improvement Association, flourished side by side with writers like Cullen, Hughes, Hurston, Johnson, Toomer, and Nella Larsen. But most white writers who ventured into Harlem regarded the lives and the culture of people of color as exotic, if not comic, profligate, or primitive. The language of race thrived in the twenties, and it worked to denigrate as well as marginalize recent immigrants as well as black writers.

In "The American Sense of Humor" (1910), Katherine Roof articulates a set of propositions that found an expanding audience in the twenties by locating another threat. The "American mind," Roof said, was becoming "more forceful perhaps in certain ways, but of coarser grain" because of "the tremendous influx of Continental foreigners," who represent "the raw and often the waste material of the countries they came from" and who possess "minds of a different color." Such people remain "essentially un-American" even after a generation or two, she notes, in terms that bear striking resemblance to statements made by prominent leaders like Madison Grant, Lothrop Stoddard, Hiram Wesley Evans, and A. Mitchell Palmer. Immigrants, whom Santayana had praised as the most restless, energetic, and adventuresome people in the world, had become the world's refuse.

Civilization in the United States (1923), edited by Harold Stearns, consists of thirty-three essays decrying the "emotional and aesthetic starvation" of the nation. In an effort to call people back to their historic destiny, writers like Van Wyck Brooks, Lewis Mumford, H. L. Mencken, John Macy, and George

Jean Nathan exhort and blame, warning that the nation's materialism, cultural incoherence, and anti-intellectualism must be overcome. What is most remarkable about *Civilization in the United States,* however, aside from the exuberance of its disappointment, are the two scapegoats it singles out. One is the Puritan: a repressed pioneer gobbling up land transformed into a repressed businessman gobbling up money and power. The other is woman, as we see especially in Stearns's indictment of the intellectual life of the United States, where women are depicted as feminizing social life:

> When Professor Einstein roused the ire of the women's clubs by stating that "women dominate the entire life of America," and that "there are cities with a million population, but cities suffering from terrible poverty – the poverty of intellectual things," he was but repeating a criticism of our life now old enough to be almost a *cliché.* Hardly any intelligent foreigner has failed to observe and comment upon the extraordinary feminization of American social life, and oftenest he has coupled this observation with a few biting remarks concerning the intellectual anaemia or torpor that seems to accompany it.[17]

Elsewhere in *Civilization in the United States,* in an essay on sex, Elsie Clews Parsons notes "the commonly observed spirit of isolation or antagonism between the sexes" and urges better understanding. But Stearns's sense of the debilitating influence of women on culture, and his corresponding distress before the sad plight of the male intellectual in the United States, rules out rapprochement. Men have finally realized, he asserts, that what women seek is total domination: "Where men and women in America to-day share their intellectual life on terms of equality and perfect understanding, closer examination reveals that the phenomenon is not a sharing but a capitulation. The men have been feminized."

The consequences are, of course, terrible, for men and for culture. "I have by implication rather than direct statement contrasted genuine interest in intellectual things with the kind of intellectual life led by women," Stearns writes. Women, he concludes, are too preoccupied with "one's enlarged social self" to resonate to the "mystery of life," too self-involved to be disinterested, and too utilitarian to be metaphysical. As a result, they diminish everything they touch. They turn intellectual life into an "instrument of moral reform," leaving culture "crippled and sterile," and men repressed and debilitated. Hope lies not in the liberation of women but in the liberation of culture from women and the "dull standardization" they force upon it, making it a "spiritual prison."

If the anxieties present in Stearns's essay had been his alone, they would require little comment. But the language of male anxiety was almost as widespread as the language of race; and among intellectuals, it was more respectable. It found expression in books and in the limited roles women were allowed to play in professional organizations, on college campuses, and in literary circles. A woman who did not know how to cook, announced Edward Bok, editor of *Ladies Home Journal,* simply lacked the "real knowledge that every normal woman should possess." Women who sought "Higher Education," said Charles William Eliot, president of Harvard, should be content with learning things that contributed to the "improvement of family life." American literature is being "strangled with a petticoat," Joseph Hergesheimer announced in 1921 in the *Yale Review,* in an essay titled "The Feminine Nuisance in American Literature." Echoing Stearns and Hergesheimer, Robert Herrick wrote three essays in *Bookman* (in December 1928, March 1929, and July 1929), urging men to resist "the feminization of our literature" and reassert the values of masculine culture. The "penalty" of feminization, he concluded in his third essay, "in art as in nature is sterility, extinction." The protagonist of Edmund Wilson's *I Thought of Daisy* (1929) thinks of himself as a literary rebel who wants "to leave behind the constraints" of middle-class society and the "shame of not making money." But he also conceives his "whole life" as a protest against "those forces of conservatism and inertia" that women epitomize. Seven years later, John Crowe Ransom wrote a piece called "The Poet as Woman," later reprinted in *The World's Body* (1938), echoing Stearns. Since women are "indifferent to intellectuality," he asserts, they are "safer as a biological organism."

Before the war, suffrage had become a rallying cry for men as well as women. With the war and suffrage won, women hoped to move from success to success in reconstituting society. But they quickly found themselves reassigned to traditional roles as defined by people like Bok and Eliot. Dorothy Canfield Fisher's novel *The Home-Maker* (1924) is built around the difficulties that Evangeline and Lester Knapp face – and the lies they must tell and try to shape their lives by – in order to defy tradition: the notion that men have been put "in the world to get possessions, to create material things, to see them, to buy them, to transport them" and that women have been put in it to nurture children and take care of their homes and husbands. But defiance of the sort practiced by the Knapps – in which Lester becomes a happy, competent housekeeper and homemaker, and Evangeline becomes an ambitious, successful, and fulfilled businesswoman – remained rare in art as well as life. And when it occurred, it sometimes drew fire from women as well as men. Some younger women advocated sexual freedom and even practiced it. But most older women opposed it, and some, especially those accustomed to thinking of women as purer than men – not so much repressed as blessed in being less passionately endowed – regarded the new sexuality, epitomized by the flapper, as a betrayal of a trust sanctioned by nature, culture, and God. Even efforts to find common ground in a war to obliterate prostitution and poverty proved disappointing. "I know of no woman who has a following of other women," said Democratic committeewoman Emily Newell Blair, nor any "politician who is afraid of the woman vote on any question under the sun."

In 1792, responding to Rousseau, Mary Wollstonecraft wrote *A Vindication of the Rights of Women.* Her aim, she said, was to give women power "over themselves," not "power over men." But male fear of being engulfed and displaced, having declined during the Lyric Years, flourished in the twenties.

In James Branch Cabell's *Jurgen* (1919), a failed poet is carried back to youth with his middle-aged frustrations intact. Jurgen shares the decade's infatuation with youth and its conviction that women enforce taboos invented by their mothers for the purpose of crippling men. The only women interested in recognizing and meeting his deepest needs are figments of his aging, lecherous imagination. His story, which is clearly allied with pornography, displays throughout a thinly veiled hostility toward women. In 1932 the implications of that convergence gained further clarity in Nathanael West's *Miss Lonely-hearts*. The "lady" writers that West's male writers complain about bear such suggestive names as Mary Roberts Wilcox and Ella Wheeler Catheter. What they need, the reporters agree, is a "good rape."

What writers of the twenties feared in any further move of women into the world of literature and art, especially as makers of major novels and poems, was both social displacement and impugning of their besieged masculinity. For two hundred years, since the day in Boston when Benjamin Franklin's father "saved" him from being a poet, business and politics had been regarded as proper work for men in the United States, culture and family as the proper concerns of women. Even in London, Ford Madox Ford remarked, "a man of letters [was] regarded as something less than a man." Such breathing room as existed in an increasingly materialistic society required that men retain their status as makers of art and that women content themselves with being help-mates, caretakers, and consumers of it. As pressure from women mounted, resistance in men deepened. "I was never a member of [the] 'lost generation,' " Louise Bogan observed, looking back on the twenties from the thirties. Soon women like Bogan found themselves forming enclaves within enclaves, in Paris as well as New York. In her Paris letters, Janet Flanner, Paris corre-spondent for the *New Yorker,* writes more as a sojourner or guest in the republic of letters than as a citizen, and more as an interested yet detached observer of the literary scene than as a full-fledged participant in it.

During the twenties, no black writer and no recent immigrant made it into Cowley's group of "admired writers." But one woman, Gertrude Stein, did, as one of the least conventional, most experimental writers of her time. Unlike her unconventional and experimental precursor Emily Dickinson, who never left home, Stein left the United States for Europe, as did Djuna Barnes, Natalie Barney, Sylvia Beach, Caresse Crosby, H.D., Janet Flanner, Jane Heap, Mina Loy, and Anaïs Nin, to name a few. What links many women writers of the twenties, however, in addition to the drift of their lives, is a haunting dis-crepancy between their very considerable creative talents and their stifled, neglected achievements. Those who managed to break through to expression tended, like Nin and Flanner, to excel in marginal genres or, like H.D. and Stein, to become self-consciously and even aggressively experimental.

Gertrude Stein knew one big thing: that the twentieth century differed radically from the nineteenth less because of its discoveries and the things it knew to be new than because of its losses – the things it no longer knew or had decided deliberately to forget. Stein enjoyed playing the part of an enthusiastic anarchist. A champion of the new, she remained clear about the provisional kinds of stability that her world permitted: "Let no one think that anything has come to stay," she said. A restless searcher, she persisted in shaping everything she could find, from strange, erotic, and forbidden experiences to "the language of dishes and daylight," into sentences that are sometimes abstract and hermetic, and sometimes simple and lucid. Her barbed opinions about food and parties, paintings and painters, writing and writers made her famous. A year after she published *The Autobiography of Alice B. Toklas* (1933), which is filled with witty and sometimes scathing judgments, a group of Parisian writers and artists countered with *Testimony Against Gertrude Stein*. But Stein recognized her opinions for what they were – temporary, improvised certainties – and so attributed real but limited value to them. "You see why they talk to me," she said, explaining her success in conducting a seminar at the University of Chicago in 1934, "is that I am like them I do not know the answer. . . . I do not even know whether there is a question let alone having answers for a question." "What is the answer?" she said on her death-bed, just before her remarkable energies failed completely, and hearing no answer murmured, "In that case, what is the question?"

Stein's world is full of clauses and phrases strung together one after another without coordinating or subordinating connectives for the same reason that it is full of gerunds: because it is a world where nothing – neither things perceived nor the consciousness that apprehends them, neither the moment of apprehension nor the fluid words in which an apprehension is rendered – stands still. Using various abstract ideas and hermetic codes, she makes art a celebration of the "thing seen at the moment it is seen" in order to force us to examine relations not simply between things and words but also among the processes of the world, the processes of consciousness, and the processes of composition. One result was a radical expansion of the speaking subject to include the reader by making the process of reading, as another process of consciousness, a process of recomposition. "I had in hundreds of ways related words, then sentences then paragraphs to the thing at which I was looking," she said, without adding that she had also broken most known rules governing punctuation and syntax and many governing diction, both as a part of her effort to make things new and as a part of her effort to draw readers into the process of renewal. The playfulness of her mind comes through in everything from her subtle ways of interlacing sexuality and writing to her aggressive ways of making us pay close attention to even the simplest words.

The verbal dexterity of Stein's art – which enables her to move back and forth between the familiar and the strange, and between a rage for order and a love of fluidity – is characteristically devoted to locating what she called the "bottom nature" of our identities as human beings. She uses familiar and often monosyllabic words to confront us with fundamental distinctions, between being and remembering, for example, or between consciousness and self-consciousness, or between both of these and the process of fashioning a self. We see this when she invites us to add commas to lines like this one from

What Are Masterpieces (1940) – "At any moment when you are you[,] you are you without the memory of yourself because if you remember yourself while you are you[,] you are not for the purpose of creating you" – and then reminds us that what we have done is arbitrary as well as plausible.

It is probably not too much to say of such sentences, first, that no other writer of Stein's time could have written them, though many learned from them, sometimes by writing poorly disguised imitations; and second, that a battery of marginalizing forces – being a Jew, being an American in Paris, being a lesbian – helped to shape the mind and imagination that formed these words, but that none of these was more important than being a female artist in a world dominated by male artists. In Stein's work, as in that of Edith Wharton and Ellen Glasgow, two versions of the self – a voluntarist self devoted to working in culture and creating it, and a determinist self concerned with its status as a victim of a rigidly gendered society – contend with one another. In her stylistic idiosyncrasies, Stein plays with her sense of herself and her work as at once marginal and central. In a similar move, she plays with a notion crucial to modernism, where surface complexity vies with formal coherence, tentatively endorsing and directly challenging a notion that later found expression in the New Criticism – namely, that the reader's proper task is to ensure that coherence triumphs over complexity.

Juggling words in ways that defied conventions which, among other things, gendered them in advance, Stein fashioned an art whose dialectical dexterity embraced its own predicament and processes. From *Three Lives* (1909), where we see "realism" and "naturalism" in a process of decomposition, through the verbal collage of *Tender Buttons* (1914) and *The Making of Americans* (1925) to *What Are Masterpieces* and *Wars I Have Seen* (1945), no writer remained more persistent and few were more inventive in finding ways of displaying the determined efforts of impacted consciousness to reach a liberating understanding of itself. In *The Geological History of America* (1936), Stein insists that in the modern world "the important literary thinking is done by a woman" because she believed that as a woman writer who was both Jewish and lesbian and who had lived in exile she understood the forces that affected freedom and the costs of trying to gain it. In her art, she authorizes the eye and the conscious mind to dominate the ear and the unconscious mind because she regarded control as essential to freedom, which remained her cause. Similarly, she celebrates our human need for invention by inventing in ways that call attention to the process of invention or, more precisely, to her activity as an artist engaged, playfully and seriously, in the act of inventing. In her hands, invention as consciousness's imposition of meaning becomes, clandestinely, an invitation extended to the reader to join in the act of invention, which for her always begins with an act of consciousness. She knew, furthermore, that the act of invention, or at least the illusion of it, was a necessary fiction to the reader–critic–interpreter as well as the writer. In this, her world resembles the one Jorge Luis Borges locates in a fragment of Heraclitus: "You shall not go down twice to the same river." We admire the dexterity of this line, Borges observes, "because the ease with which we accept the first meaning ('The river is different') clandestinely imposes upon us the second ('I am different') and grants us the illusion of having invented it."

In *Wars I Have Seen,* Stein uses what she called the "continuous present" to replace the notion of history as a story of decline or advance. She rejects these views, however, not simply in order to incorporate the past into the present, though there is an imperial aspect to what she does, nor merely in order to remind us that the past is always with us and that it is always being modified by the actions of the living, though she clearly wants to do this too, but also in order to free us from all nostalgic, determinist, and utopian views of history. Her mythmaking cannot be nostalgic, if only because as a woman she possesses no golden age to look backward to with longing; and she remains skeptical of great conquests, the stuff of progress, because she sees women as always lined up among the dispossessed. Yet, though she remains skeptical of all familiar orderings of history, she rejects historical determinism because she wants to preserve the possibility that art is transformational, if not revolutionary.

The expectations – literary as well as social – that enwrapped women of the twenties were no less confining for being the opposite of great, as Stein clearly knew. One expectation, the more sinister for being unexamined, was that women should write, as they should live, in a minor key, if not journals then "sentimental" novels or "sweet" lyrics about "domestic" affairs. "She is feminine," Robert Spiller's *Literary History of the United States* (1948) later reported of Marianne Moore, "in a very rewarding sense, in that she makes no effort to be major" – a formulation that perpetuates attitudes which flourished in the twenties. Women who modestly conformed to such expectations, or at least appeared to do so, could safely be praised as authors of minor masterpieces; those who refused, like Stein, were likely to be thought of as strange aberrations, roles some of them took delight, and others refuge, in playing. In Anäis Nin's *Diaries* (1966–74), we witness an unresolved tension between the desire to express herself in a major key, by establishing herself as subject, which men as different as James Joyce and Henry Miller were able to do in their fiction, and the pressure to meet social expectations by giving up any attempt to be major and, thus, any attempt to be a subject. Nin clearly understands which of these alternatives is culturally sanctioned for women. She also recognizes that conformity holds out the promise of acceptance as well as limited recognition – rewards that are psychological, social, and economic. The alternative, of seeking independent status and recognition as an artist and colleague among artists and colleagues, she clearly recognizes as culturally off-limits, as she signaled by showing only selected portions of her diaries to men. "There is not much future in men being friends with great women," Hemingway later remarked in *A Moveable Feast* (1964), reiterating male anxiety as though it were a law of nature; "and there is usually even less future with truly ambitious women writers."

7. MARGINALITY AND AUTHORITY / RACE, GENDER, AND REGION

The resemblances that might have fostered recognitions among writers of the twenties – white of black and male of female – worked more often to divide them. Cowley's group of "admired writers" coveted the power that accompanied recognition, and once they had achieved it, they held tightly to it. In addition, however, they wanted to claim as their own the sense of being marginalized. "That was always my experience," Fitzgerald observed in 1938: "a poor boy in a rich town; a poor boy in a rich boy's school; a poor boy in a rich man's club at Princeton. . . . I have never been able to forgive the rich for being rich, and it has colored my entire life and works." Ten years earlier, T. S. Eliot had written Herbert Read, giving his twist to the experience of being an outsider:

> Some day I want to write an essay about the point of view of an American who wasn't an American, because he was born in the South and went to school in New England as a small boy with a nigger drawl, but wasn't a southerner in the South because his people were northerners in a border state and looked down on all southerners and Virginians, and who so was never anything anywhere and who therefore felt himself to be more a Frenchman than an American and more an Englishman than a Frenchman and yet felt that the U.S.A. up to a hundred years ago was a family extension.[18]

Several things leap out of Fitzgerald's and especially Eliot's words, including a whole range of exclusionary principles – money and position; gender, race, region, and language; and a sense of moral, cultural, and racial superiority and condescension. Submerged in all of them, however, for both writers, is recognition that marginal voices possess special authority. Eliot, who was more patrician by heritage and experience than a writer like Fitzgerald even wanted to be, nevertheless claims for himself the experience of being excluded: of being looked down on and even, if we take full measure of his racial slur, of feeling despised and of being forced to see himself, as W. E. B. Du Bois had put it, in anger, pity, fear, and contempt, "only through the eyes of others" who possess some inherited cultural authority.

Behind the persistence with which writers like Fitzgerald and Eliot exaggerated their own marginalizing pressures lay more than the familiar desire to think of themselves as self-made or, more radically, as self-originating. Grave differences in personal experience separated them from black women writers like Nella Larsen and Jessie Fauset. But Fitzgerald and Eliot claimed the experience of being excluded because they thought it charged with creative potential. Their mood was more imperial than conciliatory. Actually feeling despised might be painful and even humiliating, but claiming it could spur creative response, based on recognizing oneself in despised others, and despised others in oneself.

Like the boundaries governing race and gender, the regional boundaries that continued to divide the nation – putting the Midwest at odds with the East, and the South at odds with the North, which from the South's vantage point included the upper Midwest as an already incorporated extension of the East – correlated with privilege and subjugation. After the Civil War, sectionalism had dissolved into competition among regions because, as William Dean Howells saw, in losing the political power to declare themselves separate nations, New England and the Midwest as well as the South had forfeited the hope of perpetuating distinctive cultures. "New England has ceased to be a nation unto itself," Howells wrote, in *Literary Friends and Acquaintances* (1900), and so had lost the chance of having "anything like a national literature." For a time, the South, stubborn as well as abject in defeat, tried to hold on to its identity: even the distinction of being defeated, it decided, was better than no distinction at all. And New England – hoping to claim the spoils of victory without succumbing to the centripetal forces that had made victory possible – tried vainly to cling to a sense of itself as distinctive. But eventually both discovered that the nation's new political economy meant the end of cultural independence.

During the late nineteenth and early twentieth centuries, writers of the South and the Midwest as well as New England continued to draw on fading regional folkways, hoping to delay homogenization. New England tended to look down on other regions of the United States as England had once looked down on it as a colony, but it remained toward them more imperial than conciliatory. Van Wyck Brooks matched Sarah Orne Jewett's effort to preserve the region's "local color" by launching an effort to establish New England's literature as "American literature." Like New York, New England continued to function as a cultural magnet. Many writers moved from the Midwest or South to Boston or New York; few moved from Boston or New York to Minnesota or Mississippi. Yet as they became modern cities, Boston became less and less New England's provincial capital; New York, less and less its commercial outlet. New lines of transportation and communication muted regional differences as they incorporated new territories.

In an era increasingly dominated by cities, New York quickly became the symbol of everything that was new, exciting, alluring, troubling, and confusing. Its skyscrapers, like those of Chicago, became temples to the power of people to impose and imprint themselves on their world. At some point in its growth, however, scarcely discernible until after it had been passed, New York became not a community but a collection of communities. "London is like a newspaper," Walter Bagehot remarked in 1858, "everything is there, and everything is disconnected" – a remark that fits both New York in the twenties and the magazine it inspired.

Henry Luce (1898–1967) and Briton Hadden (1898–1929), classmates at Yale, first planned to call their magazine *Facts* and then decided on *Time. Time* would be adapted to the "TIME" that "BUSY MEN" could give to keep themselves "INFORMED." No "article will be written to prove any special case," Luce and Hadden announced in 1923: "This magazine is not founded to promulgate prejudices, liberal or conservative." In practice, however, *Time* became a collection of unsigned, disconnected essays – on "National Affairs" (later "The Nation"), "Foreign News" (later "The World"), "Books," "Art," "The Theater," "Cinema," "Music," "Education," "Religion," "Medicine," "Law," "Science," "Finance" (later divided into "U.S. Business" and "World Business"), "Sport," "The Press," and "Milestones," which featured information about births, marriages, divorces, and deaths of the rich and famous – that were held together less by an announced consistency in style ("curt, concise, and complete" was *Time*'s slogan, though not its practice) than by an unacknowledged ideology. Here, to take one example, is *Time*'s curt, concise, unprejudiced description of one of President Coolidge's trips, complete with echoes of *Hiawatha* (August 29, 1927): "To his haughty redskin brothers, to the haughty strong Sioux nation, with his wife and son beside him, with big medicine in his pocket, came the pale Wamblee-Tokaha, New White Chief and High Protector – otherwise Calvin Coolidge, 29th U.S. President, but first President ever to visit any Amerindians on one of the reservations set aside for them by their Caucasian conquerors."

Like the city of busy men for whom it was designed, *Time* was held together, from section to section and issue to issue, not by human bonds but by a productive economy and the interests it generated. It gave expression to a people who were morally confused, economically at odds, and yet increasingly interdependent and crowded. If the barrage of overlapping yet competing sights, sounds, and smells of New York intensified one's awareness of oneself as a sentient receiver of impressions, the sheer mass of other people in it intensified awareness of oneself as an object of observation, scrutiny, and analysis. At the end of Cummings's *The Enormous Room* (1922), the New York on which the protagonist looks out is filled with "tall, impossibly tall, incomparably tall" buildings that shoulder their way "upward into hard sunlight" and lean "a little through the octaves of its parallel edges," emitting "noises of America" and throbbing "with smokes and hurrying dots which are men and which are women and which are things new and curious and hard and strange and vibrant and immense." Writing in Paris in the thirties but drawing on earlier experiences in Berlin as well as on the poetry of Baudelaire, Walter Benjamin noted that cities were teaching people new ways of seeing – reflected not only in impressionist paintings and the movies but also in the avid yet anxious ways in which people hurried about, gazing at the scenes of life. Other very different responses to the barrage of confusing yet exciting, discontinuous yet overlapping impressions and temptations included the rush to receive anonymous advice – in newspaper and magazine columns, for example – and the desire to take refuge in the long, willed sleep, or psychic anesthesia, that we encounter in novels as different as Nathanael West's *Miss Lonelyhearts* (1933) and Robert Penn Warren's *All the King's Men* (1946). By contrast, the second form of self-consciousness thus fostered – consciousness of oneself as an object of gazing – produced two contrasting results: the hope of being discovered as a star and transformed into a celebrity, and the danger of being exposed as a dangerous rival or enemy.

If Jay Gatsby's rise tracks the curve of modern hope, his murder at the hands of a virtual stranger tracks the curve of modern danger. Similarly, if in Sister Carrie's rise we see an early realization of that hope, in her careful retreat from view, when she sits alone, sheltering her life, we see her recognition of her world's peculiar danger. In these two characters we observe the matched hopes and fears of the modern world: the hope of discovery and celebrity that inspires a willingness to perform conspicuously, to project oneself forcefully, to make an entrance and become a "somebody" whom strangers whisper about; and the danger of being exposed or recognized as a rival or enemy that fosters the desire to protect one's privacy or, more drastically, to remain anonymous by wearing nondescript and even unisexual uniforms of the day, to go incognito or travel in disguise, in short, to become a nameless, voiceless "nobody." What we observe in the fiction of Fitzgerald no less than in the poetry of Eliot is the sense that urban, mass society calls forth increasingly calculated, self-conscious responses that include both Gatsby's extravagant, audacious performances and Prufrock's painful diffidence and self-abnegation. Gatsby throws grand parties, poses as "the host," seeks to marry the golden princess, and tries to challenge the power of his world; Prufrock wears the uniforms of his class, worries about the appropriateness of his words and the fit of his trousers, fears women, and avoids disturbing his world.

Another innovation owed something to the sheer mass of the city and more to the burgeoning "productive process" that undergirded it. Advertising was spawned as a new industry by a productive process that needed new ways of making itself and its products desirable or even indispensable. "I am in advertising because I believe in business and advertising is the voice of business," Bruce Barton (1886–1967) said. Born in rural Tennessee, where his father was a Congregational minister, Barton acquired in his youth a need to excel and a need to clothe his life with moral purpose. Having thought briefly of becoming a history professor, he drifted into advertising in Chicago, where quick success earned him a trip to New York, the advertising capital of the world. There he wrote advertising copy for Colliers' Five-Foot Shelf of Harvard's Classics that convinced people that Dr. Charles William Eliot, president of Harvard, could give them "the essentials of a liberal education in only 15 minutes a day." Later he wrote several series of inspirational articles for *American Magazine* that became books called *More Power to You* (1917), *Better Days* (1924), and *On the Up and Up* (1929). In addition, he served in Congress, ran for the Senate, and was discussed as a possible presidential candidate. But his genius lay in understanding the role advertising would play in the modern world. "He came as close as anyone will," Alistair Cooke wrote at the time of Barton's death (1967), "to achieving a philosophy of advertising, because he saw the whole of human history as an exercise in persuasion."

Discourse was history for Barton, and history, as we see in his story of the life of Jesus, *The Man Nobody Knows* (1925), was discourse. In *Babbitt* (1922), Lewis presents a parody of a Protestant minister bent on revitalizing religion by allying it with "masculinity" and "business" in editorials called "The Manly Man's Religion" and "The Dollars and Sense Values of Christianity." In this way, "the Reverend John Jemmison Drew, M.A., D.D., LL.D.," hopes to keep "old Satan" from monopolizing "all the pep and punch" of the modern businessman. Earlier, around the time of Barton's birth in 1886, the nineteenth century's long quest for the historical Jesus had culminated in popular interpretations that depicted Him as everything from a bourgeois moralist and a preacher of unforgettable sermons to a peace-loving social democrat and a revolutionary spokesman for the proletariat. In Barton's hands, Jesus becomes a progressive businessman, not a "killjoy" but the world's finest conversationalist, a model interlocutor, and thus "the most popular dinner guest in Jerusalem." Far from being a weak "failure" who must die, Jesus emerges as a practical-minded leader who "picked up twelve men from the bottom ranks of business and forged them into an organization that conquered the world."

First published in serial form in the *Woman's Home Companion, The Man Nobody Knows* became a best-seller. Barton was in advertising, he said, because he believed that "the larger development of business and the gradual evolution of its ideals" constituted "the best hope of the world." "Advertising sustains a system that has made us leaders of the free world," he added: "The American Way of Life." Such thinking made Barton a champion of most of the things Lewis satirized, including business and businessmen, promoters and salesmen. For generations, Protestant sons had been taught that men who produced goods and saved money were culture's true heroes. Barton became a heroic figure by recognizing that the new age of consumption belonged to the persuasive manner of the salesman and even more the persuasive voice and pen of the ad man. Yet his piety – which he employed in persuading people that Jesus wanted them to enjoy the products of the production system that was drawing them to its cities – was no less fervent for being secular. What he spoke with his mouth and wrote with his pen he witnessed to with his life. He became the persuading "voice of business."

Expansive, unsettled, and dynamic, truly "cinematographic" in its style, New York was prepared to play its role as the new capital of the nation's literature precisely because it was the deregionalized home of Barton's reified message. It drew aspiring writers from across the country, as settlers had once been drawn to the United States, and it became the locale of their temporary homes. It was a world of flats, apartments, and hotels. It felt as comfortable with change – the flow of the strange and the spectacular, the "tradition of the new" – as with its unchallenged position as the seat of capital investment and the center of burgeoning publications and communications industries. In one way or another, virtually every writer of the country had to come to grips with it, not because it nurtured them but because it published them and, even more, because, as a window to the future, it seemed to hold within itself signs of everything that was to be in the century with which they identified.

John Dos Passos was born in a Chicago hotel on January 14, 1896, the illegitimate son of Lucy Addison Sprigg Madison and John Randolph Dos Passos, a wealthy Chicago attorney. Raised by his mother with his father's generous support, Dos Passos lived a comfortable "hotel childhood" that included long stays in Europe. Having prepared in private schools in England and Connecticut, he attended Harvard, where he read Veblen and Dreiser, as well as Pater and Flaubert, and wrote reviews for the *Harvard Advocate* of John Reed's *Insurgent Mexico* as well as the early poetry of Pound and Eliot. By the time he graduated in 1916, he had cultivated two interests – experimental art and reform politics – that gave focus to the rest of his life.

Having opposed the entrance of the United States into World War I, Dos Passos remained skeptical of the "mountain of lies" produced to support it. But the war drew him both as an adventure and as an introduction to the "senseless agony of destruction." "I want to be able to express, later – all of this – all the tragedy and hideous excitement of it. I have experienced so little I must experience more of it, & more. The gray crooked fingers of the dead, the dark look of dirty, mangled bodies." First in *One Man's Initiation: 1917* (1920), then in *Three Soldiers* (1921), and again in *1919* (1932), the second volume of his trilogy *U.S.A.,* Dos Passos focused on "Mr. Wilson's War" with bitter fascination.

In *Manhattan Transfer* (1925), Dos Passos places the impact of World War I against the transformation of the United States from a predominantly rural, agricultural, republican, traditional culture into an increasingly urban, industrial, commercial, centralized, secular, and diverse one. This story, of a changing nation, became the backbone of his best fiction. Sinclair Lewis said of *Manhattan Transfer* that its composition was based on the "technique of the movie, in its flashes, its cut-backs, its speed." And in fact Dos Passos's art bears many traces of the movie, particularly the collage techniques of Sergei Eisenstein and D. W. Griffith, as well as the modern painting to which he was exposed early in life and the modern poetry he began reading in college. The narrative shifts and the absence of transitions, combined with varied engagements with history, which became his trademarks, also have much in common with Pound's *Cantos* (1915–70), Eliot's *The Waste Land* (1922), and Hart Crane's *The Bridge* (1930). In his overwhelmingly urban world, made for and by people, the strange and the familiar intermingle until the distance between the imaginary and the real begins to close, as it does in Freud's theory of the uncanny, in which the fulfillment of things wished for becomes terrifying. Later, in *The Culture of Cities* (1938), Lewis Mumford wrote of human desires being transformed into patterns of conduct and systems of control as well as "signs and symbols" of these things. In Dos Passos's novels, the city consists not only of patterns and systems – marvels of architectural design, civil engineering, social planning, and human governance – but also of noisy, disordered, congested, conflicted scenes in which repressed anxieties and animosities return to insist on being recognized. The uncanny thus becomes more terrible, and curiously more alien, because it is old as well as new, familiar as well as strange, personal as well as public. Its shock is redoubled – as are our encounters with all extreme forms of human madness and cruelty – precisely because it comes to us as recognition of something we somehow already know.

The uncanny is, of course, one thing in fiction and another in life, as Freud observed, in part because "a great deal that is not uncanny in fiction would be so if it happened in life" and in part because we have better means of controlling or distancing the uncanny in fiction. Like Baudelaire and Zola, however, Dos Passos reminds us that encounters with the uncanny increase and intensify in the homemade world of cities, where the gap between imagination and reality has already begun to narrow. Dos Passos narrows that gap further by making the processes of his fiction mirror the processes of the external, urban world. He features people engaged in making and remaking their world, as well as people engaged in perceiving and interpreting it. In an effort to work his way out of the dead end at which "realism" and "naturalism" seemed to him to have arrived, he employs new techniques for conveying the rapid pace, the sharp contrasts, and the abrupt shifts of urban life. Skyscrapers serve as signs of society's determination to assert its domination, subways as signs of subterranean forces that seem about to erupt. In countless places, in unfamiliar voices as well as in machines, he locates strange sounds. In "Experimental Music" (1958), John Cage speaks of the efforts of composers to open "the doors of music to the sounds that happen to be in the environment," their aim being not disorder but "a harmony to which many are unaccustomed." Charles Ives, one of the composers Cage refers to, blends new sounds with rhythms taken from old hymns or, in the case of his Scherzo for string quartet, from a song called "The Streets of Cairo" that was first performed at the 1893 Columbian Exposition, which Ives attended with his uncle Lyman Brewster. A comparable desire – that of opening literature to new sounds that happen to be in the environment – informs Stein's work from at least *Three Lives* on. Humans, Kenneth Burke once remarked, are "rotten with perfection" – and then added that language is "in its distinctive ways" as "intrinsically perfectionist" as its maker. The special quality of Dos Passos's art lies in this: that it remains "intrinsically perfectionist" even as it seeks to incorporate harsh and alien sounds, including mechanical and industrial noises as well as strange accents that happen to be in the environment of the city. Like Ives, Dos Passos wants not only to incorporate and amplify new sounds but also to endow them with something resembling order, if only by bringing them into the presence of remembered refrains drawn from the nation's past.

Offended by its picture of life, Paul Elmer More, philosopher-author of *Shelburne Essays* (1904–21) and an architect of the "New Humanism," likened *Manhattan Transfer* to an "explosion in a cesspool." But *Manhattan Transfer* is in fact deeply romantic as well as emphatically modern. In *The 42nd Parallel* (1930), the first volume of *U.S.A.*, Dos Passos continued to adjust his fiction to the nation's rapid transformation of itself from a "storybook democracy" to a "mass society" by finding new ways of making it reflect the processes of the external world as people were coming to know it. He weaves the scenes of his narrative together in ways that "expand in the reader's mind," as the poet Delmore Schwartz once observed, to "include the whole context of experience." He thus gives a new twist to Henry James's remark that the novelist would succeed "to the sacred office of the historian" and to Wyndham Lewis's remark that artists are "always engaged in writing a detailed history of the future" out of their awareness "of the nature of the present." *U.S.A.* is, as Dos Passos put it, a "collective" novel about "the march of history," made up mostly of "the speech of the people." Diverse in style and panoramic in scope, it reaches from the prewar years into the thirties and stretches from New York to California, from Chicago to Mexico, from the United States to Europe. In some moments, it moves with dizzying speed – which Dos Passos likened to "the trembling joy that is akin to [the] terror" one experiences in constant travel. In others, it stops abruptly to provide close-ups of imagined faces and scenes or offer biographies of famous lives. *The 42nd Parallel* focuses on the story of a new generation in a new and hopeful century in a "New America." *1919* follows a trail of carelessness and deceit to the ceremonial burial of the Unknown Soldier, the nation's representative of all the faceless, nameless dead of its wars – except, of course, certain outsiders: " 'Make sure he aint a dinge, boys, / make sure he aint a guinea or a kike.' " *Big Money* presents an increasingly manipulative and materialistic society in which banality, hypocrisy, corruption, violence, and injustice punctuate history. *U.S.A.* thus traces a declining history, from an age of hope (1910–17) through a war and stacks of betrayals to the deaths of Sacco and Vanzetti. In one sense it is a national epic; in another, it is a jeremiad.

Lewis, Fitzgerald, and Hemingway, among others, also wrote social fiction. But Dos Passos's works – from his early war novels on, but especially from *Manhattan Transfer* on – anticipate the social fiction of the thirties in ways that few works of the twenties do. In Dos Passos's novels, the lingering hope of the Lyric Years fades, but it never disappears. Like other writers of his time, Dos Passos knew that history and society work on and in people, shaping and misshaping their lives. But for him, that awareness possessed an edge many writers missed. His artists, even those who think of themselves as possessing a spectatorial attitude and achieving an almost mountainous detachment, are implicated, entangled, and sometimes complicit in the society they observe, especially as it becomes more centralized in its control and more sophisticated in its use of the mass media and advertising. Having studied the new media, Dos Passos incorporated them in his art because he realized they were instruments of power that could be put to the purpose of producing and manipulating a "mountain of lies." Yet he held to the conviction that the United States, and by extension, the modern world, could be reformed, if rebel artists and social reformers would again unite in directing human energies toward something other than the process of making and spending money. His spectatorial "I" was his stronghold against total incorporation into a society that insisted upon naming one either a "failure" (the victim as victim) or a "success" (the victim as victimizer, often of oneself as well as others).

U.S.A. confronts class conflict, and it examines the trauma inflicted by rapid modernization on both the fabric of social life and the individual human psyche. But it also explores the intellectual and aesthetic implications of rapid incorporation and commercialization. In it the act of living for art and literature emerges as a process of constructing new paradigms, models, and theories about almost everything: from "consciousness" and "reality" to "psychic needs" and "biological urges" to "social forces" and "natural laws." Few novels in history have done as much to survey the varied, ingenious ways in which human beings have used their minds and imaginations to impose their wills on one another: through the stories they tell, the advertisements they create, and the propaganda they generate as well as the wars they wage. It is in this sense that U.S.A. is a political novel. In confronting the many faces of power, it brings everything, including art, under the aspect of the political. Committed though he is, furthermore, to the claims of the community, Dos Passos reserves his deeper sympathy for the beleaguered, individual self. His circle of life is more urban than natural, this being a part of the large cultural transformation that had taken place between the age of Emerson and the twenties. But Emerson remained one of his heroes, and even when Dos Passos's faith in reform and his belief in human progress were most threatened, Emerson helped to sustain his faith in the self's ability to protect its own integrity and maintain the semi-independence of its soul, even against the sometimes subtle and sometimes crude pressures of an increasingly administered society.

8. WAR AS METAPHOR: THE EXAMPLE OF ERNEST HEMINGWAY

Writers whose art drew more from the customs and dialects of a region – as Jewett's and Frost's did from New England, Anderson's and Lewis's did from the Midwest, and Faulkner's did from the South – had their own reasons for resisting New York. Even those who came to regard New York as a second home – as both Fitzgerald, born in St. Paul, Minnesota, and Langston Hughes, born in Joplin, Missouri, did at times, and as Anzia Yezierska, born in Plinsk, Poland, did more completely – continued to draw sustenance from the provincial cultures they carried with them. Writers from the South carried the additional burden of a history haunted by slavery, guilt, poverty, and defeat wherever they went, and nothing that happened in the twenties lightened their load. To Mencken, the Midwest was a "forlorn country" of yokels and hypocrites. The "truths" that Carol Kennicott, protagonist of Main Street (1920), discovers were, Mencken reported, simply the truth: "the contentment" of the Midwest was "the enchantment of the quite dead." The Midwest was "negation," "prohibition," and "slavery": it was "dullness made God." But

Mencken spoke for the nation in making the South his favorite target of ridicule. The South epitomized the "idiocies of the Bible Belt," he said, and surpassed in hypocrisy and benightedness every civilization in history.

The Midwest's advantages over the South, which were considerable, derived ironically from the middle-class prosperity and ethos into which Mencken had been born and spent his life trying to escape. As a result, despite Mencken, the Midwest retained a political and economic as well as moral self-assurance that the South's aristocratic pretensions ruled out. "What we call the middle classes are for the most part the church-going classes," John Dewey observed. "The 'Middle West,' the prairie country, has been the center of active social philanthropies and political progressivism," he added, "because it is the chief home of this folk." The Midwest still felt a sense of cultural inferiority toward the East, played on by Mencken, to which writers were especially sensitive. It also felt some latent guilt for having transformed Turner's "great American West" into another scene of production to benefit big business. But it retained the self-confidence reflected in Dewey's statement. And that self-confidence was sometimes employed in resisting its own ethos, as Dreiser, Anderson, and Fitzgerald made clear in their ways, and several women made clear in theirs. Now and then, for example, in stories and novels by Fitzgerald and Hemingway, or more concertedly in a long string of novels by Zane Grey, the old strategy of trying to overcome isolation by both eroticizing and spiritualizing the landscape reappears in the fiction of the twenties. But in the works of Willa Cather and Zona Gale, we encounter subtle subversions of the male strategy of celebrating male protagonists engaged in conquering natural scenes that are associated with female beauty and fecundity. And in this, the novels of Cather and Gale parallel the paintings of Georgia O'Keeffe, which throughout the twenties and thirties associated nature's resistance to such mastery with the presence in it of charged images of obdurate female sexuality.

But other modes of resistance dominated fiction in the twenties, particularly among writers of the Midwest, who resented the authority of the past even more than they resented eastern domination. By a "generation," Fitzgerald wrote, speaking for Cowley's group of "admired writers,"

> I mean that reaction against the fathers which seems to occur about three times a century. It is distinguished by a set of ideas, inherited in moderated form from the madmen and outlaws of the generation before; if it is a real generation it has its own leaders and spokesmen, and it draws into its orbit those born just before it and just after, whose ideas are less clear-cut and defiant.[19]

Fitzgerald liked the notion that he and his generation had rejected the funny-looking clothes and outmoded social concerns of "those born just before" them and the notion that they had preempted those born "just after" by reaching back selectively to claim certain "madmen and outlaws" of the past as the true progenitors of the modern. One result was another reinvention of the literary history of the United States. At times, writers of the twenties merely reiterated what Randolph Bourne and others had stated before the War. Puritanism, for example, remained a scapegoat for most known forms of provincialism, greed, and repression. One purpose of the historical and critical works of the twenties – including broad-gauged studies such as D. H. Lawrence's *Studies in Classic American Literature* (1922), Lewis Mumford's *The Golden Day* (1926) and *The Brown Decades* (1931), and William Carlos Williams's *In the American Grain* (1925), and works on individual writers, such as Van Wyck Brooks's *The Ordeal of Mark Twain* (1920) – was to identify prophetic dissenters of the past. In Claude Bowers's *The Tragic Era* (1929) the period following the Civil War was identified as an analogue of the twenties. But most writers of the twenties showed less interest in identifying a dominant tradition than in finding precursors of the disenchantment and the spectatorial attitude that the Great War had endowed with special authority.

The sense of a world still at war, or at least deeply wounded by the war, hovers over the fiction of the twenties. Hemingway and Dos Passos were among those who had seen some fighting. Fitzgerald and Faulkner were among those who had volunteered for service only to be left behind. Faulkner's bitterness at the inadequate fate of being one on whom "they had stopped the war" found direct expression in several of his early stories and his first novel, *Soldiers' Pay* (1926). In addition, it entered several extravagant inventions – tales of daring training-camp escapades and even of heroic combat ordeals – through which he tried to correct the clumsy work of "the sorry jade, circumstance" (another phrase from *Soldiers' Pay*) that had robbed him of his chance at glory. "Like most of my generation, I was obsessed with the idea of 'War' as the test of your courage, your maturity, of your sexual powers," Christopher Isherwood (b. 1904) later remarked, in words that help us to gauge what Faulkner and others were trying to claim for themselves in the heroic tales they concocted. Even Hemingway, who volunteered for ambulance service and then stretched its boundaries to the point of becoming a decorated hero, felt driven to improve on his adventures.

Spectatorial attitudes possess remarkable elasticity, as we see in novels like *Sister Carrie,* and they had roots in cultural changes that had begun long before the Great War, as we see in Poe's "A Man of the Crowd" (1840). But the war altered and reinforced them – by penning people in trenches for long days and nights or putting them in ambulances, where waiting, watching, and cleaning up seemed to exhaust possible responses. Spectatorial attitudes were also reinforced by the rapid rise of movies, spectator sports, and even radio broadcasts, which turned people into audiences for reports on labor disputes, race riots, and gangland wars. For many survivors, however, the basic sense of being a more or less terrified yet helpless observer went back to the war. Scarred by that experience, the protagonist of Dorothy Canfield Fisher's *The Deepening Stream* (1930) thinks of herself as a permanent refugee. *Children of Fate* (1917), by Marice Rutledge, pseudonym for Marie Louise Gibson Hale, recounts the experiences of a woman who, realizing that she has been duped by "governments and capitalists" into supporting the war, feels sickened with shame and declares something like a "separate peace" of her own. In Dos Passos's *Three Soldiers* (1921), we enter the "heroic fantasies" of a character named Fusselli shortly before he encounters the "reality of war," only to realize that his false expectations have been shaped by "long movie reels of heroism." In E. E. Cummings's *The Enormous Room* (1922), traditional heroic fantasies dissolve and then re-form as paranoid nightmares. In Dos Passos's *1919* (1932), Fred Summers describes the war as a tour gone awry. "Fellows," he keeps saying, "this ain't a war, it's a goddam madhouse . . . it's a goddam Cook's tour." Gone, as though forever, we learn in Hemingway's *A Farewell to Arms* (1929), is a world where words like "sacred, glorious, and sacrifice, and the expression in vain" could be spoken without embarrassment. Gone, too, are places like the barn Frederic Henry remembers playing in as a boy, where adventure and security coexist. "You could not go back," Henry says, shortly before realizing that he will have to go forward with trepidation, knowing that the next may be his final inch.

In Thomas Boyd's *Through the Wheat* (1923), that preview features a world as strange, surreal, and deathlike as T. S. Eliot's "Unreal City," where crowds of people shuffle about "under the brown fog of a winter dawn." Boyd's protagonist, William Hicks, begins with the familiar hope of seeing "some real action" and becoming a real hero. But his first encounter is with the unglamorous odors of military latrines, and his next is with a war zone in which every semblance of order and coherent authority has vanished. Over-whelmed by the spectral quality of the world around him, in which he must perform tasks with no discernible purpose or clear consequence, he begins to suffer from a form of neurasthenia, a recoil as it were, in which the self becomes numb and the scenes of what is left of life become weightless, insubstantial, unreal. Objects appear and disappear, as images might, without rhyme, reason, or explanation. At the end of *Through the Wheat* we see Hicks in "No Man's Land," tramping

> on through the field, dimly sensing the dead, the odors, the scene. He found his knife where he had thrown it. As he picked it up, the ridge swarmed with small gray figures, ever growing nearer. He turned and walked toward his platoon. The breath from his nostrils felt cool. He raised his chin a little. The action seemed to draw his feet from the earth. No longer did anything matter, neither the bayonets, the bullets, the barbed wire, the dead, nor the living. The soul of Hicks was numb.[20]

From Paris to London to the American Midwest, people wrote letters, journals, and diaries about the war that now seem like prefaces to the chronicles of disillusionment written after it. Even writers of the Lyric Years like Genevieve Taggard and Joseph Freeman, who continued to hope that a collective effort of will might change society, shared the sense of being "refugees" and "exiles." War, Bourne had observed, was "not a relation between men, but between powers." For many writers of the twenties, the Great War seemed to have changed the fabric of social life by defining social existence as a set of relations among powers rather than among people. What they sought in response were ways of distancing or protecting themselves from governments, bureaucracies, and businesses. Their enclaves were less advances than retreats, where they could try in one motion to force some pleasure out of life and in another to turn their negative experiences into art.

"The peace intensified that moral and intellectual nihilism which the war had generated," Freeman observed. Some writers took refuge in an aesthetic cult that extolled the "Fleeting Moment" of intense experience, of which Pierrot – the clown lover of Italian opera and pantomime whom French writers like Charles Baudelaire and Jules Laforgue had claimed for modern literature – became the "tragic symbol." For them, all delight became "a poignant sorrow, all beauty a snare to the flesh and a thorn in the spirit, all success at best a not ignoble failure." Faulkner, among others, appropriated the figure of Pierrot early and carried it with him through the twenties. But aestheticism made its appeal side by side with a desire to become an active public figure. What Freeman called the "dualism between poetry and politics," as a version of the "dualism which pervaded all Western civilization," intensified. To many writers the hope of being both a citizen in "The Republic of Letters," devoted to the arts, and a citizen of society, active in social and political life, seemed to exist only as an impossible possibility. Yet almost everywhere they looked – to the reclusive Emily Dickinson, the public Walt Whitman and Mark Twain, and the detached Henry Adams – they found precursors who had been willing to grapple with that task even though they knew that a not ignoble failure was as much as they could hope for in wrestling with tensions that could not be resolved.

Hemingway built his life and his art around that effort more conspicuously than any other writer of the twenties. Many people have commented on Hemingway's egotism, in part because no other writer – not Whitman, Stein, or Fitzgerald, not even Norman Mailer – tried with more success to thrust his life upon the reading and even the nonreading public. Creating a public persona was central to his effort to become a force in the larger social world. In his last painful years, he was haunted by fear that time, age, illness, and injuries had robbed him of his powers as a writer. But he was also troubled by the recognition that he could no longer bear the weight of the public image he had created for himself. Much has also been made of his competitiveness, in part because few writers have matched the rancor he expressed toward other writers. His attacks in *A Moveable Feast* (1964) are tame compared with remarks he made in letters to his editor, Maxwell Perkins. Even in *A Moveable Feast,* where his skills as a memoirist are displayed with penetrating wit, he reveals a sad need to get even with Gertrude Stein for the jabs she directed at him in *The Autobiography of Alice B. Toklas* (1933) and an even sadder need to persuade the world that Fitzgerald was inferior to him as both a man and a writer.

In truth, Hemingway saw virtually every situation and relationship as a contest waged with some threatening "other" who was bent on destroying him as a man and as an artist. Nature, with its scenes of beauty and terror;

society, with its rituals of work, play, and love, of striving, courting, and mating, as well as its scenes of open warfare; and the in-between worlds of hunting, fishing, and bullfighting: all of these were populated with creatures, including human creatures, male and female, who harbored – or, as it often seemed to Hemingway, flaunted – needs and desires that made them rivals he had been put on earth to test himself against and overcome. Reared in a proper bourgeois home that often seemed on the edge of war, in the proper bourgeois suburb of Oak Park, Illinois, just west of Chicago, where according to its slogan "the saloons end and the churches begin," Hemingway began early to depend upon excursions into nature that sooner or later either skirted, as in "Big Two-Hearted River," or gave way, as in "Indian Camp," to violence.

In 1951, more than twenty years after his father's suicide and two days after his mother's death, Hemingway wrote Carlos Baker, his biographer, about how happy he and his siblings had been as very young children, before "everything went to hell in the family." But for him that early fall had been so decisive that memories of the brief period of happiness preceding it gradually lost their force. He characteristically thought of families as destructive scenes. "Sometimes you can go quite a long time before you criticize families," he notes in A Moveable Feast, "your own or those by marriage." But families do such "terrible things" and inflict such "intimate harm," he adds, that no one can escape their force forever: "Even when you have learned not to look at families nor listen to them and have learned not to answer letters, families have many ways of being dangerous."

Hemingway retained his sense of moving in harm's way for as long as he lived, and in this as in much else his art measured his life. In The Autobiography of Alice B. Toklas, Stein taunts Hemingway, noting that for a tough man he seemed to get hurt a lot. In a similar vein, Dos Passos added that for a virile lover he seemed to spend most of his time in bed recovering from injuries. But Hemingway's wounds were not less real because he went out of his way to suffer them, nor was his tough public persona less telling for being so contrived. Without ever being a soldier, he managed to serve in World War I, the Spanish civil war, and World War II, in the first of which, as a Red Cross worker, he was badly wounded by shrapnel. What can we conclude from this except that he was driven to prove himself to himself as well as to others? "Wounds don't matter," he wrote his family from a Milan hospital. "I wouldn't mind being wounded again so much because I know just what it is like." He was in fact driven to test himself; and he was also remarkably accident prone. In 1953 he crash-landed in Africa, only to have the rescue plane crash and burn shortly after it picked him up. When he got to Nairobi for treatment, he was suffering from severe injuries to his spine and several internal organs and was bleeding from his ears, nose, mouth, and anus. Yet this was one episode among many. Everywhere he went – Italy, Spain, France, Africa, Wyoming, Montana, the Florida Keys, Cuba – something happened to him. By the time he killed himself in Idaho in 1961, his body was a personal geography of wounds.

Among the most intense of Hemingway's early experiences, to judge from the memories he carried with him, were those that centered on the hunting and fishing he did near the family's cottage on the upper peninsula of northern Michigan, where he learned the ritual of the hunt and the code of the hunter. His father, an accomplished marksman, fisherman, and woodsman, was a tough teacher who insisted that his children – his daughters as well as his sons – learn to hunt and then to eat what they killed, even if it was muskrat. Violations of his code meant punishment, and serious violations meant punishment with a razor strop, after which his children were expected to kneel and ask God for His forgiveness. Hemingway's mother preferred churches to saloons, sidewalks to running streams, suburbs to woods, and almost anything that seemed feminine to anything that seemed masculine – except memories of her father and a favorite uncle, which she could control. Having named her first son Ernest for her father and Miller for the favored uncle, her father's brother, she began to play with her son's sense of himself as male. At times she seemed pleased by his already conspicuous efforts to demonstrate his masculinity. On other occasions, she dressed him in dresses and fancy hats.

Pressured to choose between his father's rigid clarity and his mother's mercurialness, Hemingway drew closer to his sisters, especially one named Ursula, who became the model for both Littless in "The Last Good Company" and the sister whom Nick Adams refers to in "Fathers and Sons" as the only member of his family "he liked the smell of; one sister." Littless and Nick "loved each other," we read in "The Last Good Company," "and they did not love the others. They always thought of everyone else in the family as the others." Led by the more adventuresome Littless, Nick enters a series of conversations about sex that culminate, first, in talk about their becoming common-law husband and wife and, second, in talk about androgyny. "It's very exciting," Littless says, after she has cut her hair so short that she looks "like a wild boy of Borneo." "Now I'm your sister but I'm a boy."

In both the music room at home and at a friend's house, Hemingway sought his own kind of clarity by setting up boxing rings in which, with his sisters watching, he practiced the manly art of self-defense. Later he bragged of having pitted himself against several well-known boxers. In fact, he preferred opponents he knew he could beat. For there was already within him not only a reservoir of poorly repressed hostility and an insatiable need for dominance, which his easy smile masked, but also a drive to display the hostility he felt and gain the supremacy he needed. As a result, he developed a genuinely histrionic sensibility: he liked to perform and wanted to be watched, as though by proving himself to others he could convince himself as well. As one part of this, he acquired a flair for conspicuous heroism. At Oak Park High, he saved three girls, the Oak Park newspaper reported, from "flying to destruction" down the shaft of the lunchroom dumbwaiter, by grabbing the rope and holding on, blocking it at the top of the pulley with his bare hands, until other boys could help pull the girls to safety.

World War I confirmed Hemingway's darkest suspicions: that violence and terror are parts of nature and parts of us, and parts of us not only as societies and nations but as individuals. On one level, he saw these things within people, goading, pushing, and dividing them. In his deepest self, Hemingway was at war. "As to Ernest as a boy . . . ," Fitzgerald wrote in his *Notebooks*, "it is undeniable that the dark was peopled for him" – and, we might add, the silences, too. In World War I, the shaping political drama of his generation, he located a scene that corresponded to his sense of the conflicts he saw around him, pitting a single, vulnerable, solitary self against the world. Whether this correspondence was a discovery or a projection is, of course, a vexed issue. For Hemingway's art, however, as well as for his life, the balance between discovery and projection scarcely matters. He was at war, and he saw a world at war. Of what he felt and what he saw, he wrote novels and stories in which death and danger – found in scenes of hunting, fishing, and bullfighting, of boxing and war, and between different genders, classes, and races, and thus on streets and in bars and bedrooms everywhere – push themselves on us as disclosures of what in our secret selves we are and what in our public performances we secretly want to become. His art was thus born of deep reciprocities as well as deep conflicts in which the several faces of fear loom large. He not only succeeded in making varied scenes of violent conflict visible to us. He also made his capacity for pain, injury, and recovery the world's, and the world's his. Someday, Fitzgerald remarked, Hemingway will be read "for his great studies in fear." Even the wit and nostalgia of *A Moveable Feast* coexist with darknesses born of fear. Nothing Hemingway ever wrote wholly escapes that note.

In the structure of *In Our Time,* we move back and forth between interchapters that are public and stories that are private. In "Chapter I," we see a "whole battery" going along a road "in the dark . . . to the Champagne." In "Indian Camp," the first story in the book, Nick Adams holds the basin while his father uses a jackknife to perform a cesarean on a frightened young Indian woman, without anesthesia, and then closes the incision with nine-foot, tapered gut leaders. Horrified, Nick turns his head away, so as not to see what his father is doing. Once the ordeal is over, they discover that the woman's husband, who has been in the bunk above her, listening to her cries, has cut his throat from ear to ear.

> "Why did he kill himself, Daddy?"
> "I don't know, Nick. He couldn't stand things, I guess."
> "Do many men kill themselves, Daddy?"
> "Not very many, Nick."
> "Do many women?"
> "Hardly ever."
> "Don't they ever?"
> "Oh, yes. They do sometimes."[21]

In December 1928, Hemingway's father shot himself in the right temple with a Civil War "Long John" revolver that he had inherited from his father. During

Hemingway's last years, as the voices that filled the darknesses of his life became more and more real and uncontrolled, his behavior became markedly paranoid. On July 2, 1961, he loaded both barrels of a double-barreled shotgun and obliterated his cranial vault. In the fall of 1966, Ursula, his favorite sister, poisoned herself. In 1982, his only brother, Leicester, killed himself with a single shot to the head.

After World War I, Hemingway exaggerated his war experiences, including the combat he had seen, the wounds he had suffered, and the heroism he had displayed – in part, perhaps, because no heroism could match his needs and in part because like Krebs, the protagonist of "Soldier's Home," he felt driven to lie to people who had heard so much propaganda that truth, even about genuine heroism, no longer interested them. It seems likely, too, that having lied he felt what Krebs feels, a distaste for the things "that had happened to him in the war," including "the times so long back when he had done the one thing, the only thing for a man to do, easily and naturally, when he might have done something else." And this at least is clear: that he was seriously wounded by shrapnel from enemy fire and that, in the words of the citation of the Italian government, which awarded him, among several medals, its Silver Medal of Military Valor, he showed "courage and self-sacrifice" in assisting Italian soldiers before allowing himself to be evacuated from the scene of battle. Subject though it was to later exaggeration, furthermore, what he felt then almost certainly deepened the prophetic sense growing in him that for people deprived of belief in God fear of dying would hang like a dark cloud over life. Finally, however, what haunted him was not only fear that in an age of disbelief people would be unable to find anything to believe; it was fear that when they became truly desperate they would believe in anything, including vain words and empty promises.

We cannot finally separate Hemingway's success as a writer from his success in imposing on us as readers his fascination with intimate harms as well as dramatic ones – as things private and public, inherited and invented, discovered and projected. Nor is there any way to separate this from his success in forging a prose style, still widely imitated and parodied, that became one of the most recognizable literary "trademarks" in modern literature. Hemingway began to master the immediacy we associate with representational realism, to which modern reporting aspires, while working on the *Kansas City Star,* fresh out of high school, under the direction of C. G. (Pete) Wellington, who insisted that reporters write fresh, direct prose in short, forceful sentences, free of adjectives and jargon. Later, under the tutelage of Anderson, Pound, and Stein, he read widely in modern writers – James Joyce, for example, as well as Stephen Crane, Joseph Conrad, and Henry James – and began to join what he had learned from Wellington with qualities that run contrary to conventional "realism." But his originality lay in forging relations, between writer and work and between reader and writer, in which care and restraint become necessary for the preservation of our shared humanity. Style was for him a stronghold against formidable forces that threatened to inculcate a sense of disillusionment and cynicism and obliterate a sense of hope and purpose. The issue of words and how we use them became for him a test of how we face living and dying.

"In writing for a newspaper," he reported in *Death in the Afternoon*,

> you told what happened and, with one trick or another, you communicated the emotion aided by the element of timeliness . . . ; but the real thing, the sequence of motion and fact which made the emotion and which would be as valid in a year or ten years or, with luck and if you stated it purely enough, always, was beyond me and I was working very hard to get it.[22]

Hunting, fishing, and bullfighting were subjects that lent themselves to ordered movement from one detail to the next. Writing about them, Hemingway found a way of renewing and even purifying language. If a part of his commitment was to putting "down what really happened," another was to "knowing truly what you really felt," however ugly it might be, "rather than what you were supposed to feel" or had been taught to feel. He was drawn to the "simplest things" because they were fundamental; and in a violent world "one of the simplest things of all and the most fundamental," he said, "is violent death."

In Hemingway's self-conscious style, including his practice of using simple words in economical ways, we also recognize a passion, both American and modern, for technique. Hemingway treats language as a tool or an instrument. He calls attention to new ways of using familiar words, much as modern painters call attention to their brush strokes and colors. In a 1958 interview, he described his sense of how a writer makes things new: "From things that have happened and from things as they exist and from all the things that you know and all those that you cannot know, you make something through your own invention that is not a representation but a whole new thing truer than any thing true and alive." "Big Two-Hearted River," to take an example, is grounded in his knowledge of fishing the Fox River north of Seney, Michigan. But in writing the story, he told Stein, he was "trying to do [his] country like Cezanne" had done the Provence in paintings that helped shape cubism.

Convinced that his wounds were necessary preparations for serious writing, Hemingway assumed that in one way or another wounds were necessary to others, too. We are all wounded "from the start," he wrote Fitzgerald in 1934. "But when you get the damned hurt use it – don't cheat with it. Be as faithful to it as a scientist." Faithfulness in Hemingway's case meant bringing style as technique to bear on fear. His deepest subject turned on the analogy he created between the performance of a writer and that of a person – soldier, hunter, bullfighter – facing danger and even death. "Writing, at its best, is a lonely life," he observed in a letter accepting the Nobel Prize. For a writer "does his work alone and if he is a good enough writer he must face eternity, or the lack of it, each day." The bullfight, as we see in *Death in the Afternoon*, epitomized this fundamental life-and-death predicament for him because he thought it the only art "in which the artist is [literally] in danger of death and in which the degree of brilliance in the performance is left to the fighter's honor." In the bullring, style ("purity of line") and courage ("grace under pressure") become inseparable. But similar control is also necessary for good writing because writing always tests the limits of the writer's courage and integrity. Hemingway stripped his style bare because he believed that beauty required control and knew that control was difficult. In *In Our Time* (1925), and especially in "Big Two-Hearted River," we become aware that Nick is holding tight to details of the landscape and the rules that govern such simple activities as making a camp and building a fire in order to cope with the darknesses welling up within as well as around him. As his taut actions find expression in sharp, clear, precise prose, we feel the encroachment of a legacy of losses so severe that life has become a killing field in which a single slip spells disaster.

Hemingway considered naming *The Sun Also Rises* (1926) "The Lost Generation." And the novel quickly became, as Edmund Wilson observed, the era's favorite expression of romantic disillusion and the source of its favorite poses – of stoic heartbreak, grim, nonchalant banter, and heroic dissipation. In bars from New Orleans and Memphis to Chicago, New York, and Paris, young people tried to sound like Hemingway's characters as they drank evenings away, hoping somehow to force more pleasure, or at least gratification, out of life. But *The Sun Also Rises* does not trace the advent of a new era of pleasure. It modifies the disillusionment of the twenties by introducing a depth of feeling and sentimentality that are almost wholly absent in *In Our Time*. The stoicism that Hemingway adopts in one sense and that his protagonists adopt in another serves as the last shield of truly vulnerable people who feel more than they dare admit. Brett Ashley and Jacob Barnes know themselves to be living in a world that has lost its way. Personal desires and public rituals are all they have and less than they need. Behind them lies a better life somehow already lost. "Could we but live at will upon this perfect height . . . ," said the Irish poet Lionel Johnson, "then we were all divine." But fleeting glimpses of such moments are all that any of Hemingway's characters can hope for, and few can hope for that. Even the luckiest move from one approximation to the next, trying to find a way to comport themselves in a harsh world. The style they seek to master provides them a way of carrying on, the hope that life lived under proper pressure will yield them some understanding of themselves and their world.

The ending of *A Farewell to Arms,* of which Hemingway wrote more than thirty versions, takes us back toward the war, and it is even more crippled than the ending of *The Sun Also Rises*. It leaves Frederic Henry alone, in the grips of an advanced form of neurasthenia, in which, as Anaïs Nin observed, life and art seem to be slipping away, leaving people alone, drifting with time and fighting with shadows. Overmatched, Henry declares a separate peace of his own, hoping to make withdrawal and disengagement the center of his life. When he first meets Catherine Barkley, a beautiful young English nurse whose manner resembles Brett Ashley's, he sees her merely as a substitute for going out "every evening to the house for officers where the girls climbed all over you and put your cap on backwards as a sign of affection between their trips upstairs with brother officers." When he finally realizes that Catherine is drawing him out of his protective shell, everything turns over inside him. "We could be close," he says, "when we were together, alone against the others." In the end, however, after Catherine and their child die, he is left alone again, completely cut off. Sitting in the darkened room with Catherine's body, he tries to feel something but cannot. The closest he comes to real emotion is envy for the child that has died at birth, choked by its own umbilical cord. In short, he is even farther gone than Krebs, the protagonist of "Soldier's Home."

> He [Krebs] would have liked to have a girl but he did not want to have to spend a long time getting her. He did not want to get into the intrigue and the politics. He did not want to have to do any courting. He did not want to tell any more lies. It wasn't worth it.
>
> He did not want any consequences. He did not want any consequences ever again. He wanted to live alone without consequences. Besides he did not really need a girl. The army had taught him that.[23]

Death, not love, became Hemingway's true subject – including the kind of death that starts as a consuming desire for release and becomes a consuming desire for peace. Style became his means of confronting death as well as his means of holding out against it because it offered him the possibility of controlling even moments of maximum pressure.

In the introduction to *Paris Was Yesterday: 1925–1939,* Janet Flanner recounts a conversation with Hemingway in which the two of them shared the fact that their fathers had committed suicide:

> Our talk ended with the mutual declaration that if either of us ever killed ourself, the other was not to grieve but to remember that liberty could be as important in the act of dying as in the acts of living. So, years later, I . . . had automatically recognized that fatal gunshot as his mortal act of gaining liberty. But I grieved deeply when the pitiful facts of his final bondage were made public. . . . At Ernest's death, I grieved most because he died in a state of ruin.[24]

At the end of *For Whom the Bell Tolls* (1940), Hemingway pictures Robert Jordan alone, badly injured, waiting for the enemy to come, hoping that his wait will not last long because he does not know how much pain he can bear. "Oh, let them come, he said. I don't want to do that business that my father did." Later, thinking again about suicide, he says that perhaps it would "be all right" to get "the whole thing . . . over with." Still he waits, trying to think about other things – about his comrades, or about Montana or Madrid – hoping to blot out the mounting pain. It would be all right, he says, to end it, but waiting, holding out is better as long as there is something one can do that may make a difference: "*One thing well done can make –*" he thinks, as he holds on. At the book's end we see him, "his heart beating against the pine needle floor of the forest," waiting with his submachine gun in the crook of his arm, as nameless and almost faceless enemies come up the trail toward him, knowing that when he fires, they will fire, and then it will all be over.

By the time he died, Hemingway was ravaged more by disease, injuries, and weariness than by age, and he had lost control of his art as well as his life. His career, having suffered a decline, had undergone a revival with the publication of *The Old Man and the Sea* (1952), in part, as Delmore Schwartz observed, because people found just enough in it to remind them of what a great writer he had been at his best. In fact, however, he published few works after the twenties that were as good as *In Our Time, The Sun Also Rises, Men Without Women* (1927), and *A Farewell to Arms,* and all of them were short stories: some of those in *Winner Take Nothing* (1933), for example, and later still "The Snows of Kilimanjaro" and "The Short, Happy Life of Francis Macomber." In them we see again his effort to reclaim simple, spare, disciplined prose for art – and his effort to make the act of writing a model of how a truly vulnerable self can make its way against great odds, long enough to do something worthwhile. "I know you don't like the sort of thing I write," he wrote his father in 1927, recalling the hurt he had felt when his mother condemned *The Sun Also Rises*. But "I *know* that I am not disgracing you in my writing but rather doing something that some day you will be proud of. . . . you cannot know how it makes me feel for Mother to be ashamed of what I know as sure as you know that there is a God in heaven is *not to be ashamed of.*" "Suicide is prepared within the silence of the heart," Albert Camus wrote, "as is a great work of art." In books punctuated by violence, loss, death, and disillusionment, Hemingway not only illumined his world. He also held out against the final act of destruction that drew him, sustained by faith, not in art's power to redeem social life in his time, but more modestly in the power of writing to provide models of effective resistance for writers like himself and for readers like the sister he called "Littless," in their uneven contests to protect their shared humanity.

PART THREE

The Fate of Writing during the Great Depression

1. *THE DISCOVERY OF POVERTY AND THE RETURN OF COMMITMENT*

When the Crash of October 1929 ended the biggest speculative binge in the nation's history, it brought the Roaring Twenties to a close. Scary economic indicators had been gathering for years. Farm income and industrial wages remained low throughout the twenties, and by 1929, with 35 percent of all personal income going into the pockets of 5 percent of the population, even the middle class was showing signs of stress. Residential construction, consumer spending, industrial production, commodity prices, and employment were going down while business inventories were going up. Looking back on the late twenties from the vantage point of the early thirties, F. Scott Fitzgerald located signs of anxiety in everything from the "nervous beating of feet" and the sudden "popularity of cross-word puzzles" to the remembered faces of Princeton classmates who had disappeared "into the dark maw of violence" before the Crash, including one who had jumped from a skyscraper and another who had "crawled home" to die at the high-toned Princeton Club after being beaten in a Manhattan speakeasy. But it took a crash to counter what Zelda Fitzgerald called "the infinite promises of American advertising." Borrow to buy was one message, borrow to invest, another. Bankers, brokers, and political leaders directed the campaign; newspapers, magazines, and radios executed it. McNeel's of Boston was one of countless "financial service" operations that specialized in persuading people they could get rich on borrowed money – a message politicians in Washington endorsed. On December 4, 1928, in his last address to Congress, President Coolidge assured the nation that it could "regard the present with satisfaction and anticipate the future with optimism."

In terms of technical training, business experience, and public service, Herbert Hoover was better prepared to be president than Coolidge had been. But he believed in the alliance forged between business and government during the twenties and saw no reason to change anything. "We in America," he said during his campaign, "are nearer the final triumph over poverty than ever before in the history of any land. . . . Given a chance to go forward with the policies of the last eight years, we shall soon with the help of God be in the sight of the day when poverty will be banished from this nation." "I have no fears for the future of our country," he added in his inaugural address, echoing Coolidge again. "It is bright with hope." And so the nation splurged and the market soared. On September 11, 1929, with signs of trouble spreading, the *Wall Street Journal* gave the nation this "thought for the day," borrowed from Mark Twain: "Don't part with your illusions; when they are gone you may still exist, but you have ceased to live."

During the Lyric Years, the nation's citizens – "the almost chosen people," as Lincoln called them not long before he died – had assumed that peace and prosperity would last. Following the tainted peace of Versailles, they cut foreign entanglements in order to concentrate on becoming history's heirs. Caught up in speculation and self-indulgence, they began making, spending, and investing money at a record pace. In 1923 the volume of sales on the New York Stock Exchange topped 236 million shares for the first time. In 1928 it exceeded 1.1 billion shares. Through the early fall of 1929, the market continued to rise, as droves of new investors entered the fray, many of them on money borrowed in a tight credit market. Meanwhile, millions followed the market as spectators, dreaming of the day when they, too, would get rich. In the first eight months of Hoover's administration, the *New York Times* average of selected industrial stocks jumped from 250 to 450.

Late in September and again in mid-October, the market shuddered, and on the 23rd it began a slide that neither the bankers and brokers in New York nor the politicians in Washington could halt. Within two weeks, the *New York Times* average of selected industrial stocks fell 228 points, from 452 to 224, triggering a fall in which securities listed on the New York Stock Exchange lost more than 40 percent of their total value. Words of assurance continued to float out of President Hoover's mouth. "America is sound," he insisted. But his words had lost credibility. "Yes, America is sound," replied Gilbert Seldes. "The sound is hollow."

By 1932, after years of decline, it seemed that everyone was either in trouble or threatened by it and that no one – neither the president and his secretary of the treasury, Andrew Mellon, nor the governors and mayors – knew what to do. In three years following the Crash, national income fell from $81 billion to $41 billion; new capital issues fell from $10 billion to $1 billion; 85,000 businesses, with liabilities of more than $4.5 billion, failed; and 5,000 banks closed, wiping out more than 9 million savings accounts. In 1931 alone, 2,294 banks failed, an average of 45 per week. Between 1930 and 1934, unemployment tripled, leaving between 13 and 16 million people out of work. Farm income, already low, fell 65 percent and the value of stocks traded on the New York Stock Exchange fell 78 percent.

By the winter of 1932–3, the nation was mired in the deepest crisis it had faced since the Civil War. As unemployment rose, social and economic mobility plummeted, particularly for women, the urban poor, and all people of color. Meanwhile, two shifts in population began reversing themselves. In 1932 emigrants fleeing the "land of opportunity" outnumbered immigrants entering it three to one. Similarly, the migration of people from farms to cities, which had been spurred for six decades by the nation's rapid incorporation of itself, slowed and then reversed, as people lost faith in the promise of their new urban, industrial civilization and turned back toward the land. In literature, a revival of agrarian utopianism gained in popularity in the North as well as the South, the Midwest, and the West. Meanwhile, in bread lines, soup kitchens, and shantytowns, called "Hoovervilles," people who had grown accustomed to thinking of themselves as proud and self-reliant learned to beg for assistance.

Spurred by anger and despair, hundreds of thousands of men and young boys as well as thousands of women left their homes to ride the rails, seeking release in motion. Some of those who stayed at home gathered around radios purchased in better days to hear the latest antics of Amos 'n Andy or the smooth sounds of Duke Ellington and Benny Goodman; others sought relief in the darkness of local picture shows. "Motion pictures offered several avenues of escape" from the burdens of "hard times" and "daily woes," the *New York Times* reported in December 1935: Clark Gable in *Mutiny on the Bounty,* Errol Flynn in *Captain Blood,* Gary Cooper in *Lives of a Bengal Lancer,* Greta Garbo in *Anna Karenina,* Marlene Dietrich in *The Devil Is a Woman,* Bette Davis in *Dangerous,* and the Marx Brothers in *A Night at the Opera.* Meanwhile, readers made best-sellers of novels like Hervey Allen's *Anthony Adverse* (1933), which entertained them with the glamorous adventures of a hero in Napoleonic Europe, and Kenneth Roberts's *Northwest Passage* (1937), which carried them back to a time when the nation's sense of shared purpose had been rising rather than falling.

By contrast, confidence in the future plummeted: during the thirties, the marriage rate fell sharply, the birthrate plunged to its lowest level in history, and the suicide rate rose. Soon ordinary people began to fear that the whole political economy might collapse, while those more radical, or more skeptical, began to suspect that there was something fundamentally wrong with the nation's way of life. By 1932 – when 15,000 veterans joined a protest march on Washington and more than 1 million voters cast votes for candidates on the radical fringes of the political spectrum – ordinary people were listening to drastic solutions. Some followed leaders like Huey Long and Father Charles Coughlin. Others listened to leaders of the Communist Party. "I wish we might double the number of Communists in the country," said Father John Ryan, "to put the fear, if not of God, then . . . of something else, into the hearts of our leaders." In cities, hunger marches sprang up; in the country, farmers banded together to protect their homes and farms from foreclosures. Bankers and businessmen, objects of adulation in the twenties, became objects of scorn. People challenged their right to collect bills, denounced their high-sounding ideals as self-serving, and repudiated their claims to be the nation's rightful leaders.

Given their ebullience and considerable cultural achievements, the twenties, once gone, were sure to evoke nostalgia of the kind we hear in Fitzgerald's "Echoes of the Jazz Age" (1931). Yet writers as different as Frederick Lewis

Allen, Malcolm Cowley, Josephine Herbst, Genevieve Taggard, and James Thurber soon expressed a sense of relief that the long splurge had come to an end. Not having shared the booming prosperity of the United States, England and Europe were spared the startling reversal that inspired wry signs of the kind Thurber spotted in a small shop on 14th Street: "Busted & Disgusted." But George Orwell located in England a shift that bears striking resemblance to the one that took place in the United States, from "the twilight of the gods into a sort of Boy Scout atmosphere of bare knees and community singing." Soon writers were acting more like eager-minded schoolchildren bent on studying the past and organizing reform movements than like cultural refugees left with nothing to fall back on except the lonely discipline of writing and the shared pursuit of pleasure and prosperity: "If the keynote of the writers of the 'twenties is 'tragic sense of life,' " Orwell noted, "the keynote of the new writers is 'serious purpose.' "

Stark economic realities and new political intensities distanced the twenties from the thirties. But the abrupt shift spurred efforts to examine the past as a way of understanding the present. With the sense that a dramatic break had occurred came the sense that the lost world lay close by – Only Yesterday, as Frederick Lewis Allen put it in a book published in 1931. As heirs of a bloodless tradition that drained literature of social responsibility, "palefaced aesthetes" were in bad repute. Refugees of the twenties apologized for having thought of art as above politics, and they sought what writers of the twenties had shunned: a sense of continuity with the immediate past. Looking backward, Herbst saw the twenties not as a unified period of parties, miracles, satire, jazz, and art, but as a jumble in which unfashionable ideas like social service had continued to attract champions. She found, in other words, a world that resembled, beneath its surface, the "soul-shattering" world of the thirties, "which had come in like a hurricane," sweeping a whole generation into "violent protest." Dos Passos's U.S.A. reaches back through the twenties to the Lyric Years in order to set the loss that the Crash inflicted against the gains it opened up, by making the carelessness that prevailed in the twenties the only possible starting point for understanding the commitment of the thirties.

That commitment remains difficult to gauge, however, in terms of its depth and ideological grounding. Shortly after writing "Echoes of the Jazz Age," describing the twenties as having "no interest in politics at all," Fitzgerald began what he thought of as a serious study of the writings of Karl Marx. "To bring about the revolution," he observed in his Notebooks, "it may be necessary to work inside the communist party." Hoping to infuse his fiction with his new politics, he wrote a note to himself describing Dick Diver of Tender Is the Night as "a communist-liberal-idealist, a moralist in revolt." Fitzgerald had in fact always thought of himself as a "liberal-idealist"; even in the twenties he occasionally called himself a "socialist." In the changed world of the early thirties, the call for political commitment appealed to him. But he remained ill-suited for party work of any kind and ill-equipped for critical engagement with ideologically based theory. By 1934, when he finished his elegiac story of Dick Diver's decline in *Tender Is the Night,* he had decided to give up politics once again, leaving it, as he had in the twenties, to people like Edmund Wilson, whom he called his "intellectual conscience" – first, because worrying about politics drained his waning energies; second, because he found it impossible to infuse his fiction with any explicit ideology; and third, because he had begun to suspect that the "Great Change" he believed in conflicted with his "allegiance to the class" he was "part of."

The speed of Fitzgerald's conversion and recantation was extreme even in a decade characterized by quick moves. But it is telling on several counts, not least because it reminds us that in terms of relations between politics and literature the thirties differed in significant degree but not in kind from the twenties. Looking back on the twenties, Herbst saw "crumbs and pieces which completely contradict each other." "It was all flux and change," she concluded, where even "ideas of social service, justice, and religious reaction had their special spokesman." Such words suggest what Herbst believed: that the novels of writers like Anderson, Cummings, Dos Passos, Fitzgerald, Hemingway, Lewis, and Stein remain deeply if not overtly political. But they should also warn us to be skeptical of such familiar terms as "the Red Decade" or even "the Angry Decade."

Many writers of the thirties made conscious moves toward the political Left, and they often stayed there longer than Fitzgerald. Ideology played a far more conspicuous role in their fiction than it had in the fiction of the preceding decade. But few if any writers of the thirties – Kenneth Burke, who was, of course, also a writer of the twenties, being a possible exception – made significant contributions to radical theory. And most of the representative works of the period, including those identified with the radical Left, are more deeply infused with fervent feeling – the sense of working together in the name of loosely defined yet fervently held ideas and beliefs; the sense, in Cowley's words, of "being not leader, but just one in the ranks of the great army that was marching toward a new dawn" – than with any clear revolutionary commitment or specific political strategy. For a time, they helped to tilt the country away from its fascination with material possessions and its habit of judging human worth as well as success in terms of money. The nation was less materialistic and more community-minded during the thirties than in any other decade of the twentieth century. But strong countercurrents, individualistic and even antinomian, continued to find expression in the thirties, and so did a kind of nativism or nationalism. Even writers whose work was most revisionary – writers who managed to reconceive the nature of culture and rethink the issue of how it worked and who it served – retained a fascination with the nation's culture that was at bottom a form of loyalty to it. The drastic change they hoped to accomplish they thought of as rooted in native soil. Pressing forward "toward a new dawn," they looked to the past – to the Lyric Years, especially, but also to abolitionists and to Emerson, Whitman, and Thomas Paine, among others – for guides who could help them decide what "serious purpose" might mean.

2. THE SEARCH FOR "CULTURE" AS A FORM OF COMMITMENT

Political commitment found expression in explorations of the national mood such as Louis Adamic's *My America* (1938), Sherwood Anderson's *Puzzled America* (1935), Nathan Asch's *The Road: In Search of America* (1939), Theodore Dreiser's *Tragic America* (1932), and Edmund Wilson's *American Jitters* (1932). It found expression in explicitly proletarian writing that Granville Hicks and others collected in *Proletarian Literature in the United States* (1935). It found expression in numerous "radical" novels – many of them autobiographical and all of them more fervently felt than rigorously "proletarian" – which included Nelson Algren's *Somebody in Boots* (1935), Thomas Bell's *Out of This Furnace* (1941), Robert Cantwell's *Land of Plenty* (1934), Jack Conroy's *The Disinherited* (1933), Edward Dahlberg's *Bottom Dogs* (1930), Daniel Fuchs's *Summer in Williamsburg* (1934), Michael Gold's *Jews Without Money* (1930), Albert Maltz's *The Underground Stream* (1940), Tess Slesinger's *The Unpossessed* (1934), and Clara Weatherman's *Marching! Marching!* (1935). And it found expression in a vast "documentary literature": films, recordings, and paintings as well as books about the lives, mores, and values of "the people" that culminated in a series of striking collaborations between writers and photographers, including James Agee and Walker Evans's *Let Us Now Praise Famous Men* (1941); Sherwood Anderson's *Home Town* (1940), for which Edwin Rosskam selected Farm Security Administration photographs; Margaret Bourke-White and Erskine Caldwell's *You Have Seen Their Faces* (1937); Dorothea Lange and Paul S. Taylor's *An American Exodus* (1939); Archibald MacLeish's *Land of the Free* (1938), which used FSA photographs; and Richard Wright's *Twelve Million Black Voices* (1941), for which Edwin Rosskam again selected FSA photographs.

The vast documentary movement of the thirties extended the boundaries of "literature" and also exposed the problematics imbedded in U.S. radicalism. Documentary works vary in quality. None of them, not even Agee's, is sophisticated ideologically. At times, for example, they move toward a kind of agrarian utopianism that runs so contrary to the basic urban thrust of modern history as to seem both nostalgic and anti-ideological. Much of their considerable power derives from a fascination with the culture they inscribe. They look to the future by locating grounds of hope in the painful present and the failed past. Each of them is in this deep sense an act of critical loyalty. They are "revisionary" primarily because they redefine "culture" so as to reclaim it for "the people." Having queried, judged, and dismissed the distinction between "high" and "low" culture, they go on to make a discovery that alters the meaning of "culture" itself. Implicit in Nick Carraway's tone, as well as in Sinclair Lewis's and H. L. Mencken's, is an elitist notion of "culture" that often echoes some of Matthew Arnold's famous definitions – of "criticism," for example, as a "disinterested endeavour to learn and propagate the best that is known and thought in the world," and of "Culture" as consisting of the "best that has been known and said in the world, and thus with the history of the human spirit." What writers of the thirties move toward is a sense of the interrelatedness, or seamlessness, of culture as the interactive play of all the institutions and organizations that make up the political economy of a society and all the mores, manners, and customs, all the rules and regulations, both legal and moral, all the tools and gadgets, all the games and dreams as well as the art, music, philosophy, and literature that shape and express the work, play, and love of a people. In different ways, two terms that gained currency during the thirties – "the American way of life" and "the American dream" – reinforced this sense of the seamlessness of culture. But documentary works also performed, more or less surreptitiously, another set of tasks. They defined the process of building a culture as a quest for value and meaning, they assumed that quest to be collective, and they pointed to haunting discrepancies between the promises and the realities of life in the United States. Ironically, however, in documenting the failures of the nation's industrial civilization, they reiterated its promise.

One part of the broad, eclectic reassessment of the New World as no longer new unfolded as a search for rhetorical ties with the past. This search – which found expression in novels by Herbst, Dos Passos, and scores of others, as well as in travel writings, autobiographies, biographies, and histories – is a tribute to how scary the thirties were and to how resourceful its writers became. Biographies, particularly of people forced to grapple with crises, multiplied – of John Brown by Robert Penn Warren, of Jefferson Davis and Stonewall Jackson by Allen Tate, of Abraham Lincoln by Carl Sandburg, and of Mark Twain by Bernard De Voto, to name a few. When looking toward the past, writers of the twenties had specialized in finding stories of frustrated or deflected purpose. Their novels trace the adventures of people who voluntarily uproot themselves and become nomadic exiles. Writers of the thirties, feeling more threatened as well as more entangled, wrote less as spectators and observers armed with irony than as citizens committed to telling the stories of heroes who deal successfully, or at least gallantly, with social crises. When they turned to stories of marginal people, as they frequently did, they focused on the truly marginal – people aware of their lack of status and their vulnerability. Protagonists of the thirties do not move from place to place voluntarily, pulled by hope – as Isabel Archer, Carrie Meeber, Jim Burden, George Willard, Jay Gatsby, and Nick Carraway do; they move involuntarily, driven by privation, anger, or despair, or pursued by the same law that lets Tom and Daisy Buchanan go free. As the thirties lengthened and the grip of the Depression held, Van Wyck Brooks, in *The Flowering of New England, 1815–1865* (1936) and *New England: Indian Summer* (1940), turned his ransacking of the past into a search for both obscure and well-known heroes of difficult hope. Summing up a many-faceted effort in *The Ground We Stand On* (1941), Dos Passos found words that enact the search for rhetorical ties that they also proclaim: "In times of change and danger, when there is a quicksand of fear under men's reasoning, a sense of continuity with generations gone before can stretch like a lifeline across the scary present."

With the Great War behind them, political leaders like Harding and Coolidge had begun talking as though both the idea of prosperity and an economy of plenty were their own inventions, paying little attention to the debts their ideas owed to the nation's past or the debt the prosperity they administered owed to the Progressive Era. Practicing their own form of willed forgetfulness, writers of the twenties declared themselves cut off from everything except a few madmen and prophets of the past, largely ignoring the roots their remarkable stylistic and formal experiments had in the prewar poetry of Frost, Eliot, and Pound and the prewar prose of James, Dreiser, and Stein. Feeling bereft was critical to their identity. In fact, however, the real if sometimes shaky confidence that sustained them possessed cultural roots as well as generational ties. Fitzgerald and his contemporaries assumed that the literature of the United States was coming of age, and they knew that the country was emerging as one of immense power and prosperity. Yet they continued to write "jeremiads," lamenting almost to the point of strange ecstasy the nation's failings. And in doing so they brought success under the aspect of failure, failure under the aspect of success, and both under the aspect of restless yearning, the emotion most deeply imbedded in the country's sense of itself as a land of tinkerers, inventors, and dreamers. Even writers who stayed in Europe long enough to draw sustenance from it – Stein and Hemingway, to take very different examples, or Eliot and Pound – tended to think of Europe as a world of endings and of the United States as a world of beginnings. In *The Making of Americans,* Stein presents her family's move from Europe to this country as a move from the world's old center to its new center, which is to say, from the past toward the future. Her story, she says, is not simply hers or her family's or her nation's; it is "everybody's history."

The literary potential of the cultural predicament that writers of the twenties claimed as their own emerged in statements like John Peale Bishop's assertion that Hemingway had written the drama of the disappearance of the human soul "in our time." Bishop's remark assumes that dramatic cultural events require imaginative works strong enough to trace them. More surreptitiously, it assumes that imaginative works require critical discourse strong enough to make visible their tracings. Bishop signals both the coming of age of literature in the United States and the professionalization of its study. "In opulent and commercial societies," Adam Smith predicted, thinking and writing will become "like every other employment, a particular business, which is carried out by a very few people, who furnish the public with all the thought and reason possessed by the vast multitudes that labour." The production of novels, for example, like the production of thought and reason, became a specialized function. Novels spread as the institution of commercial publishing spread to produce and distribute them as commodities. In 1928 Paul Rosenfeld left the prestigious *Dial,* which was devoted to international modernism, to become editor of *American Caravan*, which was dedicated to publishing new young American writers. A year later, after nearly five years of planning, Jay B. Hubbell and others announced the establishment of *American Literature: A Journal of Literary History, Criticism, and Bibliography*.

Writers of the thirties wanted to reorient the tasks of producing and distributing creative and critical texts, first, by making more explicit the ties between cultural events and imaginative discoveries and, second, by using critical discourse to make visible the social logic of literary discoveries. At their best, they also sought to clarify the ties between literature's social logic and the imaginative discoveries that accompanied them by rooting the present in the past and by tying literature to the culture of which it was a part. Cowley's work changed in the thirties, and so did Edmund Wilson's, as he moved from *Axel's Castle* (1931) through *The American Jitters* (1932) and *Travels in Two Democracies* (1936), based on his visit in Russia, toward *To the Finland Station* (1940). Kenneth Burke's work not only changed; in its deep concern for the social, political power of rhetoric, symbol, and myth, it found its proper home in the thirties. In her path-breaking work, *American Humor: A Study of the National Character* (1931), Constance Rourke sought to discover the roots of the nation's culture not in a few great, isolated figures of the past but in the larger cultural patterns in which ordinary people lived their lives and from which writers drew their material.

"Change the world" became a slogan of the thirties, Herbst observed, because "the world had changed." Joseph Freeman, heir of the Lyric Years, continued to talk as he always had. Hope for him still lay in calling on the working class of the United States to resume its revolutionary "path toward the New World." But "the great knife of the depression," as Robert and Helen Lynd observed in their update of *Middletown*, *Middletown in Transition* (1937), had cut through "the entire population cleaving open lives and hopes of rich as well as poor." And for a time, especially in 1932 and 1933, the world seemed to tremble with possibility. "I'm afraid, every man is afraid," said Charles Schwab of U.S. Steel. It was, Edmund Wilson announced in the *New Republic* in January 1931, as if life had come suddenly under a shadow so dark that the nation's "whole money-making and -spending psychology" had finally become discredited, leading people to "put their idealism and their genius for organization behind a radical social experiment."

In the large cultural task of placing the call for social experimentation, literature broadly defined – historical studies, personal reminiscences, and critical discourse as well as poetry, drama, and fiction – played a crucial role. Movements sprang up on the Right as well as the Left. But most writers, old as well as young, followed the advice of Michael Gold in an editorial in *New Masses* in 1929: "Go Left, Young Writers." By 1932, with hunger and bankruptcy spreading as though by invisible means, leaving millions of once-proud people desperate, "communism" loosely defined was on the rise. To a few, including Lincoln Steffens, Russia was a model of the kind of "faith, hope, liberty, a living" that the United States had once advocated and ought to copy.

To others – John Dos Passos and James T. Farrell, for example – Marxist thought seemed valuable primarily as an analytic tool. In 1932 Cowley and Wilson joined Waldo Frank, Mary Heaton Vorse, and others in supporting Kentucky's striking coal miners. What they saw – several miners shot and several supporters, including Frank, beaten – pushed them farther to the Left. That same year, Cowley, Herbst, and Wilson joined fifty other writers, including Sherwood Anderson, Dos Passos, Langston Hughes, and Steffens, in issuing a pamphlet, *Culture and Crisis,* that described the nation as "a house rotting away."

For many people, however, communism was more attractive as a secular religion, preaching an old morality of self-denial and sacrifice in service to a noble cause, than as a program for action. People who joined the Party, Cowley later remarked, were listened to, even by people like himself, who did not, "as if they had received advice straight from God." To a considerable degree, however, their authority depended on their vagueness. Recognizing the psychological as well as the social impact of the Depression, Party leaders welcomed almost anyone committed to reform, whether or not they understood the Party's tenets. Political tracts, manifestos, and petitions proliferated, but few of them were rigorous in theory or clear about strategy. Specific issues of real import tended to divide the Party, and clearly stated positions on tough issues regularly led to defections from it.

Franklin Delano Roosevelt was born in 1882 and began his study of politics during the Progressive Era, when the written word and traditional discourse, not the radio or newsreel, dominated political campaigns. In his speeches of 1932, Roosevelt anticipated several programs that became parts of the "New Deal." He sketched plans for the Civilian Conservation Corps and advocated both social welfare legislation and government regulation of utilities. There was considerable vagueness in what he said, however, and some contradiction. Still, he carried forty-two of forty-eight states, including every state west and south of Pennsylvania, which is to say, those farthest from his own center of activity. The vote, though clearly a rejection of Hoover, was also a triumph for Roosevelt. And it anticipated others to come by demonstrating his skill as a rhetorician in dominating the radio as a medium.

Roosevelt not only recognized the possibilities of the radio and its networks in a new era of sound; he also understood the importance of using actions and words as symbols. "Let it be symbolic," he told the cheering convention that had nominated him, "that I broke the tradition," calling attention to his unprecedented decision to fly to Chicago to accept the nomination in person. Henceforth, he added, let it be the "task of our Party to break foolish traditions." Later, first in his inaugural address and then in his famous "fireside chats," he entered the "homes" of "the people" to make them feel that he was speaking specifically to them of their hopes and fears, and that he was mindful of their places in and their dependence upon the land he was pledged to renew. In the process, he created a new kind of presidency, of unprecedented political and social power, based on his ability to persuade the people that, in pledging to discard the foolish, reform the outmoded, save the essential, and create the new, his voice was theirs. In the crucial campaign of 1932, in calling for a new era of bold experimentation, he showed himself to be more rhetorically and more historically minded than either Coolidge or Hoover. The urge to tinker and experiment – the desire to foster change and embrace the new – lay, he insisted, at the heart of the nation's great historic tradition. In his only use of the keyword "revolution" in the crucial year of 1932, he stayed within that tradition: "the right kind, the only kind of revolution this nation can stand for," he said, was a "revolution at the ballot box." Once elected, his New Deal emerged slowly as a mix of humanitarianism, realistic politics, and economic common sense. But with the help of the radio, it found a name, taken from a throwaway line in an early speech, that was consistent with the spirit of "bold, persistent experimentation" that he had rediscovered for and reawakened in "the people."

The New Deal was neither as radical as some have charged nor as timid as others have claimed. Given time to emerge and work, it saved the country's capitalist political economy by modifying it and created new social arrangements by redefining what democracy might mean. Part of this it owed to Roosevelt's ability to conceive government defining ends and taking actions that Hoover could not imagine. But much of it depended on his genius for finding words that rooted his reforms in the nation's past and then using the radio to dispatch those words into homes across the land. "Every man has a right to life," he said in September 1932, "and this means that he has also a right to make a comfortable living. . . . Our government, formal and informal, political and economic, owes to everyone an avenue to possess himself of a portion of the plenty" created by our society "sufficient for his needs, through his work." "Republican leaders not only failed in material things, they have failed in national vision, because in disaster they had held out no hope," he told cheering delegates at the Democratic Convention in Chicago. "Let me assert my firm belief," he said, in the most famous line in his inaugural address, "that the only thing we have to fear is fear itself."

At first, Walter Lippmann, author of *The New Imperative* (1935) and *The Good Society* (1937), was skeptical of Roosevelt. Roosevelt was pleasant, Lippmann wrote in 1932, but he was highly impressionable, lacked strong convictions, and possessed no important qualifications for the office he aspired to hold. Shortly after Roosevelt's inauguration, however, Lippmann sensed a turnabout that struck him as earned. "At the beginning of March," Lippmann wrote, "the country was in . . . a state of confused desperation." By June it was regaining "confidence in the government and in itself." Broad restoration of confidence came slowly, of course, and complete economic recovery took years. Even after 1935, when some of the worst signs of the Depression had vanished, apprehension continued to run high. But the reforms that became the New Deal began quickly, with legislation designed to put agriculture and industry on sounder footing and to bring relief to hard-pressed home owners (the Home Owners Loan Act) and unemployed workers (the Civilian Conservation Corps). As radios continued to carry Roosevelt's voice into homes throughout the country – not only in his own news conferences and "fireside chats" but also in Henry Luce's "March of Time," founded in 1931 as a radio program and then changed to a newsreel in 1935 – more and more people identified his ameliorating reforms with what "American" radicalism meant.

As the New Deal gained support, literary radicalism began to function more as a mode of cultural criticism than as a means of promoting radical action. One sign of this unfolded as something we might call the Americanization of Karl Marx, or, more broadly, of Marxist thought. "I can only welcome Communism by converting it into my own vocabulary. I am, in the deepest sense, a translator," Kenneth Burke wrote. "I go on translating, even if I must but translate English into English." A brilliant student of rhetoric, Burke knew that some things get lost in translation. But he also believed that many were saved and a few discovered. At the famous American Writers' Congress in April 1935, he examined the social function of revolutionary symbols and myths as tools that enabled carpenters and welders to discover "a sense of interrelationship by which . . ., though differently occupied, [they] can work together for a common social end." By 1935, however, Roosevelt was proving himself more effective in using symbols and myths than the Party was, and his aim was ameliorative, not revolutionary.

On this count, as on several others, literature followed politics more than it led. As signs of recovery increased, writers began drawing on "native" traditions and idioms – "translating," as it were – with curious results. "I felt myself to be a radical, not an ideologue," Alfred Kazin later recalled in *Starting Out in the Thirties* (1965). "I was proud of the revolutionary yet wholly literary tradition in American writing to which I knew that I belonged," he adds, assuming that a revolutionary tradition can remain wholly literary. In short, several forms of innocence survived the battering thirties just as they had the disillusioning twenties, and they inspired writers to try odd things. "What young writers of the thirties wanted," Kazin wrote,

> was to prove the literary value of our own experience, to recognize the possibility of art in our own lives, to feel we had moved the streets, the stockyards, the hiring halls into literature – to show that our radical strength could carry on the experimental impulse of modern literature.[1]

Versions of what Kazin called a literature of "strong social argument, intellectual power, [and] human liberation" turned up repeatedly. In their expressed desire to embrace previously nonliterary scenes and subjects, writers changed "realist" fiction and contributed to the emergence of documentary literature. But Kazin's statement is also notable for tensions it leaves unresolved, and these too are representative – particularly those between personal experience and ambition, on one side, and social realities and responsibilities, on the other. Ultimately, Kazin locates his hope for deliverance in words employed, not as Burke advocated or as Roosevelt practiced, but as poets were thought always to have used them. Power was not what came out of the barrel of a gun; it was not even what shaped the complex bartering that went on among businessmen, government agents, and union leaders in their efforts to control the flow of products, manipulate demand, and distribute profits. Power was the word, somehow "American" and yet "wholly literary," "modern" and yet timeless – which is to say, enriched by overlapping histories yet free of all historical contaminations. "Salvation would come by the word, the long-awaited and fatefully exact word that only the true writer would speak," Kazin concluded.

How to square nonelitist, revisionary aims with elitist assumptions was not a question the thirties successfully addressed. In declaring his faith in the power of *writers* to *speak* with fateful precision, Kazin appeals to Edmund Wilson, and through him to Marcel Proust, as Wilson describes Proust in *Axel's Castle* (1931): "the little man with the sad appealing voice, the metaphysician's mind, the Saracen's beak, the ill-fitting dress-shirt and the great eyes that seem to see" everything. For Kazin, Proust represented the power of art, or more precisely the power of the novel, to provide searching accounts of "the loves, the society, the intelligence, the diplomacy, the literature and the art of the Heartbreak House of capitalist culture." Yet how to bridge the gap that separated the lives of Proust's characters from those lived in the streets, stockyards, and hiring halls of the Great Depression went almost unnoticed. Westerns, which flourished in the thirties, turned back toward a world divided along different lines. Detective novels, which came of age in this decade, redirected an individualistic, separatist, antinomian tradition, which Henry Miller's fiction put to very different ends. "Proletarian" fiction used "class" as a lens for measuring that distance, often by insisting that the obliteration of "class" was the key to closing it. Documentary literature recorded and dramatized the fact of it, and also examined its human costs. The most self-consciously experimental works of the era – Henry Miller's *Tropic of Capricorn* (1939), Djuna Barnes's *Nightwood* (1936), Dos Passos's *U.S.A.* (1930–6), Faulkner's *The Sound and the Fury* (1929), *As I Lay Dying* (1930), *Light in August* (1932), *Absalom, Absalom!* (1936) and *Go Down, Moses* (1942), Nathanael West's *Miss Lonelyhearts* (1933) and *The Day of the Locust* (1939), James Agee's *Let Us Now Praise Famous Men* (1941), Richard Wright's *Uncle Tom's Children* (1938), Zora Neale Hurston's *Their Eyes Were Watching God* (1937), to name a few – directly engage poverty, race, gender, sex, caste, and class as critical social problems that are also crucial correlates of selfhood. Formal experiments of the thirties regularly embrace political and social themes. When they focus on the past, their authors work as amateur historians. When they examine the present, they often work, as Sinclair Lewis had, as amateur sociologists. Yet much of the explicitly political writing of the time, including political fiction, remained loyal to the reform spirit – the tradition of "good hope" – that reached back to the Lyric Years and beyond. And this loyalty, to what Kazin called the "revolutionary yet wholly literary tradition in American writing," often had the effect of taming if not blunting their protest.

Novels of the thirties remain divided in their depictions of the nation's culture. Protest dominates their mood. Silence plays an even larger role in the literature of the thirties than it does in *Winesburg, Ohio,* because it serves as a sign of blighted lives and of a grim resolve that sometimes bears striking resemblance to resignation. Having become less dependent on clever satire and irony, humor, like scorn, became a means of overcoming bleak, inadequate fates. In one way or another, it helps to shore up the lives even of the most damaged and threatened human beings – Djuna Barnes's women, Henry Miller's antiheroes, William Faulkner's forgotten people, black and white, James Agee's sharecroppers, Richard Wright's angry rebels, and Zora Neale Hurston's resilient black women. But humor also helped to deflect the anger and despair such characters express, muting protest and making acquiescence bearable.

At times, of course, art, like life, seemed merely to be going on. For some writers, including Hemingway and Fitzgerald, the bleakness of the thirties was more personal than historical. Hemingway "is quite as nervously broken down as I am," Fitzgerald remarked shortly after he published "The Crack-Up," adding that Hemingway's breakdown inclined itself "toward megalomania" while his own tilted "toward melancholy." In what remained of their best writing – for Hemingway stories like "The Snows of Kilimanjaro" and "The Short, Happy Life of Francis Macomber" and for Fitzgerald *Tender Is the Night* – they wrote of endings with such resonance that sooner or later we realize that, like Proust, they are writing about the end of an era, or perhaps a way of life, more or less clearly situated in "the Heartbreak House of capitalist culture." Other writers of the twenties, including Dos Passos and Herbst, found their social concerns affirmed by the thirties. And others – including Katherine Anne Porter (b. 1890), Henry Miller and Zora Neale Hurston (b. 1891), Djuna Barnes (b. 1892), and William Faulkner (b. 1897) – who were slower to develop than Hemingway and Fitzgerald, found that the search for culture fit their imaginations as well as it fit those of younger writers like James Agee (b. 1909), Henry Roth (b. 1906), and Nathanael West (b. 1904), and so made the thirties, bounded on one side by the Great Crash and on the other by the century's second great war, another distinctive multigenerational literary era.

3. THREE RESPONSES: THE EXAMPLES OF HENRY MILLER, DJUNA BARNES, AND JOHN DOS PASSOS

By 1930, when he left New York for Paris, Henry Miller thought of himself as one of the last heirs of the Lyric Years' commitment to the value of childlike innocence and unmediated feelings. Bored with things like Spenser's *Faerie Queene,* he had dropped out of City College into a series of dreary jobs – including brief stints with a cement company and his father's tailoring business, and five years as supervisor of Western Union's messenger service. But it was New York's street life that engaged him, and its burlesque shows and dance halls, in one of which he met a hostess named June Smith, who became the subject of much of his writing. Later, gaining confidence, he denounced bookishness in order to celebrate direct experience, spontaneity, and instinct. But his writings – from his early studies of outcasts, derelicts, and prostitutes to the series of novels that made him famous, *Tropic of Cancer* (1934), *Black Spring* (1936), and *Tropic of Capricorn* (1939) – are in fact highly self-conscious performances. They are shaped as much by the books he had read, of Walter Pater and Henry James as well as Whitman, Dreiser, Norris, and London, whom he more or less owned up to, as by the things he had done and seen. And they demonstrate what his carefully constructed persona, introduced in New York, perfected in Paris, then transported to California, at once denied and suggested: that his doctrines of spontaneity and instinctivism and his celebrations of unmediated experience coexisted with an active, irrepressible aestheticism.

Less apparent but no less pervasive than the aestheticism that tied Miller to the twenties were a set of social concerns, also rooted in the Lyric Years, that blossomed in the thirties. Before leaving New York for Paris, he had seen the country slide into an economic slough that matched his sense of its dismal spiritual state. Over the next several years, living in exile, he wrote a series of novels designed to smash the middle-class mores and the false dreams promulgated by the Horatio Alger stories. That, as it turned out, was the extent of Miller's social commitment. He believed, as George Orwell noted in 1940, "in the impending ruin of Western Civilization," but he had no intention of trying to stop it. Irresponsibility, an extreme form of antinomianism – a celebration of the single, solitary, pleasure-seeking, self-aggrandizing self over against a society that is corrupt and enslaved as well as corrupting and enslaving – became his cause. No group and no cultural tradition, except the one that authorized his resistance to traditions, elicited his loyalty. His only commitment was to himself as a refugee, and as the refugee-hero of his books.

Employed as an employment supervisor for the Cosmodemonic/Cosmococcic Telegraph Company of New York, Henry Miller's fictitious Henry Miller acts as the first-person narrator of *Tropic of Capricorn* (1939). Having launched a plan for improving the lives of the messengers he supervises, he is thwarted by a vice-president whose concerns are fixed by the narrow interests of a market economy. If you want to help the messengers, the vice-president says to Miller, write a Horatio Alger story for them. "I'll give you an Horatio Alger book," Miller thinks to himself. "I will give you Horatio Alger as he looks the day after the Apocalypse, when all the stink has cleared away" – a line that captures as fully as any the temporal setting and harsh humor of fiction of the thirties. After requesting a leave, Miller's protagonist spends three weeks writing:

> I sat riveted to my desk and I traveled around the world at lightning speed, and I learned that everywhere it is the same – hunger, humiliation, ignorance, vice, greed, extortion, chicanery, torture, despotism: the inhumanity of man to man: the fetters, the harness, the halter, the bridle, the whip, the spurs.[2]

Armed with this knowledge, he discovers a personal vocation that takes him as close as he ever comes to a social mission – that of writing, as he put it in *Tropic of Cancer* (1934), antibooks that record "all that which is omitted in books." Having quit his job with the Cosmodemonic/Cosmococcic Telegraph Company, he goes to Paris to become an undersider and outsider and write books that will "wipe Horatio Alger" and his cultural lies "out of the North American consciousness" forever.

The Tropic of Capricorn earned Miller an outsized reputation for sexual explicitness. Although there had been a discernible increase in sexual explicitness in the twenties, there had also been much disguise, as we see in Stein's *Three Lives* (1909), much disgust and violence, as we see in Dos Passos's *Manhattan Transfer* (1925), and much shallow irony and titillation, as we see in James Branch Cabell's *Jurgen* (1919). Coming later, Miller's novels stretched the limits of the forbidden to the breaking point; they were frequently banned, especially in English-speaking countries, and were not published legally in the United States until the 1960s. But his novels are not merely full of often repetitious sex. They are also full of ugly, poorly repressed anxieties and hostilities, including anti-Semitism, racism, and sexism.

Miller presents himself as a bohemian, devil-may-care artist who scorns worldly success and as a neglected, impoverished genius who settles scores. There is, however, a kind of self-criticism at work in his novels, as well as self-promotion. In *Tropic of Cancer* he launches a deliberate assault on the whole set of middle-class values built around the celebration of hard work and the fear of sex. But he also attacks all forms of transcendent hope, including aestheticism: "a gob of spit in the face of Art, a kick in the pants to God, Man, Destiny, Time, Love, Beauty . . . what you will" is a part of what he has in mind. He thus reminds us that radical novels can attack almost any target, including political responsibility, social allegiance, revolutionary ardor, bourgeois guilt, and aesthetic commitment. In part an epitaph, as Edmund Wilson observed, to all the writers and artists who left the United States for Europe, saying that they wanted to "experience" life and "serve" art, *Tropic of Cancer*'s sad yet playful report focuses on people, including Miller's self-protagonist, whose long bouts of drinking, eating, talking, and fornicating are broken by brief interludes devoted to reading books or visiting exhibitions. Still, a kind of truth seeking emerges from Miller's exaggerations, just as a kind of comic irony emerges from his "confessions." And both of these things help to define his notion of what art should do. His celebration of his ego, which is full of distortions disguised as disclosures, constitutes a means of countering the alienation fostered by modern mass society, just as his wildly incorporating, self-aggrandizing ego constitutes a way of countering the modern world's diminution of the self.

Miller's "divine stuttering," as he calls it in "The Third and Fourth Day of Spring," is the work of an imagination that is given to repetition and allusional density as well as irony and humor, including three forms of these things – self-reflexivity, intertextuality, and authorial anxiety – that make Miller a forerunner of "postmodernism." His novels are megalomaniacal in their self-involvement and self-absorption. They affront, assault, and offend. Together, however, *The Tropic of Cancer, Black Spring,* and *The Tropic of Capricorn* form one large interreflexive assault on the bureaucratized, overdetermining modern world by celebrating a new kind of defiant if still imperial self: "For me the book is the man and my book is the man I am, the confused man, the negligent man, the reckless man, the lusty, obscene, boisterous, thoughtful, scrupulous, lying, diabolically truthful man that I am."

Miller's iconoclastic "truthfulness" frees sex of all romance. It treats most other people – all women and many men – as interchangeable parts, differentiated only by the names and acts he assigns them. Disappointments and anxieties tilt even his most lyrical prose toward ugliness: "O world, strangled and collapsed, where are the strong white teeth? O world, sinking with the silver balls and the corks and the life-preservers, where are the rosy scalps? O glab and glairy, O glabrous world now chewed to a frazzle, under what dead moon do you lie cold and gleaming?" But his antipoetic poetry, like his antiheroic hero, reflects a sense of personal urgency that stems from the threat of personal annihilation. Experience and words, together with the books that preserve them, are all that he as a doomed body and beleaguered imagination has left. His experiences and his words, soiled by repetition, fit the beleaguered protagonist who knows that he is not and never was autonomous, knows in fact that even with the bravest and most cunning of struggles, semiautonomy is the most he can hope for. His protagonists use words as they use acts of sex: to protect themselves by asserting themselves. They survive only as damaged goods or suspect commodities, to which terrible things have always already happened.

Miller's novels are, in short, Depression novels: they are written out of as well as about economic deprivation, political corruption, and historic catastrophe. The force of the large, gangrenous world enters his novels in two large ways. It enters as an alienating force that culminates in the hard-won detachment that enables him to write about his world as though it were an apocalyptic fantasy and a dark comedy of earthly despair and about himself in the first person as though he were a visitor from another planet. But it also enters as a force that has transformed the purpose of art and sex by making them the last possible strongholds of the self and its imagination against the forces of domination and control. Since assimilation always means annihilation of the individual for Miller, and since the historical forces marshaled in its behalf, like the economic interests they serve, include almost everything – government and the manipulative media of the world; countless false notions about sex, perpetuated by culture, including literary culture, as epitomized in all romantic notions about it; and most art, as epitomized in the Horatio Alger stories – the odds against the individual's marginal survival become almost insurmountable. The darkness and savagery of Miller's humor fit the darkness and savagery of the world he renders. His characters move under dead moons that lie "cold and gleaming," and they spend most of their time picking either the scabs that dot their own bodies and souls or those that dot the bodies and souls of people around them. Those who succeed in the world's terms, even as writers, lose their mortal bodies in relinquished sex, and their mortal souls in reading and writing false stories – and so do most of those who fail. Miller speaks, therefore, both for and to a remnant who battle long odds and more or less survive by remaining suspicious of the conquests they cannot live with or without.

Like other important writers of the thirties, including Dos Passos, Barnes, West, Agee, and Faulkner, Miller sought to adjust the special preoccupations of the twenties to a world darkened by the Depression. He flaunted his irreverence for the doctrines of the impersonality and the transcendent powers of art, as epitomized by its so-called triumph over history. Other important possibilities lay imbedded, however, in the notion of art as iconoclastic counterstatement, or what Miller called "divine stuttering," and two of them met a curious fate in his fiction.

The dominant culture Miller faced as adversary not only celebrated self-reliance, privileging self-realization and diminishing the claims of community; it also assumed its representative individual to be white and male, not black and not female. In short, it based privilege on race and gender. And in these crucial ways – in its celebration of the single, solitary, self-aggrandizing self; in its embrace of absolute individual rights as essential to the individual's resistance to assimilation and, therefore, annihilation; in its wholesale reduction of all claims of community as intrusive and abusive; and in its casual assumption that the only self that matters is gentile, white, and male, not Jewish, not black, and not female – Miller's fiction reiterates the dominant culture it presents itself as attacking. Despite their self-proclaimed iconoclasm, his novels repeat crucial prejudices of the culture they attack and reiterate its fear of all efforts to defend individualism as socially desirable. As a result, much of their significance lies hidden in what they ignore. To read them fully, we must read them for their elisions.

The two crucial elisions that give Miller's trilogy, written between 1934 and 1939, its special importance play central roles in two very different novels – Djuna Barnes's *Nightwood* (1936), which is so oblique and private as to seem subterranean, and John Dos Passos's *U.S.A.* (1932–6), one of the most open, inclusive, public novels ever written. If Barnes may be said obliquely to confront the consequences of female subjugation and repression by using enforced obliqueness as one sign of those consequences, Dos Passos may be said to make the fragmented, mixed form of his novel a sign of the absence of community in the land whose story he tries to tell.

Nightwood centers on a group of expatriates in Paris and Berlin. Through Felix Volkbein, it evokes the search for history and family; through Dr. Matthew O'Connor, an unlicensed Irish-American gynecologist, it parodies the rise of modern therapeutic culture. O'Connor's alcoholic, melancholic, apocalyptic monologues on war, the modern world, and the bodies and minds of women and men are scattered throughout the novel. But the action of the novel centers on the relations between Robin Vote, who is married to Volkbein, and Nora Flood, who becomes Robin's lover, and Jenny Petherbridge, for whom Robin leaves Nora. Like Robin, however, the novel's action remains shrouded, in part because Robin's beauty makes her vulnerable to the women as well as the men who look upon her with desire, letting their needs define her. Desire, depravity, and violence hover over *Nightwood*. As we become implicated in trying to read it, furthermore, we begin, like Dr. O'Connor and Nora Flood, to fix our gaze on Robin, as though determined to know and possess her. Yet the harder we push that endeavor, the more Robin, as though sensing her vulnerability, recedes before our eyes, leaving signs and traces that we can scarcely help misconstruing.

Finally, no one in the novel escapes the sexual politics of a world ruled by possession and suppression. Sexual acts are everywhere desired, feared, anticipated, and alluded to, but none is ever seen. What we see are the consequences, in the lives of men and women, of the suppression of women and the repression of female desire. Juxtaposed to the aggressive, assaultive sexuality of *Tropic of Capricorn,* the oblique, thwarted sexuality of *Nightwood* becomes even more clearly a story about the fate of women in a world in which only white males are authorized to express, in actions and words, the full range of their desires. If Miller's novel is a testament to authorized expression and aggression, Barnes's is a testament to enforced evasion and obliqueness. Together they make clear the dual logic of performance as it comes to bear on men who feel required to express and women who feel required to suppress desire. Both novels are filled with characters who function as actors, some of whom become skilled quick-change artists or experts in cross-dressing, changing accents, and switching languages. "Henry Miller's" performance is the virtuoso performance of a character who assumes that he is linear and stable despite his internal contradictions. *Nightwood,* by contrast, focuses on the oblique gestures, hidden acts, and reticent performances of women who remain conscious of themselves as too tentative, hesitating, provisional, multiple, and fluid even to be called "selves." In 1939, shortly after finishing his first trilogy, Miller left Paris for Greece, and in 1940 he returned to the United States, where he went on telling and retelling versions of his story for forty years, eventually in another self-celebrating trilogy, *Sexus* (1949), *Plexus* (1953), and *Nexus* (1960), collectively entitled *The Rosy Crucifixion.* Five years after finishing *Nightwood,* Barnes left Paris for New York, where she lived alone, maintaining herself in silence, as a last resort of the oppressed, until she died in 1982.

If *Nightwood* exposes one set of elisions that alter the cultural significance of Miller's fiction, *U.S.A.,* which includes three novels – *The 42nd Parallel* (1930), *1919* (1932), and *The Big Money* (1936) – exposes another by making scattered particulars of the social life and the patchwork culture of the United States visible. In *The Big Money* we see women singing out of lost love,

> I hate to see de evenin sun go down
> Hate to see de evenin sun go down
>> Cause my baby he done lef' dis town

men singing out of uncertainty,

>> Oh tell me how long
>> I'll have to wait
>> . . . .
>> Do I get it now
>> Or must I hesitate
>> . . . .
>> Oh tell me how long

and workers singing out of pain,

>> While we slave for the bosses
>> Our children scream an' cry.[3]

At times Dos Passos seems to speak in his own voice about a nation hopelessly divided ("all right we are two nations") or hopelessly lost ("we stand defeated America"). Yet neither he as a narrator possessed of a discrete voice nor any of his characters succeeds in mastering the entangled historical forces that we encounter in *U.S.A.* Historical figures interact with fictional characters, blurring the line between history and fiction – and with it, the line between documentary reports and imaginative stories. Dos Passos refuses to separate history and fiction or to privilege one over the other, and he resists the temptation to view life as objectively determined yet subjectively free. Dialectical play among contrastive principles and contradictory wills is what he explores and, in his own way, celebrates. *U.S.A.* thus absorbs in its juxtapositional form several concerns of the twenties and most concerns of the thirties by recasting the large-scale cultural shift of the United States – from a predominantly agrarian, traditional society toward an increasingly urban, industrial, commercial, and secular society – into a story that culminates in open conflicts between a small group of rich, powerful people who know how to manipulate the economic forces that shape history and a large group of poor, almost powerless people who know what it feels like to be buffeted by them. A dispiriting story, *U.S.A.* reports on a nation in decline. At its end, we see an almost nameless young man called Vag standing by a road, trying to hitch a ride, and recognize in him the wreckage of broken promises and self-betrayals, so interlinked as to be inseparable, left in the wake of the Great Depression.

Upton Sinclair thought that Dos Passos's technical innovations diluted his political message; Hemingway thought that the message got in the way of the fiction. But Jean Paul Sartre, whose sympathies included reform politics and aesthetic innovations, called Dos Passos one of the century's greatest novelists and named *U.S.A.* his supreme achievement – in part, we may assume, because he recognized the significance of Dos Passos's efforts to acknowledge the force of history while celebrating the authority of fiction and in part because he recognized the significance of Dos Passos's concern for the fate of communities as well as individuals in a secular world where money becomes the only countervailing force to helplessness that people really believe in.

4. COWBOYS, DETECTIVES, AND OTHER TOUGH-GUY ANTINOMIANS: RESIDUAL INDIVIDUALISM AND HEDGED COMMITMENTS

The elitism that found expression in T. S. Eliot's famous description of himself as a "classicist in literature, royalist in politics, and anglo-catholic in religion" survived in the thirties. Worldly in its wit and reach, as it gathers fragments in different languages from different times and places, and world-weary in its tone, as it laments the loss of artistic tradition and religious faith, Eliot's style largely defined literature for shapers of the "New Criticism." Art should be cosmopolitan yet imperial in its claims (meaning that it should claim everything high-up and good) and aristocratic in its exclusions (meaning that it should condemn everything middle class, mean, or vulgar). But the thirties witnessed the revival of three overlapping forms of populism that had flourished during the Lyric Years and then languished in the twenties. One of these, more or less Marxist in tendency, descended from writers like Upton Sinclair, Randolph Bourne, Floyd Dell, John Reed, and Jack London. A second came from some of the same writers, especially London, and was primitivistic in logic. And a third, more "realist" than "naturalist," found expression in the heirs of William Dean Howells – writers like Willa Cather and Sherwood Anderson, who made fiction out of the manners and foibles, the aspirations and hypocrisies, the symbols and myths of the maligned middle class. During the twenties, when the vocabulary of idealism fell into disrepute, the untested truce between populist and elitist tendencies fell apart. Mencken became almost typical in treating the "Middle Class" with contempt and all politics, including reform politics, as a farce.

In the thirties, fiction moved – backward or forward, depending on one's persuasions – toward "realism," not as a slice of life but as an organized selection of observed reality, and in the process it moved toward a reassessment of life as always political. Writers like Michael Gold spoke of formalists and aesthetes – "escapists, abstractionists, Freudians, and mystics of art, foggy symbolists, clowns and trained seals and sex-mad pygmies of the pen" – with undisguised contempt. But many writers of the thirties worked the same tension that writers of the twenties had worked: the tension between the principle that implicated the novel in history by defining it as a genre created to account for social phenomena and historical existence, and the principle that freed it from history by defining it as a genre devoted to free imaginative play and semiautonomy, if not transcendence. What changed was the balance between these principles, which tilted toward the first.

In sweeping away the affluence of the twenties, the Crash temporarily derailed the hope of the nation's middle class – of buying radios, refrigerators, fashionable clothes, and Fords today, shares of stock and who-knew-what tomorrow, in pursuit of the good life. But it also dashed a related hope shared by many writers – of securing without crippling compromise a life of comfortable bohemian sufficiency, if not glamorous affluence. Gone, too, as though in the same motion, was the sense that writers could ignore, or even take pride in ignoring, the widening gap between their concerns and those of ordinary people. Within prose fiction, "realism," with its ties to social and historical phenomena, pulled fiction toward a larger if still somewhat specialized audience, while "surrealism," with its links to myth and symbol, to dreams and the unconscious, and thus to the unpredictable terrain of subjectivity, pulled it toward a smaller group of elite aficionados, educated, as it were, by people like Eliot. Gold's gifts for mixed metaphors occasionally got out of hand when he was debunking literary elitism as a sign of bourgeois decadence: "Even at their best, in the supreme expression of the bourgeois individualist, in a James Joyce or T. S. Eliot, defeat follows them like a mangy cur. They are up a historic blind alley and have no future." But his statement reminds us of at least three things: that writers of the twenties worked in an economy that allowed waste and encouraged privatization as well as specialization; that waste, privatization, and specialization shaped lives lived as well as words written; and that ties between the literature and the dominant culture of the twenties can be observed in literary celebrations of the claims of the individual against the community.

During the twenties, social irresponsibility was condoned in the few places where it was not in vogue. People wasted time and energy as well as money, and some of them wasted lives, on the ultimate privatistic assumption that one's life is wholly one's own, even to throw away. In the very different economy of the thirties, writers continued to take risks. They smoked, drank, made love, had sex, and traveled; they stayed up late and boasted of burning their candles at both ends. But given the scarcity of money and jobs, everyone – especially young people who were starting out – had to be more careful, a burden that differed markedly from that of being sophisticated, which in the twenties often seemed almost synonymous with sounding cynical. Merely being clever, amusing, or novel was no longer enough. By 1932 works of art and even casual remarks were checked regularly for the range of social concern they reflected.

Vigorous forms of aestheticism continued to flourish in the work of writers as different as Kenneth Burke, Wallace Stevens, and William Faulkner, as well as in music and movies. But they flourished side by side with new political intensities. Writing of the thirties bears the marks of "strangers" and "outsiders" – Southerners, Jews, blacks, and women – for whom writing was necessarily a way of testing and transgressing boundaries. Dos Passos found the peculiar intensities of the thirties more congenial than he had ever found the privatism of the twenties. Slower to mature as a writer, Faulkner emerged as a major literary figure in the thirties, in part because the history of his family and his region had put him on familiar terms with poverty, failure, fear, and defeat and in part because his own experience had taught him that a sense of entanglement could coexist with and even support a sense of estrangement.

Writing for the *New Yorker* late in 1930, Robert Benchley announced that sex was "as tiresome as the Old Mortgage" and should not be "mentioned ever again." He was bored by rebellious youths and Victorian parents and gave not a hang whether all the young women in the country got ruined, wanted to get ruined, or kept from getting ruined. All he asked was an end to plays recounting their dilemmas. But such humor belonged more to the twenties than the thirties. Even when it focused on sex, the new humor was likely to be darker, like that of Nathanael West or Henry Miller. Self-conscious sophistication like James Branch Cabell's seemed almost as dated as Sinclair Lewis's scorn for rampant materialism. Amid a spreading threat of privation, worldliness seemed as shallow as world-weariness. "We prefer crude vigor to polished banality," Jack Conroy announced in *Anvil,* one of the era's better proletarian magazines. "It ain't a fit night for man or beast," W. C. Fields remarks in *The Fatal Glass of Beer.* "The time has come to take the bull by the tail and face the situation," he adds, evoking the comic tradition, shared with Groucho Marx, of turning confusion, ineptitude, failure, and pain into laughter.

Even lives thrown away were likely to be regarded more as public statements than as private acts. In April 1932, Hart Crane walked to the stern of the steamship *Orizobe,* which was bound from Mexico to New York by way of Havana. Standing there, he removed and folded his coat and then climbed to the ship's rail, where he balanced for a moment before diving into the sea. For years Crane had inveighed against the repressive, commercial society that had wounded him. And he had also gone on drinking hard – sometimes to evoke the visions that he could turn into poetry and sometimes to blot out what he had done the night before with the sailors he sought out as homosexual partners. He was, he told his friends repeatedly, "caught like a rat in a trap." Who knows what he thought at the end – that he had squandered his gifts, that he had done all things he could do, that only the sea could deliver him from the intimate harms he had suffered during the broken intervals that constituted his life? He left no message, and his body was never recovered. Still, his death, like his life, came almost immediately to seem rhetorical, a final act as word, and so reached across the thirties – as we see in David Wolff's poem, "Remembering Hart Crane" (1935), where Crane becomes the epitome of the poet-hero hurt by the incorporation of culture, first into poetry and then into the oblivion of the "smooth imperial Caribbean" to die.

Even more typical were acts of violence that were public from the start. In 1931, roughly a year before Crane's death, nine black teenagers, ranging in age from thirteen to nineteen, were arrested in Scottsboro, Alabama, and charged with raping two white women. Both the black teenagers and the white women were drifters, out riding the rails, searching for who knows what. They were people, as Kay Boyle put it, "that no one had use for, had nothing to/give to, no place to offer." The series of trials, appeals, and retrials set off by the Scottsboro arrests, along with the protests that accompanied them, stretched across the thirties as a long reminder of what Richard Wright called the "plight of black folk." "Freedom don't mean a thing to me," one of the defendants said; life outside is "no different than prison." In 1934, while the Scottsboro tragedy was still unfolding, gangster violence reached a peak: on the afternoon of May 23, on a little-traveled road outside Shreveport, Louisiana, a posse of Texas Rangers pumped more than fifty bullets into the bodies of Bonnie and Clyde Parker; on the evening of July 22, in front of a Chicago movie theater, featuring Clark Gable in a gangster movie, federal agents gunned down John Dillinger; on the morning of October 22, on a farm in Ohio, federal agents shouted "Halt" and then filled the body of Charles "Pretty Boy" Floyd with bullets from machine guns and pistols; on November 28, following a gun battle in rural Illinois in which two federal agents died, the bullet-riddled body of George "Baby Face" Nelson was found abandoned in a ditch outside Chicago.

Violence runs through documentary works, self-consciously "proletarian" novels, "radical" strike novels, and historical novels of the thirties, and the threat or fact of it dominates two of the period's most popular forms of fiction, Westerns and detective stories. Like writers of the ancient world, Milton and Shakespeare borrowed plots from history, including several that had already been turned into art. Both sin and the idea of sin, as encoding the story of the human fall into time, mortality, and exile, were familiar to Milton's readers. But Milton assumed that he could surprise his readers all over again. More recent formula stories, including detective stories and Westerns, owe their existence to modern publishing, modern circulation, and modern marketing. We find them in magazines and we read them on trains, subways, buses, and airplanes, in barbershops and beauty parlors, or in the waiting rooms of doctors and dentists. Like older writers, however, their authors begin with received formulas and then surprise us with some distinctive twist in a familiar plot or some distinctive act of style that sets writer and protagonist apart. Yet their works differ from earlier formula stories in ways that expose one of the crucial secrets of the twentieth century: our fear that both authentic community and authentic individualism, far from coming to us as gifts of culture, come into existence against great odds – the first as an act of human contrivance, the second as an act of human will.

On the near side, as it were, of formula stories (including historical romances) stand isolated readers who feel trapped in routine, regimented lives. During the thirties, the sense of entrapment was compounded by economic circumstances that robbed people of the saving hope of the twenties: the hope that they might somehow enter the house of have. From one point of view, we may say that Westerns and detective stories exploited the need that Depression readers felt for "escapist" entertainment. But we may also say – neither more nor less neutrally – that they presented imaginatively constructed alternative worlds. Writers of Westerns go back in time, as Cody and Turner had, to reinforce a modern assumption, embedded in the nation's formative myths, that adventures essentially don't happen to people who stay at home. They take us out of our familiar worlds into adventure's or even harm's way, but they do so, as Cody had, at safe remove. In seclusion and comparative safety, we identify with characters who confront mystery, peril, and even death, or a failure of nerve that is a form of death. At the same time, however, Westerns deliver us from ultimate terror – first, by presenting a world that yields to outsized courage and skill and, second, by telling a story that works variations on a familiar formula, without finally disorienting us. Having taken us on an adventure, they deliver us from it.

There is, however, another cultural task that detective stories as well as Westerns perform. Drawing on several traditions, including classical political theory and biblical religion, their protagonists reiterate the right and respon-sibility of individuals to judge everything for themselves. In them, civil community, or more broadly culture itself, depends for its survival not on civic-minded citizens but on individualists who live by codes of their own. The cowboy drifters and outsiders of Zane Grey (a dentist who "fell in love with the West") and the estranged detective heroes of Dashiell Hammett and Raymond Chandler serve society reluctantly because, though they honor com-munity as an ideal, they reject it in its actual, fallen state in which both the threat of punishment and the lure of money, power, and pleasure inculcate "false" (sometimes "capitalist" and sometimes "feminine") values. If "false" society serves as the villain of Westerns and detective stories, "true" culture persists as their impossible dream.

Long before Dos Passos wrote *Big Money* (1938) – "they are stronger   they are rich   they hire and fire the politicians . . . all right we are two nations" – the popular fiction of the nation was virtually shouting about a crippling division between men and women. "Domestic" novels were written primarily by, for, and about women. Women are their main characters, and young women, frequently orphans, are their protagonists. Their settings favor en-closed, private spaces such as kitchens and sitting rooms. When nature makes an appearance, it typically enters as a pastoral landscape or a quiet garden. The real struggles of "domestic" novels are internal. Instruction designed to dispel internal confusion plays an important role in them and so, therefore, do reading books, singing hymns, and saying prayers. Introspection, we learn, lies near the heart of young female life as it gropes its way toward maturity. Whether one will or will not marry or, more painfully, will or will not become wise – first, by learning to remain chaste in thought as well as word and deed and, second, by learning to subordinate oneself to an appropriate husband – are the big issues. Religion and culture are inseparable, and women are the principal bearers of both. In service to them, and thus to family, lies perfect "female" freedom.

Westerns, following Owen Wister's *The Virginian,* were generally written by, for, and about men. They, too, stress proper devotion as the test of all things. But in them religious moorings are loose. Even in the late nineteenth and early twentieth centuries, British novelists, especially women novelists, continued to present ministers as heroes and to use them as authorial voices. Novels in the United States, going back to Nathaniel Hawthorne, subject them to harsh scrutiny. When characters of spiritual force appear, they are usually women. B. M. Bower, pseudonym for B. M. Sinclair, a woman who wrote stories about the Flying U Ranch, is a notable exception to the tendency for Westerns to be written by men. She is also an exception in that she concentrates on an almost prefallen community,

> [a] peaceful... little world tucked away in its hills, with its own little triumphs and defeats, its own heartaches and rejoicings; a lucky little world, because its triumphs had been satisfying, its defeats small, its heartaches brief, and its rejoicings untainted with harassment or guilt.[4]

Bowers's Flying U stories anticipate the agrarian utopianism that flourished in the thirties. By contrast, Zane Grey's social world is fallen. Though it remains largely preindustrial, it is not quite premodern. For it is already deeply conflicted about the "progress" of industrial civilization and sometimes about religion. In Grey's novels, devout women remain spiritually strong and retain religious authority. But most men, including men of the cloth, tend to use religion as they use everything else, for enlarging their fortunes and increasing their power, as we see especially in *Riders of the Purple Sage* (1912) in the contrast between Jane Withersteen and Elder Tull. Grey's heroes are drawn toward action rather than introspection, and they value integrity more than power, or even their own lives. In town, they prefer secular public spaces – livery stables, land offices, courthouses, railroad stations, or saloons – to homes and churches. But they give their deeper loyalty to a still almost untouched and, therefore, uncorrupted nature. Restlessness is one of their trademarks, isolation another. Taciturn and stoic in manner, they rarely feel desire, let alone reverence, for anything except "pure" women and unspoiled natural scenes – wide rivers, open prairies, majestic mountains, or the big sky – which they sometimes think of as vaguely feminine. Their own lives they govern by a stern code of honor they think of as masculine.

In *Riders of the Purple Sage,* ruthless Mormon elders control almost everything. In *Nevada* (1928) and *West of the Pecos* (1931), officers of the law are in cahoots with crooked, land-grabbing ranchers. In *Code of the West* (1934) a young eastern woman named Georgiana Stockwell goes West, reeking of "modern" opinions: that traditional standards of conduct are "back numbers" and that "our sisters and mothers and grandmothers have been buncoed by the lords of creation. By men!" Determined to dress, talk, and act as she pleases, Stockwell advocates liberation and encourages Eastern jazz dancing whenever she gets a chance. Some of the conflict in *Code of the West* comes from old-style rustling and land grabbing. The rest Georgiana stirs up – until, of course, she learns the valuable lessons of a fading but not yet lost frontier and so puts behind her "her pitiful little vanity of person, her absorption of the modern freedom, with its feminine rant about equality with men," and starts "longing to make amends." Thus chastened, she becomes a perfect wife – attractive and seemingly spirited yet cowed.

In classic Grey novels, male identity is (re)asserted and male hegemony is (re)established in a less overt and less strained way than in *Code of the West*. But even in them society rarely appears in an admirable light: the more developed it becomes, the more rotten it is apt to be. In novels like *Nevada* and *West of the Pecos,* society's rottenness is a secret that must be exposed. Grey's heroes belong to no community, if by community we mean a society possessed of a remembered past, knit together by shared commitments and hopes, and ordered by social justification of individual rights. Such memories and loyalties as they carry with them are their own, and so is their code of honor. By the time Grey picks up their stories, they are usually grown, and they are always courageous and resourceful enough to perform any deeds circumstances require. Their hard pasts, often known through rumors, are etched in their faces. Despair threatens them more than fear because it threatens the resolve that keeps them from sliding into criminality. Only a personal code of honor and a lingering desire to help good people build simple homes and establish nuclear families keep them going straight. The hope that somehow they may yet share such things remains faint because, preferring loneliness to compromise, they will accept wife, home, and family only on their own terms. Deeper than the threat of loneliness or even death is the threat of losing their hard, manly virtues, of which their guns often serve as signs. "Give me my guns," Venters says to Jane Withersteen in *Riders of the Purple Sage,* as she talks to him of forbearance, mercy, and forgiveness. "I'll die a man! . . . Give me my guns." Those who affirm Christian beliefs do so selectively, refusing to let gentle persuasion threaten their masculinity. The codes they live by – and with which they hope to save society for "real" men and "good" people – they think of as allied with nature and, therefore, as older than the religions that gentle women espouse and greedy men exploit. They want to save society from the greed of men gone bad and from the misguided softness of women because they want to enter it, if not as gods at least as gods might be, virile as some savage source.

Nevada begins with its hero in flight from the law, knowing that he has saved the lives of his best friend and the woman he loves: "Whatever might be the loneliness and bitterness of the future, nothing could change or mitigate the sweetness and glory of the service he had rendered." Later, Nevada saves his friend and his beloved once again, and with them an entire community, by defeating a conspiracy of killers, thieves, and crooked law officers. But this time he is permitted to join the life he has secured. Unlike the humble lives to which domestic novels characteristically commit their heroines, however, Nevada's leads him to something like an apotheosis: " 'Arizona is smilin' down on us,' " Nevada says in the book's closing lines, as he gazes "down at the sunset glow upon [the] rapt face" of the woman who loves him. " 'Nevada is smiling down upon me,' she replie[s], dreamily."

Detective stories have several things in common with Westerns, including their habit of taking us for a walk on the wild side where we meet both gangster-outlaws and a variety of outsiders who are almost outlaws. In detective stories it is merely a matter of time before we discover that society is rotten from top to bottom. Although the lines that separate victims from victimizers and avenging angels from hired gunmen are often blurred, they remain crucial, as does the line that separates the strict code of the detective hero from the slippery ethics of everyone around him, including a fair share of prominent citizens, civic leaders, and public servants who turn out to be venal, greedy exploiters of the society they pretend to serve. Often failures in conventional terms – failed policemen, for example – detective heroes are not only wily, tough, resourceful, and dependable; they are also lonely.

Though thoroughly urban, detectives, like cowboys, are social minimalists. They hark back to a culture that valued the young and the masculine more than the polished and the sophisticated. As amateur historians, however, they know that every present has a secret past. And since they remain, in one important respect, distant descendants of traditional Christians, they think of that hidden past as evil and assume it will provide clues to understanding evil in the present. Cynicism and despair threaten them because they believe in sin but not in redemption. "Man is conceived in sin and born in corruption," says Willie Stark, of Robert Penn Warren's *All the King's Men* (1946), to his reluctant detective Jack Burden; "and he passeth from the stink of the didie to the stench of the shroud. There is always something" – by which he means that evil reaches up into respectable society as surely as it reaches down into the rapacious criminal underworld and that everyone is entangled in it.

Like cowboy heroes, detective heroes work against long odds. A life of hardship marks their faces and their bearing. They know that society undermines integrity with specious promises of happiness and fulfillment, and that sooner or later it destroys those it fails to corrupt. Money and sex are chief among its false lures. With sex goes the promise of pleasure, or possibly of love, intimacy, and even marriage. With money goes the promise of luxury, power, and status. From one or another of these, detectives are always under siege. Only their code and their sense of integrity protect them. The more determined and resourceful they prove to be, the further they are drawn into the darkness of a world that breaks those it cannot buy.

Detectives work in societies that are far more advanced in their capitalism than are any that Western heroes face. Most of the people they encounter are entrepreneurs on the make. As city folk, they live without the solace of space or the consolation of nature's beauties. Yet they too speak with the special authority of the truly marginal, and they too reassert masculine identity and hegemony as counters to feminine invasions of public spheres. Since women often mix the lure of pleasure and comfort with the lure of money and security, detectives regard them with redoubled suspicion. As modern knights, however, they display a special fondness for women in distress, along with other almost lost causes. Since experience has taught them that money is corrupting, they bring an especially hard eye to bear on modern capitalism. In their world, money and guilt go hand in hand, iterating and reiterating the fear that, given the intensity with which Americans worship success and fear failure and the readiness with which they measure everything by money, they will do anything to get it.

Despite their cynicism, however, detective heroes retain a commitment to the idea of urban society and the possibility that the right kind of resourceful male individualists may somehow save it. Like Sister Carrie, they divide their lives between public performances and private retreats. A terse, taciturn lot, they specialize in the discourse of individualism, and the self-reliance that goes with it, rigorously controlling all emotions, needs, and desires that it leaves unexpressed. Only their sentimentality about good women and men of integrity, another trait they share with cowboys, attests to the large reservoir of needs that that discourse leaves unexpressed. Yet it too is crucial to the balancing act that defines their lives. If irony hardens their sentimentality, pushing them toward isolation, sentimentality softens their irony, carrying them toward community and the causes that sustain them, of rescuing the not-yet-corrupt and saving the not-yet-wholly-lost.

Striking a balance between the irony that keeps them detached and the sentimentality that keeps them humanly involved is, as it turns out, crucial to everything detectives do. Rationality, another legacy of their nineteenth-century origins, is one of their tools. But their rationality is tempered by experience, as we see in the scars that mark their bodies and the shadows that haunt their minds, reminding them of corruption and death. With them as our guides, we travel down into the underworld and up into high society, to see life as it really is. And with them, as with Henry Miller, we learn "that everywhere it is the same – hunger, humiliation, ignorance, vice, greed, extortion, torture, despotism." Detectives resist the temptations having to do with sex, money, and fear by accepting loneliness and meagerness, and by facing death; and they resist the temptation posed by cynicism in order to go on fighting the corruption that surrounds them and the doubt that lurks within them. "I've got a hard skin all over what's left of my soul," says the Continental Op, detective hero of Dashiell Hammett's *Red Harvest* (1929), whose purity and detachment extend even to his name, "and after twenty years of messing around with crime I can look at any sort of murder without seeing anything in it but my bread and butter, the day's work. But this . . . is not natural to me. It's what this place has done to me." Detectives persevere primarily for the satisfaction of knowing that they have refused to sell out or give in. "What did it matter where you lay once you were dead?" we read at the end of *The Big Sleep* (1939) a title Raymond Chandler coins as a synonym for death. "You were dead, you were sleeping the big sleep, you were not bothered by things like that. Oil and water were the same as wind and air to you. You just slept the big sleep, not caring about the nastiness of how you died or where you fell."

Heroes of such knowledge rely principally on courage, resourcefulness, and a hard code of justice. Feared and even grudgingly respected by men, admired and desired by women, they need determination to keep them going straight and a tough skin to keep their souls alive. Sometimes, like cowboys, they live almost celibate lives. The women of Hammett's *The Maltese Falcon* (1930) can be taken as representative: Iva Archer is a selfish bitch; Brigid O'Shaughnessy is a beautiful, tempting murderess; and Effie Perine is a good woman or, as Sam Spade puts it, in paying her the ultimate compliment, "a damned good man, sister." Having ticked off six or seven reasons for deciding to send Brigid over to the law, turning his back on what might have been – "the fact that maybe you love me and maybe I love you" – Sam Spade remains faithful to the special code by which he lives, silently assuming that Brigid will silently endorse what he is doing and why – an assumption his author makes about us as readers. Like Grey's cowboy-heroes, Spade clings to the idea of romantic love as a necessary fiction, without which cynicism might engulf him. But he is even more reluctant than Grey's Nevada to test that fiction by trying to live it. In the end, he finds himself not merely alone but lonely and almost dead to feeling. "I don't believe in anything," says his successor, Ned Beaumont in Hammett's *The Glass Key* (1931), "but I'm too much of a gambler not to be affected by a lot of things."

Raymond Chandler's style, basically ironic and often bitter, resembles the mood of his hero, Philip Marlowe, who moves back and forth, balancing the need to be tough against the need to remain vulnerable. Tempted by the lure of money and power, he protects himself. "To hell with the rich," he says, "they make me sick." Tempted by pleasure, his response is similar. "This was the room I had to live in," he says, as he throws the naked Carmen Sternwood out of his bed. "It was all I had in the way of a home. In it was everything that was mine, that had any association with me, any past, anything that took the place of a family." Marlowe thus reminds us that for him family is less a dream than a memory. And so, as it turns out, is being a knight. Life's not a "game for knights," he says. He commits himself to saving women who, however fair and beautiful, are almost always already corrupt because he is determined to cling at least to the *idea* of romantic love. With similar irony, he remains loyal not only to himself and his code but also, after his fashion, to society as an idea, not because society deserves his loyalty but because he deserves something to which he can be loyal. He knows that the corrupt society around him is committed to practices that turn people against one another. But he clings to the hope that the sacrifices of the select company of the tough and vulnerable may somehow create a culture that enlarges human happiness because it is the only thing that keeps him going.

The magazine *Black Mask* was announced in 1919 and began publication in 1920 for the purpose of featuring "mystery, detective, adventure, western, horror, and novelty" stories. By the mid-twenties, the "private eye" had emerged as the new savior of society, and so had *Black Mask*'s ability to find and foster talent. Beginning in 1929, Hammett published four important novels – *Red Harvest, The Dain Curse, The Maltese Falcon,* and *The Glass Key* – each of which was serialized in *Black Mask*. Detective novels, like Westerns, blossomed in the thirties. They owed much to writers like Jack London, who used a violence of principle to offset and even defeat a violence of greed; and to writers like Ernest Hemingway, who early in his career, in *In Our Time* (1925) and *The Sun Also Rises* (1926), gave new authority to vulnerable, battered heroes who become tough in order to cope with the ugly world around them. Stories like "The Killers," "Fifty Grand," "After the Storm," and "In Another Country" pushed the emergence of Hemingway's "tough-guy" protagonists. One alternative to resistance was a steady carving away at life until there was nothing left to lose. A man "must not marry," runs a line from "In Another Country," a story in which life becomes the art of avoiding entanglements. "He cannot marry.... He should not place himself in a position to lose. He should find things he cannot lose," Hemingway's protagonist says. Another possibility was becoming tough enough to survive crippling losses. During the thirties, as Hemingway's hold on his art slipped, he began taking more risks in life and fewer in fiction, with mostly sad results. But he continued to take some risks of both kinds. *To Have and Have Not* (1937), he joked a few years after its publication, was a "frail volume... devoted to adultery, sodomy, masturbation, rape, mayhem, mass murder, frigidity, alcoholism, prostitution, impotency, anarchy, rum-running, chink-smuggling, nymphomania and abortion." But its real subject, he told Maxwell Perkins, was the "decline of the individual." Later, following his involvement in the Spanish civil war as a pro-Loyalist reporter, he wrote *For Whom the Bell Tolls* (1940), a long, uneven work that marked his reaffirmation of faith in the possibility of human solidarity and worthy social causes. In *To Have and Have Not,* however, his only Depression novel and his only novel set in the United States, his bleakness seems almost total, as though, having lost faith in the discourse of radical individualism, he could find nothing to replace it. His protagonist, Harry Morgan, who has tried and failed to earn an honest living, becomes an outlaw and starts smuggling rum and illegal aliens into Cuba, only to discover that, in his dying words, "One man alone ain't got no bloody f—ing chance." Looking around after Harry's death, Maria, the novel's main female character, sees only "this god-damned life."

Similar sentiments found expression in the hard-boiled fiction of James M. Cain and Horace McCoy, who lived and worked on the fringes of Hollywood, where scores of writers – Fitzgerald, Dorothy Parker, Stephen Vincent Benét, Dos Passos, and Faulkner, to name a few – worked on and off, primarily because Hollywood paid well even during the Depression. "Excess of sorrow laughs," Blake wrote, or seeks other relief, as Hollywood understood. Maxwell Anderson, Robert Sherwood, and Thornton Wilder all found Hollywood money too good to pass up, though none of them was ever hounded by dollars in the way that Fitzgerald was in the thirties or Faulkner was in and beyond the same decade. Most writers, even minor ones earning outsized salaries, found Hollywood offputting, or felt obliged to say they did, in part because screenplays, like movies, were collaborative ventures in which individual writers played minor roles. Stories were not stories in Hollywood,

Benét remarked; they were conferences. "Imagination is free or it is not free," Cain said, simplifying a bit, "and here it is not free." Writers mattered to some directors and producers, but they did not matter much because the industry's task was to make money for the parent corporations that owned the studios.

Cut off from almost everything except sick fictions about women and society, Cain's protagonists slouch their way through their commercialized worlds toward death. Cain's novels – particularly *The Postman Always Rings Twice* (1934) – enjoyed considerable popularity. And since they are bleak reports on the destruction of virtually all values, one must ask why so many people liked to read them. Cain's protagonists, including the self-conflicted artist John Howard Sharp in *Serenade* (1937), are not so much tough as ruthless. His female characters tend to be either seductive or infantile, or both. Greed, lust, and boredom dominate their lives, until the desire for adventure triggers something like free play. Intrusions – unexpected visitors who drop in and stir things up – play crucial rules in Cain's novels, and so do emotional explosions, acts of passion in which violence and desire merge. A "drop of fear," Huff says in *Double Indemnity* (1936), is all it takes "to curdle love into hate."

Cain's novels turn on three basic relationships, male–female, artist–society, individual–society, in each of which the *other* promises fulfillment yet poses a mortal threat. Cain's characters strain toward relationships that fall apart largely because his men fear that any relation they do not completely control will entrap and destroy them. As genuine possibility – as a larger wholeness in which the self is fully expressed, and yet more than the self is expressed – relationships do not exist. Dramas of arrested development are all we have: people who act out adolescent or even infantile obsessions in an adult world that has become cynical without having attained maturity. The representative agents of society are as familiar, anonymous, and predictable as the uniformed postman who always rings twice. Cain's characters, outsiders who hope to get into the world of meretricious glitter, are driven by greed and lust, in lethal combination with boredom. Even those who try for very little stand convicted of wanting too much and so must be punished, if not by society's uniformed agents then by one another.

Finally, however, society is not only alien to Cain's characters; it is also a dark twin. In his preface to *The Butterfly* (1947), Cain speaks of himself as the poet of the "wish that comes true" – "for some reason," he adds, "a terrifying concept, at least to my imagination." Many of his women and most of his men are more at odds with themselves than with society – society having in a sense already won. In *Butterfly*, a father's incestuous love for his daughter awakens in her an incestuous desire for him. The novel's force is both abstract and corrupting. Although we suspect from the beginning that the characters cannot survive the acting out of their desires, we cannot help wanting to see what will happen when they try. In *The Postman Always Rings Twice* we encounter – in Nick, the dark-skinned alien "other"; in Frank, the "American" as outsider and finally outlaw; and in Cora, a woman who feels and expresses more desire and ambition than any woman is expected to feel or express – one of the most clearly doomed triangles in the literature of the United States. Nick, Frank, and Cora fight losing battles with their own unconscious desires as well as with one another. The forms of destruction toward which they move, even when they seem unexpected, also seem inevitable because they emanate from the premises of Cain's text, which succeeds in making fatalism entertaining. In *Serenade,* John Howard Sharp, the Artist, is afraid of what people may see in him: "There would be something horrible mixed up in it, and I didn't want to know what it was." "It," as it turns out, is double: both a homosexual attraction to a man named Winston, who is socialized almost beyond the point of seeming human, and a fearful desire to have his wish known, ostensibly in the hope that someone may be able to exorcise it.

The deepest truths about Cain's world, and the conflicted hopes that drive it, emerge in the resolution of Sharp's predicament, which is cultural as well as private. In a bullfighting scene, Juana, a primitive, archetypal female, saves Sharp by killing Winston. Making Sharp's hidden wish her own, Juana flees civilization with him and takes him as her lover, but they are then destroyed by mundane developments: they grow old, their love dries up, and their lives run down. Sharp's eyes weaken, and his body turns to fat; Juana becomes a fat old hag and dies.

Horace McCoy (1897–1955), another "poet of the tabloid murders," to borrow Edmund Wilson's phrase for Cain, was less popular than Cain. But on one occasion he became a more effective artist – in part because he felt less threatened by the "feminization" of culture than by its political economy. *No Pockets for a Shroud* (1937) grew out of his work as a crusading journalist in Texas in the twenties and early thirties. From Texas he went to Hollywood, hoping to make money writing screenplays while also writing serious fiction. A successful screenwriter, he continued to call himself a "Hollywood hack" and his work a kind of "whoring." Of his four novels – *They Shoot Horses, Don't They?* (1935), *No Pockets for a Shroud* (1937), *I Should Have Stayed at Home* (1938), and *Kiss Tomorrow Goodbye* (1948) – the first is the strongest. Now largely forgotten except as a movie, it remains important, in part because some of its evasions can be traced in McCoy's revisions.

Recalling the background of *They Shoot Horses, Don't They?* McCoy said, "There were decadence and evil in the old walkathons – and violence. The evil, of course, as evil always has and always will, fascinated the customer and the violence possessed a peculiar lyricism that elevated the thing into the realm of high art." Gloria and Robert, the two principal characters of the novel, enter a danceathon to win money. Gloria comes from West Texas, "a hell of a place," as she calls it. Having read about Hollywood in movie magazines, she has moved west, hoping to live a glamorous life on the edge of the Pacific. Being "discovered" is one possibility; "getting married" is another. If such dreams are one gift of her inadequate culture, her passive strategy, of waiting for the right man to discover her or propose to her, is another. Filled with yearning, she follows the kind of advice offered young women by Marjorie

Hillis in *Live Alone and Like It: A Guide for the Extra Woman* (1936). Women can be delivered from loneliness and insecurity, Hillis instructs, if they first assemble a proper wardrobe – including "at least two negligees" – and then learn how to wear makeup and mix martinis and manhattans the way men like them, until the right one comes along.

Made vulnerable by her yearning and desirable by her beauty, Gloria becomes an easy target for the unscrupulous men who rule Hollywood. In an early draft of the novel, she relates a "laughable" fact about her love life: "I've never been laid on a bed in my life," she tells Robert. Later, in a line McCoy kept in the final version, she stands, anticipating her death, knowing that her life is already over: "This motion picture business is a lousy business. . . . I'm glad I'm through with it," she says. "I never paid any attention to her remark then," Robert says later, as he listens to the judge sentence him to die, "but now I realize it was the most significant thing she had ever said."

Gloria's hard-earned knowledge gives her voice authority for Robert and the reader. The weight of the many things that have happened to her is felt in almost every word she utters. As a result, she becomes the big thing that happens to Robert, a confused boy from Arkansas, who remains surprised by "how it all started" and mystified by how it ends. It "seems very strange," he says, adding that he still can't "understand it all." By being ruthless about herself as well as her world, Gloria earns her bitterness. "The whole thing is a merry-go-round. When we get out of here we're right back where we started." More specifically, she speaks to Robert as a woman seared by the experience of living in a world run by men. Robert feels compelled to listen to her, he remarks in an unpublished short story from which the novel came, "because she talked to me the way I would talk to a boy if I were a girl." This remarkable line helps to make clear why Gloria becomes Robert's great teacher. She pits her bitterness and her inverted egotism against his shallow optimism and conventional egotism. "Now I know how Jonah felt when he looked at the whale," Robert says, as Gloria's lessons begin to unfold. Within a few hours she has convinced him that the grand abstractions he clings to, hope and truth and justice, are empty; that the few parts of life, including his and hers, that are not obviously ugly are "just showmanship"; that he, a chance acquaintance, has become "her very best friend . . . her only friend," because he has listened to her story and heard her voice; and that he, therefore, must do her the favor of shooting her, because, as he says to the officers who arrest him, "They shoot horses, don't they?" meaning hopelessly crippled ones.

Marathon dances were a zany fad of the twenties that became a cruel racket in the thirties. Yet McCoy deleted from his novel a number of references to breadlines and other signs of the Depression in order to expose the deeper logic of a political economy that seemed to him to regard the right to property and profit as more important than the right to life, let alone what Roosevelt called a "decent living." This entangling of public context with private lives comes through in *They Shoot Horses, Don't They?* in the marathon dance, which provides the structure of the central narrative of the novel, and in the trial of Robert for the murder of Gloria. Each of the novel's thirteen chapters is preceded by words of the judge as he pronounces Robert guilty and sentences him to die. By robbing Gloria's and Robert's fates of suspense, McCoy focuses his novel on the implicit trial of society as one in which the vulnerable sooner or later fall in love with death. Gloria's decision to go west to Hollywood, she tells Robert, came from reading movie magazines while she was in a hospital recovering from an attempt to poison herself. Thinking of her in the moment of her death, "in that black night on the edge of the Pacific," Robert remembers her as relaxed and comfortable and smiling: "It was the first time I had ever seen her smile," he says.

Like Cain's *Serenade*, McCoy's *They Shoot Horses, Don't They?* is built around characters who speak to us from the grave. In two executions – Robert's of Gloria and the court's of Robert – we witness the threatened end of the vulnerable, yearning, young American. Together, Gloria and Robert remind us that to be sustained one's hope must be sanctioned by one's culture. And they also remind us that we should not speak of a historical culture without trying to see it through the eyes of its unendorsed victims.

5. *THE SEARCH FOR SHARED PURPOSE: STRUGGLES ON THE LEFT*

Novels emanating from the radical Left shared some of the detective novel's cynicism and most of Horace McCoy's bitterness. Behind them lay a native tradition that reached back to I. K. Friedman's *By Bread Alone* (1901) and *The Radical* (1907), Upton Sinclair's *The Jungle* (1906), Charlotte Teller's *The Cage* (1907), and Jack London's *The Iron Heel* (1908). But reform was what held the Left together, and reform depended on hope. In 1937 – two years after Kenneth Burke urged the American Writers' Congress to make "the people" rather than "the worker" their "basic symbol of exhortation and allegiance" – Nathan Asch published *The Road: In Search of America*. Both parts of Asch's double adventure, of seeing "America" and then writing a book about it, unfold as a search for "the people," whom he finds in a young Mexican couple in Denver, Colorado, who live lives of resigned desperation; in a middle-aged man in Eureka, California, who hopes to become sick enough to qualify for charity before he had his wife starve to death; in Henry John Zorn, who has been left to rot away "underneath Montana"; and in a black family in Lost Prairie, Arkansas, who live "in a sieve-like empty house amid a world of cotton." Such people, Asch insists, are not "exceptional" cases but "usual and everyday and common." Trapped in misery and dispossession, they resemble the residents of a flophouse that Sherwood Anderson describes in *Puzzled America* (1935), where people lie breathing "in and out together" in "one gigantic sigh." They are average in their suffering and average in their resistance to it, and they are victims of common enemies they have not yet learned how to name: the "very rich and very smart" people who live in Washington and New York and run the country for their own personal pleasure and profit. Unable to name their enemies, Asch's victims cannot map effective strategies for opposing them. But Asch also stops short, deferring active resistance to a putative future, a "someday," in which "the people" will unite in naming and resisting their enemies.

Like Asch's *The Road* and Russell Lee's photographs of "homesteaders," Jack Conroy's novel *The Disinherited* (1933) shuns self-conscious artifice. Its protagonist, a worker named Larry Donovan, moves from job to job, spurred less by hope of finding meaningful work that can restore his sense of purpose than by fear that unemployment will sap his dwindling reserve of self-respect. Separated from the objects that his labor produces and the profits they yield, he is left to measure his efforts entirely in terms of falling wages. In some moments, Donovan treats real adventures as trivial games, a bit like Tom Sawyer. Finally, however, he is closer in spirit to Huck Finn, not because his life leads him to a grand flight west, away from civilization, civilization now being everywhere, but because he locates his proper home in his beginnings, among the "disinherited and dispossessed of the world."

There is, however, a basic confusion at work in *The Disinherited*. While capitalism remains Donovan's avowed enemy, Conroy's tone slips back and forth between angry protest and wide-eyed wonder. One explanation for this almost certainly lies in Conroy's divided loyalties. He thought of himself as a Marxist, but simply looking "at *Das Kapital* on the shelf gave" him a "headache," he once remarked. His own writings he thought of as belonging to a native tradition of radicalism, associated with "Whitman's injunction to vivify the contemporary fact," in which a strong strain of individualism survived. In a scene between a widowed mother and her son, who becomes Conroy's protagonist, age is set against youth, work against play, duty against freedom, and social organization against the single, solitary self. "You've got to be a man now. You're the only man I've got left," says the mother – to which her son responds by running out to play a game that begins with a familiar chant: "Bushel o' wheat / Bushel o' rye; / All not ready / Holler 'I.' "

Hollering "I" survived during the thirties both as an old tradition and as a principle of resistance to assimilation, including assimilation by the organization that represented Marxist thought. James T. Farrell's troubled relations with the radical Left became a familiar story. Studs Lonigan, Farrell's strongest protagonist, lives a life of swaggering individualism. Through his own brand of social realism – particularly and most forcibly in *Young Lonigan* (1932), *The Young Manhood of Studs Lonigan* (1934), and *Judgment Day* (1935) – Farrell preserved the novel as a source of information about the harsh realities of urban life. Torn between old neighborhood institutions – family, home, church, and school – and new neighborhood institutions – the playground, the poolhall, and street gangs – Studs Lonigan becomes part disappointed romantic and part tough-minded realist. From family, church, and Father Gilhooley, he acquires a graphic sense of evil, but he has been born too late to share hope of redemption. Truly buffeted, his life seems almost foreclosed. Both the romantic possibilities that he associates with Lucy Scanlon and the religious possibilities that his mother associates with the priesthood seem to him empty compared with the gang speech and gang adventures that turn antisocial behavior into a social organization.

Since the impoverishment of Studs's world is imaginative and moral as well as economic, emptiness is as much his enemy as want. The countless trivial, mundane things that happen to him are iterated and reiterated in a life that traces in its descending action the sad story of an "American destiny in our time." Finally, his descent seems neither better nor worse than the rise of Farrell's Danny O'Neill. The protagonist of *A World I Never Made* (1936), *No Star Is Lost* (1938), *Father and Son* (1940), and *My Days of Anger* (1943), O'Neill is more successful than Studs. Yet he is not so much better as merely different. The characteristic bleakness of Farrell's fiction comes through in both series, which, despite their overdependence on the massing of details, create a sense of indignation that is moral as well as social, as we see especially in Studs's yearning for what he calls "something else."

In the early thirties, the Communist Party recruited many people. But some of the conversions were halfhearted and faded rapidly. Even Lincoln Steffens's *Autobiography* – published in 1931, when the house of want was becoming more and more crowded – is divided in its allegiance: dogged in its adherence to the major tenets of the Party yet committed to a native tradition of protest exemplified by Jack London and Randolph Bourne. Looking back, Ben Hagglund saw the "collective spirit" winning a temporary victory in the early thirties. But then "when things eased up a bit, the old individualistic spirit got us again, and we were right back at each other's throats," he said. Proletarian "literature" also suffered, as Nelson Algren noted, because it was dominated by intellectuals like Michael Gold and Steffens rather than by artists. Most novelists remained on the blurred borders of the Party, some closer than Farrell, others farther away. Daniel Fuchs's trilogy – *Summer in Williamsburg* (1934), *Homage to Blenholt* (1936), and *Low Company* (1937) – sets the shaping and misshaping force of place and circumstances, as they bear down on the lives of young people to teach them their limitations, against the residual hope that somehow the earth's poor may still "reign as consuls of the earth." Robert Cantwell's *Land of Plenty* (1934) focuses on young people who are trapped in a brutal strike and so must move from one darkness – "Suddenly the lights went out" runs the novel's first line – to the next, until at the novel's end three of them huddle together, "their faces dark with misery and anger, . . . waiting for the darkness to come like a friend and set them free." In Ira Wolfert's *Tucker's People* (1943), poverty kills hope in some people but makes others "frantic for money and frantic to hunt it down." Once Wolfert's people have joined in the "game of marauding for profits," which seems to them to hold the "whole earth" in its grip, the line between legal and illegal capitalistic ventures blurs and then vanishes, making each a version of the other. In his trilogy about the Stecher family, which began with *White Mule* (1937), William Carlos Williams keeps the large-scale corruption that attracted Wolfert in the background in order to focus on the subtle ways in which the pursuit of money, power, and status makes people "become callow and selfish," starting them "down the road of rationalizations and self-justifications," until countless small compromises finally leave them without any firm principles to live by.

The strengths that set Henry Roth's *Call It Sleep* apart from most novels of the thirties derive in part from Roth's gift for evoking the sights, sounds, and smells of Lower East Side Manhattan. The sense of place and the impinging force of environment, including the force of poverty, dominate *Call It Sleep*. But Roth's novel is focused in another way, too: it recounts three years in the childhood of David Searle, a small, vulnerable, and very human animal. In one sense, it is a story of the emerging consciousness of a physical, social creature who must learn what it means to live in a gigantic and confusing world "created without thought of him." Although *Call It Sleep* confronts pain and suffering, it remains free of self-pity and is rich in the tenderness and terror that wonder makes possible. Its deeper richness comes, however, from Roth's skill in depicting the forces and voices within David that begin to contest external forces.

To editors of *New Masses*, Roth's concern with David's consciousness was a sign of decadent bourgeois individualism. *Call It Sleep*, they declared, was both "introspective and febrile." But Roth's story is a social novel about a young boy's effort to survive in a world of broken promises. Written during the thirties, it takes us back to the Lyric Years just before World War I, when the national dream seemed to embrace almost everyone, except recent immigrants like David Searle's dislocated and divided parents. Roth's own Marxist sympathies are everywhere present – in his treatment of debased sexuality and David's violent, frustrated father, and in his rendering of the kind of bleak, brutal scenes we associate with urban naturalism. But his concern with David's uneven effort to become a force among forces dominates his story.

Power, as Roth renders it, comes from the play of an unfolding self as it interacts with other selves. The characters of *Call It Sleep* feel controlled by external forces, which they try to control. But the crucial political question that Roth confronts is whether the idea of agency – or of the self as independent agent – makes sense in a world where people come to consciousness by becoming aware of myriad forces impinging upon them. David's awakening consciousness knows itself only in its contingencies, as something impinged upon by a conflicted past that is not its own and a violent social world that it can never hope to measure.

In *Call It Sleep*, the emergence of a self and the emergence of the self's voice become interrelated, interactive developments. David's world is not only one of overlapping urban sounds; it is a world of speech, part polyglot and part pidgin, that has been damaged by loss of tradition and a trail of broken promises. The words David hears emanate from a conflicted world. Those he acquires convey vague intimations of his yearnings and desires. They fit neither his experiences nor his needs. The silence into which he slips at the novel's end seems promising primarily because his young consciousness is still trying to gather the sights and sounds of his days. The "glint on tilted beards . . . the tapering glitter of rails . . . the glow of thin blond hair . . . the shrill cry, the hoarse voice, the scream of fear, the bells" exist for him as things "to cull again and reassemble" in a new state of mind – lying somewhere between willfulness and submission, assertion and acquiescence, the sheer fabrication of details and the mere recording of impressions – that we have no word for and so "might as well call sleep." David's struggle to improvise a temporary, evolving self, like Roth's struggle to create an unfolding narrative, thus comes to us as an act of compromise as well as resistance.

Novels like Roth's, which begins by recalling the small steamers that brought millions of uprooted immigrants from Europe to the United States in the late nineteenth and early twentieth centuries, look at the past in light of a present in which something has gone drastically wrong. One theme that personal writings – memoirs, letters, and personal essays – of the thirties shared with public writings was a sense of astonishment that the country's money culture, having promoted the belief that everything depended on money, had suddenly stopped producing any. Michael Gold disapproved of *Call It Sleep*. But in his own writings he grappled in a more formulaic way with many of the same tensions that drove Roth. In *Jews Without Money* (1930), he stacks one brutal experience on top of another and then concludes with a formulaic celebration of the great revolution that will finally set all the East Sides of the world free from poverty, exploitation, and misery. As editor of *New Masses,* he sentimentalized writers who seemed determined to bear witness to life's hard facts. "A first book like yours, of a young working-class author, cannot be regarded as merely literature," Gold wrote Edward Dahlberg about *Bottom Dogs* (1930). "To me it is a significant class portent. It is a victory against capitalism," he continued, unperturbed by the issue of agency. "Out of the despair, mindlessness and violence of the proletarian life, thinkers and leaders arise. Each time one appears it is a revolutionary miracle."

The key words in Gold's tribute – "working-class," "proletarian life," "revolutionary miracle" – often produced crude critical judgments that privileged the "realism" of the articulate victim. One unexpected result, exemplified by Gold, was a blurring of the line that separated autobiography, with its focus on the individual, from social fiction, with its focus on social forces. To locate the point at which a witness intersects social history, both Conroy's *The Disinherited* and Gold's *Jews Without Money* combine autobiographically based fiction with autobiographically informed journalism. Lorry and Lizzie Lewis, the chief protagonists of Dahlberg's early fiction, are also the subject of his late, more openly autobiographical *Because I Was Flesh* (1964).

By privileging social-minded writing based on personal experience, writers of the thirties were able to adjust the social tenets of Marxism to circumstances and traditions of the United States. But leaders of the Left often construed that possibility rigidly. What the United States needed, Gold argued in "Go Left, Young Writers" (1929), were writers toughened by life – "a wild youth of about twenty-two, the son of working-class parents, who himself works in the lumber camp, coal mines, and steel mills, harvest fields and mountain camps of America." Where in Mr. Thornton Wilder's fiction, Gold later asked rhetorically in "Prophet of the Genteel Christ" (1930), are the city streets, the cotton mills, "the child slaves of the beet fields," and "the passion and death of the coal miners"? Such questions reinforced the authority of the tough-guy, bottom-dog male writer at the expense of men like Wilder and, almost casually, of virtually all women writers. In *Heaven's My Destination* (1934), Wilder traced the journey of George Brush across the much-mixed world of the thirties – its trailer camps, shantytowns, and bawdy houses, its courtrooms and trains, its countryside and small towns. *Heaven's My Destination* bears interesting comparison with Dahlberg's exploration of the bottom-dog world of freight cars, hobo jungles, and flophouses; and it deserved more attention than it received from readers like Gold, if only because it explores, with considerable wit, the fate of goodness in a corrupt as well as depressed world. But George Brush's work as a traveling textbook salesman failed to interest Gold. And since less than 25 percent of women and only 15 percent of married women worked outside homes during the thirties, most of what women knew about poverty, pain, fear, and indignity struck him as narrow.

As though mindful of Gold's advice, Josephine Herbst made a conscious effort to write social fiction, only to discover that it was harder to write such fiction about women. Conroy could write, she observed, about "the feel of what it's like to work, how you handle a machine," and "how it feels to be without work, and with the imminent fear of starving," confident that his account of such ordeals would be accepted as socially significant. She could write of women who were willing to take chances and "be guilty of folly." But she could not write as a "witness of the times" who had seen firsthand "the passion and the death of the coal miners." Herbst, Meridel Le Sueur, Martha Gellhorn, Tillie Olsen, Mary Heaton Vorse, and scores of other women were welcomed to the ranks of the politically engaged. But leaders of the Left, including the editors of journals, possessed a clear sense of what wild poets should look like, and no woman resembled it. Unlike *Anvil* and *New Masses, Partisan Review* tried to blend political concerns of the thirties with aesthetic concerns of the twenties. Acknowledging that literature is always political, it also insisted, as its editor William Phillips put it, that the imagination cannot "be constrained within any orthodoxy." But *Partisan Review* helped to keep literary radicalism a largely male preserve. Looking back on her position as the *Partisan*'s drama critic, Mary McCarthy remembered herself as "a sort of gay, good-time girl" whose position reflected the sense that "the theater was of absolutely no consequence." Serious writing by women, including fiction that dealt with what Gold had called "the despair, mindlessness and violence of the proletarian life," usually seemed "narrow," "narcissistic," and "defeatist" to male readers, simply because it featured the private spaces women knew best. Looking back, trying to account for the strange fate of her long-deferred novel called *Silences* (1978), which she began in the thirties, Tillie Olsen recalled the pressure exerted on her by the Young Communist League to submerge her "writing self" by turning her interests from fiction to journalism. Herbst and Le Sueur felt similar pressures, as did Tess Slesinger and Ruth McKenney, author of a careful investigation of social and economic conditions in Akron, Ohio, called *Industrial Valley* (1939).

Assured that their experience possessed social significance, men wrote countless narratives – memoirs that resemble novels and novels that resemble memoirs – confident that their works would be greeted as revolutionary miracles. Dahlberg's *Bottom Dogs* is about coal miners; Thomas Bell's *Out of This Furnace* (1941) is about steelworkers; Pietro Di Donato's *Christ in Concrete* (1939) is about bricklayers; Conroy's *The Disinherited* moves from coal mines to railroad shops to rubber plants. But each of them is the story of a witness who has seen up close the wounded, damaged lives they recount. They rely heavily on the accumulation of brutal scenes, a literary equivalent of stockpiling, calculated to make readers pity the victims of a brutal political economy. Their language, which comes from ghetto streets, slums, mine shafts, and factories, seems almost as misshapen as the lives of the people who speak it. In them the Great Depression threatens to engulf everything except the counterforce of angry protest that they exemplify. During the thirties, that protest also found expression on the sides of freight cars ("HOOVER – CAPList Dog"), in store windows ("Coolidge Blew the Whistle / Mellon rang the bell / Hoover pulled the throttle / And the country went to hell"), on placards carried by striking workers ("This is your country dont let the big men take it away from you"), and in songs sung by people like Sarah Ogan, the "Girl of Constant Sorrow," from Elys Branch, Kentucky:

> They take our very life blood, they take our children's lives,
> Take fathers away from children and husbands away from wives.
> Coal miners won't you organize, wherever you may be,
> And make this a land of freedom for workers like you and me.
> Dear miners, they will slave you till you can't work no more.
> And what will you get for your labor but a dollar in the company store?
> A tumble-down shack to live in, snow and rain pouring through the top,
> You'll have to pay the company rent, your payments never stop.
> I am a coal miner's wife, I'm sure I wish you well.
> Let's sink this capitalist system in the darkest pits of hell.[5]

Eventually, the Communist Party gained strength even in hard-to-reach areas of the rural South. After 1933, however, as the New Deal gained momentum, defections picked up. Some people were pulled by Roosevelt's appeal to native roots; others were pushed by the Party's early denunciation of the New Deal as "social fascism." A few, including Ruth McKenney, were kicked out of the Party for "deviationism." Realizing that their strategy was backfiring, Party leaders tried to claim Tom Paine and John Brown as precursors and to endorse Conroy's celebration of Whitman. Communism, they said, was "twentieth-century Americanism." But the Party continued to lose ground even after it blurred its message. Some writers who had supported William Z. Foster and his running mate James Ford in the election of 1932 never voted for Roosevelt. As late as 1936, a majority of the American Writers'

Congress supported Earl Browder, the Communist Party candidate, while others supported Norman Thomas, the Socialist Party candidate. But the drift toward accommodation was strong. In 1937 the Communist Party itself officially endorsed Roosevelt's reforms.

Three important developments influenced this turnabout. First, despite the spread of proletarian sentiment and fiction, many writers recognized that the United States was of all places, as Herbst put it, "the least likely to produce" an organized proletariat. Its myth of affluence and mobility were deterrents, and so was its tradition of individualism and self-reliance. Second, they recognized that the nation was benefiting from the programs of the president they did not completely trust. "Preserving capitalism," wrote Leslie Fiedler, another writer who started out in the thirties, "the New Deal also preserved us who had been predicting its death and our own." Third, the drift of international events – especially the rise of Hitler's Germany and the surprising moves of Stalin's Russia – forced reappraisal. For a brief time, the first American Writers' Congress (April 1935) and the League of American Writers benefited from Hitler's presence as a common enemy, as Kenneth Burke later stated directly. With Stalin's atrocities still hidden, people who remained divided on many issues were united against Hitler, especially after reports of the staggering persecution of Jews began to drift across the Atlantic and as thousands of people, some of them writers, musicians, artists, scientists, and philosophers – people like Hannah Arendt and Thomas Mann – arrived, seeking refuge. But the fall of the Spanish Republic (March 1939) and the signing of the Hitler–Stalin Pact (August 1939) left many radicals, as Fiedler put it, feeling like casualties of a "failed apocalypse."

By the late thirties, defections from the Party and its fringes were almost commonplace. Nelson Algren and James Gould Cozzens moved on to become commercially successful writers. Robert Cantwell, author of *Land of Plenty* (1934), joined the editorial boards of *Time, Life,* and *Fortune* and later became the first managing editor of *Sports Illustrated.* Saul Bellow, Bernard Malamud, and Arthur Miller began forging links among urban writers of the thirties and those of the forties, fifties, and sixties. Premature death saved a few writers, including Nathanael West, from having to carry on after the prophecies had failed. Haunted by personal problems, the contours of which remain obscure, Henry Roth lapsed into silent hibernation, waiting for a later generation to rediscover him. By the early forties, Dos Passos and Farrell had begun sounding like garrulous, complaining shadows of their former radical selves.

John Steinbeck suffered a similar fate, though with a lighter touch, in part because he had less to feel disappointed about. Though aligned with the Left, he had always worked primarily out of a native tradition of protest, different parts of which have since been traced in books like Louis Hartz's *The Liberal Tradition in America* (1955), Alice Felt Tyler's *Freedom's Ferment* (1944), Richard Hofstadter's *Age of Reform* (1955), Daniel Aaron's *Men of Good Hope* (1951), and *Writers on the Left* (1961). Starting out in the thirties, he had persisted in drawing on his own sense of history, which was dominated by the nation's westering impulse, and he often presents "the people" whose stories he tells as history's heirs. Sharing the angry decade's sense of itself as having suffered a terrible reversal of fortune, he presents capitalism as a perverting force that violates the heavenly valleys of California – the Old World's as well as the New World's last Eden – as we see not only in his "strike" novel *In Dubious Battle* (1936) but also in *The Grapes of Wrath* (1939). Yet to read him as a realist, a naturalist, or a proletarian novelist is to misread him.

Having acquired an early suspicion of realism ("I never had much ability for nor faith nor belief in realism," he remarked. "It is just a form of fantasy as nearly as I can figure"), Steinbeck remained a deeply literary writer. He borrowed titles from Milton (*In Dubious Battle*), as well as hymns and the Bible. In *Tortilla Flat* (1935), he engages in an extended evocation of Malory's tales of King Arthur and the Knights of the Round Table. *The Grapes of Wrath* is full of literary evocations – of Jefferson, Emerson, and Whitman, among others – some of them so obvious as to seem crude. In short, Steinbeck wrote about conflicts and out of them. If some of his loyalties came from his reading of Emerson, whom he thought of as having unified man and nature as soul, others came from the influence of Edward F. Ricketts, a marine biologist and naturalist whom he met in 1930 and from whom he learned an early version of sociobiology that changed his sense of relations between individuals and groups. For Steinbeck it was as though Ricketts had disclosed something he had always known: "I have written this theme over and over and did not know what I was writing." "Group-men are always getting some kind of infection," says the Doctor in *In Dubious Battle*. "Every man wanted something for himself," says the pioneer grandfather, "The Leader of the People," in *The Long Valley* (1938), before he goes on to depict "a whole bunch of people" who collectively want "only westering" as transformed "into one big crawling beast."

A poet of sorts, Steinbeck wanted to search out the sociobiological determinants of human behavior while also celebrating his belief in "the people." In some moments, the perils of individualism seem to dominate his range of vision; in others, all forms of collectivism seem to strike him as poisonous. Thus divided, he became for a brief time one of the most prominent writers in the United States. Like his fellow Californian Jack London, he was drawn to portrayals of people of reduced states of consciousness because he wanted to situate the human spirit within nature and to locate nature's force within human animals. Animal imagery pervades his novels, from the pirate in *Tortilla Flat*, who lives in a kennel with his dogs, through "The Leader of the People," to the famous description of a turtle crossing a highway in *The Grapes of Wrath*, where we see life as a biological process that has always been historical and as a historical process that has always been biological.

The Grapes of Wrath became one of the most influential and controversial novels of the thirties. It was banned by libraries and denounced by schools and churches as well as U.S. senators; and it was extravagantly praised by

Michael Gold in *New Masses* as proof that the "proletarian spirit had battered down the barricades set up by the bourgeois monopolists of literature." At the heart of its story lies the journey – the exodus or odyssey – of the Joad family from the dust bowl of Oklahoma through camp after camp, seeking California's heavenly valleys. Left without jobs and clear roles to shore up their sense of dominance, Steinbeck's men become bewildered and baffled. Challenged, his women – especially Ma Joad – become more assertive. At his most searching, Steinbeck senses, as Roth had, links between class oppression and gender oppression. But he consistently hesitates in the presence of his own insights, and then begins to resist them. His female characters become empowered only when his male characters falter; they exercise power only in order to save the family as a patriarchal institution; and they therefore surrender power as soon as the men of the family are ready to resume their roles as protectors and providers. In short, Steinbeck brings the central problematic of his novel, which has to do with the distribution of power, under the aspect of gender, only to retreat, in part by feminizing nature in a way that allies women with passive dependence. The fate of the land emerges as a crucial issue in *The Grapes of Wrath*. But for Steinbeck, the issue is whether it is to be raped for profit by large impersonal, conglomerate, male-dominated agricultural corporations or tilled with loving care by individual, humane male farmers. Given such alternatives, neither Steinbeck nor we have much choice. But in saying that, what have we said if not that Steinbeck betrays his own insights? After celebrating Ma Joad's strength and allowing her to become the center of her abused, dislocated family, he confines her again to the nurturing role he temporarily permits her to transcend. The "naturalness" of that role, set up by his depiction of nature, he reiterates in the novel's last scene, where Rose of Sharon, Ma Joad's daughter, nurses a starving man with milk meant for her stillborn child.

Steinbeck was at his most awkward when he engaged in self-conscious symbolism (featuring overburdened turtles, tractors, and crosses) and large gestures (such as the one with which *The Grapes of Wrath* ends). His strength lay in describing natural scenes that are imbued with human qualities and in depicting characters who feel more than they understand about the natural forces and social institutions that bind them together. At his best, he is more clinical than sentimental about people because his most telling loyalty was to the processes of life. He values social movements, including strikes and protests, in the name of social justice, but even more in the name of loyalty to life. In his fiction, however, that loyalty, which opened his eyes to some things, closed them to others. It allowed him to picture men behaving like natural animals, as Lennie does in *Of Mice and Men* (1937); like social animals, as the "group-man" does in *In Dubious Battle;* and like "natural" leaders, as Tom Joad and Jim Casy do in *The Grapes of Wrath*. But where women are concerned, his focus on the processes of life, featuring cycles of death and rebirth, extinction and renewal, reiterates confinement.

Unlike Dos Passos, Farrell, and Steinbeck, all of whom lived to write weaker

novels in another era, Nathanael West died in 1940, just before the Great
Depression disappeared in the economic growth spurred by the century's
second great war. Born in New York City in 1903, the son of prosperous
Lithuanian Jewish immigrants, Nathan Weinstein began early to dash his parents' hopes. He preferred baseball to synagogue, and books by writers like J.
K. Huysmans, Friedrich Nietzsche, and Feodor Dostoyevski – or even out-
of-the-way medieval Catholic mystics—to the Torah and homework. Having
left high school without a diploma, he gained admission to Tufts University
with forged documents and then withdrew with failing grades, before entering
Brown University on the borrowed credentials of another student named
Nathan Weinstein. Freed from onerous requirements in science and math,
which the other Nathan Weinstein had satisfied, West finished at Brown, took
his degree, and left for Paris, where he spent two years reading and trying to
write. Back in New York, he continued to fend off parental attempts to draw
him into his father's construction company, choosing instead to clerk in small
hotels, where he cadged free rooms for writers like Caldwell, Farrell, and
Hammett. Set free when the Depression destroyed his father's business, he
followed Horace Greeley's advice – "Go west, young man" – by renaming
himself. By 1931, when he published his first novel, *The Dream Life of Balso
Snell,* he was Nathanael West.

West thus began a short career that established him as a virtuoso of what
he called the "peculiar half-world" of dreams and nightmares. His world
includes people who have been made grotesque by nature, like the girl in *Miss
Lonelyhearts* (1933) who is born without a nose, and people whose weaknesses
are exploited for profit, like Peter Doyle, the cripple in *Miss Lonelyhearts*. At
his best, however, West charges the pathos of his fiction with two kinds of
political meaning. He contextualizes it by surrounding it with a sick, money-
mad society in which the exploitation of nature for profit goes hand in hand
with the exploitation of human beings for profit; and he internalizes it by
presenting his characters as victims who harbor hidden affinities, learned from
a corrupt world, with the secret causes of their own predicaments. As a result,
West's is a world in which the most basic of all commitments – the commitment
to life itself – is under siege.

The Dream Life of Balso Snell is a deeply parodic comedy built around the
adventures of a poet who enters the belly of the Trojan horse through its anus
and discovers a strange new world populated by writers searching for audiences. An act of apprenticeship, a declaration of independence, and a confession
of guilt, *Balso Snell* launched West on a career dedicated to exploring the fate
of art as well as life on a morning after the apocalypse, when artistic conventions
and social precepts survive only in fragments, or in broken, disfigured bodies,
or in maimed memories. In *Miss Lonelyhearts* virtually everything – travel, art,
philosophy, and religion; the primitive and the decadent; urban life and agrarian
utopianism; good hope and cynicism; hedonism and stoicism, a fondness for
the pleasures afforded by food, drink, and sex, as well as willed abstinence
from them – come to us as escapist activities, addictions, or signs of disease.

The country's whole therapeutic culture, rather than signaling a love of life, becomes in West's fiction a sign of fear and anxiety or, more drastically, a symptom of fundamental dis-ease with life.

The newspaperman who agrees to write his paper's "Miss Lonelyhearts" column, hoping to advance his career, is transformed and then destroyed by a fatal conjunction between his paper's desire to exploit the pain and suffering of its readers, his desire to rise in his profession, and his readers' desires to find a quick fix to their problems or, failing that, to find a well of pity in which to drown themselves. West thus turns several of the nation's favorite myths – of pursuing wealth, practicing self-reliance, and finding ways to get well quick – upside down and inside out. Part newspaper gimmick, part rhetorical device, and part comic strip character, Miss Lonelyhearts becomes both a fool of pain and a mad, ludicrously inadequate Christ whose only work is to expose as false the myths that inform his life and the life around him.

A Cool Million (1934), West's third novel, exposes the American dream in general and the Horatio Alger myth to further mockery, by tracing the sad misadventures of Lemuel Pitkin. A poor honest farm boy, Pitkin begins life confident that with energy, talent, and hard work he can become anything he wants to be. But he discovers that the land which seems to lie before him like a dream is a nightmare world of exploitation. An anachronistic threat to that world, Pitkin is robbed, wrongly imprisoned, and then slowly dismembered. Having lost his teeth, one eye, one thumb, one leg, and his scalp, he is finally shot, whereupon a false version of the story of his life and death is cynically used by the forces that have destroyed him in order to persuade others to live the dream he has tried to live so that his society can go on being itself.

The Day of the Locust (1939), West's best work, has often been compared to Fitzgerald's The Last Tycoon (1941) because they were written in and about Hollywood at roughly the same time. But The Day of the Locust has more in common with Horace McCoy's They Shoot Horses, Don't They? (1935) and even John O'Hara's Hope of Heaven (1938), Paul Cain's Fast One (1933), and Raoul Whitfield's Death in a Bowl (1930) – novels that focus not on Hollywood's rich moguls but on its bitter lost dreamers who expose its marketed love affair with stardom as a love affair with death. In these novels, Hollywood is a land of illusions that promote self-deception as well as false dreams. They feature characters who are crippled or destroyed by the things they dare to do or by those they are afraid to try. In them audacity leads to lives that are short and violent, diffidence to lives that are empty. Rather than liberating people, the nation's new sexuality increases anxieties and manipulation. Jardin, the protagonist of Whitfield's Death in a Bowl, lives alone because he sees his world for what it is. Time and again, he stops himself short of allowing his feelings to become words, let alone deeds, lest he become entangled in a world that is drifting toward death. Resistance becomes the dominant principle of his life, isolation, the dominant strategy.

Early in West's The Day of the Locust, Tod Hackett begins to think of himself as the appointed artist of Hollywood's failed dreams and botched lives. At times he is tempted to become an active hero or lover. Occasionally, he even wishes he could set society straight. But learning to see and render his world are the tasks he sets for himself. Offended by the deception, decadence, and crime that surround him, he spends most of his time studying his world and trying to capture it on canvas. West himself was drawn to active participation in organized politics, and his writings sometimes reflect a tendency that marks other books of the thirties, where the caboose of literature follows the engine of social events. The gap between event and expression had closed during the Great War. Convinced that they were witnessing history as well as living it, young people started taking notes while the shells were still falling. During the twenties, the gap between event and expression widened, but during the thirties, it closed once again, as we see in writers like Clifford Odets, whose political sympathies were close to West's. Odets's plays were occasional in a special sense. Most of the things that happened to him – what he saw in the streets of New York and what he read in newspapers and magazines about events in Europe as well as other parts of the United States – fed his sense of urgency. *Waiting for Lefty* (1935) was a direct response to the New York taxi drivers' strike of 1934. In 1935, on the night after he read a report on Hitler's Germany published in *New Masses,* he started and finished *Till the Day I Die.*

For several years after moving to Hollywood, West concentrated on writing screenplays. When he took up fiction again, he brought the scenes he was witnessing under the aspect of full-scale apocalypse, as his title, *The Day of the Locust,* which comes from the Bible, clearly suggests: "And in those days men will seek death and will not find it; they will long to die, and death will fly from them." Like McCoy's characters, West's come from the margins of Hollywood. They include a dilapidated comedian who ekes out a living selling shoe polish while trying to market his daughter for a fortune; his daughter, a film-struck beauty who shuffles through a stack of old dreams while waiting to be discovered; a forlorn, middle-aged hotel clerk from Iowa who has left his meager life behind, hoping to find happiness in Hollywood before time runs out; a screenwriter from Mississippi who lives in "an exact reproduction of the Old Dupuy mansion near Biloxi"; a feisty, irascible dwarf; a cock-fighting Mexican; a Hollywood cowboy; a Hollywood Indian; and, as narrator, Tod Hackett, a young Yale graduate, who studies the bizarre life of Hollywood in hope of becoming its painter.

West's Hollywood emerges as a quintessential expression of a political econ-omy that depends on its ability to promise more than it can deliver. It thus raises to visibility the nation's will to disguise and exploit for profit its two deepest secrets: a fatal entangling of sex and violence, and a fatal fascination with money as the measure of all things. Neither the nation's new eroticism, built around free expression, nor its old romanticized sexuality, built around enticing restraint on the part of women and licensed aggressiveness on the part of men, escapes the web in which sexual desire merges with the will to dominate, making it a commodity. What is lost, the hope of intimacy, res-onates in an emptiness that haunts West's world, where all life is reduced to mean-spirited contests. Some of these games are subtle; some, such as cock-fights, are crude. But a fatal confluence of sex, violence, money, and power lurks in all of them. In the novel's last scene West's pathetic, repressed, almost wholly ineffectual former hotel clerk commits a senseless act that provokes mob hysteria and riot.

Shortly after he arrives in Hollywood to study set and costume design, Tod Hackett begins to focus on a few people who masquerade as victors and on several whose failure is as obvious as the cheap clothes they buy from mail-order houses. But his main interest focuses on the disenchanted who have come to the land of dreams hoping to find happiness before they die: "They were the people he felt he must paint." In the bedlam of the novel's last scene, when poorly repressed frustrations erupt, people begin to act out their dream-nightmares in an orgy in which inflicting death and suffering it become almost interchangeable experiences. Observing the scene around him, Hackett thinks of his masterpiece, "The Burning of Los Angeles," which is based on the innumerable sketches he has "made of the people who come to California to die."

West's own subject, the United States at the end of the road, brings the novel as near as it can come to apocalypse. In it, several important distinctions begin to dissolve, including those between dream and nightmare, living and dying, life and art. California in general and Hollywood in particular – the places Americans dream of going and go to dream – become the places they go to kill or die. "The Burning of Los Angeles," Hackett's drawing of a surreal land of lies, begins to merge with the "actual" scene of his life, just as he, West's designated artist, begins to merge with his world. As he is being carried off in a police car, Hackett remembers his painting and then sees it all around him in the bedlam he is actually living. Hearing the car's siren, he thinks that he is making the noise he hears. Feeling his lips with his hands, he discovers that they are clamped tight, then begins to laugh hysterically, and then begins to imitate the sound of the siren as loud as he can.

In April 1940, shortly after *The Day of the Locust* was published, Nathanael West and Eileen McKenney, subject of Ruth McKenney's *My Sister Eileen* (1938), were married and began a short, happy marriage that ended in December when they died in an automobile accident near El Centro, California. *The Day of the Locust* earned good reviews and poor sales, and then dropped from sight, in part because its surreal strangeness, brought to bear on the nation's last fairyland, seemed too savage for people still trying to recover from the Depression. But West's art reminds us that grim awareness means nothing without matching comprehension. His best novels, *Miss Lonelyhearts* and *The Day of the Locust,* are guidebooks of a sort. They flaunt their freedom from the detachment we associate with photographs while also insisting on their reportorial accuracy. They enable us to confront the despair that fills the lives of people, even those with money, who know that they are truly home-less, as well as the violence that feeling lost and hopeless can provoke. And they surprise us with the consequences of ordinary emptiness. Horrors run amok in them. But their deepest horror derives from West's insistence that the despair that drives people toward death can also drive them to commit any atrocities they are capable of conceiving, including those that center on the pursuit and the deferral, the deferral and the pursuit, of inflicting death and suffering it.

6. DOCUMENTARY LITERATURE AND THE DISARMING OF DISSENT

Photography began acquiring documentary authority in the nineteenth century, when the daguerreotype first appeared. Later, as equipment improved, it began to assert itself as an art form that tied artistic fidelity to passivity. Later still, having joined forces with literary realism and naturalism, it reinforced aesthetic doctrines of direct presentation and authorial impersonality. During the thirties, it allied itself with history, as a recording instrument, and to a lesser extent with sociology, as an analytic tool. Large-scale efforts, including several funded by such government agencies as the Farm Security Administration, were launched to create photographic records of faces and scenes. In a related move, with the example of the camera in mind, writers tried to use words to record and preserve objects, faces, and scenes. Like Asch's *The Road* (1939), Louis Adamic's *My America* (1938) reports without photographs, but the recording instinct of the social reporter informs his work, and so does the example of the camera. In books like Margaret Bourke-White and Erskine Caldwell's *You Have Seen Their Faces* (1937), Dorothea Lange and Paul S. Taylor's *An American Exodus: A Record of Human Erosion in the Thirties* (1939), Archibald MacLeish's *Land of the Free* (1938), and Richard Wright and Edwin Rosskam's *Twelve Million Black Voices* (1941), words and photographs comment on one another. In each of these books, however, the text tends to become subordinate to the photographs, as MacLeish acknowledged by saying that, having begun as "a book of poems illustrated by photographs," his project had become "a book of photographs illustrated by a poem." Lange and Taylor in particular celebrate an aesthetic built on the clear, vivid, and seemingly detached art of photography.

Documentary literature in the thirties used the camera as an instrument, invoking the authority of its nascent aesthetic, in order to preserve a fading past and tame a threatening present. Like the new social sciences, including new forms of history, art and journalism joined the effort to preserve "the American way of life." In the process, often unwittingly, they contributed to the success of Roosevelt's New Deal. Roosevelt's style of leadership, featuring experimentation, or "statesmanship as adjustment," depended on his ability to learn as he groped. But it also depended on his ability to persuade "the people" to learn as they groped by persuading them, in large part rhetorically, that by groping he and they were doing three things at once: continuing traditions of the past, saving the present, and shaping the future. Most of the "alphabet agencies" of the New Deal, including the FSA (Farm Security

Administration), the CCC (Civilian Conservation Corps), and the WPA (Works Progress Administration), which included the FWP (Federal Writers' Project) and the FTP (Federal Theater Project), were parts of a large campaign in which action and persuasion reinforced each other. In them the line between agency and message, or propaganda, blurred.

The quality of the outpourings that resulted from the nation's large push to preserve its story, like the motives behind the government's initiatives, were mixed, and they remain difficult to assess. Recalling his own debt to the FWP (1935–42), Saul Bellow described it as belonging to a "day before gratitude became obsolete," when writers unexpectedly became beneficiaries of federally sponsored programs. Other writers viewed the government's programs as more or less subtle co-optive moves, and grateful artists as willing or not so willing dupes. Though some works produced were of marginal value, others were important. Richard Wright's *Uncle Tom's Children* (1938) won a prize from *Story* magazine for the best work by an FWP writer, and Pare Lorentz's documentary *The River,* which influenced both Steinbeck and Faulkner, was produced by the FSA. Certainly, the scope of government-sponsored projects was impressive. During its four-year existence, the FTP employed nearly 13,000 people and presented more than 42,000 performances, with a repertoire that ranged from *Macbeth* to *Hansel and Gretel;* from a folklore-based ballet of "Frankie and Johnny," which featured pirouetting pimps and prostitutes, to scores of new plays by FTP writers – including Paul Green's *Hymn to the Rising Sun,* George Sklar's *Stevedore,* Theodore Brown's *Lysistrata,* Elmer Rice's *Prologue to Glory* (a play about Lincoln), and W. E. B. Du Bois's *Haiti* (about a revolt against Napoleon) – several of which were condemned by Martin Dies's House Un-American Activities Committee. Conrad Aiken, Arna Bontemps, Erskine Caldwell, Ralph Ellison, Margaret Walker, Eudora Welty, Edmund Wilson, Richard Wright, and Frank Yerby were among hundreds of writers employed on federal projects, some of whom worked in cooperation with teams of photographers to produce guidebooks that surveyed the people, land, history, and culture of each of the forty-eight states and Alaska. Simply in terms of accumulated data, the results were impressive. But in addition to the guidebooks, on which nearly 12,000 researchers, writers, and coordinators worked, hundreds of biographies, histories, compilations of folk songs and folk stories, accounts of expeditions and explorations, and a variety of documentary reports were produced.

The documentary enterprise sponsored by the New Deal reinforced an impression with which it may fairly be said to have begun: that the nation's culture had done and was doing too little for "the people." But it also enlarged the need it set out to meet – the need to recover, in Alfred Kazin's words, a sense of "America *as an idea.*" As a result, it stimulated a remarkable outpouring of creative energies. In its conjoining of words and photographs, furthermore, it encouraged further examination of the complex relations between scenes of life, on one side, and forms of human perception, feeling, and expression, on the other. Having brought the desire to recover the past into contact with efforts to record images of the nation's spaces, it gave new weight to a notion dating back to Plato, that human creativity begins with a sense of place. In addition, it recalled moments when empty spaces had become named places, including one when an expanse of land so large no wanderer could think the end of it, under a sky that seemed as big as time itself, had become the "Great Plains."

Following a visit in 1926, the Dutch historian Johan Huizinga observed, in "Life and Thought in America," that in this country serious fiction (Cather, Wharton, Dreiser, and Lewis are among the writers he mentions) exposes the cheap optimism and boosterism of the nation's society and protests its puritanical prohibitions and crass materialism. But he also noted that its culture tended to reassert its power by assimilating and neutralizing even its most acidic critics, often by making their roles ornamental. London, whom Huizinga does not mention, has this in common with Wharton, Dreiser, Cather, and Lewis, whom he does mention: that he became read and rewarded only to find in large popularity what they had experienced in more modest success – that the United States was surprisingly resourceful in resisting the implications of what he wrote.

The documentary movement of the thirties, though in part an effort to recover "America *as an idea*," was also an effort to make art – image and word – more than ornamental, first, by making it more responsible to social realities and, second, by making it an integral part of the effort to survive. In this way it sought to counter the process by which art loses force as it earns praise. By deciding to make *Land of the Free* "a book of photographs illustrated by a poem" rather than "a book of poems illustrated by photographs," MacLeish came close to making it another version of the reiterative art practiced by writers like Farrell, which relies heavily on the quantitative piling up of similar scenes. Two books for which Edwin Rosskam selected FSA photographs – Sherwood Anderson's *Home Town* (1940) and Richard Wright's *Twelve Million Black Voices* – also present verbal texts that illustrate visual texts. They depend less on juxtaposition and progression than on the accumulation of discrete images. But other works – notably Lange and Taylor's *An American Exodus* and Bourke-White and Caldwell's *You Have Seen Their Faces* – accomplish more by remaining divided and even conflicted.

Both Lange and Bourke-White thought of the camera as the perfect instrument of documentary art because they believed in its directness and passivity. "With a camera," Bourke-White said, "the shutter opens and closes and the only rays that come in to be registered come directly from the object in front of you." The "truth of the times," as the phrase went, could emerge through a camera, untainted by bias that no writer could escape, even by taking the camera as a model: "I am a camera with its shutter wide open," Christopher Isherwood said, "quite passive, not thinking." But Lange and Bourke-White accomplished more than their theory allowed, often by violating it. They began with the aim of recording the crippling effects of poverty on the suddenly visible poor: those who were "burned out, blowed out, eat out, tractored out," as one farmer interviewed by Lange and Taylor put it. The Great Depression was a leveling experience as well as a harsh one. It left a fair number of bankers and large landholders trapped in milder versions of the same hopeless, moneyless mess that robbed farmers of land and laborers of jobs. The results proved wrenchingly divisive. Several months after the Historical Section of the Resettlement Administration published a photograph made by Walker Evans in Bethlehem, Pennsylvania, in 1935 – of a cemetery against a backdrop of tenement houses, with a large steel mill looming in the background – a woman appeared at the Washington office of the Resettlement Administration and asked for a copy of the photograph so that she could send it to her brother, a steel executive in Pennsylvania, bearing a message: "*Your* cemeteries, *your* streets, *your* buildings, *your* steel mills. But *our* souls, God damn you."

Photographers like Lange, Bourke-White, and Evans played major roles in recording the faces of the Great Depression, but they did so by allowing their practice to outstrip the theory. Among the several large lessons of the Depression, one of the largest is this: that even in near disaster people find unexpected ways of refusing to be reduced to silence or passivity. In the thirties, photography and documentary literature not only helped to make these lessons visible; they also enacted art's versions of them. They recorded the faces of weather-beaten, almost vanquished people – urban and rural, black, brown, and white – whom hunger, fear, and anger had taught how not to smile. They celebrated the resilience of former "hyphenated-Americans" and former slaves side by side with once "native sons" and once-proud farmers. They recorded the personal narratives of former slaves and the folk music – songs of protest, drinking songs, and gospel songs – of people from the hills of Kentucky, Tennessee, North Carolina, and Georgia to the streets of New York, Detroit, Chicago, and San Francisco. In this vast undertaking, they made words and photographs work together in ways that have little to do with objectivity.

Like Bourke-White, Lange associated her art with passivity. But her famous "Migrant Mother," one of several photos she took of Florence Thompson on a wet March afternoon in 1936, in a migrant labor camp in Nipomo, California, gathers power from several sources, including their central figure, a mother weary of consideration and worn by privation, sheltering her shy, frightened, and almost helpless children. Both nature's force, which is felt directly, and society's indifference, which is felt as abnegation, come to bear on vulnerable human beings. But Lange's photograph also confronts its always more comfortable viewer with the suffering of people who ask, in all but words, what they may make of their diminished lives. The children convey a sense of vulnerable yearning that privation has not extinguished, the mother, a strength and faithfulness that weariness has not destroyed. At the same time, Lange's photograph depends on and even registers the vulnerability and faithfulness of an artist who refuses to let privilege drain her of compassion or near helplessness drain her of resolve. There is a felt correspondence, a reciprocity, between the Migrant Mother and Lange, as we see even more clearly when the most famous of the photographs is viewed in the context of the six that she made on that rainy afternoon. This dimension of Lange's art – its quiet celebration of art's engagement with life as the form that art's faithfulness to life and to itself must take – runs counter to the notion that photography's force depends on objectivity. And in this, it discloses the deeper significance of the documentary impulse: its determination that art be more than ornament.

Some documentary works – Ruth McKenney's *Industrial Valley* (1939) and George Leighton's *Five Cities* (1939), for example – as well as some more overtly imaginative works – including George Maltz's *The Underground Stream* (1940), a novel about automobile factories, and Thomas Bell's *Out of This Furnace* (1941), a novel about steelworkers in Pennsylvania – leave us with the sense of writers who feel almost overwhelmed by their tasks. "I, for one, considered myself a witness to the times rather than a novelist," said Jack Conroy. Under the double pressure of a "radical world view" and the "urgency of the times," imaginative acts seemed almost futile, Herbst remarked. Some writers tended, D. H. Lawrence noted, in speaking of Dahlberg, to be content with dramatizing their own defeat, as though they were in love with themselves in their "defeated role." But in the era's more remarkable collaborations – of Lange and Taylor, Bourke-White and Caldwell, Wright and Rosskam, and especially Walker Evans and James Agee – the pressures against passive objectivity mount. Both Walker Evans and James Agee wanted, as Agee put it, "to perceive simply the cruel radiance of what is." But each of them wanted to know it, as though for the first and last time, as artists working with and through their different media. One sign of this is Evans's curious mix of clearly posed and seemingly unposed photographs. Another is Agee's strained and even painful effort to integrate all of the motives as well as the means of his perceiving and recording into the story he tells. The result, *Let Us Now Praise Famous Men* (1941), constitutes one of the most remarkable encounters with the United States in crisis yet written. Agee analyzes the shame and pitiableness even more than the anger and fear of the Ricketts and the Gudger families of Alabama. He exposes the sexual desire that he feels for and attributes to the people he writes about. Gender, class, and race as facts of life and as social constructions also come into play, as does the force of privation. Yet Agee also celebrates the endurance and even the obdurate privacy of the families into whose lives he intrudes. Having anticipated the deprivation he encounters, he finds himself surprised by dignity.

Like several other writers of the thirties, Agee preferred native traditions of radicalism, in part because he wanted to subordinate both the aesthetic concerns of the twenties and the political concerns of the thirties to a new kind of reporting in which the lines between history and art and between nonfiction and fiction blur. In one sense, the meaning of the sharecroppers' lives resides in the bare facts of their existence; in another, it is discovered as well as preserved through the intrusive acts that record them. Agee could and did describe his art as a teasing out of the "cruel radiance of what is," as though the radiance in question were prior to the act of writing – which is to say, were already wholly present in the object described. But he remained an almost painfully self-conscious artist who could and did speak of his art in very different terms; and in practice he worked through a far more complicated predicament.

Agee's effort to transform the invisible struggles "of an undefended and appallingly damaged group of human beings," first, into visible and, then, into famous lives draws on lessons gathered from several sources, including Whitman's injunction to vivify the facts, Dos Passos's insistence on the disjunctions between human lives and human scenes, and a range of rhetorical traditions of the South. As a result, he violates facile notions about the objectivity of documentary literature from the first page of his book to the last. His text not only interacts with Evans's photographs. It employs a wide range of discourses – ethnographic, sociological, phenomenological, theological, historical, autobiographical, poetic, novelistic – and utilizes an astonishing range of styles – realist, naturalist, impressionist, expressionist, surrealist, cubist, and visionary. He takes the radiance of the real seriously by taking the reconstitutive power of art seriously.

Power in fact emerges as one of Agee's great themes. We witness and thus become complicit in the power of words and of photographs to invade and impose themselves on human lives as well as to represent, fix, and transform them. The power of words and photographs to represent and construct are a part of what *Let Us Now Praise Famous Men* critiques. The book depends on those powers, and on the willingness of the poet and the photographer to use them in representing those who cannot represent themselves – cannot speak in their own voices or name their own enemies, cannot defend their interests or assert their rights, and certainly cannot impose their needs and desires upon their world. Agee discovers and confronts the presumption implicit in his effort to represent the unrepresented. He exposes, in a kind of confession, his own mixed needs – in which sexual desire, economic and professional ambition, and social condescension mingle – and acknowledges that he cannot hope faithfully to do all that needs to be done. He realizes that he belongs to the privileged world that has sentenced to silence and privation those whose lives he presumes to invade and condescends to honor. But like Lange and Evans, he persists in doing his work while making his confession because he believes that what he is doing is better done than not done.

Agee assumes that words become images and images, words; and he assumes that the world to which he belongs depends upon the power of words and images to shape as well as represent life. He knows, in short, the power of words like "art" and "artist" as well as "sharecropper," "tenant farmer," and "redneck," just as he knows what interests profit from such words. When his manuscript, which was commissioned and then rejected by *Fortune* magazine, was first submitted to Harper Brothers in late August 1938, its title was *Cotton Tenants: Three Families*. But as Nazi armies swept across Poland, preempting the world's attention, Harper Brothers lost interest in the book. When it finally appeared, published by Houghton Mifflin in 1941, Agee had exchanged its descriptive title for a poetic one and had also given up hope of having the book produced in newsprint so that tenant farmers could afford to buy it. Together, these changes reflect his awareness of the oddity and power of his work and his awareness of the gulf that separated him and his readers from the people of whom he had written and for whom he wanted to write. *Let Us Now Praise Famous Men* is, in short, a deeply self-conscious work. It is a meditation on the cruel radiance of what we see and a meditation on the cruel fact that with all the goodwill we can muster we can never recognize and acknowledge more than a part of what we see. And it is also a meditation on the limits of what, among the things we see and recognize, we can directly record or indirectly evoke with images and words. In it, even omission and silence come under inspection. What objects do to subjects, and subjects do to objects – the Rickettses and the Gudgers to Evans and Agee, as well as Evans and Agee to the Rickettses and the Gudgers – emerge as twin themes. Agee's narrative becomes confessional and autobiographical because under pressure it must: the objects of his observations – of his snoopings, spyings, and pryings – invade him, calling him and his vocation into question, forcing him to present both himself and his work for inspection and examination. One set of tensions he plays with has to do with social and economic class; another has to do with race and caste; another with sexual desires, his own as well as those of the Rickettses and Gudgers, both as they exist and as he renders them; and another with journalism and art, even "honest" journalism and "selfless" art, since Agee knew that the struggle for money and fame is never far from the artist's view.

Among prose works of the thirties and early forties, only Faulkner's greatest novels are as unrelenting as *Let Us Now Praise Famous Men* in scrutinizing the social and vocational predicament of literature and the writer. The guilt that Agee carries through his story is in part the guilt of a survivor. But it is also the guilt of that privileged creature, the artist, for whom suffering and loss become, among other things, art's occasion and subject: if the Rickettses and Gudgers *had* life – had expressive voices, decent spaces, and decent livings of their own – Agee seems to say, they should have no need of art or artists. Agee's irony constantly turns back on the self and work of the artist by positing indirectly an ideal state in which the Gudgers and Rickettses of the world so fully possess life – and with it, force – that they possess the only radiance worth having and so have no need of Evans or Agee and their arts of image and word. There is, as a result, deep ambivalence in *Let Us Now Praise Famous Men,* and a hovering silence as well. The self-reflexivity fostered by Agee's double commitment – to the limited radiance of life itself and to the limited radiance of what art can do with and for broken, stunted lives – alters the boundaries between nonfiction and fiction by clouding them, and so invites those who read his book to question themselves and their motives.

Agee and Evans opened the documentary tradition to directions that are still being explored. In doing this, however, they also defined the limits within which radical thought tended to work in the thirties. The widening web of suspicion that we associate with Marx and Freud – of social institutions and of personal and family relations – threatened at times to silence Agee. Privilege of the kind he had known at Phillips Exeter and Harvard became suspect to him, along with many familiar human motives, including those of artists and reformers. Not even loyalty and valor, human feeling and truth seeking wholly escaped the web of his suspicion. He remained a sojourner everywhere he lived. But despite his doubts, he went on trying to enter the lives, hear the voices, and speak the language of those among whom he moved; and despite his desire for privacy and his fear of exposure, he went on inviting others to examine his. He found his finest moments as a human being and as a writer in *Let Us Now Praise Famous Men* because he found in it a way of holding on to diminished life and imperfect art by making diminished life serve imperfect art, and imperfect art enhance diminished life.

7. THE SOUTHERN RENAISSANCE: FORMS OF REACTION AND INNOVATION

Facing a world that seemed in danger of losing its way, shapers of the documentary movement in the thirties brought to culmination the most extensive literary and artistic effort ever launched to record, examine, and change the life and values of the people of the United States. The guidebooks sponsored by the WPA present the thirties as a casualty of the past. They focus on dusty, windblown streets and peeling storefronts; on dried-up towns and eroded farms; on segregated water fountains and restrooms; on houses whose windows and doors are shut; and on faces that are gaunt, blank, or even battered. Reiterating the messages conveyed by the titles of books like Dreiser's *Tragic America* (1931), Wilson's *The American Jitters* (1932), and Anderson's *Puzzled America* (1935), they provide correctives, as Robert Cantwell noted, "to the success stories that dominate our literature." At the same time, they exemplify energy and resolve. Simply by bringing photography into innovative conjunctions with new modes of reporting, Bourke-White and Caldwell, Wright and Rosskam, Lange and Taylor, and Agee and Evans added a new dimension to the "bold, persistent experimentation" that was the trademark of the New Deal. In the process, they helped to salvage and rehabilitate both "America" and "the People" as ideas of genuine force.

Moved by a similar sense of crisis, historical novelists like Kenneth Roberts searched through the nation's past, looking for heroes. Documentary works of the thirties focus on the average suffering of the neglected and voiceless poor – and, if only as putative presences, on the intent, inquiring faces of writers and photographers jerked to attention by that suffering. Historical novels focus on the triumphs of heroic men, or occasionally a heroic woman, who command our attention by virtue of superior status or achievement. As putative presences, historical novelists sometimes lapse into the role of distracted dreamers born out of season, turned toward some distant home of the mind. But the role they covet blends the talents of a detective with the motives of a moralist who wants to make giants of the past serve as models for the present. In a series of novels – *Arundel* (1930), *Rabble in Arms* (1933), *Northwest*

Passage (1937), and *Oliver Wiswell* (1940) – Kenneth Roberts presents heroes who turn turmoil and trial into triumph. His books helped the nation retain a sense of itself as young during the first decade in which it felt old.

In the mid-thirties, as conditions began to ease some, several writers launched a counterattack against the negative reports that Cantwell thought of as needed correctives. Disaffected intellectuals who persisted in depicting the nation as puzzled, jittery, and tragic were labeled "misleaders" by Van Wyck Brooks. During the Lyric Years, Brooks had launched his career with *The Wine of the Puritans* (1908) and *America's Coming of Age* (1915), in which he used past failings to point American culture toward its true destiny. During the thirties, with the nation mired in disillusionment, he began writing success stories. Shortly after writing *The Life of Emerson* (1932), his first tale of literary triumph, he launched a five-volume series on "Finders and Makers" with *The Flowering of New England, 1815–1865* (1936) and *New England: Indian Summer, 1865–1915* (1940). The "goldenrod rises again in its season, and the folk-poem recovers its meaning, when the nation, grown old, returns to its youth," we read in *New England: Indian Summer,* in a line that captures almost perfectly a theme – of hope rooted in memories – that nudged its way into books like Louis Adamic's *My America* (1938). People are free, Brooks wrote in *The Flowering of New England,* sounding another shared theme, when "they belong to a living, organic, believing community, active in fulfilling some unfulfilled, perhaps unrealized purpose" rooted in the past. Dos Passos remained more skeptical than Brooks. But by 1937, a year after completing *The Big Money* (1936), he too decided to turn his long-standing fascination with the nation's past to the task of defining its "hope for the future." *The Living Thoughts of Thomas Paine* (1940) was one result, and *The Ground We Stand On* (1941) another. We "must never forget," he wrote in the latter, "that we are heirs to one of the grandest and most nearly realized world-pictures in all history."

It remained, almost by default, the task of the South to keep alive the darker view of history with which the thirties – buried in failed banks, dried-up farms, and blighted lives – had begun. World War I had changed the region. Thousands of young Northerners, including Fitzgerald, had taken basic training there, and thousands of Southerners, including one of Faulkner's brothers, had traveled north en route to France. At the Great War's end, a large migration from the depleted soil of the South to the streets of the North was still under way, particularly among southern African-Americans. But the region's lingering resistance to the incorporating Union – typified by its persistence in voting Democratic while Republicans were running the country – preserved its isolation, and in 1920 the collapse of the agricultural market pushed it deeper in debt. As affluence and rumors of affluence continued to spread across the land, the South began to crack under the strain of being the only poor region in the world's richest nation. Hoping to make belated peace, a new generation of leaders intensified their efforts to attract industries from the North, particularly textile factories from New England. But nothing seemed to go right. In 1927 the heavens opened up, devastating the richest farmlands the South had left with a record-breaking flood, and then closed in a widespread, three-year drought that lasted through 1930, intensifying the impact of the Depression.

Merging as they did with the military buildup of World War II, the federally administered economic reforms of the New Deal changed every section of the United States. But they changed the South most because the South had farther to go. To be fully incorporated into the Union, the South had to change its values as well as its political economy. Agencies such as the Agricultural Adjustment Administration, the Civilian Conservation Corps, the Federal Emergency Relief Administration, and the Tennessee Valley Authority, to name a few, helped to keep the South solidly Democratic. They also accelerated its integration into this country's version of the modern world. Some Southerners thought of Roosevelt as a "prophetic figure"; others, resistant to the end, rejected everything he stood for. Most federal programs fell short of their goals. Some failed badly, especially among those most in need of help. Southern African-Americans called the NRA (National Recovery Act) the "Negro Run Around" and "Negroes Ruined Again." But the New Deal accelerated a transformation, tilting the South farther away from its old, dispersed, agriculturally based form of capitalism toward a new industrial, commercial, and centralized political economy administered from its own centers of communication and transportation as well as political, economic, and commercial exchange, such as Atlanta, Georgia. This rapid transformation triggered a sense of betrayal and a sense of hope that informed the emergence of the South's new literature.

The Southern Renaissance – the most striking literary development of the thirties – arose from an improbable confluence of events. On one side, the Crash brought the United States closer to the experience of the South, which had all along been closer to the experience of the world at large, making southern experience suddenly more pertinent. On the other, it sped the South's integration into the Union, triggering dislocations and ambivalences similar to those found in literary modernism. Looking back on his own beginnings as an experimental painter, Robert Motherwell noted that he and his colleagues had been "formed by the Depression, when the American Dream lay in pieces on the floor," making the "possibility of making money . . . inconceivable to us." What he and his friends had sought instead, he added, was "to use the standards of international modernism as a gauge" in order "to make painting that would stand up under international scrutiny." In many respects, Motherwell's aim was shared by Faulkner and several of the Southern Agrarians, including the early editors of the *Southern Review*. But it was shared with differences that can be accounted for only when we recognize that local history shapes literature, particularly the novel, far more directly than it shapes painting.

When the Crash came, bringing the nation down almost into the dust, it found the South waiting there, already on familiar terms with history's great negative lessons of poverty, failure, defeat, and guilt. Beneath the surface of the nation's official history lay thousands of brutal stories – of people captured and enslaved; of people robbed of their land and herded onto reservations; of pioneers whose backbreaking labors had done little more than scar the plains; of women ignored, belittled, dominated, and abused; of working masses huddled in ghettos; of gaunt tenant farmers and itinerant day laborers. "It is not till you live in America, and go a little under the surface," D. H. Lawrence observed, "that you begin to see how terrible and brutal is the mass of failure that nourishes the roots of the gigantic tree of dollars." Yet "when we think of America," he noted, we think first of "her huge success" and "never realize how many failures have gone, and still go to build up that success."

When we think of the South, by contrast, we think first of failure and defeat. In the days of the Revolution and the early republic, the South's story had been almost one with the nation's official story. It was a story of westward expansion, and it was a story of success piled on success. During the age of George Mason, George Washington, James Madison, and Thomas Jefferson, the South had been rich even in letters. Edgar Allan Poe and Mark Twain possessed ties to the South; and T. S. Eliot seems at times to have thought he did, particularly when he was writing about Mark Twain or was searching for a cultural explanation for the tensions that divided him and the sense of dispossession that haunted him – when, in short, he wanted to understand why he felt central by family heritage yet marginal by temperament. In fact, however, unlike Eliot's family, the South had begun living an almost separate history even before the fateful decisions that led it into secession. Its dream of an agrarian society built on the backs of black slaves and crowned by a white landed aristocracy set it squarely against the nation's egalitarian rhetoric and its headlong rush to transform itself into a model of corporate capitalism built on the backs of laborers and crowned by an aristocracy of wealth.

The South's decision to declare itself separate and commit itself to the institution of slavery intensified its regional differences. Four years of decimating war followed by twelve years of occupation left it sequestered in shame and resentment and poor in everything except subregions, dialects, and the great negative lessons of history, all of which both cut across and sharpened divisions based on class, caste, race, and gender. What the South dreamed was one thing, but what it directly knew was another. In 1929, despite several decades of slow recovery, the South remained guilt-ridden yet defiant. But it also remained internally conflicted, in part because its experience of defeat seemed inseparable from the only claims to distinction it had left.

During the late nineteenth and early twentieth centuries, when for the nation at large being an "almost chosen people" seemed clearly to mean being chosen for wealth and power, the South made small gains and yet fell farther behind. By 1929 it was in large part a land of hominy grits and hookworms, sharecroppers and subsistence farmers, moonshine whiskey and feuding clans, cultural backwardness and a strict and often brutal system of racial segregation. When, infrequently, the larger nation paused to think about the subject, it regarded the South as an embarrassment. If northern industry went with virtue, southern backwardness went with vice; the South's failure had been moral before it became military or economic. H. L. Mencken fancied himself an iconoclastic deflator of his nation's self-deceptions. Yet in virtually every word he uttered about the South, even in asides, he reinforced one of the North's deepest assumptions: that compared with the South, it was virtually spotless. Such assumptions carried weight in the South as well as the North, furthermore, because one thing the North and South shared was a religious tradition that had never been able to decide whether salvation was a wage for good works or a gift of grace.

The South's deepest fear derived from its share in this basic confusion. Neither its religious fundamentalism (another of its trademarks) nor its almost separate history had wholly separated it from the nation's dream of innocence and wealth. Yet to a region whose identity revolved around lessons of loss, what could that dream do except redouble self-doubt? In posing repeatedly the question Miss Rosa Coldfield raises in Faulkner's *Absalom, Absalom!* (1936), of why God let the South lose the war, the South raised repeatedly the half-repressed question that haunted it even more than losing the war itself: of whether in a nation that thought of itself as commissioned by God to become a model of confidence, industry, and prosperity, it had been chosen to stand as an antitype of guilt, sloth, and poverty. The deep alienation that stands at the heart of southern writing in the thirties has several sources, including the ambivalence the South felt about the nation's headlong rush toward secularism, progress, prosperity, and power. At its best, however, particularly in the fiction of Faulkner, it includes several kinds of ambivalence, including one generated by recognition that its mixed history contained literary possibilities that were lying there, waiting to be exploited.

The result was a literature of divisions that are intensely if not peculiarly modern: stories about the hope of being chosen and the pain of being excluded; stories about being, and being doomed to remain, *other;* and stories in which defeat – as a kind of death, as well as a principle of exclusion – becomes a spur to the imagination. These stories were nothing if not commodious. They made room for crucial questions about language and forms of storytelling and the ties of both of these to place or region. They made room for issues of class, caste, race, and gender, and thus for the language of power as well as the power of language. As a result, with the thirties as backdrop, the South was able to create a literature that laid claim to the future by studying out its past and by examining the moment to which that past had somehow led.

In 1922 a group of professors and students at Vanderbilt, led by John Crowe Ransom, a Tennessean educated at Oxford, founded a magazine called the *Fugitive* and began publishing verse characterized by wit, irony, restraint, impersonality, and formal precision – which is to say, verse that was more "modern" than "southern." By 1929, however, the Fugitives were prepared to join in a remarkable flowering that adjusted "modern" preoccupations to "regional" concerns. In that year – in which Hemingway published *A Farewell to Arms* and Lewis published *Dodsworth* – Joseph Wood Krutch of Tennessee published *The Modern Temper,* Ellen Glasgow of Virginia published *They Stooped to Folly,* Evelyn Scott of Tennessee published *The Wave,* Allen Tate of Kentucky published *Jefferson Davis: His Rise and Fall,* Robert Penn Warren of Kentucky published *John Brown: The Making of a Martyr,* Thomas Wolfe of North Carolina published *Look Homeward, Angel,* T. S. Stribling of Tennessee published *Strange Moon,* and William Faulkner of Mississippi published both *Sartoris,* the shortened version of *Flags in the Dust* (1973), and *The Sound and the Fury.* The decade that followed – which witnessed the continued work of Ransom, Scott, and Glasgow, the maturation of Stribling, Grace Lumpkin, Donald Davidson, Erskine Caldwell, Andrew Lytle, Katherine Anne Porter, Margaret Mitchell, and Zora Neale Hurston, as well as Warren and Young, and the emergence of writers like James Agee, Lillian Smith, Eudora Welty, and Richard Wright, as well as historians and sociologists like W. J. Cash, Frank Owsley, Howard Odum, John Ballard, and C. Vann Woodward, together with several great novels by Faulkner – belonged to the South as no decade before or since has. Many novels of the thirties – not only strike novels, detective novels, and hard-boiled fiction, but novels by writers as different as Djuna Barnes, Henry Miller, James T. Farrell, John Dos Passos, and Nathanael West – are angry in mood. Yet most of them remain interrogative. Despite their bluster and their surface confidence, they remain tentative even when, borrowing from documentaries, they are most concrete or, following early modernists, they affect great formal control. "Why, why is God letting this happen to us?" they ask in a thousand ways.

It was, strangely, on such questions, which in a sense can never be answered, that southern writers suddenly began to think of themselves as expert witnesses. In villages, where the South still lived in 1929, they had observed people who lived in slow time and acquired a sense of sequence and shared knowledge. But they had also seen history batter people with failures and defeats, leaving them with the sense of being entangled in messy stories whose beginnings and endings were hazy and whose meanings, like their margins, were blurred.

By 1929 more and more Southerners were ready to buy into the dream of becoming rich and powerful enough to impose their will on their environment. Having lost hold on the old sense of living in a world made for them, they began grabbing at the possibility of making one for themselves. The considerable ambivalence provoked by this effort can be observed in novels as different as Erskine Caldwell's *God's Little Acre* (1933) and Ellen Glasgow's *Barren Ground* (1925). It can also be seen in Faulkner's novels, where backward-looking ghosts vie with forward-looking parvenus for our attention. Many Southerners drawn toward the great project of bending the world to fit human desire still felt the pull of a world of which they could say what Faulkner said of North Mississippi – that its glory lay in the fact that God had done more for it than man had yet done to it. And when, having opted for the Union's way, they saw the nation's economy fall apart, their ambivalence was deepened by frustration. Faulkner became the most inventive of the nation's novelists of the twentieth century in part because, like Wallace Stevens, he learned to make expression the subject of expression and invention the subject of invention. In the process, he gave space to oppressed lives and expression to submerged voices, including occasionally those of people born poor, female, or black. But the South's ambivalence also triggered reaction. In 1930 a group of Southern Agrarians denounced the great technological project of the United States in a manifesto called *I'll Take My Stand,* which includes contributions by Davidson, Ransom, Tate, Warren, and Young, bearing titles like "Reconstructed but Unregenerate."

I'll Take My Stand is reactionary on several counts, including its denial of voice and space to black, female, and lower-class Southerners, as well as its strong preference for the agrarian way over the industrial-commercial way, for "high" culture over "low," for privileged classes over the dispossessed, and for timeless "literature" over mere writing. Only in "art" – and cautiously there – is innovation praised. Yet, by recoil, as it were, Davidson, Ransom, Tate, Warren, and Young clarify their moment. Where life is concerned, slow time is their aim. Having helped to invent a past in which a landed, educated, and sternly self-disciplined aristocracy ruled, as opposed to a merely landed one (though a merely landed one seemed to them superior to one dominated by industrialists and bankers), they propose that we turn back the clock and then slow it down by funneling human inventiveness into art. Even there, they want to subject it to a hard and, as it seemed to them, masculine rationality – which is why they tended to prefer Donne to Shakespeare, clean, clear poetry to noisy, messy fiction, and any number of inferior writers to William Faulkner. With time, of course, the Agrarians changed: Ransom more than Davidson, Tate more than Ransom, and Warren more than Tate. But as young men writing in an old country and a dry season, they made recoil their principal mode.

Try as they might, however, they could not master the South's negative heritage simply by declaring it a cultural model. Tate's and Warren's writing improved when they realized that the South's most useful literary resource was its negative identity: that the authority, moral as well as aesthetic, of marginality, failure, guilt, and shame was about all the South had to offer as imaginative capital, and that, in this fate, it had much in common with most other peoples of the earth, including in the thirties many other Americans. Such overlap made it appropriate that the South should become the nation's dominant literary scene for the first time during the Great Depression. As scenes of publishing and marketing writing, Memphis, Nashville, New Orleans, Atlanta, Chapel Hill, Baton Rouge, and Charlottesville remained small, provincial capitals, and Oxford, Mississippi, and Eatonville, Florida, mere frontier outposts, of Boston, New York, and Chicago. But as scenes of writing and as settings for stories, they became dominant.

The South's literary task was complicated, however, by its desire to find some way of honoring its lost causes while it chased prosperity and power. It wanted, in short, to live out of its past in the double sense of claiming ties to it while becoming free of it. From 1935 to 1942 Robert Penn Warren and Cleanth Brooks edited the *Southern Review* out of Baton Rouge and made it an example of what the new literary South, as an extension of the New South, aspired to be. They published the work of several of the Fugitives – Ransom, Tate, Davidson – as well as other southern writers, including Andrew Lytle and Eudora Welty. Some of the work they published harks back to the kinds of resistance celebrated in *I'll Take My Stand,* and its appeal remained largely regional. But some of it points to enlarged ambitions that are reflected in the six fine stories by Welty published there between 1937 and 1939. Welty's stories are grounded in a strong sense of place. But they focus primarily on the South's little people – its traveling salesmen and its hairdressers – not on members of old families burdened with memories and aristocratic pretensions. And they are written out of the formalist tradition that we associate with international modernism, and thus mirror the larger literary ambitions of the *Southern Review.* Despite its regional ties and name, the *Southern Review* of the thirties was not provincial; it was imperial. Kenneth Burke, R. P. Blackmur, and F. O. Matthiessen, whose audiences were broadly American, published there, and so did Ford Madox Ford, Herbert Read, Aldous Huxley, Mario Praz, and Paul Valéry, whose audiences were international. The *Southern Review* thus mirrored the new aspirations of the region whose name it claimed. Despite its talk about aristocracy, the South had always been a preponderantly middle-class society, like the world of Welty's fiction and, for that matter, the rest of the United States. Although it wanted to honor its past as myth as well as fact, with words and monuments, it also wanted to collapse into a few short decades a process of industrialization that, by 1929, was a century old in New England and at least half again as old as that in England: it wanted to move from the old-style agrarian capitalism it had built around plantations to a new-style capitalism built around banks, railroads, factories, and industrial corporations. It wanted to turn its preindustrial republic into a modern, incorporating political economy, so that the future could at last be *now*.

One set of consequences of this shift in allegiance from the Old and toward the New South can be seen in the dislocations, discontinuities, and confusions that directly enter its fiction – the trilogy of T. S. Stribling, for example, called *The Forge* (1931), *The Store* (1932), and *Unfinished Cathedral* (1934), as well as the Snopes trilogy of Faulkner, *The Hamlet* (1940), *The Town* (1957), and *The Mansion* (1959), and virtually all of the fiction of writers like Thomas Wolfe and Erskine Caldwell. Having written essays and documentary works as well as stories, Erskine Caldwell made his mark with *Tobacco Road* (1932) and *God's Little Acre,* both of which are set in the brutalized countryside of the Piedmont, previously more ignored than forgotten. Caldwell's Piedmont remains oblivious to the South's preoccupation with cultural distinctiveness. Its history is felt in entrenched meagerness rather than haunting memories of lost elegance. And its present includes the New South's hope that industrialism may pave the way to greater wealth – and even to a fairer distribution of it. A traveler and a listener, Caldwell writes of despised and oppressed people, with as little adornment as possible and with almost no sense of mannered style. His land is a land of worn-out soil and new industry, including textile mills lured away from a declining New England; and it is a land of exploited, misshapen people who characteristically act with a minimum of reflection and a maximum of yearning and desire, whether they seek gold or sexual pleasure, respectability or justice. None of them understands either the cultural and economic deprivations of their lives or the inadequacies of their dreams. They claim our attention because, despite everything, they are not yet wholly inured to privation. They lead meager lives and have almost no education. But they hold fast to some waning aspiration (in *Tobacco Road,* Jeter Lester's dream of a good tobacco crop; in *God's Little Acre,* Ty Ty Walden's dream of finding gold on a worn-out piece of ground, Will Thompson's dream of securing a fair wage, and even Jim Leslie's pitiful dream of becoming respectable) as though to one last, fading dream. Simply by holding out, they give meager meaning to their lives.

Unlike Caldwell, many southern writers found themselves in a double bind: they wanted to pay homage to the South's past and also participate in deserting it. This tension enters southern fiction of the thirties in many ways. In Margaret Mitchell's *Gone with the Wind* (1936), it emerges as a struggle between what we might call a poetry of the past and a poetry of the future, and it makes Mitchell's novel considerably more interesting than its popularity has led us to believe. Mitchell's poetry of the past emanates from the historical struggle about which she writes – the Civil War – and it remains the ostensible subject of her novel. Her poetry of the future emanates from the historical struggle out of which she wrote, which in her own day had entered a new phase and was nearing a decisive moment. That struggle, which Mitchell surreptitiously seizes as a sequel to the old war, makes itself felt in two very different ways – one an act of recognition, the other an act of suppression.

The recognition enters through the tension (which occasionally comes close to open conflict) between the unconventional, untraditional, pragmatic, self-involved, forward-looking, sentimental yet tough-minded, heroine-protagonist, Scarlett O'Hara, on one side, and the South's conception of itself, on the other. Scarlett's sentimentality surfaces in her regressive love for Ashley Wilkes and her nostalgia for Tara. But there is a sense in which Scarlett belongs more to the novel's future – which is to say, Mitchell's present – than she does to its ostensible present. She begins as a spunky, vain, willful young woman. But socialized by her changing world, she becomes not the woman the Old South would have her be, "a lady," but the opportunistic creature whom Mitchell presents the South as needing and secretly wanting: one who takes whatever quarter she can get but never gives any. Scarlett thus tilts *Gone with the Wind* toward Mitchell's present, when the South was emerging as a region anxious to make its way in the world but anxious, too, about the political and social emergence of blacks. On this count, *Gone with the Wind* remains an emphatically white novel, which is to say an emphatically reactionary one. It suppresses blacks not only as political agents but as independent agents of any kind – this being Mitchell's way of turning the clock back and slowing it down.

Mitchell's persistence in making Scarlett respond unconventionally to familial and personal pressures as well as large social forces makes more striking her persistence in having Scarlett share the South's determination to keep black people in subordinate, subservient roles. Mitchell thinks of Scarlett, and sometimes has Scarlett think of herself, as a rebel, and so in some ways she is. She breaks several rules that govern the behavior of women in her society. But she remains an ardent defender of her confused society, which thinks of itself as aristocratic and traditional even when it acts like the middle class on the make. Scarlett loves the land, but she's willing to leave it if by doing so she can enhance her chance of becoming affluent. She pays lip service to the forbearance and self-denial of women like Melanie, but it is her father's willfulness that she adapts to changing circumstances, in the name not of mere survival but of dominance. The Yankees are right about one thing, she remarks: it takes "money to be a lady," with which admission she embraces the New South emerging around her and turns her back on the Old South, in which money, like sexual desire, was something a "lady" did not talk about.

Like Mitchell's Atlanta, Scarlett is young, headstrong, and ambitious. Tara belongs to an older, agrarian world, where land was the only thing that counted because, allied as it was with family, class, and continuity, as well as the South's concept of "lady," it was the only thing that could be counted on. But Atlanta, where Margaret Mitchell in fact lived not as a lady, is the scene Scarlett makes her own, and it gives her special ties to the new world rising out of the ashes of the old, and to its poet, Margaret Mitchell. *Gone with the Wind* thus engages the story of the South in the extended moment that began with the South's defiance of the North and ended with its full incorporation by it. That moment embraces both the crisis of the Civil War and the crisis of the war's long aftermath, in which crucial questions of race, gender, and justice, as well as unbridled ambition, the fear of poverty, and the worship of success, came into play. On these questions, *Gone with the Wind* combines remarkable recognitions with remarkable evasions and suppressions, because Mitchell, like her region and even her nation, was not prepared to face them.

In discussing Dorinda Oakley, the heroine of *Barren Ground*, Ellen Glasgow praised the old-fashioned virtue of fortitude. Dorinda "exists wherever a human being has learned to live without joy, where the spirit of fortitude has triumphed over the sense of futility." Dorinda's hard choice – to limit and control all personal relationships with men and women in order to avenge and assert herself by reclaiming unproductive land from proliferating broomsedge – comes after she has been betrayed by a wealthy young man named Jason Greylock; and it is apt to strike us as more surprising and troubling in a woman than in a man. If that is our problem, however, Dorinda's is this: that for her, as for men, it leads to a strikingly truncated life. Having disciplined herself to go without many things, she becomes strong yet cold and even hard. The other side of her self-determination and self-assertion is ruthless self-denial –

in all of which she resembles Faulkner's Thomas Sutpen in *Absalom, Absalom!* Disappointed in love, she snaps back to triumph in life and so wins our sympathy, just as she won Ellen Glasgow's. She is a model of resilience as well as iron will. But it tells us much about the logic of Glasgow's art – and by implication Dorinda's life – that as it moved toward *They Stooped to Folly* (1929) and *The Sheltered Life* (1938) it became more distrustful of youthful unrest, and more committed to fortitude – and the resignation that fortitude makes possible – than to joy. Glasgow's heroines and heroes form purposes and sustain culture, together with its institutions and its values, despite the buffeting they receive from nature and history. But as Dorinda puts it, they triumph by keeping themselves "untouched and untouchable." What matters most is a vein of iron called *will,* which teaches the yearning self that denial is the only route to self-realization.

Transformed if not reinvented by her own needs in conjunction with the exigencies of a great cultural crisis, Scarlett O'Hara becomes at least as ruthless as Dorinda Oakley. But she never willingly practices resignation. She wants and is determined to try for everything, including pleasures and comforts, if not intimacies, that Dorinda forgoes. Like Dreiser's Carrie, she is sustained by the hope of tomorrow even when everything goes wrong. The clearest embodiment of self-willed energy in her world, she emerges as the only hope the South has of beating the North at its own game. In some moments, she comes to us as an old-fashioned character who acts as a force by making choices, charting her own course, and changing her world. In others, she comes to us as a newfangled personality, buffeted by the forces that surround and in a sense shape her. Too hurried to be reflective, she assumes that playing well the only game she's been given is better than choosing, like Ashley, to play no game at all simply because the one he prefers has been taken away from him.

Gone with the Wind is, as almost everyone knows, "romantic," not "realistic." But it shares important ground with the great historical novels written in the nineteenth century by Stendhal, Tolstoy, Balzac, Trollope, Dickens, and others, which gained power by tapping the political force of nationalism. In part because it is so accessible, and with the help of Hollywood has become so popular, it has endured as a vehicle for claiming and defining something like a *national* identity for the only despised region of a rich and powerful nation. Mitchell went on living in the New South, of course, even while she was thinking and writing about the Old South, a fact that helps to account for Scarlett's being the strongest part of *Gone with the Wind,* its history, the weakest. Yet even as history *Gone with the Wind* is in one way more accurate than Allen Tate's *The Fathers* (1938). Tate studied history and wrote biographies. But he was finally more a moralist than a historian. What he valued were aristocratic forms of feeling that he thought of as having been crushed by change in Europe and England during the late eighteenth and early nineteenth centuries. The South's hope lay in trying to re-create them. Faith, tradition, and order lent dignity to life by creating high culture and making poetry possible. Although Tate settled for a position in a university, what he wanted for all good writers was a place in society. In his dream, economic sufficiency was enough, so long as literature was accorded a place of honor that recognized its sacred task, of preserving a sense of the past and preparing the hearts and minds of men – and to a lesser extent, those of women – for the proper work of the future: the perpetuation of high culture. The South that Tate called into existence in his writings had committed itself to these things, only to abandon them. Betrayal haunted his mind even more than defeat. But the South he evoked in his essays and poems as well as in *The Fathers* had never been fully achieved even by the most blessed of Virginia's plantation owners. It was a necessary invention of a moralist searching for some adequate means of scolding both the South and the modern world into a program of conservative restoration.

Thomas Wolfe's struggle with the South was more tortured than Mitchell's and less historical than Tate's. For Wolfe was, to borrow the title of an openly autobiographical essay that he wrote and rewrote, "God's Lonely Man." Eugene Gant, his representative protagonist, traces his roots back to a scene in which as a small boy his father had watched southern soldiers marching toward Gettysburg. But Gant's deeper wounds are more recent, and they resemble Wolfe's in being familial, personal, and mortal. Like Wolfe, Gant is an expert on the intimate harms done to children by parents and on the ingenious ways wounded children find of settling scores with their parents. Wolfe wrestled all of his life (he died in September 1938, not quite thirty-eight) and in all of his fiction with the pain of his youth, unable to make peace with it. Like Wolfe, Gant carries his grievances with him, and when they surface, they pour forth in a flood of poetic prose filled with adolescent yearnings as well as old grievances. At odds with his world, Gant is also self-conflicted. Union, the thing he most wants, is denied him as though by some smudge of fortune. Yearnings fill his attenuated life both as a prelude to extravagant spendings of his words and as a hedge against exhausting them.

If in Gant's story we seek Wolfe's image of the South or, more broadly, his image of the United States, we don't have far to go. The United States existed for Wolfe as something present in the "forms we see on every hand of fear, hatred, slavery, cruelty, poverty, and need" and as an idea of free fulfillment too long deferred. Recognizing the otherness of the past, and the way in which it is always already lost, Wolfe tried to create voices that could incorporate old refrains in cadences that belonged to the present: "I believe we are lost here in America, but I believe we shall be found," he wrote in his last letter to "Foxhall Edwards" in *You Can't Go Home Again* (1939).

> And this belief, which mounts now to the catharsis of knowledge and conviction, is for me – and I think for all of us – not only our own hope, but America's ever-lasting, living dream. I think the life which we have fashioned in America, and which has fashioned us – the forms we have made, the cells

that grew . . . – was self-destructive in its nature, and must be destroyed. I think these forms are dying, and must die, just as I know that America and the people in it are deathless, undiscovered, and immortal, and must live.

I think the true discovery of America is before us. I think the true fulfillment of our spirit, of our people, of our mighty and immortal land, is yet to come. I think the true discovery of our own democracy is still before us. And I think that all of these things are as certain as the morning, as inevitable as noon.[6]

Wolfe's books fit together as parts of one long, ragged story written by a person convinced that, by some miracle of election, he is both privileged and doomed to seek words for the lost meanings of his world. His various narrators speak in voices that resemble one another, and they echo his favorite poets. Together they help us locate Wolfe's overarching theme in a conflicted self whose paradoxical fate it is to be the center of a world – family and community – from which he feels almost hopelessly cut off.

Wolfe characteristically begins his stories as he began his life, in a traditional world of small communities where people remember their ancestors, live textured lives in extended families, and accept the past as a guide to the future. But he and his protagonists quickly move away from home into a boarding-house, out of an old, warm world into the modern world of open and endless seeking, yearning, and experimenting. Easy surrender to alienation as well as flight and death play familiar roles in his novels, as we see in Ben and Helen in *Look Homeward, Angel,* and so does the routine, vengeful seeking of recompense, as we see in Luke's mad pursuit of money and position. Wolfe's own version of this was a tortured search for a lost home and a lost father: "We are so lost, so naked and so lonely in America," he wrote. "Immense and cruel skies bend over us, and all of us are driven on forever and we have no home." "And which of us shall find his father, know his face, and in what place, and in what time, and in what land? Where?" These possibilities, the only ones that matter for Wolfe, exist primarily as ideas and are felt primarily in rhetoric – this being another sign of what being cut off means. Wolfe wrote on and on, retracing his loss and his hope again and again.

From one angle, we may say that the profligate quality of Wolfe's fiction, his rhetorical and poetic responses to want born of loss, resembles deficit financing. But his fiction, like Whitman's poetry, centers on his effort to locate and exploit correlations between his story and the nation's story. And his sense of that story brought the United States and his own life under the aspect of the South and the Great Depression into a tale informed, as he once put it in a letter, by an "intolerable memory" of "violence, savagery, immensity, beauty, ugliness, and glory," on one side, and an unfinished quest for wisdom and strength, on the other. Wolfe's art lacks the historical depth and the social reach of Faulkner's, and it misses these things both as enriching resources and as principles of order. But his transitory world still manages to remind us of the fate of regions in the United States. By the time Wolfe wrote, his South was fading as a distinct region. What had happened to New England, the

Midwest, and the West was happening to the South, which had committed itself to being incorporated. If, furthermore, the ever-expanding Union, driven by its logic of incorporation, presents one problem, the South's ambivalence presents another. Wolfe's South, like Mitchell's, wants the Union, which is to say the modern, as much as the Union wants it, and so is prepared to leave to art both its distinctive and largely negative heritage of failure and its prized if largely imagined heritage of glory. Some of Katherine Anne Porter's better stories – "Flowering Judas" and "Noon Wine," for example – trace the descent of people into erotic willfulness and economic opportunism and confront the effects of privation on the lives of marginalized farmers as they erupt into violence. Others, including "The Old Order, "The Grave," and "Old Mortality," are "southern" in their attention to family, tradition, land, and the past. But their focus is on the creation and preservation of a sense of these things, not on the remembered possession of them. Throughout her life, Porter spread misrepresentations about her family and childhood, evoking family traditions that bore little relation except as compensatory strategies to the uprooted life she began in 1890 in a small L-shaped log cabin in Indian Creek, Texas. In its restraint, clarity, and control, her art is closer in style to Fitzgerald's, Hemingway's, and Cather's than to Wolfe's. Her South is not in transition; it is preserved in fabrications disguised as memories of an era of merriment and style that neither she nor her family had ever directly known.

8. HISTORY AND NOVELS / NOVELS AND HISTORY: THE EXAMPLE OF WILLIAM FAULKNER

Speaking in 1964, Ralph Ellison described William Faulkner as the novelist who had brought "the impelling moral function of the novel and . . . the moral seriousness of the form . . . into explicit statement again." On one level, Ellison described this move as consonant with what the "American novel at its best" (Melville, Twain, James, Fitzgerald, Hemingway are among those he mentions) had always done. On another, he described it as consonant with the "specific concerns of literature," including explorations of "new possibilities of language." But he also described it as a move that was natural and even necessary for Faulkner because he had "lived close to moral and political problems which would not stay put underground."

Faulkner's fiction owes something to his powers of observation and his ear for dialect, and something to his sense that human lives are always shaped by natural and social forces, which is to say, by instinct and by culture. His stories are rooted in history as both natural scene and cultural construct. In addition, his fiction owes much to stories and poems he had read and tales he had heard, some of them about the adventures of his own prominent family in North Mississippi. As stories based on direct observation, his novels come to us as more or less organized reports on observed realities. As stories rooted in history, they remind us of the historicity of all deeds done and all words spoken. As stories anchored in individual consciousnesses – the memories and imaginations of narrators of diverse needs and desires as well as mixed strengths and weaknesses – his novels seem necessary and revealing in some moments, tricky and even deceitful in others.

Faulkner thus engaged, obliquely in some moments, more openly in others, the varied formal preoccupations of international modernism in the late moment of its turning back on itself in skepticism and critique as well as continuing celebration. In his fiction, as opposed to his early poetry and sketches, his concern with his own expressive drive manifests itself in his willingness to examine expressive acts. By repeating different versions of the same story and proliferating different narrative voices, he extends and explores the old tales and talking, the core stories and the language – the dialects and the voices – on which his novels depend. His fascination with human creativity culminates in examinations of the need and occasion of human inventions. What sets his fiction apart, however, as the most remarkable of its time and place, are the varied ways in which it brings technical sophistication, often centered on what Hannah Arendt has called "incessant talking," to bear on great social and moral problems – such as poverty and violence, race, gender, caste, and class – that are deeply but not peculiarly southern, and so makes visible to us what Ellison calls the "moral function of the novel" and the "moral seriousness of the form."

Looking back on the trilogy she began in 1933 with *Pity Is Not Enough,* Josephine Herbst thought of it as damaged by the "urgency of the times," which deflected and even discredited the interests ("crumpled" is her term) with which she had begun, including language and the idioms in which she was writing. More isolated than Herbst, Faulkner retained the complex set of interests with which he began. By the end of World War II, Sherwood Anderson, F. Scott Fitzgerald, Ellen Glasgow, Nathanael West, and Thomas Wolfe were dead, and so were W. B. Yeats, James Joyce, and Virginia Woolf. The fifties belonged to a new generation of writers, including several – Welty among them – who had started out in the thirties. But Faulkner's great novels, which began with *The Sound and the Fury* (1929) and ended with *Go Down, Moses* (1942), coincided with the Great Depression, and in their own way gave expression to it.

Faulkner was an amateur historian, genealogist, and folklorist as well as a "failed poet" before he became a novelist. English poetry of the Renaissance and English and French poetry of the nineteenth and early twentieth centuries strongly influenced him, as did English and European novels from Cervantes's *Don Quixote* to Joyce's *Ulysses.* In addition to a remarkably retentive mind, he possessed an ear for dialect and an eye for folkways. He studied the history, geography, vegetation, and wildlife of North Mississippi, in part by collecting from oral traditions different and even contradictory versions of tales about his family and region. In the process, he came to think of literary culture as regional in its origins and historical in its thrust. He remained a weak poet in part because he remained dependent on words, rhythms, and even themes borrowed from distant poets. He became a strong novelist when he turned from the shared scenes and themes of *Soldiers' Pay* (1926) and *Mosquitoes* (1927) toward the largely unexplored territory of North Mississippi, where his need to think of himself as a radical originator, another sign of the "modern," was more easily sustained. Neither his great-grandfather, the "Old Colonel," W. C. Falkner, author of *The White Rose of Memphis* (1880), nor Stark Young, contributor to *I'll Take My Stand* (1930) and author of *So Red the Rose* (1934), a popular romance set in Mississippi during the Civil War, posed a serious threat to a writer who was prepared to create, name, and populate an imaginary county – Yoknapatawpha – as a correlate to the world he understood too well to love or hate.

Provincial shyness contributed to the uneasiness Faulkner felt in New York's literary salons; even the French Quarter in New Orleans got on his nerves after several months. So for the most part he stayed in Oxford, without feeling at home there, as though convinced that his art depended on his ability to achieve intimacy without being drawn into any union he did not largely control. His art is broad in its allusions, analogues, and reach. It brings the culture, society, and political economy of one imaginary North Mississippi county into the broad sweep of U.S. history, which he had studied in much the way Stein, Dos Passos, Herbst, and Warren had. The smaller worlds of his extended families, disfigured as they are by exploitation, privilege, and subjugation, are tied to larger worlds that are similarly disfigured. The logic of virtually every entangling word he wrote reiterates, then qualifies, and even disavows both the peculiarity, or regional otherness, of his fictional world and the dominance that he claimed for himself, on his hand-drawn map of Yoknapatawpha, as its "Sole Owner & Proprietor." Faulkner draws us into his major novels – *The Sound and the Fury* (1929), *As I Lay Dying* (1930), *Light in August* (1931), *Absalom, Absalom!* (1936), *The Hamlet* (1940), and *Go Down, Moses* (1942) – with acts of style that seem simultaneously to assume that human experience is accessible to words imaginatively employed and to acknowledge that human experience remains incommensurate with words and resistive to imaginations. Words "go straight up in a thin line, quick and harmless," Addie Bundren insists in *As I Lay Dying,* while doing moves "terribly . . . along the earth, clinging to it, so that after a while the two lines are too far apart for the same person to straddle from one to the other." Yet Addie remains a creature of memories and words as well as deeds done. She remembers and re-remembers, trying to make words serve her needs. That effort, of seeking words that are commensurate with a life lived, a faithful record of emotions felt and deeds done, remains for her as much a part of what it means to be human as feeling and doing.

Faulkner knew, however, as Addie insists, that words follow a line and lead a life of their own. And with some trepidation, he wanted them to do just that because he wanted them to serve not only as a record or critique of life but also as an enhancement of it or, more radically, as a supplement to it. Readers familiar with Faulkner's fiction know that he felt a special affinity for young, white, southern males born, as he had been, into families whose best days lay behind them. Privileging such people seemed natural to him. Yet few writers have set so varied a cast of characters – rich and poor; illiterate, literate, and even literary; female and male; white and black; old and young – loose in search of words to fit their varied and often more or less desperate needs, or shared with so many characters his sense that our search for words is a part of wisdom and a sign of our humanity – an act of living as well as the heart of our art. His characters struggle – like Addie and with him – to confess their mixed success in achieving some triumph over the limits of language as well as life.

We might begin with *The Sound and the Fury*, which forces us to surrender our most basic categories of understanding – space, time, and causality – in order to confront us with the relinquished, almost vanquished lives of four children named Compson: Benjy, Caddy, Quentin, and Jason. Looking back, Faulkner described his novel as an effort, several times repeated, to match his "dream of perfection." "It's not the sum of a lot of scribbling," he said; it's the dream of writing "one perfect book" that drives an artist. Yet in its first two sections *The Sound and the Fury* ignores every requirement of a well-told, logocentric, linear story. Its words seem not so much to follow a line of their own as to move in several directions at once. Even its familiar title, evoking Macbeth's sense of life – as "a tale / Told by an idiot, full of sound and fury, / Signifying nothing" – turns out to be *dis*orienting. For it not only leads us into a world where our most familiar categories of understanding no longer apply; it also leads us into a world in which art becomes entangled with life rather than rising above it. Having defied our desire for a well-told tale, it goes on to defy our sense of one well concluded: closure, the sense of a well-wrought ending, is another of the things Faulkner fails to provide. Imperfect success – in which stories divide and propagate, as one telling leads to another – emerges as the end of a novel whose striking means consist of fleeting glimpses, partial knowledge, and flawed expression. *The Sound and the Fury* seems at times to flaunt its willfulness in refusing to establish its coherence. It circles and repeats in one motion, and avoids and evades in another. And this is especially true where its missing center, Caddy – the only character who combines sexual energy and a spirit of adventure with a capacity for nurturing love and a spirit of caring – is concerned.

For Caddy is given little space of her own and less voice. She comes to us primarily through the felt needs of her three brothers – Benjy's need for shelter or, more broadly, for *home* as a place he does not have to earn; Quentin's need for deliverance from the desperation of a young man whose several hallucinations spring, on one side, from his rage for order and, on the other, from his rage for ecstasy, which is to say, his need to find both a principle of love and a person to love; and Jason's need to find someone to blame and punish for the dirty tricks he thinks of life as having played on him. Otherwise, the novel approaches Caddy only to pull back, reenacting as well as rendering a process by which a male author conspires with his male characters to marginalize black servants descended of black slaves and also white women. Yet there is gain as well as loss in Faulkner's decision to give Caddy privacy rather than full expression. *The Sound and the Fury*'s refusal of full disclosure, like its refusal of perfect coherence, is essential to its freedom, just as its freedom is essential to its generosity. Few novelists have given readers larger roles in literary transactions and none has shared more fully the process of creation with them. By approaching Caddy and then avoiding her, disclosing her and then concealing her, Faulkner draws his readers into his own imaginative processes, making his art an art of conjecture and surmise, and his reader, his hidden double.

Unlike *The Sound and the Fury*, *As I Lay Dying* begins as a straightforward linear tale. In the book's opening lines, we follow Darl and Jewel as they walk a dirt path "straight as a plumb-line, worn smooth by feet and baked brick-hard by July, between the green rows of laid-by cotton," toward the place where a brother named Cash is building a coffin for their mother, Addie Bundren. Focused on a single family, the novel traces a continuous action that begins at twilight, on a country farm, just before Addie dies, and then takes us on a bizarre journey through fire and flood to Jefferson, where it ends shortly after Addie has finally been buried and Anse, her husband, has bought a new set of teeth and found a new wife.

If, however, the action is in one sense continuous, in another it is fragmented. For it comes to us in fifty-nine sections recounted by fifteen different narrators, including friends and passing acquaintances as well as all seven members of the Bundren family. Together, its various narrators engage in, and occasionally parody, every possible activity of consciousness – intuitive, rational, and imaginative, primitive, conventional, and idiosyncratic. And though each narrator helps to advance the action, several also delay it in order to take us back into the past where, for example, we re-see enough of the strange courtship and marriage of Addie and Anse and glimpse enough of Addie's buried life to see that private histories have worked both with and against entrenched poverty and rigid class and gender lines to lead to the rigid, truncated, confused, and diffuse lives of Anse, Addie, and their wounded children: Cash, Jewel, Darl, Dewey Dell, and Vardaman.

Like *As I Lay Dying*, *Light in August* begins in the "hot still pinewiney silence" of rural Mississippi, as another traditional, straightforward, linear, logocentric tale. "I have come from Alabama: a fur piece," Lena Grove says in the book's opening line as she sits by a country road leading to Jefferson, having traveled for almost four weeks across the slow, deliberate world of the still largely rural and partially traditional South, carrying her unborn child and looking for its runaway father. Lena is never "for one moment confused, frightened, alarmed," Faulkner later remarked. So confident is she of her own resourcefulness that pity never enters her mind even as something she does not need. Having got to Jefferson, she finds help, first, from an un-Byronic lover named Byron Bunch, who immediately falls in love with her – an obviously unwed pregnant woman – "contrary to all the tradition of his austere and jealous country . . . which demands in the object physical inviolability";

and then from a failed minister and failed husband named Gail Hightower, D.D. – which means, the townspeople tell Byron, "Done Damned." With Byron as a self-appointed protector and Hightower as a midwife, Lena gives birth to her illegitimate son and then sets out traveling again. "My, my. A body does get around," she says in the novel's last lines. "Here we aint been coming from Alabama but two months, and now it's already Tennessee."

In fact, however, *Light in August* had its own beginnings in a manuscript called "Dark House," home of the outcast minister, Gail Hightower, who is so crippled by his obsessions with his family's history that he has failed his calling, his congregation, and his wife. As an unwed pregnant woman who becomes an unwed mother, Lena too is something of an outcast. And Joanna Burden and Joe Christmas, toward whom the novel moves with a strong sense of fatality, are not only the most emphatic and compelling strangers in all of Faulkner's fiction; they are also among the most divided and doomed.

The last member of a family of stern, self-righteous, life-denying New England Puritans, Joanna Burden is descended, on one side, from almost invisible women and, on the other, from violent, domineering men, bearing names like Calvin and Nathaniel, who have come to the South to save it from the sins of sloth and pleasure seeking as well as the evils of slavery. "I'm not ready to pray yet," Joanna says, after she and Joe Christmas have begun one of the strangest love affairs in all of fiction. "Dont make me have to pray yet. Dear God, let me be damned a little longer, a little while."

Drawn into an affair with each other, Joanna Burden and Joe Christmas begin all over again to feel fated and doomed. Joe shares some of Joanna's sense of sex as fascinating and repugnant, irresistible and forbidden. But he is self-conflicted and unsure of himself on other grounds, including the crucial question – unresolvable in his case – of whether he is or is not part black. Abused, pursued, and finally mutilated by men, drawn to, befriended, and yet offended by women, fearful of progeny, Joe Christmas travels country roads that turn out to be more deadly than the "thousand savage and lonely streets" he has already traveled, where "memory believes before knowing remembers. Believes longer than recollects, longer than knowing even wonders." Toward the end, we see him carrying his fragile life with him "like it was a basket of eggs." Years later, referring to the fact that Joe Christmas's racial identity remains unresolved, Faulkner described Joe's story as the tragedy of a man who "didn't know what he was" and had "no possible way in life . . . to find out."

Faulkner's concern with race had emerged before *Light in August,* and it would emerge again, especially in *Absalom, Absalom!* and *Go Down, Moses.* But it was in *Light in August* that he first directly confronted his sense that a racist society magnifies race as a crucial correlate of identity simply by being racist. By defining black people as the dark, forbidden *other* and then seeking complete control of them, Faulkner's South not only makes race a crucial personal problem, the central correlate of personal identity; it also institutionalizes race as a crucial social problem and then contrives, as an elaborate rationalization, a historical justification for what it had done that reaches back through the Bible to the beginning of human time. In Joanna Burden, we see inscribed a similar process with regard to gender. On this count, however, which comes to us through Joanna Burden's family history, the North and the South are one. Both regions fear female desire, and both map strategies for ensuring male domination of it. The women of Joanna Burden's family are almost as male-dominated as the wives of Doc Hines and Mr. McEachern, Joe's grandfather and stepfather. Joanna Burden is descended of New England abolitionists who have come to the South to save it from its sins. When in middle age she takes a lover for the first time, she breaks every rule of propriety she has been taught: she takes someone she thinks of as younger in age, lower in class, and forbidden by caste. When she is finally destroyed, it is not because she holds unpopular views on race. It is because she has insisted on expressing as well as feeling sexual desire and on trying to control her own life.

The work of culture in inculcating attitudes about age, class, and caste visibly touches every character in *Light in August,* especially Joe and Joanna. In language, thought, and feeling, Joe and Joanna internalize attitudes about race, gender, and human sexuality that are so inimical to their lives that they figure directly in their destruction. In different ways, each of them tries to escape the web of associations that holds them. But they fail, in part because, as another sign of culture's work, they display a crippling fear of ambiguity and a matching desire for clarity, which we see especially in their dependence on bipolar distinctions (white–black, man–woman, salvation–damnation) that they cannot live with or without.

These destructive traits, as it turns out, including the deadly preference for clarity over truth, run deeper in the men of Yoknapatawpha than in the women. One sign of this is the way in which Joanna seems almost manlike when she displays them. Another is the way in which she seems so exclusively the child of her visible male forebears. And another is the fact that it is especially in Joe Christmas – in his responses to men and women and their responses to him – that the full force of Faulkner's novel is felt. The moment Joe chooses the hard, ruthless clarity of his stepfather McEachern over the tender concern of his stepmother – accepts the one as harsh yet reliable, the other as soft, insidious, and unpredictable – we come to see fully the crucial relation Faulkner sensed between a man's attitude toward women and his disposition toward life. For that moment tilts Joe toward the two fatal moments that mark the end of his life, in the first of which he kills Joanna Burden and in the second of which he is murdered and mutilated by Percy Grimm, a deputized as well as self-appointed defender of purity and clarity.

Joe Christmas and Joanna Burden are paired in *Light in August* as lovers and as victims. But while Joe is the novel's only male victim, Joanna Burden is one of several female victims – Joe's mother, his maternal grandmother, his stepmother, and Gail Hightower's wife being others – all of whom are victims of men: husbands, fathers, stepfathers, ministers, and deputy sheriffs. Lena Grove's triumph can be described in various ways, and since she is a limited heroine, it remains a limited triumph. But it is not negligible. It depends upon her steady refusal to permit anything – hardship and privation, elderly parents who die too soon, a harsh brother, a worthless lover who deserts her, a rigid, judgmental society, or condescending readers – to turn her into a victim. And there is a sense in which it sets her free. Her journey, which begins and ends the novel, takes her into and out of Yoknapatawpha, an escape few characters in Faulkner's fiction ever manage. And though it, too, can be variously described, there are clear signs, especially in her treatment of Byron Bunch, that it includes two things of importance – a youthful desire to get around and see her world before she settles down, and a stubborn resolve to make a home unlike any she has ever seen.

Like the worlds of *The Sound and the Fury*, *As I Lay Dying*, and *Light in August*, those of *Absalom, Absalom!* and *Go Down, Moses* are in debt from the beginning. Their principal inheritance – of loss, defeat, guilt, and poverty, as seen in dark, dilapidated mansions, disintegrating families, weathered tombstones, shadows, and ghosts – haunts the lives of Faulkner's characters in a thousand ways. Not even Marcel Proust, James Joyce, and Thomas Mann give a larger role to crippling memories than Faulkner. The strange sentences with which *Absalom* begins move in fits and starts, looking back in one moment, pressing forward in another.

> From a little after two oclock until almost sundown of the long still hot weary dead September afternoon they sat in what Miss Coldfield still called the office because her father had called it that – a dim hot airless room with the blinds all closed and fastened for forty-three summers.[7]

The force of place and of nature's rhythms, the weight of tradition, the burden of names, and the authority of naming mingle with dangling facts – "forty-three summers" – that the reader must work to understand. Hemingway, too, had started out in the twenties. But by the middle of that careless decade, he had mastered the spare, lean, cut-to-the-bone style that made him famous. Faulkner's distinctive style was slower to emerge, and when it appeared in *Sartoris* (1929) – later published in its original, uncut form as *Flags in the Dust* (1973) – and, more decisively, in *The Sound and the Fury*, published on October 7, 1929, on the eve of the Great Depression, its rhetorical extravagances came as a counterresponse to the hard, dried-up South of the thirties. Faulkner spends his words freely, as though determined somehow to reclaim his almost vanquished world and its bound, unfree descendants and their dead yet restless progenitors.

Absalom, Absalom! is, on one side, the story of the rise and fall of Thomas Sutpen, who was born in 1807 in the mountains of West Virginia and died in 1869 at Sutpen's Hundred, northwest of Jefferson. Born into a poor white family, in a primitive mountain community where the concept of property does not even exist, Sutpen, still a boy, has tumbled with his family down the mountainside into Tidewater Virginia, where property is the foundation on which society is built and the measure by which the worth of all human beings is determined. There, where black people are property and poor, propertyless white people are serfs, Sutpen learns to see himself and his family as the landed gentry see them: as underclass people, evacuated into a world "without hope or purpose" for them, where they are expected to perform work that is "brutish and stupidly out of proportion to its reward." Affronted, Sutpen decides to acquire all of the things that give the people who possess them the political and economic power to exploit and the social right to despise those who do not. On one side, he wants to endow the lives of his ancestors with purpose; on the other, he wants to ensure that his and their descendants will be set forever free from "brutehood." In the process of working toward this, however – in acquiring a plantation, a mansion, and slaves, and establishing a family – Sutpen becomes even more ruthless and arrogant than the Virginia plantation lord who first hurt him into action. He becomes, in short, an extender of the same patriarchal, slave society that has victimized him, his family, and his ancestors. A radical individualist, he affronts and insults not only his slaves and the children he has by them, but also his wives and his legitimate children, sons and daughters alike. Then having abused everyone else, he betrays the trust of a poor, propertyless white man named Wash Jones, whose life recalls his own beginnings, by seducing and then casually discarding his granddaughter, Milly. Whereupon, Wash Jones, himself at last outraged, cuts Sutpen down with a rusty scythe.

At one point, with defeat staring him in the face, Sutpen recapitulates the basic facts of his life, hoping to understand where his plan went wrong. But telling his story belongs primarily to other people in *Absalom, Absalom!* It belongs to Miss Rosa Coldfield, his sister-in-law, who is herself one of the insulted and injured people left in the wake of his fatally flawed project. It belongs to Mr. Compson, son of General Compson, Sutpen's contemporary and friend. It belongs to Quentin Compson, suicidal brother of Caddy in *The Sound and the Fury*, whom Faulkner recruits to serve first as audience and interlocutor to Miss Rosa and his father, then as a tutor on southern history and culture to Shreve, who becomes Quentin's audience and interlocutor and then begins to tell the story himself. And it belongs to Sutpen's daughter, Judith, a woman of few words, who makes her plotting of the Sutpen family cemetery another commentary on the human consequences of Sutpen's scheme for giving meaning to his life.

The proliferation of interlocutors – of characters who listen and query, then comment and narrate – enlarges as well as enriches *Absalom, Absalom!*, which becomes a novel about storytelling as interpretation. Miss Rosa's account is a demonology in which Sutpen ("man-horse-demon") "abrupts" upon a peaceful world that he proceeds to savage and ruin. On one level, Sutpen's ruthlessness gives Miss Rosa a way of understanding the fate of her lost South, but her motives are personal as well as cultural. And on another level, Sutpen's ruthless hurry gives her a way of understanding the forces that have blighted her life. Through her demonology, she wins sympathy and achieves revenge. What she cannot do is reconstitute her life. From the novel's first scene on, we think of her as sitting in a too-tall chair like a "crucified child," wearing "eternal black," as though in anticipation of her own funeral, going over and over Sutpen's story, unable either to resolve it or to let it go.

To Mr. Compson, a source of considerable information, Sutpen's story belongs in part to the aborted hopes of the South and in part to the ages. Soured by his empty life, his declining family, and the declining South, Mr. Compson is too cynical and self-pitying to seek understanding. Drawn to Sutpen's story, he protects himself from its implications by presenting it as another tale of "misfortune and folly": "a horrible and bloody mischancing of human affairs." In his hands, the search for meaning and the effort to assess responsibility seem futile, and interpretive storytelling becomes another empty game: "Perhaps that's it," he says; things don't add up, "and we are not supposed to know."

Like Miss Rosa, Quentin and Shreve go over and over Sutpen's story, and like Mr. Compson, they often feel like giving up. *"Yes, too much, too long,"* Quentin thinks, just before he begins to listen again, this time to Shreve, whose ironic tone seems at times to resemble Mr. Compson's: *"but I had to hear it and now I am having to hear it all over again because he sounds just like father."* It is, however, with Quentin and Shreve and the "happy marriage of speaking and hearing" they achieve, that *Absalom, Absalom!* begins to yield plausible explanations for the devastation Sutpen has wrought – the succession of wives and not-wives affronted; of children neglected, abandoned, and ruthlessly manipulated, until one kills another; of slaves conquered, abused, and betrayed; of friends used and discarded. Together Quentin and Shreve rewrite Sutpen's story into a tale of ruthless, self-involved ambition that leads to terrible violence both before and after it leads to desertion, fratricide, and consuming guilt.

Quentin's and Shreve's accounts of Sutpen's story are in some ways as biblical and personal as Miss Rosa's, particularly as they reach out to resonate with Quentin's agonized attachment to Caddy in *The Sound and the Fury;* and they are in some ways as classical and even literary as Mr. Compson's, particularly when they become stories about two brothers who are doomed to destroy each other and two sisters who are doomed to lives of love and faithfulness that are never returned. Finally, however, they become more daring and more plausible. They are more daring because they make imaginative leaps that tie stories of the past to those of the present and so confront dark truths that are, as Faulkner later suggested, "probably true enough." They are more plausible, first, because they seem less compromised by Miss Rosa's need to avenge and Mr. Compson's desire to escape responsibility; second, because they make better sense of the fragmentary and sometimes contradictory stories they inherit, especially about what drove one of Sutpen's sons to kill the other; and, third, because they acknowledge and even celebrate, as signs of shared humanity, the surmise, conjecture, and fabrication that enable them to extend the stories they inherit toward meaning. Such community as exists in *Absalom, Absalom!* is constituted of tales and talking that overlap one

another, in which individual acts of style and voice, which tend toward isolation, are preserved but also softened. In *Absalom, Absalom!* language – or,
more specifically, incessant talking – becomes the constitutive ground of community.

Quentin is a student of many things, including cemeteries. Midway through
Absalom, we see him remembering a visit to the cemetery where Thomas
Sutpen and Ellen Coldfield Sutpen lie buried in graves marked by "heavy
vaulted slabs" ordered from Italy, "the best, the finest to be had," paid for
by Thomas. But there are three other "identical headstones with their faint
identical lettering, slanted a little in the soft loamy decay of accumulated cedar
needles," which Judith Sutpen has arranged and paid for: one for Charles Bon,
the part-black son whom Sutpen has denied repeatedly; one for Charles Etienne
St. Velery Bon, son of Charles and grandson of Thomas; and one for Judith
herself. Judith's action, of including and providing in death for two descendants
Thomas Sutpen denied in life, comes to us as a commentary, a counterstatement, that she completes with her own grave. Having leaned down to examine
Charles Bon's grave and to ponder it, Quentin moves on to brush the cedar
needles away from the second, "smoothing with his hand into legibility" its
"faint lettering" and "graved words." But it is the third that transfixes him –
first, because it is separated from the others, "at the opposite side of the
enclosure, as far from the other four as the enclosure would permit"; second,
because it has been placed there on instructions written by Judith "when she
knew that she was going to die," as another counterstatement to Sutpen's life;
and third, because of what it says and does not say.

> He had to brush the clinging cedar needles from this one also to read it,
> watching these letters also emerge beneath his hand, wondering quietly how
> they could have clung there, not have been blistered to ashes at the instant
> of contact with the harsh and unforgiving threat: *Judith Coldfield Sutpen.*
> *Daughter of Ellen Coldfield. Born October 3, 1841. Suffered the Indignities and*
> *Travails of this World for 42 Years, 4 Months, 9 Days, and went to Rest at Last*
> *February 12, 1884. Pause, Mortal; Remember Vanity and Folly and Beware.*[8]

"Yes," Quentin thinks, "I didn't need to ask who invented that." Given the
scorching words, the telling omission of Thomas Sutpen's name, and the subtle
ways in which what is written and not written fit Judith's life, however, we
must ask, and so must Quentin. His choice – "Miss Rosa ordered that one"
– is plausible. But Clytie is another possibility, and Judith is surely a third.
Strangely, however, the indefiniteness of the author of these words redoubles
their force in a book in which authorship is so heavily gendered and yet so
widely shared, and in which language, tricky and unreliable though it is,
becomes the scene of the only happy, productive marriage we observe.

In some moments, *Absalom, Absalom!* seems to be ruled by principles of
isolation and incommensurability so severe that bits and pieces, resistant to
meaningful patterns, are all we have. In others, it seems ruled by a principle
of repetition so severe that we need not even listen, since everything we

encounter comes to us as something already known, to strike once again the "resonant strings of remembering." But flawed model though it is, Quentin's conflicted mind, torn between hope and affirmation, despair and denial, reminds us of two things. First, that though we are free to fail, we are not free to desist; and second, that, to know ourselves in our world, we must study the history that has engendered us.

In multiplying possibilities, Faulkner both gives and takes. He draws us into the search for answers, but he also erodes our confidence in the possibility of finding a final answer. He even threatens us with the possibility that he has authorially exhausted the range of possible interpretive moves, leaving us to admire his dexterity. Finally, however, only the first of these threats holds; and despite the losses it entails, it proves to be liberating. For Faulkner's formulations have this in common with Miss Rosa's and Quentin's and Judith's: they require as well as invite revisions. It is in this connection, furthermore, that these flawed and limited characters become in one crucial respect model citizens. "What you have as a heritage, now take as a task," Goethe said. "For thus you shall make it your own." "It is not required of you that you complete the work," said Rabbi Tarphon in *Pirke Aboth,* "but neither are you free to desist from it." Where Faulkner's characters pick up such admonitions as these is not, finally, hard to say. They permeate the room that Miss Rosa still calls an office because her inadequate father had called it that, they rise from the "rotting shell" of Sutpen's dilapidated mansion and failed marriages, and they are encoded in the faint lettering and graved messages found in the Sutpen family cemetery. Quentin's life is tortured in part because he lives a personal lie, particularly where his feelings for Caddy are concerned. But it is also tortured because he knows that his own life figures in larger cultural lies. His personal crisis, like Miss Rosa's and Judith's, cannot be separated from the larger moral crisis of the rank ambition and ruthlessness of his possessive, sexist, and racist society, which, like Sutpen, is intensely but not peculiarly southern. Sutpen's origins, his Scotch-English family, were American before they became southern, and they were British before they became American. Even in their migrations he and his family are intensely modern. Quentin's personal crisis provides him a way into Sutpen's culturally resonant story and its destruction of Miss Rosa and Judith precisely because his personal crisis, brought on by living a lie, prefigures the moral crisis of his society. Far from celebrating "community" and "tradition" as achievements of the South, as the Agrarians had tried to do, Faulkner presents them as ideas that weigh more heavily precisely because, given the nation's fascination with the new and the individual as well as its divisive greed, they exist only as ideas.

Quentin's conflicts are so fundamental as to *be* the only life he has. Though isolating, furthermore, they turn out to be shared by characters as different as Thomas Sutpen, Eulalia Bon, Ellen Coldfield, Miss Rosa, Mr. Compson, Henry Sutpen, Judith Sutpen, Charles Bon, Clytie, and Wash Jones. Quentin discovers scenes one piece at a time, and he passes them on in the same way, with this bit added or that altered. And he hears, word by word, stories that are filled with echoes, resonances, remarkable vacancies, and deletions, like the father's missing name on Judith's tombstone. Time and again he feels what Charles Bon seems likely to have felt at least once – namely, that the whole of his life is about to fall "into pattern." Frustrated, he grasps for something, some "integer," that will solve the "jigsaw puzzle picture," only to meet with new bafflement. To the end, despite a series of remarkable breakthroughs, he must make do with stories that are tentative, provisional, imperfect, on the assumption that they are "probably true enough."

The mood of Faulkner's great fiction remains deeply provisional because, in language as well as action, it is so deeply circumstanced by time and history, as we see in this passage from *Go Down, Moses:*

> The boy would just wait and then listen and Sam would begin, talking about the old days and the People whom he had not had time even to know and so could not remember (he did not remember ever having seen his father's face). . . .
>
> And as he talked about those old times and those dead and vanished men of another race from either that the boy knew, gradually to the boy those old times would cease to be old times and would become a part of the boy's present, not only *as if* they had happened yesterday but *as if* they were still happening, the men who walked through them actually walking in breath and air and casting an actual shadow on the earth they had not quitted. And more: *as if* some of them had not happened yet but would occur tomorrow, *until at last it would seem* to the boy that he himself had not come into existence yet.[9]

This passage comes to us as a celebration and a critique of language and storytelling. Behind it lie the loss of the old days and the old people, and terrible conflicts: between parents and children as well as two genders and three races of people; and between lives lived and words uttered or written in a certain order. The power Faulkner attributes to words is at one with the power his words display: "And as he talked *about* those old times and those dead and vanished men of another race . . . [they] would cease to be old times and would become." As Faulkner renders Sam's resonating voice, he celebrates it. Yet even as he celebrates it, rendering its power in the plenitude it adds, he insists on an anterior plenitude, prior to division and loss, whose default is the occasion of Sam's song; and he insists as well on reminding us that Sam's song is a fiction by forcing us to view it under the aspect of the phrase he thrice repeats: *as if.* What Sam finds is not the thing itself, but some more or less adequate substitute for it: it was "as if . . . until at last it would seem." Insofar as Sam's voice fills a void, it is *as if* it fills a void.

Faulkner's own effort to live for his world unfolded as an effort to work through the South's tangled story – its lost dream, its lingering guilt, its terrible lies, and its exploitation of people as well as land – by finding words for it. In the process, he not only helped to make the South visible to others; he also helped to make the deeper meanings of both the modern novel and the Great

Depression visible. His techniques include means of expansion, especially through analogical ties and associations; means of extension, especially through the proliferation of voices and tales and versions of voices and tales; and means of establishing relations, especially rhetorical relations, with his readers. They also include techniques that worked counter to expansion, extension, and connection: techniques of concentration and localization that tie his fiction, as Albert Camus once put it, to the dust and the heat of the South; techniques of regression and escape, as we see in voices such as Quentin's in *The Sound and the Fury*, which moves, not out toward other voices, but in toward his own interior; and techniques of aggression, ranging from terse, laconic understatement to ironic and parodic motions to strange convoluted flights. Through all of this, but especially through the proliferation of narrators, Faulkner's fiction displays an underlying sympathy for those who attempt to create narrative in the pursuit of meaning. That sympathy encodes a secret sympathy for those who have attempted, with limited success, to fashion a coherent self or create a coherent culture. Informing the interplay among these sympathies is the predicament of an artist who knows that we are circumscribed creatures whose needs include self-transcendence as well as self-definition, a sense of being rooted in the order of being as well as a sense of being responsible to and for something larger than our own personal status and prosperity.

Like Whitman, Faulkner celebrated the magic of the commonplace. And like Whitman's, his disaffection with life in the United States coexisted with fascination. The disaffection and alienation that mark this country's fiction run deep in Faulkner's work because he felt acutely the failure of his culture to meet those needs of mind and spirit that material possessions can never satisfy. Like T. S. Eliot, he was suspicious of the dream of creating a social system so perfect that people would no longer need to be good; and like Herman Melville, he felt more solidarity with the poor, the forgotten, and the defeated than with the rich and the victorious, though it was the latter he wanted to join. More courageously than most, he lived by writing the incongruities, conflicts, anxieties, and even the lies, that shaped his own life as well as his region and nation. One thing bequeathed by the nineteenth century, besides a suspect faith in the sufficiency of material progress, was the promise of more freedom: a willingness to blur or even dissolve all lines, restrictions, and taboos, in life as well as in art. Faulkner sought the rewards of material progress and enjoyed breaking long-honored rules, including several having to do with narrative fiction. But he remained convinced that freedom suffices only when people are spiritually sure enough of themselves to know what they truly want, and then only when what they want corresponds to their deepest needs and so matches their need for affiliation as well as attention, and their capacities for awe and wonder.

Like other writers in the United States during the early twentieth century, Faulkner was an heir less of the dominant culture of the nineteenth century than of its great rebels. Much of the daring, even the headiness, of the assaults that Darwin, Marx, Nietzsche, and Freud – to name only four – mounted

against accepted beliefs found expression in the brashness of writers like Faulkner, as they set out to invent literature anew. Faulkner's almost fierce determination to deal with the past on his own terms not only marked him as a
rebel; it also shaped his art. Like much modern fiction, his is often pessimistic
and violent, even brutal and despairing. He is a poet of deprivation and loss.
Affluence and plenty mark his work only in style and imagination. Yet we
find other things there: remnants of the good hope of the Lyric Years, which
was political as well as aesthetic; the persistence of the exuberance of the
twenties, which was experimental as well as escapist; and the difficult hope
against hope that sprang to life during the Great Depression, of creating anew
an imperfect community, knit together by imperfectly possessed and painfully
held memories and by imperfectly shared and practiced values. These things
he infused with the same boldness of spirit and moral courage that we see in
the striking formal experiments that give his fiction its special place in a great
and varied outpouring of innovative, conflicted, and often self-critical expression.

Notes

PART ONE: A DREAM CITY, LYRIC YEARS, AND A GREAT WAR

1 Henry James, *The Portrait of a Lady* [1881], ed. Leon Edel (Boston, 1963), p. 17.
2 Ibid., p. 260.
3 O. E. Rölvaag, *Giants in the Earth: A Saga of the Prairie* [1924–5], trans. the author with Lincoln Colcord (New York, 1965), p. 36; see also pp. 5, 9–10, 29, 35.
4 Theodore Dreiser, *Sister Carrie* [1900], ed. Donald Pizer (New York, 1970), p. 369; see also pp. 1, 9–11, 367–9.
5 Harriette Arnow, *The Dollmaker* (New York, 1954), p. 307.
6 Willa Cather, *My Ántonia* [1918] (Boston, 1949), pp. 352–3.
7 Dreiser, *Sister Carrie*, pp. 11–12.
8 Frederick Jackson Turner, "The West and American Ideals," *Washington Historical Quarterly*, 5 (October 1914): 245. This essay was reprinted with some revisions in *The Frontier in American History* (New York, 1920). See p. 293 for the statement I quote with "stark and strong and full of life" deleted.
9 See Turner's "The Significance of the Frontier in American History," in *The Frontier in American History*, p. 14.
10 Henry Adams, *The Education of Henry Adams* [1918] (Boston, 1961), p. 450.
11 Bertrand Russell, "The Free Man's Worship" [1902], in *Mysticism and Logic and Other Essays* (London, 1917), pp. 47–8.
12 Adams, *Education*, p. 499.
13 Quoted in Werner Heisenberg, "The Representation of Nature in Contemporary Physics," trans. D. T. Benfey, in Sallie Sears and Georgianna Lord, eds., *The Discontinuous Universe: Selected Writings in Contemporary Consciousness* (New York, 1972), p. 130.
14 T. K. Whipple, *Study Out the Land* (Berkeley and Los Angeles, 1943), p. 65.
15 Frederick Winslow Taylor, *The Principles of Scientific Management* [1911] (New York, 1913), pp. 7–8; see also pp. 25, 36–7, 59, 144.
16 Quoted in William L. O'Neill, ed., *Echoes of Revolt: The Masses, 1911–1917* (Chicago, 1966), p. 54.
17 Joseph Freeman, *An American Testament: A Narrative of Rebels and Romantics* (New York, 1936), p. 67.
18 Alan Seeger, "I Have a Rendezvous with Death," in Harriet Monroe and Alice Corbin Henderson, eds., *The New Poetry: An Anthology of Twentieth-Century Verse in English* [1917] (New York, 1939), pp. 528–9.
19 Winston Churchill, quoted in Paul Johnson, *Modern Times: The World from the Twenties to the Eighties* (New York, 1983), pp. 13–14.

20 Ezra Pound, "Hugh Selwyn Mauberley" [1920], in *Selected Poems* (London, 1928), p. 176.

21 William March, *Company K* [1933] (New York, 1957), p. 63.

22 Willa Cather, *A Lost Lady* [1923] (New York, 1972), pp. 106–7.

23 See Harry Crosby, *War Letters* (Paris, 1932); and Edward Germain, ed., *Shadows of the Sun: The Diaries of Harry Crosby* (Santa Barbara, Calif., 1977), pp. 147–8.

24 Ernest Hemingway, *A Farewell to Arms* (New York, 1929), pp. 4, 196.

PART TWO: FICTION IN A TIME OF PLENTY

1 Alexis de Tocqueville, *Democracy in America,* 2 vols., trans. Henry Reeve, with revisions by Francis Bowen and Phillips Bradley (New York, 1945), vol. 2, pp. 105–6.

2 Henry Adams, *Democracy: An American Novel* [1880] (New York, 1961), p. 55.

3 John Dos Passos, *1919* [1932] in *U.S.A.* (New York, 1937), p. 468.

4 Sinclair Lewis, *Babbitt* (New York, 1922), p. 183. For phrases quoted above, see pp. 160, 59, 143.

5 Waldo Frank, *The Re-Discovery of America: An Introduction to a Philosophy of American Life* (New York, 1929), p. 105. For phrases from *Babbitt*, see pp. 181–2, 187.

6 See Edward Earl Purinton, "Big Ideas from Big Business," *Independent,* April 16, 1921, p. 395, in George E. Mowry, ed., *The Twenties: Fords, Flappers, and Fanatics* (Englewood Cliffs, N.J., 1963), pp. 3–10.

7 Werner Heisenberg, "The Representation of Nature in Contemporary Physics," trans. O. T. Benfey, in Sallie Sears and Georgianna Lord, eds., *The Discontinuous Universe: Selected Writings in Contemporary Consciousness* (New York, 1972), pp. 131–2.

8 These words first appeared in a feature story in the *New York World,* May 13, 1927. They are reprinted in Robert P. Weeks, ed., *Commonwealth vs. Sacco and Vanzetti* (Englewood Cliffs, N.J., 1958), p. 226. This excellent compilation of documents also includes the longer statements Sacco and Vanzetti made at the time of their sentencing.

9 John Dos Passos, *The Big Money* [1936], in *U.S.A.* (New York, 1937), pp. 461–2.

10 F. Scott Fitzgerald, "Early Success" [1937], in Edmund Wilson, ed., *The Crack-Up: F. Scott Fitzgerald* (New York, 1945), p. 87. This book also contains Wilson's moving tribute to Fitzgerald as a "dedication."

11 F. Scott Fitzgerald, "The Scandal Detectives" [1935], in Jackson R. Bryer and John Kuehl, eds., *The Basil and Josephine Stories* (New York 1973), pp. 15–16.

12 F. Scott Fitzgerald, "Echoes of the Jazz Age," in Wilson, ed., *The Crack-Up,* pp. 16–17.

13 See F. Scott Fitzgerald, *The Great Gatsby* (New York, 1925), p. 23. For other quoted phrases, see pp. 39, 40, 44, 22–3.

14 F. Scott Fitzgerald, *Tender Is the Night* [1934], rev. ed. (New York, 1951), pp. 117–18.

15 Fitzgerald, *The Great Gatsby,* p. 46. For other quoted phrases, see pp. 1–2, 98–9.

16 Ibid., pp. 180–1; cf. pp. 58–60.

17 Harold E. Stearns, "The Intellectual Life," in Harold E. Stearns, ed., *Civilization in the United States: An Inquiry by Thirty Americans* (New York, 1922), p. 135.

18 Quoted by Sir Herbert Read, "T. S. Eliot: A Memoir," in Allen Tate, ed., *T. S. Eliot: The Man and His Work* (London, 1967), p. 15.

19 F. Scott Fitzgerald, "My Generation," first printed in *Esquire,* 70 (October 1968):

119, and reprinted in Matthew J. Bruccoli, ed., *Profile of F. Scott Fitzgerald* (Columbus, Ohio, 1971), pp. 4–6.

20 Thomas Boyd, *Through the Wheat* (New York, 1923), p. 266. It is worth noting that Fitzgerald played a crucial role in persuading Scribner's to publish Boyd's novel, which deserves more attention than it has received.

21 Ernest Hemingway, "Indian Camp," in *In Our Time* (New York, 1925), p. 21.

22 Ernest Hemingway, *Death in the Afternoon* (New York, 1932), p. 2.

23 Ernest Hemingway, "Soldier's Home," in *In Our Time,* p. 93.

24 Janet Flanner, *Paris Was Yesterday: 1925–1939* (New York, 1972), p. viii.

PART THREE: THE FATE OF WRITING DURING THE GREAT DEPRESSION

1 Alfred Kazin, *Starting Out in the Thirties* (Boston, 1965), p. 15. See also pp. 4–5.

2 Henry Miller, *Tropic of Capricorn* [1934] (New York, 1961), pp. 32–3; see also pp. 16, 30–1, 34.

3 John Dos Passos, *The Big Money* [1936], in *U.S.A.* (New York, 1937), pp. 19, 29, and 521. See also pp. 461–4.

4 B. M. Bowers, *Flying U Ranch* (New York, 1912), p. 47.

5 I am indebted to Allen Tullos of Emory University for callng these lines to my attention and for providing me a copy of them.

6 Thomas Wolfe, *You Can't Go Home Again* (New York, 1939), pp. 741–2.

7 William Faulkner, *Absalom, Absalom!* [1936] (New York, 1986), p. 7.

8 Ibid., p. 264.

9 William Faulkner, *Go Down, Moses* (New York, 1942), p. 171; italics added.

Bibliographical Notes

A PREFACE IN TWO PARTS

On Mikhail Bakhtin, see *Problems of Dostoevsky's Poetics,* ed. and trans. Caryl Emerson (Minneapolis, 1984), p. 17. On Tzvetan Todorov, see " 'Race,' Writing, and Culture," trans. Loulou Mack, in Henry Louis Gates, ed., *"Race," Writing and Difference* (Chicago, 1986), p. 38.

PART ONE: A DREAM CITY, LYRIC YEARS, AND A GREAT WAR

1. *The Novel as Ironic Reflection*

For James on the novel, see especially "The Art of Fiction," in Leon Edel, ed., *Henry James: The Future of the Novel* (New York, 1956), pp. 19–20; and James's preface to *The American,* in R. P. Blackmur, ed., *The Art of the Novel: Critical Prefaces of Henry James* (New York, 1934), pp. 30–4. "The Lesson of Balzac," in Edel, ed., *The Future of the Novel,* pp. 97–124, is also helpful. I also quote as indicated in the text from James, *The American Scene,* ed. W. H. Auden (New York, 1946), esp. pp. xxvi, 82–3, 106–7, 110–11, and 120–30. On Whitman, see "A Backward Glance o'er Travel'd Roads" [1888], *Leaves of Grass: Comprehensive Reader's Edition,* ed. Harold W. Blodgett and Sculley Bradley (New York, 1965), pp. 561–74. On Pound's sense of life as increasingly "cinematographic," see his review of Jean Cocteau's *Poesies, 1917–1920, Dial,* 70 (January 1921), p. 110. On Santayana, see his *Character and Opinion in the United States* (New York, 1920). On Twain's unwritten sequel, see Albert Bigelow Paine, ed., *Mark Twain's Notebooks* (New York, 1935). On Huck Finn and language, see Lionel Trilling, *The Liberal Imagination: Essays on Literature and Society* (New York, 1976), esp. p. 117. Compare Pound's sense of modern life as "cinematographic" with Vachel Lindsay's sense of modern culture as increasingly "hieroglyphic" in Lindsay, *The Art of the Motion Picture* [1915] (New York, 1970), pp. 20–1.

2. *Confidence and Uncertainty in* The Portrait of a Lady

On Alfred North Whitehead, see his *Science and the Modern World* [1925] (New York, 1967), chap. 6, "The Nineteenth Century," pp. 95–112, esp. pp. 96–7. On Heisenberg, see his "Non-Objective Sciences and Uncertainty," from *The Physicist's Conception of Nature* [1955], trans. Arnold J. Pomerans (New York, 1958), in Ellmann and Feidelson, eds., *The Modern Tradition,* pp. 444–50; his "The Representation of Nature in Contemporary Physics," trans. O. T. Benfey, in Sears and Lord, eds., *The*

Discontinuous Universe, pp. 122–35; and his *Physics and Philosophy*, all in the General Bibliography. On the broader implications of the problems Heisenberg raises, see William Barrett, *The Illusion of Technique: A Search for Meaning in a Technological Civilization* (Garden City, N.Y., 1978). On the concept of "liminality," see Turner, *The Ritual Process*, in the General Bibliography. On James's fiction, see Alfred Habegger, *Henry James and the "Woman Business"* (Cambridge, 1989), esp. chap. 7; Laurence Holland, *The Expense of Vision: Essays on the Craft of Henry James* (Princeton, N.J., 1964); Mark Seltzer, *Henry James and the Art of Power* (Ithaca, N.Y., 1984); and especially Charles Feidelson, "The Moment of *The Portrait of a Lady*," *Ventures*, 8, no. 2 (1968): 47–55. On Isabel Archer as guardian angel, see chapter 46; on Rome as a "world of ruins," see chapter 46 and compare chapters 27 and 36; on Isabel Archer as used, see chapters 51 and 52; on her resistance to renunciation, see chapter 53.

3. Lines of Expansion

On the great migrations, see Degler, *Out of Our Past*, pp. 273–303, in the General Bibliography, and Handlin, *The Uprooted*, and Higham, *Send These to Me*, in the Bibliography, Part One. On the literature of exploration, see Wayne Franklin, "The Literature of Discovery and Exploration," in Emory Elliott, with others, ed., *Columbia Literary History of the United States* (New York, 1988), pp. 16–23, as well as Kolodny, Smith, and Todorov, cited later in this note. On the Homestead Act, see Smith, *Virgin Land*, pp. 190–200, 221–3, and 238–40, in the Bibliography, Part One. On *Sister Carrie*, see Philip Fisher, *Hard Facts*, pp. 128–78, in the Bibliography, Part One, and "Acting, Reading, Fortune's Wheel: *Sister Carrie* and the Life History of Objects," in Eric J. Sundquist, ed., *American Realism: New Essays* (Baltimore, 1982), pp. 259–77; and Walter Benn Michaels, *The Gold Standard and the Logic of Naturalism* (Berkeley and Los Angeles, 1987). On "personality" as a keyword, see Warren Susman, "Personality and the Making of Twentieth-Century Culture," in John Higham and Paul A. Conkin, eds., *New Directions in American Intellectual History* (Baltimore, 1979). See also Trachtenberg, *The Incorporation of America* in the Bibliography, Part One; and Anderson, *The Imperial Self*, and Poirier, *The Performing Self*, in the General Bibliography. For Dickey on Roethke, see James Dickey, *Babel to Byzantium: Poets and Poetry Now* (New York, 1968), p. 150. On erotic connotations of exploration, see Kolodny, *The Lay of the Land*, in the Bibliography, Part One; for other connotations, see Smith, *Virgin Land*, and Todorov, *The Conquest of America*, also in the Bibliography, Part One. On Heisenberg, see the bibliographical notes to Section 2 above.

4. Four Contemporaries and the Closing of the West

On Crook, see John McPhee, *Rising from the Plains* (New York, 1986), pp. 19–20; on Sheridan, see Dee Brown, *Bury My Heart at Wounded Knee: An Indian History of the American West* (New York, 1970), esp. chap. 7, "The Only Good Indian Is a Dead Indian." See also Roy H. Pearce, *The Savages of America: A Study of the Indian and the Idea of Civilization* (Baltimore, 1965); Robert H. Berkhofer, Jr., *The White Man's Indian: Images of the American Indian from Columbus to the Present* (New York, 1978); Lee C. Mitchell, *Witnesses to a Vanishing America: The Nineteenth Century Response* (Princeton, N.J., 1981); and Slotkin, *The Fatal Environment*, in the Bibliography, Part One. On Cody, see Nye, *The Unembarrassed Muse*, pp. 192–3, 200–9, and 278–88, in the

General Bibliography; and Richard J. Walsh, with Milton J. Salisbury, *The Making of Buffalo Bill: A Study in Heroics* (Indianapolis, Ind., 1928).

5. Chicago's "Dream City"

In addition to the guidebooks mentioned in the text, the following include useful discussions of Chicago's Columbian Exposition: Banta, *Imaging American Women,* and Larkin, *Art and Life in America,* in the General Bibliography; and Fisher, *Hard Facts,* Lears, *No Place of Grace,* Trachtenberg, *The Incorporation of America,* and Ziff, *The American 1890s,* in the Bibliography, Part One. The statements by Saint-Gaudens and Wister are quoted in Trachtenberg, pp. 217–18. On the World's Parliament of Religions, one of the largest of several large congresses held at the Columbian Exposition, see Richard Hughes Seager, *The World's Parliament of Religions, Chicago, Illinois, 1893: America's Religious Coming of Age* (Unpublished diss., Harvard University, 1986), and David Burg, *Chicago's White City of 1892* (Lexington, Ky., 1976), esp. pp. 262–85. A letter from Thomas Huxley was read at the parliament, and Herbert Spencer spoke there on "social evolution and social duty." Lyman Abbott and Washington Gladden were among many other prominent speakers. Abbott's statement about how cosmopolitan Chicago and Americans were is quoted in Burg, p. 263. Barrow's statement is quoted in Seager, p. 95.

6. Frederick Jackson Turner in the Dream City

On the Homestead Act, see Smith, *Virgin Land,* pp. 190–200, 221–3, and 238–40. On the distinction between the "moralist" and the "historian," see Todorov, *The Conquest of America.* On evolutionary connotations of Turner's "thesis," see the works cited in the bibliographical notes to Section 5 above. For Howells on the Dream City, see *A Traveler from Alturia* (1894), an excerpt from which appears in Harris, ed., *The Land of Contrasts,* in the Bibliography, Part One, pp. 345–62.

7. Henry Adams's Education and the Grammar of Progress

On Adams's use of terms such as "convenient fictions," see his Letter to Charles Francis Adams, Jr., May 1863, in Worthington C. Ford, ed., *A Cycle of Adams Letters, 1861–1865,* 2 vols. (Boston, 1920), vol. 1, p. 278, and *The Education of Henry Adams* [1918] (Boston, 1961), pp. 469 and 472–3. On the emergence of pragmatism as a philosophical movement, see Kuklick, *The Rise of American Philosophy,* in the General Bibliography. On Heisenberg, see the works cited in the bibliographical notes to Section 2, above. Poe's "The Man of the Crowd" was first published in *Burton's Gentleman's Magazine* in December 1840 and was later revised for *Tales* (1845). All quotes are from the revised version. For the quotes from Paul Elmer More, see *Aristocracy and Justice: Shelburne Essays, Ninth Series* (Boston, 1915), pp. 141, 136. For the quote from *The Sun Also Rises* (New York, 1926), see p. 148. See also Lionel Trilling, *Freud and the Crisis of Our Culture* (New York, 1955), pp. 53–5.

8. Jack London's Career and Popular Discourse

For a different reading of London's career, see Lynn's *The Dream of Success,* pp. 75–118, in the Bibliography, Part One. Commager, *The American Mind* (in the

General Bibliography), Lears, *No Place of Grace,* and Ziff, *The American 1890s,* have little to say about London, but they provide valuable accounts of the popular uses to which the writings of London's various mentors and guides were being put during his lifetime. Whipple's book, *Study Out the Land* (Berkeley and Los Angeles, 1943), deserves more attention than it has received. See especially "Jack London – Wonder Boy," pp. 93–104. On Thoreau's sense of the "wild," see *Walden* [1854] (New York, 1962), p. 160, esp. the first paragraph of "Higher Laws."

9. Innocence and Revolt in the "Lyric Years": 1900–1916

On Santayana's definition of the sharp division in U.S. culture, see his "The Genteel Tradition in American Philosophy," *University of California Chronicle 13* (1911): 37–80. This essay is included in Santayana's *Character and Opinion in the United States* (New York, 1920) and *The Genteel Tradition at Bay* (New York, 1931). On "Puritanism," see Randolph Bourne, "The Puritan Will to Power" (1917), H. L. Mencken's "Puritanism as a Literary Force," and Waldo Frank's *Our America* (1919). Huneker's statement on "Puritanism" is quoted in Daniel Aaron, "Literary Scenes and Literary Movements," p. 736, in the General Bibliography. This period is unusually rich in memoirs. See Mabel Dodge Luhan, *Movers and Shakers* (New York, 1936), esp. chap. 4 and pp. 21–38; Joseph A. Freeman, *An American Testament: A Narrative of Rebels and Romantics* (New York, 1936), pp. 34–7, 49–55, 61–7, and 94–115; and Floyd Dell, *Homecoming* (New York, 1933), pp. 34–43. See also Max Eastman, *Art and the Life of Action* (New York, 1934); Susan Glaspell, *The Road to the Temple* (New York, 1927); Emma Goldman, *Living My Life* (New York, 1939); and Genevieve Taggard, ed., *May Days* (New York, 1925), a collection of pieces from *Masses,* 1911–17. On politics, see Walter Lippmann, *A Preface to Politics* (New York, 1913). On painting, see Larkin, *Art and Life in America,* chaps. 25–8, and on photography, see Trachtenberg, *Reading American Photographs,* and Stange, *Symbols of Ideal Life* – all in the General Bibliography. On Bourne's sense of "trans-nationality," see Aaron, p. 738, as cited earlier in this note. For a sense of how art and politics did and did not interact, see O'Neill, ed., *Echoes of Revolt,* in the Bibliography, Part One, and Aaron, *Men of Good Hope,* and May, *The End of American Innocence,* in the General Bibliography. Floyd Dell's *Intellectual Vagabondage: An Apology for the Intelligentsia* (New York, 1926), is a confession and examination of the failed hopes of the Lyric Years.

10. The Armory Show of 1913 and the Decline of Innocence

Several of the works mentioned in the bibliographic notes to Section 9 above deal with the Armory Show, and most of them deal with the decline of innocence. See especially Luhan, *Movers and Shakers,* chaps. 1–4, and Larkin, *Art and Life in America,* chap. 28, "Explosion in the Armory." In addition, see Milton W. Brown, *The Story of the Armory Show* (New York, 1963); William Innes Homer, *Alfred Stieglitz and the American Avant-Garde* (Boston, 1977); and George H. Roeder, Jr., *Forum of Uncertainty: Confrontations with Modern Painting in Twentieth-Century American Thought* (Ann Arbor, Mich., 1980). On the loss of innocence, see Gertrude Stein, *Paris, France* (New York, 1940), and her sense of the nineteenth century as still "sure of evolution and prayers"; and May, *The End of American Innocence.*

11. The Play of Hope and Despair

For crucial passages in *Martin Eden* [1909] (New York, 1950), see pp. 320–6, 370–5, 385–99, and 402–11. On the fiction of Dreiser, see especially the works of Fisher cited in the bibliographical notes to Section 3 above. On Dreiser's sense of determinism, see *A Book About Myself* (New York, 1922), pp. 253; and on his sense of distress in the face of suffering, see pp. 127, 140, 157, and 210. On Wharton, see R. W. B. Lewis, *Edith Wharton: A Biography* (New York, 1975), esp. pp. 13–15 and 535–9; Candace Waid, *Edith Wharton's Letters from the Underworld: Fiction of Women and Writing* (Chapel Hill, N.C., 1991); Cynthia Griffin Wolff, *A Feast of Words: The Triumph of Edith Wharton* (Oxford, 1977); and Judith Fryer, *Felicitous Space: The Imaginative Structures of Edith Wharton and Willa Cather* (Chapel Hill, N.C., 1986). On Stein, see Wendy Steiner, *Exact Resemblance to Exact Resemblance: The Literary Portraiture of Gertrude Stein* (New Haven, Conn., 1978). On "commodification" as I use it in this section and elsewhere, see Georg Lukacs, *History and Class Consciousness: Studies in Marxist Dialectics,* trans. Rodney Livingstone (Cambridge, Mass., 1971), esp. p. 100. On neurasthenia, see Lears, *No Place of Grace,* and Lutz, *American Nervousness,* in the Bibliography, Part One.

12. The Great War and the Fate of Writing

For Bourne on the youthfulness of the Lyric Years, see *Youth and Life* (New York, 1913), p. 7; for his views on the war, see *The History of a Literary Radical* (New York, 1920), p. 31 and passim. On World War I, see especially Paul Fussell, *The Great War and Modern Memory* (New York, 1975), and David M. Kennedy, *Over Here: The First World War and American Society,* in the General Bibliography. On the experiences of women during and just after the Great War, see especially Kennedy, pp. 30–1, 235, 261, 284–7. On the experiences of African-Americans, see Kennedy, pp. 29–30, 158–63, and 279–84. See also May, *The End of American Innocence,* and Hugh Kenner, *A Homemade World: The American Modernist Writers* (New York, 1975). For the quote from George Jean Nathan, see him as quoted in Loren Baritz, ed., *The Culture of the Twenties,* p. xxxiii, in the Bibliography, Part Two. On the responses of volunteer ambulance drivers, see Charles A. Fenton, "Ambulance Drivers in France and Italy: 1914–1918," *American Quarterly, 3,* no. 4 (Winter 1951): 326–43.

PART TWO: FICTION IN A TIME OF PLENTY

1. When the War Was Over: The Return of Detachment

On the publication and popularity of *The Education of Henry Adams,* see Sklar, ed., *The Plastic Age,* in the General Bibliography. On Adams's correspondence before and during the Great War, see Ernest Samuels, *Henry Adams: The Major Phase* (Cambridge, Mass., 1964), esp. pp. 552–4 and 579. For the general frame of my remarks, see Karl Barth, *From Rousseau to Ritschl,* trans. Brian Cozens (London, 1959), pp. 11–57. The poem of Wallace Stevens I allude to is "The Poem That Took the Place of a Mountain," in Wallace Stevens, *Collected Poems* (New York, 1964), p. 512. For excellent discussions of the end of the war and its aftermath, see Kennedy, *Over Here,* chaps. 5 and 6, and Leuchtenburg, *The Perils of Prosperity,* chaps. 3 and 7, in the General Bibliography. On political apathy and disillusionment, see especially Thorstein Veblen,

"Dementia Praecox" [1922], in Loren Baritz, ed., *The Culture of the Twenties,* and Walter Lippmann, "The Causes of Political Indifference Today" [1927], in ibid.

2. The "Jazz Age" and the "Lost Generation" Revisited

Malcolm Cowley's *A Second Flowering* and especially *Exile's Return,* in the Bibliography, Part Two, are works of lasting value. For Bishop's statement about Hemingway, see "The Missing All" [1937], in Edmund Wilson, ed., *The Collected Essays of John Peale Bishop* (New York, 1948), p. 75, cf. p. 66. For Ward's description of jazz, see him as quoted in Wendy Steiner, "The Diversity of American Fiction," p. 854, in the General Bibliography. On jazz more generally, see Irving Sablosky, *American Music* (Chicago, 1969), chaps. 6 and 7; J. A. Rogers, "Jazz at Home" [1925], in Baritz, ed., *The Culture of the Twenties,* pp. 67–9; Carl Van Vechten, "The Black Blues" [1925], in Cleveland Amory and Frederic Bradlee, eds., *Vanity Fair: Selections from America's Most Memorable Magazine* (New York, 1960), pp. 95–6; Nye, *The Unembarrassed Muse,* chap. 13, "Ballads to Blues," and chap. 14, "The Big Band Era"; and especially Neil Leonard, *Jazz and the White Americans,* in the Bibliography, Part Two. For general context, see Leuchtenburg, *The Perils of Prosperity,* chap. 9, "The Revolution in Morals." For a good gathering of Mencken's attacks on the "booboisie," see *Notes on Democracy* (New York, 1926). For Josephson's sense of the artist's increasingly adversarial relation to culture as "resistance to the milieu," see *Portrait of the Artist as American* (New York, 1930), p. xiii. For Wharton's remark on Lewis, see "The Great American Novel," *Yale Review, 16* (1927): 648–9. On Coolidge, see William Allen White, *A Puritan in Babylon: The Story of Calvin Coolidge* (New York, 1938), esp. pp. 21–2, 72–3, 208–9, 234, 250–3, 283–4, 325, 395–6, 412–20, and 443–4. This book remains one of our better political biographies. For Rilke's letter, see *Duino Elegies,* trans. J. B. Leishman and Stephen Spender (New York, 1939), app. 4, pp. 128–30. For Wharton's statements, see her *A Backward Glance* (New York, 1934), p. 369; *French Ways and Their Meaning* (New York, 1919), p. v; and her preface to *Ghosts* (New York, 1937), p. x. On Lewis and the twenties, see especially Mark Schorer, *Sinclair Lewis: An American Life* (New York, 1961).

3. The Perils of Plenty, or How the Twenties Acquired a Paranoid Tilt

On race and racism as issues that evoked extreme responses in the twenties, see Lothrop Stoddard, *The Rising Tide of Color* (New York, 1920); Madison Grant, *The Passing of the Great Race* (New York, 1917); and Leslie Shane, *The Celt and the World: A Study of the Relation of Celt and Teuton in History* (New York, 1917). Also of interest are Fitzgerald's review of Shane's book in *Nassau Literary Magazine, 73* (May 1917): 104–5; M. Gidley, "Notes on F. Scott Fitzgerald and the Passing of the Great Race," *Journal of American Studies, 7* (1973): 2, 171–81; and Paul L. Murphy, "The Sources and Nature of Intolerance in the 1920s," *Journal of American History, 51* (June 1964): 60–76. On U.S. nativism, see Higham, *Strangers in the Land,* in the General Bibliography; Allen, *Only Yesterday,* chap. 3, in the Bibliography, Part Two; and Leuchtenburg, *Perils of Prosperity,* chap. 9. For statements by Palmer, Evans, and others, see Mowry, ed., *The Twenties,* pp. 121–53, and Baritz, ed., *The Culture of the Twenties,* pp. 75–108, both in the Bibliography, Part Two. On the Sacco and Vanzetti case, in addition to Weeks, ed., *Commonwealth vs. Sacco and Vanzetti,* as cited in note 11 to Part Two, see G. Louis Joughin and Edmund M. Morgan, *The Legacy of Sacco and Vanzetti,* in the Bibliography, Part Two; and Paul Avrich, *Sacco and Vanzetti: The Anarchist Background* (Princeton, N.J., 1991). On Prohibition, see Allen, *Only Yesterday,* chap. 10; the several essays collected in Mowry, ed., *The Twenties,* on "the Dry Crusade," pp. 89–120; Thomas B. Gilmore, *Equivocal Spirits: Alcoholism and Drinking in Twentieth-Century Literature* (Chapel Hill, N.C., 1987), esp. pp. 96–117; and Charles Merz, *The Dry Decade,* in the Bibliography, Part Two. For Lippmann on disillusionment of the young, see his *A Preface to Morals* (New York, 1929), p. 6; for his views on "diffused prosperity," see "The Causes of Political Indifference Today" (1927), in Baritz, ed., *The Culture of the Twenties,* p. 151. Anderson's statements about himself as a teacher of "anti-success" and as a "minor figure" are quoted in Irving Howe, *Sherwood Anderson* (New York, 1951), pp. 248, 243.

4. *Disenchantment, Flight, and the Rise of Professionalism in an Age of Plenty*

On the man of letters, see Edmund Wilson's essay "Thoughts on Being Bibliographed" [1943], in *Classics and Commercials* (New York, 1950), pp. 105–20, where Wilson quotes Fitzgerald regarding the reach of his ambition (p. 110); Cowley, *Exile's Return,* esp. the Prologue and Epilogue, and "Taps for the Lost Generation," chap. 9 in *A Second Flowering.* These pieces exemplify as well as reflect on the tasks and predicament of writers. On mass-circulation magazines, see Lynd and Lynd, *Middletown,* pp. 229–40, in the Bibliography, Part Two; and Christopher P. Wilson, "The Rhetoric of Consumption: Mass-Market Magazines and the Demise of the Gentle Reader, 1880–1920," in Richard W. Fox and T. J. Jackson Lears, eds., *The Culture of Consumption,* pp. 37–64, in the Bibliography, Part Two. For the quotes from Lindsay, see *The Art of Motion Pictures* [1915] (New York, 1970), pp. 21–2. For Calkins's linking of "modernism" and advertising, see his memoir, *"and hearing not –" Annals of an Ad Man* (New York, 1946), p. 239. On Watson and the rise of advertising, see Kerry W. Buckley, *Mechanical Man: John Broadus Watson and the Beginnings of Behaviorism* (New York, 1989), esp. pp. 71, 74, and 136, for quoted phrases. On Calkins, Barton, and Watson, see also T. J. Jackson Lears, "From Salvation to Self-Realization: Advertising and the Therapeutic Roots of the Consumer Culture, 1880–1930," in Fox and Lears, eds., *The Culture of Consumption,* pp. 2–38. For a discussion of Lefebvre, see Lears, pp. 21–2. On the themes of disenchantment, estrangement, and flight, see Cowley's *Exile's Return* and Joseph Freeman, *An American Testament* (New York, 1936), pp. 172–3. On Johnson's *Stover at Yale* (New York, 1912), see esp. pp. 262–3. For biographies of Fitzgerald, see Matthew J. Bruccoli, *Some Sort of Epic Grandeur: The Life of F. Scott Fitzgerald* (New York, 1981); and Andrew Turnbull, *Scott Fitzgerald* (New York, 1962). Krutch's critique is in *The Modern Temper* (New York, 1929), pp. 160–1. For Lippmann, see the notes to Section 3, this part.

5. *Class, Power, and Violence in a New Age*

The Workers is a pioneering work of documentary sociology based on Wyckoff's determined effort to see life from the bottom up by making his way across the United States as a common laborer, a trip that began in 1891 and lasted into 1893. Wyckoff later taught at Princeton, his alma mater. On the lingering memories of the Great War, see especially Paul Fussell, *The Great War and Modern Memory.* For Fitzgerald's conflicted sense of himself as both in and out of his "generation," see "Echoes of the Jazz Age" and "Early Success," in Wilson, ed., *The Crack-Up,* esp. pp. 14–15 and 87–8. See *The Crack-Up* also on the issue of the "very rich" (p. 125). On the sources, background, and historical context of *The Great Gatsby*, see Richard Lehan, *The Great Gatsby: The Limits of Wonder* (Boston, 1990). Caspar W. Whitney's "Evolution of the Country Club," which first appeared in *Harper's New Monthly Magazine* (December 1894), is reprinted in Harris, ed., *The Land of Contrasts*. Both polo and golf figure prominently in Whitney's discussion. On Fitzgerald and the twenties, Bruccoli, *Some Sort of Epic Grandeur*, is especially good. For Fitzgerald's engagements with the history and myths of the United States, see *The Notebooks of F. Scott Fitzgerald*, ed. Matthew J. Bruccoli (New York, 1978), p. 63 and passim.

6. The Fear of Feminization and the Logic of Modest Ambition

On the broad theme of feminization and culture in the United States, see Douglas, *The Feminization of American Culture*, in the General Bibliography. Parsons's essay, "Sex," is one of two by women in *Civilization in the United States;* the other, "The Family," is by Katherine Anthony. For Cowley's sense of his generation, see his *A Second Flowering*, esp. pp. 8–18 and 240–55. On Cowley's omissions, see, e.g., Shari Benstock, *Women of the Left Bank*, in the General Bibliography; and Elaine Showalter, "Women Writers Between the Wars," in the Bibliography, Part Two. For the quotes from Blair and Bogan, see Showalter, pp. 823 and 822. For Ransom, see *The World's Body* (New York, 1938), pp. 77–8. On *The New Negro* and the marginalization of the Harlem Renaissance, see Houston A. Baker, Jr., *Modernism and the Harlem Renaissance,* in the Bibliography, Part Two. Roof's essay was originally published in *Outlook, 96* (October 8, 1910): 311–16. It is reprinted in Roderick Nash, ed., *The Call of the Wild: 1900–1916*, pp. 209–14, in the General Bibliography. On nativism, see bibliographical notes to Section 3, this part. Dorothy Canfield Fisher's *The Home-Maker* is at times awkwardly direct in what it does, but readers interested in the cultural construction of gender should read it. On women writers in Paris, Benstock, *Women of the Left Bank,* is indispensable, but its pertinence reaches beyond the important subject it directly addresses. On Stein, see Steiner, *Exact Resemblance; to Exact Resemblance*; Richard Bridgman, *Gertrude Stein in Pieces* (New York, 1970); Harriett Scott Chessman, *The Public Is Invited to Dance: Representation, the Body, and Dialogue in Gertrude Stein* (Stanford, Calif., 1989); and Marjorie Perloff, *The Poetics of Indeterminacy: Rimbaud to Cage* (Princeton, N.J., 1981), pp. 67–108. On Nin, see Benstock, *Women of the Left Bank*, pp. 5–8 and 429–37. Hemingway's remark about great women is in *A Moveable Feast* (1964), in the first paragraph of "A Strange Enough Ending." He has Stein in particular in mind.

7. Marginality and Authority / Race, Gender, and Region

For Fitzgerald on being a poor boy, etc., see him as quoted in Bruccoli, *Some Sort of Epic Grandeur*, p. 232. For W. E. B. Du Bois's statement, see *The Souls of Black Folk* [1903] (New York, 1923), p. 3. On "regionalism," see especially James Cox, "Regionalism: A Diminished Thing," in the General Bibliography. On the founding of *Time*, see Frank L. Mott, *A History of American Magazines* 5 vols. (Cambridge, Mass., 1930–68), vol. 1, pp. 293–328. For the quotations, see pp. 295–6 and 311–12. On Bruce Barton and the transformation he embodied, see Raymond Williams on "personality," in *Keywords: A Vocabulary of Culture and Society* (New York, 1976), pp. 194–7; Susman, "Personality and Twentieth-Century Culture," pp. 212–26; and

Warren I. Susman, ed., *Culture and Commitment: 1924–1945*, esp. pp. 127–30, in the General Bibliography. For Lewis's treatment of the Reverend Drew, see *Babbitt* (New York, 1922), pp. 204–5. On Dos Passos, see Cecelia Tichi, *Shifting Gears*, esp. pp. 194–216, in Bibliography Part Two.

8. War as Metaphor: The Example of Ernest Hemingway

For John Dewey on the "Middle West," see "The American Intellectual Frontier," first published in *New Republic, 30* (May 10, 1922): 388, and reprinted in Baritz, ed., *The Culture of the Twenties*, pp. 350–1. See also Lynd and Lynd, *Middletown*, pp. 7–8. For Bourne on war, see *The History of a Literary Radical*. For Freeman on the aftermath of the Great War, see *An American Testament*, pp. 154–5, 166–7, 172–3, and 180–200. On Hemingway, see both Carlos Baker, *Ernest Hemingway: A Life Story* (New York, 1969), and Kenneth S. Lynn, *Hemingway* (New York, 1987). Baker's book is especially helpful on Hemingway's relations with other writers, but Lynn's is better on his childhood and his relations with his family. For Hemingway on "families" as instruments of intimate harm, see *A Moveable Feast* [1964] (New York, 1965), p. 108. For Fitzgerald on Hemingway and the dark, see Wilson, ed., *The Crack-Up*, p. 174. Carlos Baker, ed., *Ernest Hemingway: Selected Letters, 1917–1961* (New York, 1981), is very valuable, as are Scott Donaldson, *By Force of Will: The Life and Art of Ernest Hemingway* (New York, 1977); Philip Young, *Ernest Hemingway* (New York, 1977); and Philip Young, *Ernest Hemingway: A Reconsideration* (University Park, Pa., 1966). On Hemingway and suicide, see, e.g., *Death in the Afternoon* (New York, 1932), p. 20; on "all stories, if continued far enough," as ending "in death," see p. 122; and on art as radically individual and as also allied with death, see pp. 99–100. Both "The Last Good Company" and "Fathers and Sons" are in Ernest Hemingway, *The Nick Adams Stories* (New York, 1972), pp. 70–134 and 256–68, respectively. See esp. pp. 71–2, 112–13, 115–16, and 121–2 in "The Last Good Company" and pp. 265–6 in "Fathers and Sons."

PART THREE: THE FATE OF WRITING DURING THE GREAT DEPRESSION

1. The Discovery of Poverty and the Return of Commitment

Fitzgerald's "Echoes of the Jazz Age" [1931], is reprinted in Wilson, ed., *The Crack-Up*, pp. 13–22; see esp. pp. 19–20. On the Crash of 1929, see John Kenneth Galbraith, *The Great Crash, 1929* [1955] (Boston, 1972). On the Great Depression, see Leuchtenburg, *The Perils of Prosperity*. See also Bird, *The Invisible Scar*, Schlesinger, *The Crisis of the Old Order*, and Wector, *The Age of the Great Depression*, in the Bibliography, Part Three. For quotes of Roosevelt and for Lippmann regarding him, see Frank Freidel, *Franklin D. Roosevelt: The Triumph* (New York, 1956). On reading habits in the thirties see Hart, *The Popular Book*, in the General Bibliography, and Waples, *People and Print*, in the Bibliography, Part Three. For Thurber on the thirties, see "New York in the Third Winter" [1932], in Sklar, ed., *The Plastic Age*, pp. 331–41. For George Orwell's sense of the thirties, see his splendid essay, "Inside the Whale," in Sonia Orwell and Ian Angus, eds., *The Collected Essays, Journalism and Letters of George Orwell* (London, 1968), vol. 1, pp. 493–526, esp. pp. 507–10. For Herbst's, see "A Year of Disgrace," in Saul Bellow and K. Botsford, eds., *Noble Savage, 3* (1961):140–2; 144–6; "Moralist's Progress," *Kenyon Review, 28* (Autumn 1965): esp. 773–7; and

"The Starched Blue Sky of Spain," *Noble Savage*, 1 (1960): esp. 77–80. For the quoted phrases of Zelda Fitzgerald and Ryan, see Leuchtenburg, *Perils of Prosperity*, pp. 242, 261. For Seldes, see his "Short History of the Depression," as quoted in Daniel Aaron, "The Thirties – Now and Then," *American Scholar* 35 (Summer 1966):491–2. On Fitzgerald's "radicalism," see Bruccoli, *Some Sort of Epic Grandeur*, pp. 347–8. For Cowley's sense of the form commitment took in the thirties, see the several works cited in the Bibliography, Part Three, and especially his statements in "Thirty Years Later: Memories of the First American Writers' Congress," pp. 495–520, esp. 500, 504–5, in the Bibliography, Part Three.

2. The Search for "Culture" as a Form of Commitment

On culture and commitment in the thirties, see Susman, ed., *Culture and Commitment;* see also his "The Thirties," as cited in the Bibliography, Part Three. These works, including Susman's introduction and notes to his anthology, are crucial to any assessment of the thirties. Also helpful is Reuel Denney, "The Discovery of Popular Culture," in Robert E. Spiller and Eric Larrabee, eds., *American Perspectives* (Cambridge, Mass., 1961). Arnold's quotes are from "Functions of Criticism at the Present Time" and his preface to the 1883 edition of *Literature and Dogma* (1873). Also pertinent to the issue of defining "culture" are his several essays in *Culture and Anarchy* (1869). For thirties counters to Arnold, see Susman, "The Thirties," esp. pp. 183–5, where, among other things, he discusses the remarkable popularity of Ruth Benedict's *Patterns of Culture* (1934) and the rising authority of phrases like "the American way of life." For Bishop on Hemingway, see the bibliographical notes to Section 2, Part Two. For the quote from Adam Smith, see Raymond Williams, *Culture and Society, 1780–1950* (London, 1959), pp. 34–5. For Herbst on "change," see "Yesterday's Road," *New American Review*, 3 (April 1968):85. For Schwab on fear, see him as quoted in Leuchtenburg, *Perils of Prosperity*, p. 250. For Wilson on the thirties, see *The American Jitters* and especially "An Appeal to Progressives" [1931], in *Shores of Light: A Literary Chronicle of the Twenties and Thirties* (New York, 1952), pp. 518–33, esp. pp. 528–9. For Cowley, see him as cited in the bibliographical notes to Section 1, this part. For Burke's sense of himself as a "translator," see his letter to Cowley, June 4, 1932, in *The Selected Correspondence of Kenneth Burke and Malcolm Cowley, 1915–1981*, ed. Paul Jay (New York, 1988), p. 202. His speech at the Writers' Congress was titled "Revolutionary Symbolism in America." On silence as strategy, see J. A. Ward, *American Silences: The Realism of James Agee, Walker Evans, and Edward Hopper* (Baton Rouge, La., 1985). On Roosevelt, see especially William Leuchtenburg, *Franklin D. Roosevelt and the New Deal*, as cited in the Bibliography, Part Three. For Fitzgerald on Hemingway, see his letter to Beatrice Dance, in Andrew Turnbull, ed., *The Letters of F. Scott Fitzgerald* (New York, 1963), p. 543.

3. Three Responses: The Examples of Henry Miller, Djuna Barnes, and John Dos Passos

For Orwell's sense of Miller's significance, see "Inside the Whale." This essay is valuable on the twenties and thirties as well as for its sense of Miller's achievement and the shaping influence of Whitman on Miller. See also *Tropic of Cancer* [1934] (New York, 1961), pp. 1–2; *Black Spring* [1936] (New York, 1963), p. 15; and *The Books in My Life* (New York, 1952). On Miller, see also Steiner, "The Diversity of American

Fiction." On Barnes, see Benstock, *Women of the Left Bank,* esp. pp. 230–67. On Dos Passos, see Donald Pizer, *Dos Passos's "U.S.A.": A Critical Study* (Charlottesville, Va., 1988), and Townsend Lundington, *John Dos Passos: A Twentieth-Century Odyssey* (New York, 1960). On Miller, see also Susman, "The Thirties."

4. Cowboys, Detectives, and Other Tough-Guy Antinomians: Residual Individualism and Hedged Commitments

For Eliot's self-description, see his *For Lancelot Andrewes* (New York, 1929), p. vii. Gold's attacks on aesthetes, including Eliot and Joyce, is in "The Writer in America," quoted by Marcus Klein, "The Roots of Radicals: Experience in the Thirties," in Madden, ed., *Proletarian Writers of the Thirties,* p. 135, in the Bibliography, Part Three. On W. C. Fields, see Aaron, "The Thirties – Now and Then," p. 494. On violence in the thirties, see Wilson, *The American Jitters,* pp. 13–16, 37–45, 121–31, 175–92; Frohock, *The Novel of Violence in America;* "Four Martyrs," in Jack Salzman and Barry Wallenstein, eds., *Years of Protests,* pp. 366–75; and especially Bird, *The Invisible Scar,* esp. pp. 157–61, 171–4, 188–90, and 192–6, all in the Bibliography, Part Three. On Hart Crane's death, I am indebted to John Irwin's poem, "The Verbal Emblem," in *The Heisenberg Variations* (Athens, Ga., 1976), pp. 62–5. On Westerns and detective novels, see John G. Cawelti, *Adventure, Mystery, and Romance,* as cited in the General Bibliography; idem, *The Six-Gun Mystique* (Bowling Green, Ohio, 1984); and Philip Durham and Everett L. Jones, *The Western Story: Fact, Fiction, and Myth* (New York, 1975). Especially valuable is T. K. Whipple's "American Sagas," pp. 315–20, which focuses on Zane Grey. The Depression hurt book buying: 214,334,000 new books were printed in 1929; 110,790,000 were printed in 1933. Over the same period, motion picture attendance dropped from 177,000,000 in 1929 to 60,000,000 in 1933. Westerns and detective novels held up well, however. Zane Grey in particular was one of the most widely read novelists of the thirties, and detective fiction flourished. See Hart, *The Popular Book,* esp. pp. 248–9 and 257–61. On *Anthony Adverse,* which I mention in Section 1, this part, see ibid., pp. 261–2. On *Gone with the Wind,* which I discuss in Section 7, this part, see pp. 263–4. The passage I quote from *All the King's Men* is early in Chapter 5. On the "tough-guy" extensions of detective fiction, see Madden, ed., *Tough Guy Writers of the Thirties,* as cited in the Bibliography, Part Three. I am indebted to Joyce Carol Oates's essay on Cain and Thomas Stuark's on McCoy for valuable information about these writers as well as valuable discussions of their work. I am also indebted to unpublished work of Kathye Bergin, one of my graduate students, on Cain. A former graduate student, Martha Sledge, called my attention to Marjorie Hillis's *Live Alone and Like It,* a gift for which I am grateful.

5. The Search for Shared Purpose: Struggles on the Left

For representative collections of writings of "the Left" in the thirties, see the anthologies edited by Hicks, Madden, Nekola and Rabinowitz, North, Salzman and Wallenstein, and Swados in the Bibliography, Part Three. On Conroy's reaction to *Das Kapital,* see him as quoted in Erling Larsen, "Jack Conroy, *The Disinherited,*" in Madden, ed., *Proletarian Writers of the Thirties,* p. 88. On Farrell's relations to the Left, see especially Salzman and Wallenstein, *Years of Protest,* pp. 277–93, which includes an excerpt from Farrell's "A Note on Literary Criticism." Hagglund's remark is in "The

30's, a Symposium," p. 68, in the Bibliography, Part Three. Algren's remark, made on the same occasion, is on p. 104. Farrell, Conroy, and Cowley also took part. My discussion of Roth's *Call It Sleep* is indebted to an unpublished essay by Jane Creighton, one of my graduate students. "Thirty Years Later: Memories of the First Writers' Congress," in the Bibliography, Part Three, is also valuable. On Mary McCarthy and the *Partisan Review*, see her as quoted in Showalter, "Women Writers Between the Wars," p. 831. On the *Partisan Review*'s relations to the Left, see the pieces in Salzman and Wallenstein, *Years of Protest*, pp. 294–307. For an assessment of "radical" fiction in the thirties, see Rideout, *The Radical Novel in the United States, 1900–1954*, as cited in the Bibliography, Part Three. Rideout's book includes a very useful list of "radical novels" from 1901 to 1954. On the strained relations between FDR and the Left, see especially Leslie Fiedler, "The Two Memories: Reflections on Writers and Writing in the Thirties" in Madden, ed., *Proletarian Writers of the Thirties*, pp. 3–25. On Hitler as a unifying force, see Kenneth Burke in "Thirty Years Later," p. 497. On the popularity of Steinbeck's writings, see Hart, *The Popular Book*, pp. 250 and 272. On West's ties to the Left, see Marcus Klein, "The Roots of Radicals: Experience in the Thirties," in Madden, ed., *Proletarian Writers of the Thirties*, pp. 134–57, esp. pp. 142–5. On the important issue of the roles of women in activities on the Left, see Herbst's letter to David Madden as quoted in his Introduction to *Proletarian Writers of the Thirties*, pp. xv–xxii. See also Herbst as cited in the bibliographical notes to Section 1, this part; Nekola and Rabinowitz, *Writing Red;* and Deborah Rosenfelt, "From the Thirties: Tillie Olsen and the Radical Tradition," *Feminist Studies*, 7, no. 3 (Fall 1981): 370–406. My discussions of both John Steinbeck and Nathanael West are indebted to unpublished works of Mylene Dressler, another of my graduate students.

6. Documentary Literature and the Disarming of Dissent

One of the best early discussions of the documentary movement as a search for culture is Robert Cantwell, "America and the Writers' Project," *New Republic*, 98 (April 26, 1939): 323–5, which is reprinted in Susman, ed., *Culture and Commitment*, pp. 194–5. For Saul Bellow's comments, see him in Bellow and Botsford, eds., *Noble Savage*, p. 3. The text of Pare Lorentz's *The River* is reprinted in Filler, ed., *The Anxious Years*, pp. 364–75, with a headnote by Lorentz, as cited in the Bibliography, Part Three. See Johan Huizinga, *America: A Dutch Historian's Vision, From Afar and Near*, trans. Herbert H. Rowen (New York, 1972), pp. 254–60. On documentary literature, see "The 30's: a Symposium"; Rideout, *The Radical Novel*, esp. chaps. 6, 7, and 8; and William Stott, *Documentary Expression and Thirties America*, as cited in the Bibliography, Part Three. On James Agee, see David Madden, ed., *Remembering James Agee* (Baton Rouge, La., 1974). For a work that deals in interesting ways with the impact of dehumanizing forces, see Edward Dahlberg's autobiography, *Because I Was Flesh* (New York, 1965), in which Dahlberg describes his young self as a "suffering locality rather than a person" (p. 92). Of particular value on the striking collaborations of photographers and writers of the thirties are Carl Fleischhauer and Beverly W. Brannan, ed., *Documentary America, 1935–1943*, in the Bibliography, Part Three, which includes fine essays by Lawrence W. Levine and Alan Trachtenberg; Stange, *Symbols of Ideal Life;* and Trachtenberg, *Reading American Photographs*. For theoretical context, see especially Walter Benjamin, "The Work of Art in the Age of Mechanical Reproduction," in *Illuminations*, as cited in the General Bibliography.

7. *The Southern Renaissance: Forms of Reaction and Innovation*

On the basic tensions of the thirties and how the South figured in them, see Herbert Agar, "Culture versus Colonialism in America" [1935], in Susman, ed., *Culture and Commitment*, pp. 24–42; and Herbert Agar and Allen Tate, eds., *Who Owns America?* (Boston, 1936), a sequel to *I'll Take My Stand: The South and the Agrarian Tradition* [1930] (New York, 1962). On the Southern Renaissance, see the works by James Cox in the General Bibliography and by Fred Hobson, Louis Rubin, Jr., Anne Scott, Lewis Simpson, and especially Richard King in the Bibliography, Part Three. Motherwell's statement is in the *New York Times,* July 18, 1991, p. A 12. Lawrence's statement about the United States is in his introduction to Edward Dahlberg's *Bottom Dogs* [1930] (San Francisco, 1961), p. vii. For Glasgow's statement about Dorinda, see her preface to *Barren Ground* [1925], written in 1933 and reprinted in a new release of *Barren Ground* (New York, 1985), p. x. On Wolfe, see David Donald, *Look Homeward: A Life of Thomas Wolfe* (Boston, 1987); on Porter, see Joan Givner, *Katherine Anne Porter: A Life* (New York, 1982).

8. *History and Novels / Novels and History: The Example of William Faulkner*

For Ralph Ellison's discussion of Faulkner, see "Hidden Name and Complex Fate" [1964], in *Shadow and Act* (New York, 1964), pp. 164–5. For Herbst's statements, see her letter to David Madden, cited in the bibliographical notes to Section 5 above, p xxi. For Faulkner's statements about Caddy Compson, Lena Grove, and Joe Christmas, see David Minter, *William Faulkner: His Life and Work* (Baltimore, 1981), pp. 102 and 130. On Faulkner's fiction and its relations to modernism, see especially André Bleikasten, *The Ink of Melancholy: Faulkner's Novels from the "Sound and the Fury" to "Light in August"* (Bloomington, Ind., 1990); Donald M. Kartiganer, *The Fragile Thread: The Meaning of Form in Faulkner's Novels* (Amherst, Mass., 1979); John T. Irwin, *Doubling and Incest/Repetition and Revenge: A Speculative Reading of Faulkner* (Baltimore, 1975); John T. Matthews, *The Play of Faulkner's Language* (Ithaca, N.Y., 1982); Richard C. Moreland, *Faulkner and Modernism: Rereading and Rewriting* (Madison, Wis., 1990); and Wesley Morris, *Reading Faulkner* (Madison, Wis., 1989). On Faulkner and the issues of race, class, caste, and gender, see Myra Jehlen, *Class and Character in Faulkner's Fiction* (New York, 1980); Carolyn Porter, *Seeing and Being: The Plight of the Participant Observer in Emerson, James, Adams, and Faulkner* (Middletown, Conn., 1981); and Eric Sundquist, *Faulkner: A House Divided* (Baltimore, 1983). See also my essay " 'Truths More Intense Than Knowledge': Notes on Faulkner and Creativity," in Doreen Fowler and Ann J. Abadie, eds., *Faulkner and the Southern Renaissance* (Jackson, Miss., 1982), pp. 245–65.

Bibliography

This bibliography is divided into four parts. In the General Bibliography, I include a small group of theoretical works that have been particularly helpful to me in establishing a theoretical framework for my study and a larger group of works in literary and social-intellectual history that cover most or all of the period from 1890 to 1940. In addition I include several collections of documents, most of them from the American Culture series, of which Neil Harris is the general editor, that are of great value in gaining a sense of events and of various voices that emerged during the years I examine.

Following the General Bibliography are shorter bibliographies on the literary and social-intellectual history for each of the three major parts of the study.

GENERAL BIBLIOGRAPHY

Aaron, Daniel. "Literary Scenes and Literary Movements." In Emory Elliott, with others, ed. *Columbia Literary History of the United States*. New York, 1988, pp. 733–57.

Men of Good Hope: A Story of American Progressives. New York, 1961.

Writers on the Left: Episodes in American Literary Communism [1961]. New York, 1992.

Ahlstrom, Sydney. *A Religious History of the American People*. New Haven, Conn., 1972.

Anderson, Quentin. *The Imperial Self*. New York, 1971.

Bakhtin, M. M. *The Dialogic Imagination: Four Essays*. Edited by Michael Holquist; translated by Caryl Emerson and Michael Holquist. Austin, Tex., 1981.

Banta, Martha. *Imaging American Women: Ideas and Ideals in Cultural History*. New York, 1987.

Benjamin, Walter. *Illuminations*. Edited by Hannah Arendt; translated by Harry Zahn. New York, 1968.

Benstock, Shari. *Women of the Left Bank: Paris, 1900–1940*. Austin, Tex., 1986.

Bradbury, Malcolm. *The Modern American Novel*. Oxford, 1983.

Burke, Kenneth. *Attitudes Toward History*. New York, 1937.

The Philosophy of Aesthetic Form: Studies in Symbolic Action. Baton Rouge, La., 1941.

Cawelti, John. *Adventure, Mystery, and Romance: Formula Stories as Art and Popular Culture*. Chicago, 1976.

Charvat, William. *The Origins of American Critical Thought* [1936]. New York, 1961.

Commager, Henry Steele. *The American Mind: An Interpretation of American Thought and Culture Since the 1880s*. New Haven, Conn., 1950.

Cox, James M. "Regionalism: A Diminished Thing." In Emory Elliott, with others, ed., *Columbia Literary History of the United States*. New York, 1988, pp. 761–84.

Degler, Carl. *At Odds: Women and the Family in America from the Revolution to the Present.* Oxford, 1980.

——— *Out of Our Past: The Forces That Shaped Modern America.* New York, 1959.

Douglas, Ann. *The Feminization of American Culture.* New York, 1977.

Ellmann, Richard, and Charles Feidelson, Jr., eds. *The Modern Tradition: Backgrounds of Modern Literature.* New York, 1965.

Fussell, Paul. *The Great War and Modern Memory.* New York, 1975.

Gates, Henry Louis. *Figures in Black: Words, Signs, and the Racial Self.* New York, 1987.

Geertz, Clifford. *The Interpretation of Culture: Selected Essays.* New York, 1973.

Ginger, Ray, ed. *American Social Thought.* New York, 1961.

Hart, James D. *The Popular Book: A History of America's Literary Taste.* New York, 1950.

Hartz, Louis. *The Liberal Tradition in America.* New York, 1955.

Heisenberg, Werner. *Physics and Philosophy.* New York, 1962.

Higham, John. *Strangers in the Land: Patterns of American Nativism, 1860–1925* [1955]. New York, 1981.

Hofstadter, Richard. *The Age of Reform: From Bryan to FDR.* New York, 1955.

Howe, Irving. *World of Our Fathers: The Journey of the East European Jews to America and the Life They Found and Made.* New York, 1976.

Jameson, Frederic. *The Political Unconscious: Narrative as a Socially Symbolic Act.* Ithaca, N.Y., 1981.

Kazin, Alfred. *On Native Grounds: A Study of American Prose Literature from 1890 to the Present.* New York, 1942.

Kennedy, David M. *Over Here: The First World War and American Society.* New York, 1980.

Kuklick, Bruce. *The Rise of American Philosophy: Cambridge, Massachusetts, 1860–1930.* New Haven, Conn., 1977.

Larkin, Oliver W. *Art and Life in America* [1949]. New York, 1960.

Lasch, Christopher. *Haven in a Heartless World: The Family Besieged.* New York, 1977.

Leuchtenburg, William E. *The Perils of Prosperity, 1914–1932.* Chicago, 1958.

Levine, Lawrence W. *Black Culture and Black Consciousness: Afro-American Folk Thought from Slavery to Freedom.* Oxford, 1977.

Lukacs, Georg. *The Theory of the Novel: A Historio-Philosophical Essay on the Forms of Great Epic Literature.* Translated by Anna Bostock. Cambridge, Mass., 1971.

May, Henry F. *The End of American Innocence: A Study of the First Years of Our Time, 1912–1917.* New York, 1979.

Nash, Roderick, ed. *The Call of the Wild: 1900–1916.* New York, 1970.

Noble, David. *America by Design: Science, Technology, and the Rise of Corporate Capitalism.* New York, 1977.

Nye, Russell. *The Unembarrassed Muse: The Popular Arts in America.* New York, 1970.

Poirier, Richard. *A World Elsewhere.* New York, 1966.

Porter, Carolyn. *Seeing and Being: The Plight of the Participant Observer in Emerson, James, Adams, and Faulkner.* Middletown, Conn., 1981.

Radway, Janice A. *Reading the Romance: Women, Patriarchy, and Popular Literature.* Chapel Hill, N.C., 1984.

Ruland, Richard. *The Rediscovery of American Literature: Premises of Critical Taste, 1900–1940.* New York, 1967.

Sears, Sallie, and Georgianna Lord, eds. *The Discontinuous Universe: Selected Writings in Contemporary Consciousness.* New York, 1972.

Sklar, Robert, ed. *The Plastic Age: 1917–1930*. New York, 1970.

Sollors, Werner. *Beyond Ethnicity: Consent and Descent in American Culture*. New York, 1986.

Stange, Maren. *Symbols of Ideal Life: Social Documentary Photography in America, 1890–1950*. Cambridge, 1989.

Steiner, Wendy. "The Diversity of American Fiction." In Emory Elliott, with others, ed., *Columbia Literary History of the United States*. New York, 1988, pp. 846–72.

Stepto, Robert B. *From Behind the Veil: A Study of Afro-American Narrative*. Urbana, Ill., 1979.

Susman, Warren, ed. *Culture and Commitment: 1929–1945*. New York, 1973.

Trachtenberg, Alan. *Reading American Photographs: Images as History: Mathew Brady to Walker Evans*. New York, 1989.

Turner, Victor. *Dramas, Fields, and Metaphors: Symbolic Action in Human Society*. Ithaca, N.Y., 1974.

The Ritual Process: Structure and Anti-Structure [1969]. Ithaca, N.Y., 1977.

Washington, Mary Helen. *Invented Lives: Narratives of Black Women, 1860–1960*. Garden City, N.Y., 1987.

Williams, Raymond. *Culture and Society*. London, 1959.

Marxism and Literature. New York, 1977.

PART ONE: A DREAM CITY, LYRIC YEARS, AND A GREAT WAR

Abrahams, Edward. *The Lyrical Left: Randolph Bourne, Alfred Steiglitz, and the Origins of Cultural Radicalism in America*. Charlottesville, Va., 1986.

Bertoff, Warner. *The Ferment of Realism: American Literature, 1884–1919*. New York, 1964.

Brown, Dee. *The Gentle Tamers: Women and the Old Wild West*. Lincoln, Neb., 1958.

Conn, Peter. *The Divided Mind: Ideology and Imagination in America, 1898–1917*. Cambridge, 1983.

Fisher, Philip. *Hard Facts: Setting and Form in the American Novel*. New York, 1985.

Handlin, Oscar. *The Uprooted: The Epic Story of the Great Migrations That Made the American People*. New York, 1951.

Harris, Neil, ed. *The Land of Contrasts: 1880–1901*. New York, 1970.

Higham, John. *Send These to Me: Immigrants in Urban America* [1975]. Baltimore, 1984.

Kolodny, Annette. *The Lay of the Land: Metaphor as Experience and History in American Life and Letters*. Chapel Hill, N.C., 1975.

Lears, Jackson. *No Place of Grace: Antimodernism and the Transformation of American Culture, 1880–1920*. New York, 1981.

Lutz, Tom. *American Nervousness, 1903: An Anecdotal History*. Ithaca, N.Y., 1991.

Lynn, Kenneth S. *The Dream of Success: A Study of the Modern American Imagination*. Boston, 1955.

Martin, Jay. *Harvests of Change: American Literature, 1865–1914*. Englewood Cliffs, N.J., 1967.

Mumford, Lewis. *The Brown Decades: A Study of the Arts in America, 1865–1895*. New York, 1931.

O'Neill, William L., ed. *Echoes of Revolt: "The Masses," 1911–1917*. Chicago, 1966.

Rowe, John Carlos. *Henry Adams and Henry James: The Emergence of a Modern Consciousness.* Ithaca, N.Y., 1976.

Slotkin, Richard. *The Fatal Environment: The Myth of the Frontier in the Age of Industrialization.* Middletown, Conn., 1985.

Smith, Henry Nash. *Virgin Land: The American West as Symbol and Myth.* Cambridge, Mass., 1950.

Smith-Rosenberg, Carroll. *Disorderly Conduct: Visions of Gender in Victorian America.* New York, 1985.

Todorov, Tzvetan. *The Conquest of America: The Question of the Other.* Translated by Richard Howard. New York, 1984.

Trachtenberg, Alan. *The Incorporation of America: Culture and Society in the Gilded Age.* New York, 1982.

Ziff, Larzer. *The American 1890s: Life and Times of a Lost Generation.* New York, 1966.

PART TWO: FICTION IN A TIME OF PLENTY

Allen, Frederick Lewis. *Only Yesterday* [1931]. New York, 1959.

Amory, Cleveland, and Frederic Bradlee, eds. *"Vanity Fair": Selections from America's Most Memorable Magazine – A Cavalcade of the 1920s and 1930s.* New York, 1960.

Baker, Houston A., Jr. *Modernism and the Harlem Renaissance.* Chicago, 1987.

Baritz, Loren, ed. *The Culture of the Twenties.* Indianapolis, Ind., 1970.

Beach, Sylvia. *Shakespeare and Company.* New York, 1959.

Carpenter, Humphrey. *Geniuses Together: American Writers in Paris in the 1920s.* Boston, 1988.

Cowley, Malcolm. *Exile's Return: A Literary Odyssey of the 1920s* [1934]. New York, 1951.

  A Second Flowering: Works and Days of the Lost Generation. New York, 1973.

Cowley, Malcolm, ed. *After the Genteel Tradition.* New York, 1937.

Fox, Richard W., and T. J. Jackson Lears, eds. *The Culture of Consumption: Critical Essays in American History, 1880–1980.* New York, 1983.

Gilmore, Thomas G. *Equivocal Spirits: Alcoholism and Drinking in Twentieth-Century Literature.* Chapel Hill, N.C., 1987.

Hoffman, Frederick J. *The Twenties: American Writing in the Postwar Decade* [1955]. New York, 1962.

Hoffman, Frederick J., Charles Allen, and Carolyn Ulrich. *The Little Magazine: A History and a Bibliography.* Princeton, N.J., 1946.

Josephson, Matthew. *Life Among the Surrealists.* New York, 1962.

Joughin, Louis, and Edmund M. Morgan. *The Legacy of Sacco and Vanzetti.* New York, 1948.

Kouwenhoven, John. *Made in America: The Arts in Modern Civilization.* New York, 1948.

Leonard, Neil. *Jazz and the White Americans.* Chicago, 1962.

Lippmann, Walter. *A Preface to Morals.* New York, 1929.

Loeb, Harold. *The Way It Was.* New York, 1959.

Lynd, Robert S., and Helen Lynd. *Middletown: A Study in Modern American Culture.* New York, 1929.

Merz, Charles. *The Dry Decade.* New York, 1931.

Meyer, Donald. *The Positive Thinkers: A Study of the American Quest for Health, Wealth, and Personal Power from Mary Baker Eddy to Norman Vincent Peale.* New York, 1965.

Mowry, George E., ed. *The Twenties: Fords, Flappers, and Fanatics*. Englewood Cliffs, N.J., 1963.

Murray, Robert K. *Red Scare: A Study in National Hysteria*. Minneapolis, Minn., 1955.

Parry, Albert. *Garrets and Pretenders: A History of Bohemianism in America* [1933]. New York, 1960.

Showalter, Elaine. "Women Writers Between the Wars." In Emory Elliott, with others, ed., *Columbia Literary History of the United States*. New York, 1988, pp. 822–841.

Sinclair, Andrew. *Prohibition: The Era of Excess*. Boston, 1962.

Tichi, Cecelia. *Shifting Gears: Technology, Literature, and Culture in Modernist America*. Chapel Hill, N.C., 1987.

Trilling, Lionel. *The Liberal Imagination: Essays on Literature and Society*. New York, 1950.

Ware, Carolyn F. *Greenwich Village: 1920–1930*. Boston, 1935.

Wilson, Edmund. *The American Earthquake*. New York, 1958.

  The Shores of Light: A Literary Chronicle of the Twenties and Thirties. New York, 1952.

PART THREE: THE FATE OF WRITING DURING THE GREAT DEPRESSION

Aaron, Daniel. *Writers on the Left*. New York, 1961.

Aaron, Daniel, and Robert Bendiner, eds. *The Strenuous Decade*. Garden City, N.Y., 1970.

Allen, Frederick L. *Since Yesterday*. New York, 1940.

Bernstein, Irving. *The Lean Years*. Boston, 1960.

Bird, Caroline. *The Invisible Scar*. New York, 1966.

Burke, Kenneth. "Revolutionary Symbolism in America." In Henry Hart, ed., *American Writers Congress*. New York, 1935, pp. 87–94.

Cash, W. J. *The Mind of the South* [1941]. New York, 1960.

Clurman, Harold. *The Fervent Years*. New York, 1957.

Cooke, Alistair. "Remembrance of Things Past: The 1930s." In *A Generation on Trial: U.S.A. vs. Alger Hiss*. New York, 1950, pp. 3–41.

Cowley, Malcolm. *The Dream of the Golden Mountains: Remembering the 1930s*. New York, 1980.

Degler, Carl. *Place over Time: The Continuity of Southern Distinctiveness*. Baton Rouge, La., 1977.

Filler, Louis, ed. *The Anxious Years: America in the Nineteen Thirties – A Collection*. New York, 1963.

Fleischhauer, Carl, and Beverly W. Brannan, eds. *Documenting America, 1935–1943*. Berkeley and Los Angeles, 1988.

French, Warren, ed. *The Thirties*. Delano, Fla., 1967.

Frohock, W. M. *The Novel of Violence in America*. Dallas, Tex., 1957.

Galbraith, John Kenneth. *The Great Crash, 1929*. Boston, 1954.

Gray, Richard. *Writing the South: Ideas of an American Region*. Cambridge, 1986.

Gurko, Leo. *The Angry Decade*. New York, 1947.

Hicks, Granville, and others, eds. *Proletarian Literature in the United States: An Anthology*. New York, 1935.

Hobson, Fred. *Tell about the South: The Southern Rage to Explain*. Baton Rouge, La., 1983.

Hoffman, Frederick J., ed. *Marginal Manners: The Variants of Bohemia*. Evanston, Ill., 1962.

Kazin, Alfred. *Starting Out in the Thirties*. Boston, 1965.

King, Richard H. *A Southern Rensaissance: The Cultural Awakening of the American South, 1930–1955*. New York, 1980.

Leuchtenburg, William. *Franklin D. Roosevelt and the New Deal, 1932–1940*. New York, 1963.

Lynd, Robert S., and Helen Lynd. *Middletown in Transition*. New York, 1937.

Madden, David, ed. *Proletarian Writers of the Thirties*. Carbondale, Ill., 1968.

Tough Guy Writers of the Thirties. Carbondale, Ill., 1968.

Matthews, Jane D. *The Federal Theater, 1935–39*. Princeton, N.J., 1967.

Nekola, Charlotte, and Paula Rabinowitz, eds. *Writing Red: An Anthology of American Women Writers, 1930–1940*. New York, 1987.

North, Joseph, ed. *"New Masses": An Anthology of the Rebel Thirties*. New York, 1969.

Piper, Henry Dan, ed. *Think Back on Us . . . A Contemporary Chronicle of the 1930's by Malcolm Cowley*. Carbondale, Ill., 1967.

Rideout, Walter. *The Radical Novel in the United States, 1900–1954*. Cambridge, Mass., 1956.

Rubin, Louis D., Jr. *William Elliott Shoots a Bear: Essays on the Southern Literary Imagination*. Baton Rouge, La., 1975.

Salzman, Jack, and Barry Wallenstein, eds. *Years of Protest: A Collection of American Writings of the 1930's*. New York, 1967.

Schlesinger, Arthur M., Jr. *The Crisis of the Old Order*. Boston, 1957.

Scott, Anne F. *The Southern Lady: From Pedestal to Politics, 1830–1930*. Chicago, 1970.

Simpson, Lewis. *The Dispossessed Garden: Pastoral and History in Southern Literature*. Athens, Ga., 1975.

Stott, William. *Documentary Expression and Thirties America*. New York, 1973.

Susman, Warren. "The Thirties." In Stanley Coben and Lorman Ratner, eds., *The Development of American Culture*. Englewood Cliffs, N.J., 1970, pp. 176–98.

Swados, Harvey, ed. *The American Writer and the Great Depression*. Indianapolis, Ind., 1966.

Tanner, Louise. *All the Things We Were*. Garden City, N.Y., 1968.

Terkel, Studs. *Hard Times: An Oral History of the Great Depression*. New York, 1970.

"The 30's: A Symposium." *Carleton Miscellany* (Winter 1965): 6–104.

"Thirty Years Later: Memories of the First Writers' Conference." *American Scholar* 35 (Summer 1966): 495–516.

Tindall, George. *The Emergence of the New South, 1913–1945*. Baton Rouge, La., 1967.

Waples, Douglas. *People and Print: Social Aspects of Reading in the Depression*. New York, 1948.

Wector, Dixon. *The Age of the Great Depression: 1929–1941*. New York, 1948.

Wyatt-Brown, Bertram. *Southern Honor: Ethics and Behavior in the Old South*. New York, 1982.

Index

Aaron, Daniel, 188
Abbott, Lyman, 27, 236
Absalom, Absalom (Faulkner), 159, 206, 212, 220, 222–7
Adamic, Louis, *My America*, 152, 195, 203
Adams, Charles Francis, Jr., 43, 77
Adams, Henry, 25, 29, 31–5, 61, 77–81, 137, 236, 238
  Democracy, 80
  Education of Henry Adams, The, 31–5, 38, 77–81
  on the modern city, 35, 37, 38
  Mont-Saint-Michel and Chartres, 78, 79
Addams, Jane, 26, 70
Adventures of Huckleberry Finn, The (Twain), 2
advertising, 91–2, 105–6, 128–9, 147
Agee, James, 160, 164, 207
  Let Us Now Praise Famous Men, xv, 152, 159, 199–202
Age of Innocence, The (Wharton), 95
Agrarians, 208
Aiken, Conrad, 196
Alcott, Louisa May, 6
Alger, Horatio, 45, 55, 161
Algren, Nelson, 152, 183, 188
Allen, Frederick Lewis, 150
All the King's Men (Warren), 127–8, 174
American, The (James), 1
American Caravan, 155
American Civil Liberties Union (ACLU), 97
American Exodus, An (Lange and Taylor), 152, 195, 197
American Humor: A Study of the National Character (Rourke), 155
American Jitters, The (Wilson), 152, 155, 202
American Language, The (Mencken), 86
American Literature: A Journal of Literary History, Criticism, and Bibliography, 155
American Scene, The (James), 3, 4
American Scholar, The (Emerson), xii
"American Sense of Humor, The" (Roof), 118

American Tragedy, An (Dreiser), 1, 60–1, 63, 110
American Writers' Congress, 181, 187–8
America's Coming of Age (Brooks), 49
Anderson, Margaret, 81, 103
  Home Town, 152
Anderson, Maxwell, 98, 177
Anderson, Sherwood, 3, 82, 83, 100–3, 104, 141, 151, 156, 167, 181, 202, 216
  autobiographical writings of, 101
  background of, 100–1
  Home Town, 197
  influence of, 103
  Marching Men, 101
  Puzzled America, 152, 181, 202
  Windy McPherson's Son, 101
  Winesburg, Ohio, 101–3, 160
Anthony, Susan B., 26
Anvil, 169, 186
Architecture, of World's Columbian Exposition, 24–6
Arendt, Hannah, 188, 216
  On Revolution, xiv–xv
Aristocracy and Justice (More), 37
Armory Show of 1913, xi, 50–2, 237
Arnold, Matthew, xiii, 24, 152–3
Arnow, Harriette, 15
art, 48, 50–3, 85
Art of Motion Pictures, The (Lindsay), 105
Asch, Nathan, 152, 181–2, 195
Ash Can school, 44, 50–1
As I Lay Dying (Faulkner), 217, 219
"At the Fishhouses" (Bishop), xvi
Attitudes Toward History (Burke), xv
Austen, Jane, 6
Austin, Mary, 27
Autobiography of Alice B. Toklas, The (Stein), 122, 137, 138
Awakening, The (Chopin), 26, 58, 60
Axel's Castle (Wilson), 155, 159
Ayres, C. E., 78

Babbitt, Irving, 92
Babbitt (Lewis), 87–9, 92–3, 129
Backward Glance, A (Wharton), 95–6
Backward Glance o'er Travel'd Roads, A
   (Whitman), 2
*Backwash of War: The Human Wreckage of the
   Battlefield as Witnessed by an American
   Hospital Nurse, The* (La Motte), 71–2
Bacon, Francis, 7, 31
Baedeker, Karl, 24
Bagehot, Walter, 126
Baker, Carlos, 138
Baker, Ray Stannard, 26
Bakhtin, Mikhail, xv, 234
Ballard, John, 207
Bancroft, George, 28
Barnes, Djuna, 121, 160, 164, 207
   Nightwood, 159, 164–5
Barney, Natalie, 121
Barren Ground (Glasgow), 58, 207, 211–12
Barrows, John Henry, 27
Barton, Bruce, 128–9, 241
   The Man Nobody Knows, 105, 129
Baudelaire, Charles-Pierre, 36, 137
Beach, Sylvia, 81, 121
Beard, Charles, 78
Because I Was Flesh (Dahlberg), 185
Bell, Thomas, 152
   Out of This Furnace, 152, 187, 199
Bellamy, Edward, 63
Bellow, Saul, 188, 196
Benchley, Robert, 169
Benét, Stephen Vincent, 177
Benjamin, Walter, 127
Berkman, Alexander, 65
Big Sleep, The (Chandler), 175
"Big Two-Hearted River" (Hemingway), 143
Bishop, Elizabeth, xvi
Bishop, John Peale, 82, 154
Black Mask, 176
Blackmur, R. P., 209
Black Spring (Miller), 161, 163
Blake, William, 177
Boas, Franz, 78
Bogan, Louise, 121
Bohr, Niels, 35
Bok, Edward, 119–20
Boni & Liveright, 106
Bontemps, Arna, 196
Bookman, The, 67
Books That Changed Our Minds, 78–9
Borges, Jorge Luis, 123–4
Boston (Sinclair), 98
Bottom Dogs (Dahlberg), 152, 185, 187

Bourke-White, Margaret, 197–8, 202
   view of poverty, 197–8
   You Have Seen Their Faces, 152, 195, 197
Bourne, Randolph, 46, 48, 49, 64–5, 75, 135,
   136, 167, 183
Bower, B. M. (pseud.), 172
Bowers, Claude, 135
Boyd, Thomas, 136
Boyle, Kay, 169–70
Boynton, H. W., 67
Brewster, Lyman, 131
Bridge, The (Crane), 130
Bromfield, Louis, 104
Brooks, Cleanth, 209
Brooks, Van Wyck, 47, 54, 64, 103, 126, 203
   America's Coming of Age, 49, 203
   Flowering of New England, The, 153, 203
   New England: Indian Summer, 153, 203
   Ordeal of Mark Train, The, 135
Browder, Earl, 188
Brown, John, 187
Brown, Theodore, 196
Brown Decades, The (Mumford), 135
Buffalo Bill's Wild West Show, xi, 22–3, 30
Burke, Kenneth, 94, 131, 151, 155, 158, 168,
   181, 209
   Attitudes Toward History, xv, xvi
   socialism of, 158
Burnham, Daniel, 23, 24, 25, 26, 30, 50
Butterfly, The (Cain), 178
Bynner, Witter, 98

Cabell, James Branch, 86, 169
   Jurgen, 121, 162
Cage, John, 131
Cahan, Abraham, 44
Cain, James M., 177–8, 244
   Butterfly, The, 178
   Postman Always Rings Twice, The, 178–9
   Serenade, 178, 179
Cain, Paul, 192
Caldwell, Erskine, 196, 202
   God's Little Acre, 207, 209, 210
   Piedmont of, 209–10
   Tobacco Road, 209, 210
   You Have Seen Their Faces, 152, 195, 197
Calkins, Ernest Elmo, 105
Call It Sleep (Roth), 13, 184–5, 245
Call of the Wild, The (London), 39, 40,
   42–3
Camus, Albert, 145, 228
   Rebel, The, xi–xii
Cane (Toomer), 102
Cantos (Pound), 130

Cantwell, Robert, 188, 202, 203
  Land of Plenty, 152, 183
capitalism
  in *Absalom, Absalom!*, 222–3
  in *The Financier* and *The Titan*, 62–3
  in *The Great Gatsby*, 114–15
  in *The House of Mirth*, 58–9
  in *Martin Eden*, 54–5
  and property, 36–7
  in *Sister Carrie*, 18–19, 21
Carnegie, Andrew, *Triumphant America*, 2
Cash, W. J., 207
Cassatt, Mary, 26
Cassidy, Hopalong, 117
Cather, Willa, 3, 10–11, 32, 73–4, 134, 167,
  197, 238
  Death Comes for the Archbishop, 29, 73–4, 96
  loss of premodern world, 29–30
  Lost Lady, A, 73
  My Ántonia, 12, 14–18
  One of Ours, 68, 71, 73
  O Pioneers!, 1
  Song of the Lark, 58
Cézanne, Paul, 50, 51
Chamberlain, John, 78
Chandler, Raymond, 171, 175–6
  Big Sleep, The, 175
  hero of, 176
Chang Tsu, 8, 37–8
Chicago
  growth of, 13
  World's Columbian Exposition in, xi, 23–
    7, 30, 31, 37, 236
Children of Fate (Rutledge), 135–6
Chopin, Kate, 26, 58, 60
Christ in Concrete (Di Donato), 187
Churchill, Winston, 69
cities 3–4, 43–4, 62–3, 87, 135, 174–5, 182–4
  of Adams, 34–5, 37
  of Dos Passos, 130–1
  of Dreiser, 15, 16, 18–19, 62–3
  expansion of, 13
  as "hieroglyphic," 35–6
  as human creations, 18–19, 35–6, 37–8, 126
  life in as "cinematographic," 3–4; and as
    "disconnected," 126–7, 130–1
  mass society, 94–5, 104–6, 126–8
Civilization in the United States, 118–19
class, money, and power, 8, 18, 20–1, 35,
  36–7, 40, 43, 45, 53, 55–6, 59, 60, 61,
  63, 73, 89–91, 93–4, 107, 109, 110–11
"Clean Well-Lighted Place, A"
  (Hemingway), 33
Code of the West (Grey), 172–3

Cody, William F. ("Buffalo Bill"), xi, 21,
  22–3, 30, 36, 170–1
Columbus, Christopher, 12
Communist Party, 156, 158, 183, 187–8
Company K (March), 72–3
Conrad, Joseph, 34, 39, 141
Conroy, Jack, 169, 187, 199
  Disinherited, The, 152, 182, 185, 187
Cooke, Alistair, 128
Coolidge, Calvin, 90, 100, 127, 147
Cool Million, A (West), 192
Cooper, Anna Julia, *A Voice from the South*,
  27
Cortissoz, Royal, 50–1
Cott, Carrie Chapman, 70
Cowley, Malcolm, 78, 81, 82, 98, 151, 155,
  239, 240, 241
  admired writers of, 117–18, 125, 134
  Exile's Return, 100
  socialism of, 156
Cox, Kenyon, 23, 50
Cozzens, James Gould, 188
Crane, Hart, 13, 74, 169
  Bridge, The, 130
  death of, 169
Crane, Stephen, 44, 141
  Maggie: A Girl of the Streets, 26
"Crisis in Poetry" (Mallarmé), 1
Croly, Herbert, 47
Crook, George, 21
Crosby, Caresse, 74, 121
Crosby, Harry, *War Letters* (1932), 74
Cullen, Countee, 118
Culture of Cities, The (Mumford), 130
Culture and Crisis, 156
Cummings, E. E., 46, 49, 81, 83–4, 151
  The Enormous Room, 83–4, 127, 136
Custom of the Country, The (Wharton), 61, 62,
  95

Dahlberg, Edward, 186, 199, 245
  Because I Was Flesh, 185, 245
  Bottom Dogs, 152, 185, 187
Daiches, David, 78
Darwin, Charles, 34, 40, 43
Darwinism, 32–3
Daughter of the Middle Border, A (Garland), 14
Davidson, Donald, 207, 208
Davies, Arthur, 50
Davis, Richard Harding, 67
Day of the Locust, The (West), 159, 192–4
Death in the Afternoon (Hemingway), 142–3
Death in a Bowl (Whitfield), 192

Death Comes for the Archbishop (Cather), 29, 73–4, 96
Deepening Stream, The (Fisher), 71, 135
Dell, Floyd, 44, 46, 47, 48, 49, 50, 54, 167, 237
detective stories, 170, 171, 173–7, 244
Deutsch, Babette, 98
De Voto, Bernard, 153
Dewey, John, 78, 134
Dial, 64, 104, 154
Dickey, James, 16
Dickinson, Emily, 121, 137
Di Donato, Pietro, 187
Dies, Martin, 196
Disinherited, The (Conroy), 152, 182, 185, 187
documentary movement, 152–3, 159, 170, 195–202, 245
Dollmaker, The (Arnow), 15
Doolittle, James Harold, 66
Dos Passos, John, 65, 68, 83, 98, 103, 104, 130–3, 138, 151, 153, 156, 160, 168, 188, 190, 200, 203, 207
  background of, 130
  Ground We Stand On, The, 153–4, 203
  Manhattan Transfer, 130, 131, 162
  One Man's Initiation: 1917, 84, 130
  social fiction of, 132–3
  Three Soldiers, 100, 130, 136
  urban world of, 130–1
  U.S.A., 1, 46, 81, 84, 98–9, 100, 102, 130–3, 136, 150, 159, 164, 165–7
Double Indemnity (Cain), 178
Douglass, Frederick, 27
Dream Life of Balso Snell, The (West), 191
Dreiser, Theodore, xvi, 3, 32, 48, 60–1, 62–4, 110–11, 154, 161, 197, 202, 238
  American Tragedy, An, 1, 60–1, 63, 110
  background of, 60, 61, 63–4
  Financier, The, 63, 110
  Gallery of Women, A, 86
  protagonists of, 62–3
  Sister Carrie, xiii, xvi, 12, 14–21, 60–1, 111
  Stoic, The, 110
  Titan, The, 63, 110
  Tragic America, 152, 202
Du Bois, W. E. B., 71, 118, 125, 196
  Souls of Black Folk, The, 4
Duchamp, Marcel, *Nude Descending a Staircase*, 50
Duino Elegies (Rilke), 94
Dunbar, Paul Laurence, 44
Duncan, Isadora, 47
Durkheim, Emile, xiii, 30

Eastman, Max, 48, 49, 54
"Echoes of the Jazz Age" (Fitzgerald), 149, 150
Education of Henry Adams, The (Adams), 31–5, 38, 77–8, 79–81
1890s, 1–43
  and Buffalo Bill's Wild West Show as cultural narrative, 21–3
  and Chicago's "Dream City" as cultural narrative, 23–7
  and Turner's thesis as cultural narrative, 27–9, 30–1
Einstein, Albert, 80
Eisenhower, Dwight D., 112
Eliot, Charles William, 120, 128
Eliot, T. S., 49, 63, 78, 100, 154, 167, 168, 228
  "Love Song of J. Alfred Prufrock, The" 7
  as outsider, 125, 128
  ties to South, 205
  Wasteland, The, 85, 130
Ellison, Ralph, 196, 215
Emerson, Ralph Waldo, xii, 133, 151, 189
Emma (Austen), 6
Empey, Arthur Guy, 68
Enormous Room, The (Cummings), 83–4, 127, 136
Evans, Hiram Wesley, 96, 118
Evans, Walker, 152, 198, 199, 201, 202
Exile's Return (Cowley), 100
"Experimental Music" (Cage), 131

Falkner, W. C., 217
Farewell to Arms, A (Hemingway), 74–5, 136, 143–4
Farrell, James T., 156, 182–3, 188, 190, 197, 207, 244–5
Fathers, The (Tate), 212–13
Faulkner, William, xii, xiv–xv, xvi, 3, 11, 81, 82, 83, 137, 159, 160, 164, 168–9, 177, 201, 207, 209, 215–29
  Absalom, Absalom!, 159, 206, 212, 220, 222–7
  achievement of, 227–8
  As I Lay Dying, 217–18, 219
  characters of, 217–18
  disaffection and alienation of, 228
  Ellison on, 215
  Go Down, Moses, 102, 103, 216, 220, 227–8
  heir of nineteenth-century culture, 228–9
  Light in August, 219–22
  North Mississippi of, 216–17
  observed realities of, 215–16

Soldiers' Pay, 135
Sound and the Fury, The, 216, 218–19, 223, 228
techniques of, 228
Fauset, Jean, 118
Federal Theater Project (FTP), 196
Federal Writers' Project (FWP), 196
Ferris, George Washington Gale, 24
Fiedler, Leslie, 188
Fields, W. C., 169
Fighting France (Wharton), 67
Financier, The (Dreiser), 63, 110
Finnegans Wake (Joyce), 7–8
Fisher, Dorothy Canfield, 103
  Deepening Stream, The, 71, 135
  Home-Maker, The, 120, 241
Fitzgerald, F. Scott, xvi, 3, 11, 12, 37, 81, 86, 97, 103, 104, 106, 109–10, 110–17, 133, 140, 150–1, 177, 203, 216
  "Echoes of the Jazz Age," 149, 150
  generation of, 109–10, 134
  Great Gatsby, The, xiii, 38, 81, 83, 99, 100, 107, 109, 110–17, 128
  Last Tycoon, The, 192
  in the 1930s, 147, 160
  as outsider, 125
  "Scandal Detectives, The," 107–9
  socialism of, 150–1
  Tales of the Jazz Age, 82
  Tender Is the Night, 110, 112, 150, 151, 160
  This Side of Paradise, 82, 109
  in World War I, 112, 135
Fitzgerald, Zelda, 74, 82, 111, 112, 147
Five Cities (Leighton), 199
Flanner, Janet, 81, 103, 121
  Paris Was Yesterday, 144
Flaubert, Gustave, 1
Flinn, John, 27
Flowering of New England, The (Brooks), 153, 203
Ford, Ford Madox, 47, 121, 109
Ford, Henry, 100
Ford, James, 187
For Whom the Bell Tolls (Hemingway), 144–5, 177
Four Arts Ball (Paris), 74
Foster, William Z., 187
Frank, Waldo, 156
  The Re-Discovery of America, 88
Frankfurter, Felix, 97
Franklin, Benjamin, 113, 116–17, 121
Freeman, Joseph, 46–7, 49, 61–2, 65, 66, 81, 82, 106–7, 136, 137, 155

French Ways and Their Meaning (Wharton), 95
Freud, Sigmund, 39, 78, 201,
Friedman, I. K., 181
frontier
  in Cather's work, 29–30
  closing of, 11–13, 14, 21–3, 27–8, 30, 37, 38, 235–6
  Turner's thesis of, 27–9, 30–1
Frost, Robert, 2, 49, 154
Fry, Roger, 51
Fuchs, Daniel, 152, 183
Fugitive, The, 206
Fuller, Henry, 18

Gale, Zona, 103, 134
  Preface to a Life, 101
Gallery of Women, A (Drieser), 86
Garland, Hamlin, 12, 14, 25
Gellhorn, Martha, 186
"Genteel Tradition," 2, 44–5, 48
Geological History of America, The (Stein), 123
Giants in the Earth (Rölvaag), 12, 14–18
Gilpin, William, 13, 28
Giovannitti, Arturo, 49
Gladden, Washington, 236
Glasgow, Ellen, 216, 246
  Barren Ground, 58, 207, 211–12
  Builders, The, 67
Glass Key, The (Hammett), 176
Glockens, William, 4
Go Down, Moses (Faulkner), xi, 102, 159, 216, 220, 227
God's Little Acre (Caldwell), 207, 209, 210
Gold, Michael, 98, 155, 167, 168, 183, 186, 190
  "Go West, Young Writers," 185–6
  Jews Without Money, 23, 152, 185
  "Prophet of the Genteel Christ," 186
Golden Bowl, The (James), 5
Golden Day, The (Mumford), 135
Goldman, Emma, 49, 65, 97
Gone with the Wind (Mitchell), 210–11, 212
Goodbye Wisconsin (Wescott), 117
"Go West, Young Writers" (Gold), 185–6
Grant, Madison, 118
  The Passing of the Great Race, 96
Grant, Ulysses, 78
Grapes of Wrath, The (Steinbeck), 189–90
Graves, Robert, 72
Great Crash of 1929, 147–9, 160, 204–5
Great Gatsby, The (Fitzgerald), xiii, 38, 81, 83, 99, 100, 109, 110–17, 128
Green, Paul, 196

Green Hills of Africa (Hemingway), 85
Gregg, Frederick James, 50
Grey, Zane, 171, 176, 244
  Code of the West, 172–3
  Nevada, 173
  Riders of the Purple Sage, 172, 173
Ground We Stand On, The (Dos Passos), 153–4, 203

Hadden, Briton, 126
Haeckel, Ernst, *The Riddle of the Universe*, 40
Hagglund, Ben 183
Hakluyt, Richard, 12
Hammett, Dashiell, 171, 175–6
  Glass Key, The 176
  Maltese Falcon, The, 176
  Red Harvest, 175
Hapgood, Hutchins, 48
Hapgood, Norman, 50
Hapgood, Powers, 98
Harcourt Brace, 106
Harding, Warren G., 84, 90
Harrison, Benjamin, 23
Hartley, Marsden, 51
Hartz, Louis, 188
Hay, John, 77
Hayden, Sophia, 26
Haywood, Bill, 46, 51
H.D., 100, 121
Heap, Jane, 121
Heaven's My Destination (Wilder), 186
Heisenberg, Werner, 8, 16, 34, 37, 92, 234, 235
Held, John, Jr., 85
Hemingway, Ernest, 3, 11, 68, 81, 82, 83, 103, 104, 114, 134, 135, 137–45, 151, 154, 177, 242
  accident-proneness of, 138
  "Big Two-Hearted River," 143
  "Clean Well-Lighted Place, A," 33
  competitiveness of, 137–8
  Death in the Afternoon, 142–3
  family background of, 138, 139, 140–1
  Farewell to Arms, A, 74–5, 136, 143–4, 206
  For Whom the Bell Tolls, 144–5, 177
  Green Hills of Africa, 85
  "In Another Country," 177
  In Our Time, 102, 140, 143, 177
  "Last Good Company, The," 139
  Moveable Feast, A, 124, 137, 138, 140
  in the 1930s, 160
  Old Man and the Sea, The, 145
  prose style of, 141–3
  public persona of, 137, 138

"Soldier's Home," 141, 144
  suicide of, 141, 144
  Sun Also Rises, The, 38, 82, 143, 145, 177
  To Have and Have Not, 177
  at war, 139–40, 141
  Winner Take Nothing, 145
Herbst, Josephine, 103, 150, 151, 156, 160, 186, 187, 188, 199, 216
  Pity Is Not Enough, 216
Hergesheimer, Joseph, 103, 120
Herrick, Robert, 67, 120
Heyward, Bill, 97
Hickerson, Harold, 98
Hicks, Granville, 152
Hills, Majorie, 179–80
Historical novel, 202–3
Hobbes, Thomas, 39
Hofstadter, Richard, 188
Hollywood novels, 192–3
Holmes, Oliver Wendell, Jr., 66
Home-Maker, The (Fisher), 120, 241
Homestead Act, 13, 14, 21, 29
Homesteaders, 29
Home Town (Anderson), 152
Hoover, Herbert, 147–8
House of Mirth (Wharton), 26, 57, 58–60, 61
House Un-American Activities Committee (HUAC), 196
Howells, William Dean, 2, 12, 14, 24, 29, 65, 167
  Literary Friends and Acquaintances, 126
  Modern Instance, A, 1
Hubbell, Jay B., 155
Hughes, Langston, 75, 103, 118, 133, 156
"Hugh Selwyn Mauberley" (Pound), 72
Huizinga, Johan, 197
Human, All-Too-Human (Nietzsche), 1
Huneker, James G., 46
Hunt, Richard, 24
Hurston, Zora Neale, 118, 159, 160, 207
Huxley, Aldous, 209
Huxley, Thomas, 236

I'll Take My Stand, 208, 209, 217
immigrants and immigration, 11–14, 43–4
In the American Grain (Williams), 135
"In Another Country" (Hemingway), 177
In Dubious Battle (Steinbeck), 189
Industrial Valley (McKenney), 187, 199
In Our Time (Hemingway), 102, 140, 177
Isherwood, Christopher, 135, 197
I Thought of Daisy (Wilson), 120
Ives, Charles, 131

James, Henry, xvi, 1, 2, 5–11, 12, 41–2, 53,
     77, 84, 100, 102, 132, 141, 154, 161, 234,
     235
  American, The, 1
  American Scene, The, 3, 4
  Golden Bowl, The, 5
  Lesson of the Master, The, 10
  "Passionate Pilgrim, The," 12
  Portrait of a Lady, The, xvi, 5–11, 19, 42
  Princess Casamassima, The, xiii
  social and economic forces in work of, 41–
     2
  Watch and Ward, 6
Jazz, 85–6
"Jazz Age," 81, 85–6
Jewett, Sarah Orne, 126
Jews Without Money (Gold), 23, 152, 185
John Barleycorn (London), 56
Johnson, Albert, 96
Johnson, James Weldon, 44, 118
Johnson, Lionel, 143
Johnson, Owen, 108
Joplin, Scott, 27
Josephson, Matthew, 81, 239
  Portrait of the Artist as American, 87
Joyce, James, 48, 102, 141, 216
  Finnegans Wake, 7–8
Jungle, The (Sinclair), 44, 181
Jurgen (Cabell), 121, 162

Kant, Immanuel, 39
Katzmann, Frederick G., 97, 98
Kazin, Alfred, 196
  Starting Out in the Thirties, 158–9
Kelley's Industrial Army, 39
Kesey, Ken, 38
Kipling, Rudyard, 39
Knopf (Alfred A.), 106
Kronenberger, Louis, 79
Krutch, Joseph Wood, 109, 206–7
Ku Klux Klan, 97

Ladies Home Journal, 104–5, 119
La Farge, John, 50
Laforgue, Jules, 137
La Motte, Ellen, 71–2
Laplace, Pierre-Simon, 39
Land of the Free (MacLeish), 152, 195, 197
Land of Plenty (Cantwell), 152, 183
Lange, Dorothea, 197–8, 202
  American Exodus, An, 152, 195, 197
  "Migrant Mother," 198–9
  view of poverty, 197–8

"Last Good Company, The" (Hemingway),
     139
Last Tycoon, The (Fitzgerald), 192
Laurent, Henri, 105
Lawrence, D. H., 199, 205, 246
  Studies in Classic American Literature, 46
Lawrence, William, 90
League of American Writers, 188
Lefebvre, Henri, 105
Leighton, George, 199
Lenin, Nikolai, 79
Lerner, Max, 78
Leslie, Shane, 97
Lesson of the Master, The (James), 10
Le Sueur, Meridel, 186, 187
Let Us Now Praise Famous Men (Agee), xv,
     152, 159, 199–202
Lewis, Sinclair, 86–90, 92–3, 103, 130, 151,
     152, 159, 169, 197, 206
  Babbitt, 87–9, 92–3, 129
  Main Street, 87, 133
Lewis, Wyndham, 132
Lewisohn, Ludwig, 45
Light in August (Faulkner), 219–222
Lincoln, Abraham, 148
Lindsay, Vachel, xiii, 35, 36, 43, 49
  Art of Motion Pictures, The, 105, 234
Lippmann, Walter, 45, 46, 47, 61, 100, 109,
     157
Literary Friends and Acquaintances (Howell),
     126
Literary History of the United States (Spiller),
     124
Locke, Alain, 118
Lodge, Henry Cabot, 81
Loeb, Harold, 81
London, Jack, xii, 32, 38–43, 44, 54–7, 161,
     167, 177, 181, 183, 189, 236–7
  background and career of, 38–9
  Call of the Wild, The, 39, 40, 42–3
  death of, 56
  John Barleycorn, 56
  Martin Eden, 26, 41, 45, 54–7
  nature in work of, 40–1, 42–3
  People of the Abyss, The, 39, 40
  White Fang, 40
  as writer-hero, 39–40
Long Valley, The (Steinbeck), 189
Look Homeward Angel (Wolfe), 214
Looking Backward (Bellamy), 63
Lorentz, Pare, 196
"Lost Generation," 81, 85
Lost Lady, A (Cather), 29, 73
Lowell, Amy, 49

Loy, Mina, 121
Luce, Henry, 126–7, 158
Luhan, Mabel Dodge, 44, 45, 46, 47, 51–2
  Movers and Shakers, 50, 81
Luks, George, 44
Lumpkin, Grace, 207
Lyell, Sir Charles, 34
Lynd, Robert and Helen
  Middletown, 87, 91, 105
  Middletown in Transition, 155
Lyric Years, 43–75, 151, 159, 167
  and the Armory Show as cultural narrative,
    50–2
  and the cult of the "new," 44, 47
  and the discourse of disillusionment, 68–9,
    71–5
  and the discourse of patriotism, 65–8
  and the "Genteel Tradition" and "Genteel
    Custodians," 44, 45, 46, 48, 50–1, 65–8
Lytle, Andrew, 207, 209

MacLeish, Archibald, Land of the Free, 152,
  195, 197
MacMonnies, Mary Fairchild, 26
Maggie: A Girl of the Streets (Crane), 26
Main Street (Lewis), 87, 133
Mailer, Norman, 137
Making of Americans, The (Stein), 1, 123, 154
Malamud, Bernard, 188
Mallarmé, Stéphane, 1
Malraux, André, 3
Maltese Falcon, The (Hammett), 176
Maltz, George, The Underground Stream, 152,
  199
"Man of the Crowd, The" (Poe), 35–6, 135
Manhattan Transfer (Dos Passos), 130, 131, 162
Mann, Thomas, 188
Man Nobody Knows, The (Barton), 105, 129
Marching Men (Anderson), 101
March, William, 72–3
marginality, authority and forms of, 4–5, 98–
  9, 100, 103–4, 107, 118–121, 123, 125–6,
  134–5, 153, 160, 168–9
Marne, The (Wharton), 68
Martin Eden (London), 26, 41, 45, 54–7
Marx, Karl, xiii, 40, 43, 46, 182, 201
Masses, 47, 48, 49, 52, 54, 64, 65
Masters, Edgar Lee, 49, 102
Mather, Frank, 50
Matthiessen, F. O., 209
McAlmon, Robert, 81
McCarthy, Mary, 186
McCoy, Horace, 177–181, 244
  Pockets for a Shroud, 179

They Shoot Horses, Don't They?, 179–81,
  192
McKay, Claude, 118
McKenney, Ruth, 187
  Industrial Valley, 187, 199
  My Sister Eileen, 194
McKim, Mead, and White, 24
McTeague (Norris), 63
Mellon, Andrew, 90, 100, 148
Melville, Herman, 39
Mencken, H. L., 45, 48, 73, 152, 167
  American Language, The, 86
  on Lewis, 86–7
  on Midwest, 133–4
  on South, 134, 206
Middletown, U.S.A. (Lynd and Lynd), 87, 91,
  105
Middletown in Transition (Lynd and Lynd),
  155
Midway Types: A Book of Illustrated Lessons,
  26
Midwest, 133–4
"Migrant Mother" (Lange), 198–9
Millay, Edna St. Vincent, 98
Miller, Arthur, 188
Miller, Henry, 159, 160–1, 207, 243–4
  anti-aestheticism of, 162–3
  Black Spring, 161, 163
  Depression novels of, 163–4
  and post modernism, 163
  Rosy Crucifixion, The, 165
  self-involvement/self-absorption of, 162–3,
    164
  subjects of, 160–1
  Tropic of Cancer, 161, 162, 163
  Tropic of Capricorn, 159, 161–2, 163, 165
Milton, John, 170
Mission of the North American People, The
  (Gilpin), 13
Miss Lonelyhearts (West), 121, 127, 159, 191–2
Mitchell, Margaret, 207
  Gone with the Wind, 210–11, 212
Modern Instance, A (Howells), 1
modernism and the idea of the modern, 3–4,
  8, 10–11, 32–6, 38, 41–2, 48, 50–3, 60,
  78, 83–4, 93–6, 100–2, 105–6, 121–4,
  159, 162–3, 167, 168–9, 204, 207–8, 215–
  16, 217, 228–9
Monroe, Harriett, 103
Mont-Saint-Michel and Chartres (Adams), 78,
  79
Moore, Marianne, 124
More, Paul Elmer, 37, 131
Mother Earth, 49, 97

Motherwell, Robert, 204
motion pictures
  in Great Depression, 149, 170
  in the 1920s, 106
  and World War I, 67, 68
Moveable Feast, A (Hemingway), 124, 137, 138, 140
Movers and Shakers (Luhan), 50, 81
Mumford, Lewis, 79
  Brown Decades, The, 135
  Culture of Cities, The, 130
  Golden Day, The, 135
Murger, Henri, 103
  Scènes de la vie de bohème, 103–4
music, 81, 82, 85–6, 106, 149
My America (Adamic), 152, 195, 203
My Ántonia (Cather), 12, 14–18
My Sister Eileen (McKenney), 194

Nathan, George Jean, 48, 73, 86
Nation, 50
National American Woman Suffrage Association, 70
National Recovery Act, 204
National Women's Party, 70
Native Americans, 23
  war against, 21–2
  in World's Columbian Exposition, 26
nativism, 96–9
Nevada (Grey), 173
New Deal, 157–8, 187, 188
  documentary movement and, 195–6, 202
  in the South, 204
New England: Indian Summer (Brooks), 153, 203
New Masses, 98, 155, 184, 186, 190, 193
New Negro, The: An Interpretation, 118
New Republic, 47, 48, 61, 64, 67, 155
New York City
  growth of, 13
  of Henry Adams, 35, 37
  in 1920s, 126, 127, 130
New Yorker, The, 121, 169
New York Stock Exchange, crash of, 148
Nietzsche, Friedrich, 40, 43, 46, 48, 49, 191
  Human, All-Too-Human, 1
Nightwood (Barnes), 159, 164–5
Nin, Anaïs, 121, 143
  Diaries, 124
Nineteenth Amendment, 70
1920s, 77–145, 149–50, 154
  and the authority of business, 89–90
  and the decline of reform, 89–90, 132–3

and the discourse of disillusionment, 80–1, 89
as the "Jazz Age," 81, 82, 85–6, 106
and the "Lost Generation," 81–3, 85
and mass production and mass culture, 94–5, 104–5
prosperity in, 90–1, 93–4, 106
and the return of detachment, 77–8, 80–1
and the Sacco–Vanzetti trial as cultural narrative, 97–9
1930s
  aestheticism and anti-aestheticism in, 155, 158–9, 162–3, 167, 168–9
  and the Communist Party, 149, 156, 183, 186–8
  detective novels in, 159, 170, 174–7, 244
  documentary literature and photography in, 151, 152, 153, 170, 182, 195–9, 202
  "hardboiled" novels in, 177–81
  historical novels in, 149, 170, 202–3
  and the New Deal, 156–8, 188, 195–6, 202, 204
  radical novels in, 152, 170, 181–7
  and the redefinition of culture, 152–4, 196–7, 202–3
  and the return of reform, 149–51, 155–6, 159–60, 195–9
  and the search for a usable past, 150, 151, 153–4, 165–6, 195–6
  and the South and the Southern Renaissance, 203–7
  violence in, 160–71
  and "Westerns," 159, 170–4, 244
Norris, Frank, 63, 161
  McTeague, 63
Norris, George, 53
Norton, Charles Eliot, 66
Norton, Richard, 65, 66
novel, the
  and the blurring of generic lines in, 38
  and art's "spiritual rootage," 45–6
  class in, xvi, 43–4, 110–17
  commitment to real, 1–3
  conflicted allegiances, 1–2
  and culture, xi–xiv
  detective stories, 170, 171, 173–7, 244
  and discontinuous narrative, 101–2
  documentary movement, 152–3, 159, 170, 195–202, 245
  experiments in technique, xiii
  frontier as model, 36–7, 38
  and gender, xvi, 117–24, 125–6
  Genteel Tradition, 44–6
  during Great Depression, 147–229, 242–6

historical, 202–3
in historical process, xv–xvi
as incessant talk, xiv–xv
and language, 3, 4–5, 79, 83–5, 86, 122–4, 131, 132–3, 141–4
and loss of continuities, 3–4
lyrical tradition of, 1–2, 8–10, 45–6
Lyric Years, 46–50, 54–64, 148, 237
and marginality, 4–5, 125–6
and modernism, 2–4, 32–6, 50–3, 105
narrative urge in, 2–3, 5–7, 9–11
in the 1920s, 81–145, 238–42
popularity of, xiii
protest and social reform, 44–6, 47, 48, 49
race, xvi, 43–4, 125–6
radical left, 181–95, 244–5
role of, xiv
and self-fashioning, 79–80, 107, 113
and sexual liberation, 109
Southern Renaissance, 204–29, 246
spiritual motive of, xvi
tough-guy, 177–81, 244
at turn of century, 1–5, 43–4
urban/western expansion themes in, 11–21, 235
vernacular tradition in, 10–11
during World War I, 53–4, 64–75, 238
Western stories, 170–3, 244
Nude Descending a Staircase (Duchamp), 50

Oates, Joyce Carol, 244
Odets, Clifford
    Till the Day I Die, 193
    Waiting for Lefty, 193
Odum, Howard, 207
Ogan, Sarah, 187
Of Mice and Men (Steinbeck), 190
O'Hara, John, 192
O'Keefe, Georgia, 134
Old Man and the Sea, The (Hemingway), 145
Olmsted, Frederick Law, 23
Olsen, Tillie, 186–187
One Flew over the Cuckoo's Nest (Kesey), 38
One Man's Initiation: 1917 (Dos Passos), 84, 130
One of Ours (Cather), 68, 71, 73
Only Yesterday (Allen), 150
On Revolution (Arendt), xiv–xv
O Pioneers! (Cather), 1
Oppenheim, James, 47, 48, 49, 54, 64
Ordeal of Mark Train, The (Brooks), 135
Orwell, George, 150, 161, 243
Out of This Furnace (Bell), 152, 187, 199
Owsley, Frank, 207

Paine, Thomas, 151, 187
Palmer, A. Mitchell, 96, 97, 118
Palmer Raids, 96
Paris Exposition of 1889, 24
Paris Was Yesterday (Flanner), 144
Parker, Dorothy, 177
Parkman, Francis, 28
Parrington, V. L., 78
Parsons, Elsie Clews, 119
Parties (Van Vechten), 112
Partisan Review, 186, 245
Passing of the Great Race, The (Grant), 96
"Passionate Pilgrim, The" (James), 12
Pater, Walter, 1, 161
Patria Mia (Pound), 53
Patriotic Gore (Wilson), 67–8
Paul, Alice, 70
Pearson, Karl, 31–2
People of the Abyss, The (London), 39, 40
Perkins, Maxwell, 137, 177
Personality: How to Build It (Laurent), 105
Phillips, William, 186
photography, 13, 18, 51
    in documentary movement, 152, 195, 197–202, 202
Picasso, Pablo, 51
Pity Is Not Enough (Herbst), 216
"place" of women, the, 19–20, 26–7, 44–5, 57–60, 61, 62, 70–1, 117–20, 123, 124, 125, 160, 164–5, 168, 171, 172–3, 175–6, 180–1, 186–7, 211–12, 218–19, 220–2
Pockets for a Shroud (McCoy), 179
Poe, Edgar Allan, 205
    "Man of the Crowd, The," 35–6, 135
"Poet as Woman, The" (Ransom), 120
Pokagon, Chief Simon, 26
Porter, Katherine Anne, 160, 207, 215
Portrait of the Artist as American (Josephson), 87
Portrait of a Lady, The (James), xi, xvi, 5–11, 19, 42, 235
Postman Always Rings Twice, The (Cain), 178–9
Pound, Ezra, xiii, 3, 35, 48, 49, 52–3, 100, 154, 234
    Cantos, 130
    "Hugh Selwyn Mauberley," 72
    Patria Mia, 53
Prager, Robert, 65
Praz, Mario, 209
Preface to a Life (Gale), 101
Princess Casamassima, The (James), xiii
Principles of Scientific Management, The (Taylor), 46

professionalism, rise of, 91, 154–5
Professor's House, The (Cather), 29
prohibition and crime, 99–100, 107
proletarian fiction, 159, 183
Proletarian Literature in the United States (Hicks), 152
"Prophet of the Genteel Christ" (Gold), 186
Proust, Marcel, 159
Pulver, Mary Brecht, 67
Puritanism, 46, 135, 237
Puzzled America (Anderson), 152, 181, 202

Quinn, John, 51

Race, racism, and nativism, 4, 21–3, 26, 27, 43–4, 45, 57–60, 61, 62, 70–1, 86, 96–8, 117–18, 121, 125, 151, 160, 164, 168, 169–70, 196, 206, 210–11, 213, 215–16, 217–18, 219, 220–1
Radin, Paul, 78
Raleigh, Walter, 12
Random House, 106
Ransom, John Crowe, 206, 208, 241
"The Poet as Woman," 120
Read, Herbert, 125, 209
Rebel, The (Camus), xi–xii
Red Harvest (Hammett), 175
Re-Discovery of America, The (Frank), 88
Red Man's Greeting (Pokagon), 26
Red Scare, 96
Reed, John, 46, 49, 54, 65, 66, 130, 167
Reef, The (Wharton), 58
regions and regionalism, 28–30, 47, 82, 93–4, 102–3, 125–6, 133–5
"Remembering Hart Crane" (Wolff), 169
Rice, Elmer, 196
Richards, I. A., 78
Ricketts, Edward F., 189
Riddle of the Universe, The (Haeckel), 40
Riders of the Purple Sage (Grey), 172, 173
Ridge, Lola, 98
Rilke, Rainer Maria, 94
River, The (Lorentz), 196
Road, The: In Search of America (Asch), 152, 181–2, 195
Roberts, Kenneth, 202–3
Roethke, Theodore, 16
Rölvaag, O. E., *Giants in the Earth*, 12, 14–18
Roof, Katherine, 118, 241
Roosevelt, Franklin Delano, 156–8, 187, 195
Roosevelt, Theodore, 37, 66, 71, 84
Root, John, 24
Rosenfeld, Paul, 154–5
Rosskam, Edwin, 152, 195, 197, 202

Rosy Crucifixion, The (Miller), 165
Roth, Henry, 160, 188
Call It Sleep, 13, 184–5, 245
Rourke, Constance, 155
Rousseau, Jean-Jacques, 55
Rousseau and Romanticism (Babbitt), 92
Russell, Bertrand, 34
Rutledge, Marice (pseud.), 135–6

Sacco–Vanzetti case, 96, 97–8, 132
Saint-Gaudens, Augustus, 23, 24, 50
Sandburg, Carl, 49, 153
Santayana, George, 4, 11, 118, 234, 237
Sargent, John S., 51
Sartre, Jean Paul, 166
Saturday Evening Post, 104, 105
"Scandal Detectives, The" (Fitzgerald), 107–9
Schwab, Charles, 155
Schwartz, Delmore, 132, 145
science and technology, 7, 8, 31–4, 37–8, 46, 92–3,
scientific management, 46
Scott, Evelyn, 207
Scottsboro trials, 169–70
Sea Wolf, The (London), 39
Seeger, Alan, 66–7, 68
Seemuller, Ann Moncure Crane, 6
Seldes, Gilbert, 148
Serenade (Cain), 178, 179
Service, Robert W., 68
Seven Arts, 47, 48, 54, 64, 65
Shakespeare, William, 170
Shaw, George Bernard, 39
Sherman, William T., 21
Sherwood, Robert, 177
Shinn, Everett, 44
"Significance of the Frontier in American History, The" (Turner), 27–8, 30–1
Silences (Olsen), 186
Sinclair, B. M., 172
Sinclair, Upton, 65, 166, 167, 181
Boston, 98
Jungle, The, 44, 181
Sister Carrie (Dreiser), xiii, 12, 14–21, 60, 61, 111
Sitting Bull, 21, 22
Sklar, George, 196
Slesinger, Tess, 152, 187
Sloan, John, 44
Smart Set, 47–8
Smith, Adam, 154
Smith, Bernard, 78
Smith, Lillian, 207
Smith, Louis, 48

"Soldier's Home" (Hemingway), 141, 144
Soldiers' Pay (Faulkner), 135
Son at the Front, A (Wharton), 68
Song of the Lark (Wharton), 58
Son of the Middle Border, A (Garland), 14
Son of the Wolf, The (London), 39
Souls of Black Folk, The, (Du Bois), 4
Soule, George, 78
Sound and the Fury, The (Faulkner), 216, 218–19, 223, 228
Southern Renaissance, 204–29
Southern Review, 204, 209
Spargo, John, 44
Spencer, Herbert, 236
Spengler, Oswald, 79
Spiller, Robert, 124
Spirit of the Ghetto, The (Hapgood), 48
Stanton, Elizabeth Cady, 26
Starting Out in the Thirties (Kazin), 158–9
Stearns, Harold, 118, 119
Steffens, Lincoln, 44, 155, 156, 183
  Autobiography, 183
Stein, Gertrude, 3, 39, 48, 50, 51–2, 62, 75, 81, 82, 100, 121–4, 131, 138, 141, 151, 154, 237, 241
  Autobiography of Alice B. Toklas, The, 122, 137, 138
  champion of new, 121–2
  Geological History of America, The, 123
  Making of Americans, The, 1, 123, 154
  teacher of writers, 83
  Tender Buttons, 123
  Three Lives, 62, 101, 123, 162
  verbal dexterity of, 122–123
  Wars I Have Seen, 123, 124
  What Are Masterpieces, 123
  as woman writer, 123, 124
Steinbeck, John, 188–90
  Grapes of Wrath, The, 189–90
  In Dubious Battle, 189, 190
  Long Valley, The, 189
  Of Mice and Men, 190
  in protest tradition, 188–9
  Tortilla Flat, 189
Stevens, Wallace, 168
Stieglitz, Alfred, 51
  "From the Shelton Hotel," 18
  "Steerage, The," 13
Stoddard, Lothrop, 96–7, 118
Stover at Yale (Johnson), 108
Stribling, T. S., 207, 209
Strong, Philip D., 98
Stuark, Thomas, 244

Studies in Classic American Literature (Lawrence), 46, 135
Studies in the History of the Renaissance (Pater), 1
Suckow, Ruth, 103
Sullivan, Louis, 25
Sumner, William Graham, 78
Sun Also Rises, The (Hemingway), 38, 82, 143, 145, 177
Susman, Warren, 235, 243
Swinburne, Algernon Charles, 39

Taggard, Genevieve, 46, 49–50, 82, 136
Tales of the Jazz Age (Fitzgerald), 82
Tarbell, Ida, 44
Tarkington, Booth, 60
Tate, Allen, 153, 207, 208, 213
  Fathers, The, 212–13
Taylor, Frederick Winslow, 46
Taylor, Paul S., An American Exodus, 152, 195, 197, 202
technology, 35, 37–8; see also science and technology
Teller, Charlotte, 181
Tender Buttons (Stein), 123
Tender Is the Night (Fitzgerald), 110, 112, 150, 151, 160
Thayer, Webster, 97
They Shoot Horses, Don't They? (McCoy), 179–81, 192
This Side of Paradise (Fitzgerald), 82, 109
Thomas, Norman, 188
Thoreau, Henry, Walden, 40–1, 237
Three Lives (Stein), 62, 101, 123, 162
Three Soldiers (Dos Passos), 100, 130, 136
Through the Wheat (Thomas), 136
Thurber, James, 150
Till the Day I Die (Odets), 193
Time magazine, 126–7
Titan, The (Dreiser), 63, 110
Tobacco Road (Caldwell), 209, 210
Tocqueville, Alexis de, 20, 67, 80
Todorov, Tzvetan, xvi, 235, 236
To Have and Have Not (Hemingway), 177
Toomer, Jean, 118
  Cane, 102
Tortilla Flat (Steinbeck), 189
Tragic America (Dreiser), 152, 202
Tragic Era, The (Bowers), 135
Trilling, Lionel, 35
Triumphant America (Carnegie), 2
Troeltsch, Ernst, xiii
Tropic of Cancer (Miller), 161, 162

Tropic of Capricorn (Miller), 159, 161–2, 165
Tucker's People (Wolfert), 183
Tugwell, R. G., 78
Turgenev, Ivan, 102
Turner, Frederick Jackson, 13, 27–36, 134,
    170, 236
    "The Significance of the Frontier in
    American History," 27–8, 30–1, 78
Twain, Mark, 5, 10, 12, 137, 148, 205, 234
Twelve Million Black Voices (Wright), 152,
    195, 197
Tyler, Alice Felt, 188
Tynan, Kenneth, 113
Tzara, Tristan, 48

Uncle Tom's Children (Wright), 159, 196
Underground Stream, The (Maltz), 152, 199
Upstream (Lewisohn), 45
urbanization, 11–12, 13, 14, 16, 43
U.S.A. (Dos Passos), 1, 46, 81, 84, 98–9,
    100, 102, 130, 131–2, 133, 136, 150, 159,
    164, 165–7

Valéry, Paul, 209
Van Dyke, Henry, 45–6
Van Gogh, Vincent, 51
Van Vechten, Carl, 83, 112
Veblen, Thornstein, 78, 238–9
violence, in 1930s novels, 170
Virginian, The (Wister), 36–7, 171
Voice from the South, A (Cooper), 27
Volstead Act, 99
Vorse, Mary Heaton, 49, 156, 186

Waiting for Lefty (Odets), 193
Walden (Thoreau), 40–1
Walker, Margaret, 196
Ward, A. C., 85
War Letters (Crosby), 74
Warren, Robert Penn, 153, 207, 208, 209
    All the King's Men, 127–8, 153, 174
Wars I Have Seen (Stein), 123, 124
Wasteland, The (Eliot), 85, 130
Watson, John B., *Behaviorism*, 105–6
Weatherman, Clara, 152
Weber, Max, xiii, 37
Wellington, C. G. (Pete), 141
Wells, H. G., 69
Welty, Eudora, 196, 207, 209
Wescott, Glenway, 117
West, the; *see* frontier
West, Nathanael, 160, 164, 188, 191, 194–5,
    207, 216

background of, 191
Cool Million, A, 192
Day of the Locust, The, 159, 192–4
Dream Life of Balso Snell, The, 191
Miss Lonelyhearts, 121, 127, 159, 191–2
Western stories, 170–3, 244
Wharton, Edith, xii, 3, 12, 32, 57–61, 62, 81,
    197, 238
    Age of Innocence, The, 95, 100
    Backward Glance, A, 95–6
    background of, 57–8, 61
    Custom of the Country, The, 61, 62, 95
    Fighting France, 67
    French Ways and Their Meaning, 95
    House of Mirth, 26, 57, 58–60, 61
    Marne, The, 66, 68
    Reef, The, 58
    Son at the Front, A, 68
What Are Masterpieces (Stein), 123
Wheeler, Candace, 26
Whipple, T. K., 41, 237
White, E. B., 99
White Fang (London), 40
Whitehead, Alfred North, 7, 234
Whitfield, Raoul, 192
Whitman, Walt, 2, 13, 49, 64, 137, 151, 161,
    187, 189, 228, 234
    Backward Glance o'er Travel'd Roads, A, 2
    "Death-Sonnet for Custer, A," 21
Whitney, Caspar W., 114
Wilder, Thornton, 177, 186
    Heaven's My Destination, 186
Williams, William Carlos, 63, 183–4
    In the American Grain, 135
Wilson, Edmund, 98, 103, 155, 156, 162,
    179, 196, 202, 240
    American Jitters, The, 152, 155, 202
    Axel's Castle, 155, 159
    I Thought of Daisy, 120
    Patriotic Gore, 67–8
Wilson, Woodrow, 44, 53, 54, 65, 69, 77, 99
Windy McPherson's Son (Anderson), 101
Winesburg, Ohio (Anderson), 101–2, 103, 160
Winner Take Nothing (Hemingway), 145
Winthrop, John, 12
Wister, Owen, 24
    The Virginian, 36–7, 171
Wolfe, Thomas, 207, 209, 213–15, 216
    Look Homeward Angel, 213–14
    protagonist of, 213–14
    South of, 213–15
    You Can't Go Home Again, 213–14
Wolfert, Ira, 183

Wolff, David, 169
Wollstonecraft, Mary, 120
women; see also "place" of women
  of the Left, 186–7
  of the 1920s, 119–24
  and the World's Columbian Exposition,
    26–7
Woodward, C. Vann, 207
Woolf, Virginia, 216
Workers: An Experiment in Reality – The West
  (Wyckoff), 110
Works Progress Administration (WPA), 196,
  202
World's Columbian Exposition, 23–8, 29, 30–
  1, 37, 131, 236
World War I, 53–4, 64–75, 77, 130, 135, 136–
  7, 139–40, 141–3, 203, 238, 240

Wright, Richard, 83, 152, 160, 196, 202, 207
  Twelve Million Black Voices, 152, 195, 197
  Uncle Tom's Children, 159, 196
Wyckoff, Walter, 26, 240
  Workers: An Experiment in Reality – The
    West, 110

Yeats, W. B., 48, 52, 216
Yerby, Frank, 196
Yerkes, Charles T., 63
Yezeirska, Anzia, 44, 133
You Can't Go Home Again (Wolfe), 213–14
You Have Seen Their Faces (Caldwell and
  Bourke White), 152, 195, 197
Young, Art, 49, 54
Young, Stark, 208, 217